HYDERABAD

HYDERABAD

A BIOGRAPHY

Revised and Updated Edition

NARENDRA LUTHER

OXFORD
UNIVERSITY PRESS

OXFORD
UNIVERSITY PRESS

Oxford University Press is a department of the University of Oxford.
It furthers the University's objective of excellence in research, scholarship,
and education by publishing worldwide. Oxford is a registered trademark of
Oxford University Press in the UK and in certain other countries.

Published in India by
Oxford University Press
22 Workspace, 2nd Floor, 1/22 Asaf Ali Road, New Delhi 110002, India

First Edition published in 2006
Oxford India Paperbacks 2006
Revised and Updated Edition 2012
Revised and Updated Edition 2021

ISBN-13 (print edition): 978-0-19-949245-9
ISBN-10 (print edition): 0-19-949245-X

ISBN-13 (eBook): 978-0-19-099266-8
ISBN-10 (eBook): 0-19-099266-2

Typeset in Palatino LT Std 10/13
by The Graphics Solution, New Delhi 110 092
Printed in India by Rakmo Press, New Delhi 110 020

To Bindi
who gave up all her wifely claims on
me while this book was in writing—
and subsequently got used to the dereliction

In Kyo I am
And still I long for Kyo
Oh Bird of Time!

　　　　　—Basho (1643–94)
　　　　　Japanese Haiku Poet

Contents

Photographs (between pp. 196 and 197)

Preface to the 2006 Edition

Since the stock of the book's first edition, published by Orient Longman, had long been exhausted, there was a continuing demand for a second edition. I am grateful to Oxford University Press for taking up this project.

The second edition has been thoroughly revised in the light of the comments and criticism received from various quarters. In particular, the following changes have been made:

Originally, the book was a narration in the first person by the City. It presented some difficulties in the treatment of the subject and also caused some confusion for the readers. The narrative voice has therefore been changed into the conventional third person.

Second, the book has been updated. The first edition ended with the death of Nizam VII. This edition covers the period up to the elections of 2004. The literature published on the subject since the publication of the last edition has also been taken into account.

Earlier, no footnotes or endnotes were given in the belief that they interfere with the flow of reading. In view of the suggestions received, now exhaustive references by way of endnotes have been provided. This should satisfy the demands of readers, scholars, and researchers.

These changes led to a necessary restructuring of chapters and their contents to some extent. All these make it virtually a new work. They also make it the most up-to-date history of Hyderabad—and of Andhra Pradesh.

I hope it will receive the same response which the first edition did.

It is not possible to adequately acknowledge my debt of gratitude to so many individuals and institutions. Amongst those, I would like to mention the Osmania University Library, the Salar Jung Museum, the State Central Library, the *Idara-e-Adabiyat-e-Urdu*, H.E.H. the Nizam's Trust Library, the State Archives of Andhra Pradesh—and in particular, Dr Syed Dawood Ashraf (whom I bothered a great deal), the Archaeology Department of Andhra Pradesh, the Maulana Abul Kalam Azad Oriental Research Institute, the Urdu Research Centre, the library of the Urdu daily *Siasat* and especially its editor, Abid Ali Khan, for his unstinted help at all times, the *Deccan Chronicle* daily, and a number of other institutions and organizations.

Unfortunately, while the book was still under preparation, Abid passed away. His son and successor, Zahid Ali Khan was, however, equally helpful and generous in letting me draw upon his resources, especially upon some of the old photographs.

For vetting the translation of some of the pieces of poetry and for doing the translation itself, in some cases, I am indebted to Dr B.M. Sagar. I am grateful to the indefatigable and ever-smiling Sheshu Bala and Ramana Raju, S.Q. Ahmed and his team who put all this in proper order, and to Neelamegham who went over the script with his usual meticulous care and found mistakes where I thought none existed.

I am also grateful to the celebrated painter M.F. Husain for the use of his painting on the cover page.

For the second edition, I would also like to thank R.J. Rajendra Prasad formerly of *The Hindu* daily, and I. Venkata Rao, a veteran journalist and former Chairman of the Press Academy, for their valuable inputs and clarifications.

Hyderabad,   NARENDRA LUTHER
30 October 2004

Preface to the 2006 Oxford India Paperbacks Edition

Minor changes and corrections have been made in this edition in the light of the feedback received from readers and friends. I am particularly grateful to my following friends who have gone through the book with minute care for this purpose: P. Vaman Rao, former Chief of News Bureau of *The Hindu* and editor of *New Swatantra Times*; Shankar Melkote, Managing Director of Margadarshi Marketing (P) Limited, convener of the Little Theatre and a voracious reader; Dr S.K. Rao, a distinguished economist and Director-General of the Administrative Staff College of India, Hyderabad; and Rahul Luther, Managing Trustee of Hope Trust.

NARENDRA LUTHER

Preface to the 2012 Oxford India Paperbacks Edition

The first paperback edition has undergone seven reprints. During this period a number of momentous developments have occurred in Hyderabad and Andhra Pradesh. A new edition of the book was therefore called for.

This edition brings the story up to mid-2012. This opportunity has been utilized for thoroughly revising the whole text and carrying out minor corrections, deletions and additions wherever necessary. Two more pictures have also been added.

I would like to thank the publisher and, in particular, editorial and production team at OUP for their continued cooperation and hard work in bringing the book up-to-date. I am also happy that the book is coming out as an e-book soon. Also, it is a matter of gratification that the book has been translated into Hindi and Telugu and will be published soon. I am grateful to Dr Kakani Chakrapani, Dr Durgampudi Chandrasekhar, Govindaraju Chakradhar, and G. Venkatarajum for their combining operations while translating the book. That should make the text error-free.

I hope that this edition will receive the same reception as the earlier hardback and paperback editions.

Hyderabad,   NARENDRA LUTHER
25 August 2012

Preface to the Revised and Updated Edition

When the last updated edition was published in 2012, the creation of Telangana seemed unlikely. However, events progressed sooner than expected and the new state of Telangana came into being in early 2014. Six years have elapsed since that historic development. This called for a new edition of the book. I am glad to be writing the preface for this third, updated edition. Apart from being a chronicler of the earlier part of the story of Hyderabad, I have also been a witness to the section of the story described in Part 4 of this book: 'Dawn of Democracy'. Indeed, I am now one of the few people who have seen both the birth of Andhra Pradesh and its bifurcation. For a good part of that period I was part of the administration of the state.

As the perspective becomes distant, and the dust and heat of contemporary events settle down, the need is also felt for reviewing the relative importance of some parts of the narrative. I have done that especially in light of the feedback received from readers from far and wide.

I am particularly grateful to my friend A.K. Goel, a former IAS officer and now adviser to the government of Telangana, for his inputs in the revision and updating of the sections that discuss the period leading to the creation of Telangana and later.

Hyderabad,   NARENDRA LUTHER
7 April 2020

ONE: The Beginning

Antenatal Scenario

Hyderabad sits nestled amongst one of the oldest rock systems of the world. These gneissic granite rocks are 2,500 million years old. Rain, sun, and wind have for aeons, through their collective and continuous physical and chemical action, worked them into weird shapes. Some appear perched upon each other so precariously that you feel some giant-children playing at house making must have kept them there. From times immemorial they have stayed like that without tumbling down. They will remain like that long after we are gone.

Golconda Fort was once a mere hillock, a hump of a giant camel, a mass of scattered misshapen granite. It was sheer wilderness. There, cow and goatherds used to graze cattle and sheep belonging to the nearby villages. It was so popular with graziers that it took the name of 'the hillock of the graziers'—*golla konda* in Telugu, the local language. *Golla Konda* later on became 'Golconda'. Hyderabad is the daughter of Golconda Fort which stands in ruins now, eight kilometres away from the centre of the city. The fort was built about a thousand years ago, during the Kakatiya rule (AD 1000–1321) which had its capital at Warangal—a city about 150 kilometres to the north of Hyderabad.

Rudramba Devi, Queen of the Kakatiya dynasty, ruled for 34 years from AD 1262 to 1296. She withstood the combined attacks of the Pandyas, the Yadavas, and Hoysalas with the help of her grandson, Prataparudradeva who succeeded her (AD 1296–1323).

He too was an illustrious ruler but was subjected to repeated attacks by the Sultans of Delhi: there were five during the two decades after AD 1303. Finally, he was defeated by Ulugh Khan, imprisoned and taken prisoner to Delhi. On the way he committed suicide. Ulugh Khan later became the Sultan of Hindustan and is known as Mohammad Tughlaq. Since his empire had extended to the south, Delhi was no longer the centre of political gravity. He, therefore, ordered that the capital of India be shifted from Delhi to Devagiri which he renamed as Daulatabad. For two decades this city remained the capital of India.

The people of the region did not like Mohammad Tughlaq or his rule. In AD 1346, his local centurions rebelled against him and chose a noble from amongst themselves called 'Zafar', as their King. He founded the Bahmani dynasty that ruled from AD 1347 to 1518 with its capital first at Gulbarga and then at Bidar. It was divided into *taraf*s or provinces, each under a Governor. Tilang was one of them with headquarters at the mud fort of Golconda.

During the reign of the 13th Bahmani ruler, Mohammad III (AD 1463–1482), there came a young handsome man, Sultan Quli from Hamdan across the river Oxania up in the northwest of Afghanistan.

Sultan Quli, the son of a fugitive chieftain, entered the service of the Bahmani ruler and soon impressed him both as a soldier as well as a man of letters. He rose fast and in AD 1496 he was appointed Governor of the Tilang province. In 1518 when the Bahmani ruler, Mohammad, died Sultan Quli renamed the Golconda fort as Mohammad Nagar and made it his capital. He strengthened the fort and built a number of palaces, mosques, and other buildings in it. A large number of people were attracted to settle within the ramparts of the fort. It was from this fort that Sultan Quli proceeded to expand the territory under his control. He gradually conquered about 70 forts and fortresses and extended his kingdom from Warangal to Rajahmundry on the banks of the river Godavari. He however, did not declare his independence and was known as 'Badé Malik'—the Big Chief—the title that is inscribed on his grave. He subscribed to the Shia sect of Islam.

Sultan Quli had seven sons. He imprisoned two of them for their delinquencies. One of them, Jamsheed, was confined at Golconda, while the other, Daulat, was kept at Bhongir, a hill fort about 50 kilometres away.

One afternoon Mahmud Hamdani, an accomplice hired by Jamsheed Quli, plunged a dagger into Sultan Quli's neck as he sat in prayer after inspecting the construction of the fort's cathedral mosque. To cover his tracks Jasheed struck down Hamdani and took the throne. Thereafter he also blinded his brother, Daulat Khan. In the seven years of his rule he could not escape the stigma of these acts.

His younger brother, Ibrahim, made some attempts to capture the throne. But he failed and fled to seek refuge in the neighbouring Hindu empire of Vijayanagar. There he was treated extremely well and was seated by the ruler, Ram Raja's side. He spent seven years there and also married a Hindu Princess, Bhagiriti by name.

Jamsheed died of cancer in 1550. For a while his infant son was placed on the throne but the leading nobles invited the exiled brother of Jamsheed, Ibrahim, to come from Vijayanagar and take the throne. He was given a tumultuous welcome.

Ibrahim ruled for 30 years. He brought order to the state, consolidated the territories under him, and made further additions to them. He also strengthened the Golconda fort with stone and mortar. A double rampart with a circumference of eight kilometres was added. It had 8 iron gates and 400 bastions. All this cost Rs 2.1 million. In 1565, he joined with the other three Muslim Sultans of the Deccan and this confederacy of four Sultans—of Ahmednagar, Bijapur, Bidar, and Golconda—waged a battle against Ram Raja, the ruler of Vijayanagar. The Battle of Tallikota—also known as Banihatti—ended in a crushing defeat for the Vijayanagar Empire and virtually finished it.

When Ibrahim returned victorious from the battle he had another occasion to celebrate. His wife, Bhagiriti, gave birth to a fourth child, their third son, whom they called Abu Muzaffar. Later on, Abu was formally known as Mohammad Quli, 'the Servant of the Prophet'. A chronogram was prepared for him and he was given the epithet of *bais-e-rozi-e-ahil-e-alam* ('Provider of Sustenance to the People').

Not much is known about his birth. Years later, his court-poet, Vajahi, wrote a romanticized and fabled account of Mohammad Quli's life in his book, *Qutb-o-Mushtari*. In that he described the celebrations on the birth of Mohammad Quli with usual poetic hyperbole:

On Mohammad Quli's birth, gold was distributed so liberally that it has become cheaper than dirt. So many jewels and gems were scattered all over that swans have started coming on land to pick up their food. Gold due to the fall in its value has become pale.[1]

Ibrahim was popular amongst his subjects. The Hindus used to refer to him fondly as *Malkabhiram*. During his period, the fort-city began to get congested. Hygiene could not be maintained and the health of the people was threatened. Some habitation had come up on the east bank of the river Musi and suggestions were made to set up another township there. In 1578, Ibrahim had a bridge built across the river Musi. Ibrahim played with the idea of establishing a city outside the fort. He set up a township called Ibrahimpatnam to the west of the fort about 20 kilometres away. The site was not well chosen and so it did not make any progress.

Meanwhile about eight kilometres to the east, across the river there was a small sleepy village called Chichlam. It was also on the highway to the port town of Machilipatnam and a regular stream of merchandise and caravans passed that way each day. A number of taverns and inns sprang up there. Every visitor could not enter the fort as a matter of course; it took time and money to get admission. So people, while waiting for entry, bided their time at Chichlam or thereabouts. In the same Chichlam a girl called Bhagmati was born. Bhagmati used to go to the village temple with a silver plate full of offerings, covered with a red silk-cloth. Travellers, tradesmen, and soldiers were frequently seen on the road that went past the temple at Chichlam.

One day an important noble with his retinue come galloping. Hidden from the road was Bhagmati, a 14-year-old village girl, headed for the temple with a plateful of offerings. It would not be beyond these soldiers to tease or even abduct her. She waited for them to go by. But when she emerged from her hiding place the main rider rode into view suddenly. He stopped and addressed her in a firm but gentle voice.

'Young lady, who are you?'

Bhagmati didn't look up. But she noted that the voice was of a young man. From her lowered eyes she could see the stirrups and the cloth-of-gold shoes worn by the rider.

She replied that she lived in the village and was on her way to the temple to pray and sing to the deity.

'Sing?' the rider asked, 'I shall like to hear you sing.' And then pointing to the covered plate she was carrying, he asked her, 'What is there in that plate?'

'Some sweets, Sir.'

'I am hungry. Can I eat something out of that?'

'These are for the deity, Your Highness. After I have done my prayers, they will be sanctified, become *prasad* and I shall distribute them to my family and neighbours. You could then take something out of the offering.'

'But I am hungry, young lady,' the rider pleaded with a tone of authority.

'My goddess is hungry too, Your Lordship. The sweets belong to her first. Only after she has partaken of them can they be touched by any mortal.'

'But, lady, I am ... ,' the rider stopped abruptly. Whether he merely wanted to repeat that he was hungry, or to disclose his identity, wasn't clear. 'Well,' he conceded, 'I shall wait near the temple. I hope you won't be long.'

'Yes, My Lord,' the young maiden replied as she went her way beyond the tree, her anklets tinkling rhythmically. The fond eyes of the young rider followed the damsel and he tapped the mane of his horse with each beat of Bhagmati's footstep. The ding-dong of the temple gong and a little later the notes of a melody wafted across from the sacred precincts. Soon the maiden returned and lifted the cloth covering the plate and proffered a piece of sweet to the rider.

He took the sweet respectfully with both hands. He seemed to be aware of the Hindu ritual of accepting prasad with due deference, she noted.

'You do this every day?' he enquired with a smile.

'No, Your Honour. Only once a week—on Tuesdays. Everyday I visit the temple in the morning.'

'Then I shall see you tomorrow morning,' he announced and after a short pause, added, 'I am Abu Muzaffar, Prince of Golconda. Also called Mohammad. What is your name, maiden?'

'Your pleasure, Highness. This worthless creature is called Bhagmati.'

'Bhagmati,' the Prince beamed. 'Bhagmati is a good name. And you sing beautifully.' All of a sudden he took off a string of pearls from his neck and put it in the plate she was holding.

'But, Your Highness … .' The dumb-founded maiden didn't know what to say.

'I shall be hungry again tomorrow morning. And one piece of sweet will not be enough for me, Bhagmati.'

Mohammad Quli sped off and joined his companions who stood dismounted respectfully at a distance. Bhagmati followed the Prince with her eyes. The gold and diamonds on his person shone in the morning sun. And so did the string of pearls on her plate.

A smile spread across her face as she picked up the string. 'For my goddess!' she exclaimed.

And then flushed with excitement, she scampered towards the temple again.

The priest looked at her in surprise. Why this visit again so soon after her prayers, he wondered. But before he could ask her, Bhagmati placed the string of pearls at the feet of the goddess and then told the priest. 'The Prince gave this for my Devi—my goddess.'

The next morning Bhagmati sang again though it was not her practice. When she came out of the temple, the Prince was there waiting by the side of the tree. He was alone without any escort. His horse was tied to the tree. Bhagmati bowed to him and presented to him the uncovered plate full of sweets.

The Prince sampled different sweets and then suddenly looked at Bhagmati's bare neck. 'Where is the necklace?' he asked.

'It is with the Devi, Highness.'

'But I gave it to you. It was meant for you.'

'My goddess needed it. I had promised to give her one as soon as I could, Sire.'

Mohammad smiled. Then he took off another, heavier, four-stringed necklace. 'Here is another. This one is only for you.'

'No, Sire,' Bhagmati replied coyly, 'I don't need one, I am a poor girl.'

'I agree', said the Prince, 'you don't need any ornaments. But I want to enhance the beauty of this necklace.' And no one can be poor who has a Prince for a slave,' remonstrated Mohammad.

'*Oui Ma*!' Bhagmati exclaimed as she put her finger between her teeth. 'You mock this worthless creature.'

Mohammad didn't reply. He put the necklace around Bhagmati's neck.

'But, Your Highness … ,' Bhagmati protested. He took her into his embrace and gave her a gentle kiss. She felt no urge to resist. She felt she had known him for years, for ages.

'Till tomorrow then,' said the Prince as he released her from his embrace, and turned towards his horse.

Bhagmati's mother had been dead for some years. Her father was very fond of her. Before she reached her house, she had taken off the necklace and held it in her clenched fist.

She spread open her palm before her father without uttering a word. There were tears in Lingayya's eyes. 'I know. It is the Prince. I don't know what to do. We can run away from here but we won't be able to escape. His men will seek us out.'

'But father,' she said calmly, 'there is no need to go away from here. He is not a brigand. He is a Prince. He will not do any dishonorable thing to us.'

'They are all alike—these brigands and Princes. They are predators. Take care of yourself, my daughter. You are no doubt wise for your years. But you don't know the ways of Princes.'

'Don't worry, father. I shall take care of this matter.' There was calm assurance in her tone.

The Prince didn't come for the next few days. Bhagmati wasn't at ease with herself. She often heard the galloping horses echo in her ears on the way to the temple. The necklace, that had been given to her by the Prince, had been deposited in the steel safe at home and whenever she was alone, she would take it out, put it around her neck, and admire herself in the mirror. She would put an extra piece of sweet in the plate containing her offerings, stop near the tree and look around, in vain.

It was a dream, she began to tell herself. One of those things that happen to women who end up insane. Like Chintamma, who in her deranged manner, kept on talking of the horse rider who would come to marry her, but didn't. In broad daylight and in front of many people Chintamma said he had asked for her hand. People now laughed at her. Her father was right, Bhagmati told herself. It was a passing fancy on the part of the Prince. Just a gift from him had set her day dreaming.

On Tuesday she went to the temple in the evening. She performed the usual *arti*, sang a devotional song, and danced before the deity. Today there was a special, unstated invocation in her voice and a new vigour in her movements. She emerged from the temple exhausted, unmindful of things around her. She was startled to hear her name.

'Bhagmati!' And the beaming face of Mohammad Quli emerged from the shadows. 'God be praised. You didn't tell us that you danced so well.'

'Your Highness, it is kind of you to say so. I can only amuse myself. But when did you come? Why ... ?' She wanted to ask him why he hadn't come the last week but quickly stifled the question.

'Oh, you must come to the fort and show them how well you can dance and sing.'

'I only dance before my deity, Sire.'

'We shall install a replica of your deity there.'

'But, My Lord ... .'

'Come and see the fort at least. And bring with you your friends and others you like. I shall send some palanquins and mounts the day after tomorrow.'

'Sometime, yes, My Prince. Not yet.'

'I shan't wait for long.'

Lingayya's circumstances started improving. Every other day some gift or the other would come from the fort. One day some masons came and started repairing and painting the house. Lingayya was embarrassed by all this attention. His friends in the village became respectful towards him. He felt a certain degree of formality now in their dealings with him. The village too started prospering. A new well was dug. A new irrigation channel was opened up for the fields. However, Lingayya felt, tongues wagged in the village. It was not a bad bargain for the father, said people— no not even for the whole village! One girl could mean so much to them all!

One evening the Prince held Bhagmati in his arms and though the sun had set, he wouldn't let her go. He was insistent that she come to the fort.

'My Prince,' she remonstrated, 'I cannot come there just like that. There has to be an occasion.'

'Your visit will be an occasion', said the Prince, 'I shall illuminate my palace.'

'How many times has it been illuminated before?' Bhagmati was smiling but her sarcasm was apparent. This time she did not address him with any of her customary honorific prefixes.

'Never before, my love,' the Prince drew her closer and kissed her head.

'My Master, my Lord, I shall come in broad daylight to stay. Not for a visit.'

'But, of course. I shall come to fetch you in a proper manner, my Queen.'

Then Bhagmati relaxed. She became limp in his arms. They remained locked in embrace for a long, long time. Bhagmati was still lost in raptures when Mohammad Quli detached himself from her and said: 'Bhag, where did you get those *charoli*[2] from?'

'What charoli my Prince?' she asked, somewhat confused, looking around.

'These,' Mohammad said, touching her teeth with his finger.

'Oh these, my teeth,' she felt relaxed. 'I have heard people call them pearls. But 'charoli'—that is something new.'

'Yes, you will always hear something new from me. I am a poet. I look at things differently.'

'But poets call them pearls,' protested Bhagmati.

'Yes. One poet 10,000 years ago called them pearls and then everyone adopted that simile. They are not original, these poets, Bhag, they imitate.'

'But my Prince is original,' smiled Bhagmati proudly as she pulled the young man's face down on hers.

'Wait,' said Quli, 'let me see your eyes a little longer. Your eyes, Bhag, are the drunkards sleeping under the arches of mosques.'

'*Marhaba!*' exclaimed Bhagmati, 'another original metaphor. My lover has become a poet now.'

'Your love is making me a poet, Bhag. Your lips, kernels of coconut, oh, let me eat them.'

'My eyes, my eyebrows, my teeth, my lips—all have been transformed by your imagination.'

'I can make more similes if I see more of your body.' There was mischief in his tone and passion in his touch as he pulled her towards him.[3]

'No more poetry now,' remonstrated Bhagmati as she wriggled out of his embrace.

Their love became stronger as time passed. People of the village no longer made snide remarks about Bhagmati or Lingayya. On the other hand, they came to show them greater regard. After all, everybody in the village had benefited by the new attention on account of the Prince's interest in Bhagmati.

And then they heard in the village that the old Sultan had died suddenly one evening. The Prime Minister was away at Naldurg, on a campaign. The Prince didn't visit Bhagmati for some weeks. There was tension in the village. It was heard that there were skirmishes in and around the fort. One day there was the beating of a tom-tom in the village. The crier said that Mohammad Quli—the Prince charming of Bhagmati—had become the new Sultan. There were also rumours that he had married the daughter of the Peshwa, Mir Shah Mir—the girl who was engaged to his elder brother.

These rumours reached Bhagmati also but she did not believe them. There was no way of verifying them either. The Prince—now the Sultan—had vanished from the scene, it seemed. Two months thus passed. Desolate days and nights for Bhagmati. Her father pitied her but did not broach the subject with her. The *pujari* of the temple noticed the change in her but he too kept quiet. In the village too there was discreet silence in the presence of Bhagmati and her father, but there were sniggers and also some expression of mock sympathy. Some sort of self-pity on the part of village elders too was also in the air. The development of the village would come to a stop now, said the village *patel* jeeringly.

Meanwhile, Bhagmati made her trips to the temple regularly. She sang, occasionally she danced, and sometimes she felt a resentment welling up within her. Could her Devi do nothing for her? Why? But she nipped such sacrilegious thoughts in the bud. After all the Devi knew what was best for Bhagmati. It was only appropriate that she resigned herself to her fate.

One day, when she came out of the temple lost in her thoughts, she suddenly heard a familiar voice.

'Bhag, I have come,' said Quli. He was with a number of armed guards.

'Yes, Sultan of the World,' she said with cold formality. She made a deep bow and raised her hand in salutation a number of times as is done to a King. 'This slave and the village are honoured by the visit.' And then after a pause she added with veiled bitterness, 'Congratulations, Sultan, for the coronation.'

Mohammad Quli ignored the felicitation. 'We have come to take you, Bhag.'

'But didn't the Sultan acquire a Queen only recently? I forgot to congratulate His Highness on that. My apologies.'

'Bhag, that was statecraft.'

'Marriage? Statecraft? This lowly creature doesn't understand how a wedding becomes a matter of statecraft?'

'You won't, Bhag. You don't have to. Only understand this that if I hadn't done this, I wouldn't have been alive.'

'Alive surely you must have remained, My Lord, but perhaps not become the Sultan,' Bhagmati said dryly. 'Wasn't being a Prince good enough?'

'Bhag, in our system, it is a question of everything or nothing. In order to survive as a Prince, I had to become Sultan. Otherwise, I would have been put to the sword or at least blinded and jailed.'

Bhagmati shivered. 'You had to fight, yes, but you didn't have to marry.'

'Yes, I had to. To overcome the opposition, to win support. That's how my marriage was a political move. I despise the woman and she has already been dispatched across the wall of my private apartments to the harem.'

'But, My Sultan, you could have sent me a message, some reassurance.'

'I was engaged in a battle of survival and believed that you would understand. '

All the welled-up anger in Bhagmati disappeared. It was as if the weeks of separation had never intervened. He was now the ruler and he had come to her himself. The Devi had not let her down after all.

Bhag took the prasad from her plate and gave a piece to Quli. 'Oh God, thank you. Oh Devi! Thank you, my Prince is safe. Nothing else matters.'

Quli patted the tearful girl on her head and said: 'A week more and we shall go to the palace together. We shall then illuminate it for you.'

Bhagmati flew into his arms.

The next day, a dozen messengers came bearing gifts for Bhagmati and her father. The villagers suddenly started addressing Lingayya as *chaudhary*—the head of the village.

Soon thereafter Bhagmati was married to the new Sultan. A big procession came to take her in a gold-plated palanquin. A hundred horsemen accompanied her. A number of ceremonies were held in the fort and for days there were celebrations of all sorts. People at Chichlam could see some of the fireworks in the fort. A feast was arranged in the village too, and 50 cartloads of sweets and savouries came from the fort. Some more jewels and ornaments were presented to the deity in the temple and the priest was given 5,000 hons (1 hon = Rs 4.5). Everyone in the village received presents.

Bhagmati grew even more beautiful in the palace. The Sultan was a good poet and he composed a number of poems for her. Those pleased her no end and she basked in the sunshine of his attentions. This was not uncommon. Meanwhile women came to the harem with regularity—some quietly, guests of an evening; some with pomp and show for a longer stay. But none would last beyond a few weeks. After that they were packed off across the wall, to the harem—the female quarters—where they had other discarded Queens of hearts for company and eunuchs to ensure that they remained faithful to their faithless master. There were older women and young children too. These women had nothing to look forward to. They could only nurse the memories of a brief glory when they shared the royal couch and the whole world seemed to dance around their little finger.

Bhagmati's fate would be no different, they said knowingly. She had already lasted a long while but one of these days she would walk through the great door in the wall and join the human museum on the other side. Days, weeks, months, and years passed. And the young Sultan was still mad about her. And then people started talking of the magic spell of her secret powers. She was still there. She was the Queen.

Bhagmati used to visit the village once in a year at the time of the festival of Batkamma. Her retinue had instructions to stop outside the village. In the village she was all by herself except for her three ladies-in-waiting. She would participate in the festival as in the days of her childhood and early youth and she insisted that every lady address her as 'Bhago', not as Begum or such nonsense. In 1588, when she came for the festival, she told her friends proudly that the village would soon be turned into a big city. It sent a wave of excitement through the people of the village.

Soon many officials started visiting the village. Men with all sorts of instruments for measuring land, for watching the intensity of the sunlight, digging pits, raising dunes of sand and earth here and there, descended on the site. Some petty officials set up a permanent camp. A number of Iranians also used to come accompanied by a lot of baggage. Draftsmen spent days drawing up plans. There was an unending bustle on the slopes.

Then, on an auspicious day when the moon was in the constellation of Leo and Jupiter was in its own mansion, the Sultan issued a decree ordering the establishment of a new city 'which should be a replica of heaven on earth and unequalled in the world.'[4]

The project of building the new city was entrusted to the Prime Minister, Mir Mohammad Momin. He was a *sayyad*, that is, a descendent from the family of the Prophet. He hailed from Astarabad in Iran. He had a particularly good education and acquired such renown for his learning that he was appointed a tutor to Prince Hyder, son of Shah Tahmasp, King of Iran. When, after the death of the Shah, the Prince was murdered, Momin proceeded first to Kashan and then to India. In 1581, he arrived at Golconda and secured a job at the court of the young poet-ruler, Mohammad Quli. Because of his formidable reputation as a scholar, a divine, and a man of profound wisdom, he rose rapidly and soon became Prime Minister of the state. He wrote in Persian and Arabic on subjects as diverse as divinity, prosody, architecture, and weights and measures. He was also a poet and excelled in the panegyric as well as the lyrical form. He was an aesthete and this created a special bond between him and Mohammad Quli, which he further cemented by writing *qasidas*—poems of praise—in honour of the Sultan. In an age of versatility, it was the breadth of his interests that made him a revered figure. He remained Prime Minister of Golconda for over forty years during the reign of Mohammad Quli and that of his successor, Sultan Mohammad, and died in harness. The cemetery in which he is buried is named after him. Shias consider it an honour to be interred there.

As one of the advocates of the proposal to build a new city outside the Golconda fort, Mir Momin looked forward to an opportunity to indulge in his passion for town-planning. His ambition was to create a city better than Isfahan—the most beautiful city in Iran—which he had seen grow and develop as a child. It was thus the soaring imagination of the Sultan and the vaulting ambition of his Prime Minister that was responsible for the creation of the new city.

Mir Momin plunged whole-heartedly into the project of building a new city. He invited some of the architects and master-builders whom he had known and heard of in Iran to come to Golconda to help him execute the project. Mir Abu Talib, Kamal-ud-din Shirazi, and Sheharyar Jahan were persuaded to come. Even before their arrival the preliminary work of clearing the site had been started and rough sketches drawn up. After their arrival the flurry of activity picked up.

A permanent camp of draftsmen and planners was set up near Chichlam. Construction started soon after the laying of the foundation stone.

The Sultan came on a richly caparisoned elephant followed by his courtiers and nobles to lay the foundation stone. Mir Momin received him with profuse courtesies.

'Your Majesty, this is a topographical plan of the area,' Mir Momin said pointing towards the large sheets of paper.

'We know this topography, Mir Jumla,'[5] the Sultan replied with a twinkle in his eyes. 'This is where we got the object of our heart's desire, the best gem of our palace. Yes, Mir Jumla, I know this area and I am glad the experts approved my choice. Show me how the city will be laid out.' Then looking at the sketch, he exclaimed:

'Ha! Four minarets. I hear there is one minar in Delhi—very, very tall.'

'My Lord will have four minarets at the four corners of this magnificent building.'

'Good. Go on, Mir Jumla.'

'It will be a perfect square and will have three storeys. On the roof will be a mosque facing the Mecca.'

'Subhan Allah. Mir Jumla, I like it.'

'Thank you, My Sovereign. There is more to it. The mosque will take in forty-seven persons whose seats will be marked. And more persons can also be accommodated, if necessary.' The Sultan nodded.

'And each side of the square of the building will face a road going in the four directions of your kingdom. This,' pointing to the west, he proceeded, 'comes from the fort, the seat of your gracious court and goes to the port of Machilipatnam.'

The Sultan looked in the direction of the east to check the distance and imagined the bustling port of the kingdom about 300 kilometres away.

'How far is the fort?' Mohammad asked.

'The main gate is exactly eight kilometres from this point, my Master, and from there the august palace is exactly one kilometre.'

'Good'.

'And this road goes to the north, to the river. And the other road to the Koh-e-Toor which will be about five kilometres.'

'Ah, Koh-e-Toor,' mused the ruler. 'Very bracing climate. I want a palace there, and you haven't forgotten that, I am sure.'

'Of course not, Your Majesty. That is provided for in these plans.' 'Good. Let me see the plans for that.'

'Presently, Your Majesty. First let me explain the features of this area.'

There was just a hint of boredom in the Sultan's expression as he noticed the two big tables yet to be seen.

'If My Sovereign pleases, this slave shall stop here,' suggested the shrewd Peshwa.

'No, no, go ahead. For a little while longer.' And then suddenly, turning towards the plan, he said,

'But that makes a cross, Mir Jumla. That is a Christian symbol.'

'Yes, My Lord. How sharp your observation is! But we have not made a cross in the plan. There is another intersection. Seventy-six metres to the north of this.' The Peshwa showed the next plan. 'You see it here. There will be a fountain here. Again facing the four arches, one in each cardinal direction. And now if it pleases My Lord, we will move to the next table.'

At the next table was a large plan, far bigger than the first. There were sketches of numerous buildings and far to the north was a light blue streak indicating the river Musi.

Pointing to the centre of the sketch, Mir Momin submitted: 'This site is the fountain, octagonal in shape and from here four channels will be dividing each road into two parts ... .'

'A fountain, and four channels?' the face of the young monarch brightened. 'But that is so in our sacred Garden of Eden, Mir Jumla.'

'Exactly so, My Lord,' beamed Mir Momin. 'Your Majesty fore-stalls me. It was your command to make the new city a replica of heaven on earth. And it is the humble attempt of your slave to carry it out in so far as it lies within the power of a mortal.'

'Aha!' exclaimed Mohammad gleefully.

'These four channels,' Mir Momin continued, 'symbolize the heavenly canals of pure water, pure milk, pure honey, and pure wine, Sire.'

'Indeed, Mir Momin.'

'In our sacred heaven, My Lord, by the side of the eternal fountain, there are two trees, one called *Sidr* and the other *Talha*. These trees have no counterparts on earth. I intend to plant here the coconut and betel nut tree to represent them.'

'And what about the other features?' asked the excited young monarch.

'Presently, Your Majesty. There will be four arches on four sides. Behind the western arch will be the royal palaces for the gracious abode of My Lord and his royal family. It will have an area of 1,000 square metres and extend right up to the Musi. There will be the imperial palace of justice also there. Opposite, on the eastern arch, musicians will play music and in particular, the favourite instrument of Your Majesty, the *shehnai* (wind musical instrument) four times a day. On the northern and southern arches, there will be armed guards to protect the area.'

'I see, so there will be a cross here too. Why the two crosses?'

'Sire, in our Holy Book, there is a mention of not one, but of a number of heavens, if you'd recall *Sura* 55. The two crosses represent the two heavens. On the western square will be the abode of our Sovereign Lord and on the southwestern side will be his loyal subjects, living in eternal submission to the Lord. *Sura* 56 decrees that My Lord.'[6]

'And my *houris* will be behind the western arch,' stated the Sultan by way of reassurance.

'Indeed, My Lord.'

'So, I see that you have drawn upon the holy book to design the new city. Very clever indeed!'

'That is the kindness of my Master to say so. We have also not neglected to provide for the faithful subjects of Your Majesty. There will be shops and residences, schools and mosques and inns, and a general hospital for the sick, as was the direction of Your Majesty.'

'Wonderful, Peshwa Sahib, you understand me very well. And how are you going to execute this project? Where are your experts?'

'May I have the honour of presenting the leaders of my team, Your Good Honour? I have got some of the best experts from Iran; those who helped in the planning and execution of Isfahan, the city of pride in Iran.'

'So, are we going to have an Isfahan here?'

'Better than Isfahan, Sire. Now Shah Abbas will have to send his experts here to see the city we are going to create!'

'Mir Momin, I want gardens all over. This city should be lost in the lush growth of greenery.'

'Twenty-three square kilometres of greenery will surround 2.5 kilometres of the city, My Lord. Don't I know my Master's love of gardens? And that is only appropriate. In Islam, the concept of heaven is a garden. Indeed, in Arabic, the word for garden is the same as for heaven—*jannat*.'

'Mir Jumla, I don't know whether I'll go to jannat after my death, but I want to live in jannat while I am here.'

'Your Majesty will live an eternity here. For so young a human and so noble a soul, the thoughts of the hereafter are not appropriate. We need your benign presence and your subjects adore you. Wherever you are, there is heaven for us.'

Then Mohammad lifted a shimmering cloth-of-gold coat from a tray and offered it to Mir Momin. The Prime Minister bent almost double and made a number of salaams. The Sultan then honoured Mir Jumla's three assistants—Abu Talib, Ustad Kamal-ud-din Shirazi, and Sheharyar Jahan[7]—in a similar fashion.

As the Sultan finished with the ceremony, there was a light drizzle even while the sun shone.

Everybody said it was a good omen. The Sultan himself was the first to point that out.

The people of Chichlam were given a free meal that evening from the royal kitchen. There were also magnificent fireworks.

Birth of Bhagnagar

The construction went on at a remarkable pace. Men and women, some thousands of them, worked round the clock. Material came from all over and in all modes of transport. The concentration was on Charminar and the two palaces—the Daulatkhana-e-Ali and the Khuadadad Mahal. These were major projects. Shops, and inns, and houses were small things compared to these.

In 1592, the nucleus of the city was ready: Charminar, some palaces, the Jami Mosque, the *Ashurkhana*, the four arches, and the fountain. Mir Momin had taken care to have trees and other greenery planted even when the site surveys were completed so that by the time the buildings were ready, saplings had begun to acquire strength.

The Sultan had been very eager to move to the new city. As soon as the nucleus was ready, he ordered his court to move. A grand function was held at which the Sultan addressed the assembled gentry. He had composed a poem especially for the occasion. He concluded his speech with this couplet:

> *Mera shehar logan soon mamoor kar*
> *Rakhya joon toon darya mein min ya Sami!*

> (Fill up my city with people,
> My God, just as you have filled the river with fish.)

The gathering cheered him lustily on his spontaneous expression of his sentiment. As was customary, a number of chronograms were prepared on the completion of the Charminar. A chronogram is a literary device by which a couplet, or an epigram, or a mere word or two are put together to signify an important event. Every letter has a numerical value assigned to it and the word or couplet then yields the date of the event. Those who had composed chronograms were then invited to recite their compositions. Each recitation was appreciated since it showed considerable ingenuity, and great proficiency in diction and grammar. Most of the chronograms flattered the monarch.

But the gathering was rent by shouts of *wah wah* and marhaba by the recitation of simply two words by a young man, named Hasan. He made his obeisance to the ruler, bowed to the gathering, and uttered the usual prefatory remark: 'I submit.'

It was greeted with the usual formal response from the audience: 'Be pleased to grant.'

The Sultan simply nodded his head slightly by way of permission.

Hasan looked around at the audience in a bemused manner and then said: 'Ya Hafiz.'

Saying this, he stopped; then looked around. This could have been an opening of a poem, or a prefatory invocation for a line. So people waited. But that was all. He then just smiled and surveyed his audience for their reaction. The compere made a quick calculation and got up and said, 'Your Majesty, this yields the year of 1000 H' (corresponding to AD 1592.)

A pandemonium of applause and verbal cheers broke out.

Hasan could not cope with the shouts of praise from all sides. He looked like a mechanical toy wound to raise his hand in rapid salutations.

The Sultan got up and placed his hands on the bowed head of the young man. A bag containing 1,000 hons was given to him and a robe was placed on his shoulders.

The monument got its chronogrammatic name and every one knew that the young man had started on his upward journey in the court.

The Sultan drove in straight to his palace. There the Royal Chamberlain received him while petals of roses were showered on him from all sides. A dozen young girls greeted him with silver

plates and as they waved the lighted lamps they sang a song composed by the Sultan:

> *Tumhi mere mandir soo ao aj lala*
> *Tum oopar thç joban waroon gi sau bala.*

(Come to my temple my lover
I shall squander my whole youth on you.)

Thousands of earthen lamps flickered on all the balconies and
created a chiaroscuro. At the centre of the courtyard a thousand
damsels were ready in a dance formation. As Mohammad Quli
walked up to the gilded chair high on the platform, his entourage
took seats on either side aided by liveried attendants. Two young
women wielded the *morchhals*—peacock-feather fans in silent
rhythmic sways.

Heralded by a drumbeat, the dance began with soft music
to which a thousand beautiful, lissome, young bodies swayed.
Gradually, the rhythm became faster and women fell out of the
formation and receded into the shaded passages, leaving fewer
and fewer dancers. Ultimately, only two were dancing while a
lone plaintive voice started singing and the dancers drew themselves closer still to the Sultan. When the song stopped, they fell
prostrate at the royal feet. The Sultan got up. He clapped and then
made for his private apartments.

The public ceremony was over. Now the Sultan was free from
the protocol.

Outside the palace a ten-deep file of horses came marching up
to the gate. There were 50 rows and then a palanquin carried by
eight men. Behind the palanquin were another 50 rows, ten deep.
That was the special privilege of Bhagmati. She always came to
visit the Sultan's apartments in a procession of a thousand horses.
She had been offered an elephant to ride too, but she preferred
the safer and more feminine palanquin. That way she was lost
in the march of the cavalry. It heightened her mystery. On an
elephant, the whole world could see her. From a palanquin she
was invisible, except at the points of entry and exit. People kept
guessing about her—her appearance, her dress, her gait. She was
the perfect woman. She knew how to enhance her mystique. Only
her personal attendants, the eunuchs of the harem, and the Sultan

had seen her. The Sultan of course had seen her for many years and yet he was not sated. Every time he came to her with renewed appetite. And every meeting of the two lovers was a ritual.

He would greet her with one of his own compositions—sometimes a full poem, sometimes a mere couplet. That stoked her desire for him as no spirits could. She drank sparingly and only with the Sultan, to please him. He was always in high spirits; yet he wanted her to fill his glass.

He would insist on her sipping it first. Then he would fill her glass, sip it, and pass it on to her. Mohammad Quli would gulp down his glass and ask for more. Bhagmati nursed her drink and seldom took more than a peg. 'I do not need a drink,' she often told him. 'The sight of you is enough to excite me.' The Sultan liked the compliment. He said wine redoubled his pleasures. In the background musicians played soft music from behind thin veils. Bhagmati would hum the words of some song and make the gestures of dance. Quli would not let her get up and dance. In the beginning he would himself try to dance with her. Then he would just cling to her while she still hummed the tune. Then gradually, there was no knowing from where the song and the dance got mixed. The musicians knew from the sounds of the private chambers when the music should fade out. The lights too were put out. Bhagmati was in the arms of the young ruler.

One night he groped around her bosom, opened his eyes and saw her tresses spread over her bare shoulder and her contours. 'Dark clouds,' he whispered, and shaking her tresses, he went on, 'These dark clouds are trying to climb these beautiful mountains.'

Bhagmati made a gesture of covering her bare bosom with her long scented locks. Quli brushed them aside, and teased her, 'Don't cover this part, dear. Already night is confined by the day,' and saying this he drew a circle with a finger on the breasts around the nipples. Bhagmati quivered in ecstasy.

In her sleep she ruled his world. In the morning, she woke up before her lover. She looked at the ravages of the night before. Her clothes, her ornaments, and his robes were strewn all over the hall. She didn't know they had been over so much of the room during the night. A few things were found in the balcony that overlooked the river. That was so particularly if it was a full-moon night.

Mohammad Quli had already been drinking when Bhagmati was announced in the new palace. He did not keep to his seat, as mostly he did. He got up, ran towards the door, and before Bhagmati could even make her bows, he embraced her.

'You made me wait today, Bhag.'

'I was asked to come at this time, Majesty, and I am not late.' Bhagmati gave her explanation.

'You are on time, but that doesn't mean that you did not make me wait for you.'

'I am indeed fortunate in my love.'

'You are, you are,' he teased her as he nuzzled into her bosom. 'No woman was ever loved so much!'

'You are already drunk, my Sultan,' responded Bhagmati.

'Not yet. I drink myself, but I shall get drunk only by your hand. And when I am drunk, you know I don't speak.'

'Your words of love always ring in my ears, My Lord. I am never without their resonance.'

Quli pulled Bhagmati gently by her hand. Like an excited child he took her to the arch of the main hall and showed her the inscription. 'It is your palace, Bhag!' Bhagmati looked up in surprise. The inscription read 'Hyder Mahal'.

'But ... ,' she began a feeble, confused protest.

'Yes. This is Hyder Mahal. Dedicated to you because henceforth that will be your title: Hyder Mahal.'

Bhagmati tried to make her bow of gratitude. Quli stopped her with his embrace. Then he withdrew, stood at a distance, and declared royally:

'I give you this palace. And this city. It is named after you. Let generations to come know that you once lived here and I loved you.'

'But Your Gracious Majesty ... .'

'Shh ... ,' the Sultan put his fingers on her lips. 'No Majesty, no Sultan, I am today simply Abu Muzaffar, your Abbu.'

'That is blasphemy, my love. I don't deserve all this.'

'You don't know what you deserve,' the Sultan challenged. 'Sometimes even a Sultan feels poor. I wish I had more to give you, to name after you, to be associated with your name. If I were Alexander, I would have named the entire new world after you. But I am ... .'

Bhagmati interrupted him. 'You are ruler of the whole world. You are my Master. I know nothing beyond that.'

'Enter your palace, my Queen,' Quli said as he bowed and spread out his right hand as a gesture of invitation.

This was the first time Quli had addressed Bhagmati as Queen. He had a thousand poetic terms of endearment for her. He had called her the life of his life, a houri from heaven, even a goddess, but never a Queen. Quli noticed a tremor in her frame and then two tears rolled down her eyes. In silence she coiled her arms around his neck. She felt choked. Mohammad Quli, the Sultan of Golconda, the founder of the new city, Bhagmati's lover, smothered her with kisses, then lifted her and took her across the threshold. She giggled and tried to get down but he kept on marching, holding her aloft in his arms. He stopped only to deposit her on the couch. Then he filled two glasses, gave her one and took the other himself. He raised it and declared solemnly: 'To Bhagnagar—and Hyder Mahal.'

She responded coyly: 'To my lover and the founder of Bhagnagar.'

Bhagmati was ecstatic. For the next few days she became an ethereal being. She went to her old temple to pray. She came not as Hyder Mahal but simply as Bhagmati of old, in a palanquin, unornamented, almost incognito. No one was informed beforehand. Only after she reached the temple, word spread and her old friends and companions gathered there. Gradually, the whole village began to converge there. But she did not want a crowd. Only a few people were allowed within the precincts of the temple. She danced there, a dance of gratitude, as if to herself and then, just as quietly as she came, she slipped away. She left a new gold necklace for the deity and a thousand hons for the priest.

The construction activity continued at a feverish pitch. The Jami Mosque, the Ashurkhana, and so many palaces were being built at the same time. There was a hospital as well. The palaces occupied an area of a million square metres. As each palace was built, Mohammad Quli would compose a poem describing its main features.

The city grew rapidly in every way. There were new houses, new bazaars, new shops, new buildings, and new gardens. True to his word, Mir Momin created gardens all around the city. From the Nabat Pahad (now called Naubat Pahad) to Koh-e-Toor, over 23 square kilometres in area consisted of gardens of different types.

Dad Mahal was the palace of justice. Here Mohammad Quli used to receive petitions from the general public once a week, and as far as possible, instant redress was provided to supplicants. There were over a dozen other palaces, and although each was good in its own way, two were particularly special. First, the Khuadadad Mahal which had eight storeys. Each floor had a different name and there were terrace gardens right up to the top floor. Mohammad Quli could not live without the sight of greenery. Some of the foreign visitors expressed surprise at the height of the terrace gardens. How could the arches stand so much weight and how was water conveyed to such heights!

The other remarkable palace was the Qutb Mandir. No, it was not a temple, as the name would suggest. It was a palace in which only women were allowed entry, and of course, the Sultan himself. Whereas in his poems on different palaces, Mohammad Quli described their architectural features, in the poem on the Qutb Mandir, he talked only of the attractions of the beauties there. Bhagmati never went there. She did not count herself as one of the women. She was the unique woman and she used to come on invitation and in her own special style, the way she came on the first day to the new city and to new palaces made for her. One thousand horses strutted the streets and in their midst she rode a specially ornamented palanquin. When she paid a visit to the Sultan, the whole town knew. It was an event and Mohammad Quli never recited poems about his sweethearts before her. She was so special in every way.

It was natural that many people became jealous of Bhagmati. Many Persian nobles were not happy with the name Bhagnagar. It was so pagan sounding, they objected. Once there was an uprising in the city too. This was sparked off by an incident at the Nabat Pahad. Some Mughals got drunk and entered the royal pavilion. They were driven out by the *Darogha*—the Police Commissioner— by force. In the clash, two or three Mughals were killed. This set off reprisals in the city. The darogha crushed the uprising but some disgruntled local Sunnis used this as a pretext to rise against the excessive Shia influence on the Sultan. His own brother, Khuda Banda, became the leader of the rebels. There were a number of people in this group who harboured ill will against Bhagmati.

The Sultan however, did not relent. Khuda Banda was arrested and put in jail. Others were killed. Peace was restored. To make his point Bhagmati was invited once again by the Sultan and she came through the main streets of the city with her resplendent entourage. For three days she stayed there and only the eunuchs or the attendants could see the Sultan during that period. He drank, sang, and was all the time with Bhagmati.

Then came the first of Muharram, the month of mourning for Muslims. Suddenly, the Sultan became a different person. He put on black robes, broke his wine glasses and goblets, ordered a thousand earthen lamps to be lit at the Ashurkhana. He rode out of his palace, but got down and walked barefoot about a kilometre to the Ashurkhana. All the nobles followed him in black robes. At the Ashurkhana, the congregation, after hearing the *zakir*, followed him in chorus, singing the *marsiyas*—poems of mourning for Husain and the martys of Karbala—composed by him especially for the occasion. It had a doleful beat. The hall reverberated with the sound of the beating of a thousand breasts and the deep, sonorous, rhythmic chant. Tears rolled down every eye from the excessive emotion generated by the chanting. This practice went on for ten days.

Each day another thousand earthen lamps were added to those already kept there. So on the tenth day there were 10,000 lamps. The whole place shone like a jewel. No celebrations were allowed in the city during the month. Black drapes hung from balconies and walls of houses and shops. Toddy shops were closed. Professional women shut the front doors and received their 'guests' discreetly through the back doors. He observed this practice unfailingly every year. Mohammad Quli himself composed only marsiyas during this period. If he wrote any other type of poems, he kept them to himself. It was hard on him, to undergo a complete change of lifestyle. And he would lose considerable weight during the month.

After this period of mourning, cognizant of the feelings of some of the leading nobles about the name given to the city, he

announced that the city would be given a title, a chronogrammatic epithet. This generated considerable enthusiasm amongst
the poets and learned people. Ultimately, the epithet selected was
Farkhunda Bunyad. This meant, literally, 'of auspicious foundation'. The meaning was the same as Bhagnagar in the popular
idiom. Mohammad Quli was very excited about this clever con-
trivance. It affirmed in a way the name he had chosen himself for
the city. The nobles, who had hoped for a new name, felt let down
at this. Quli called Bhagmati again and told her with great enthusiasm the story of this game of chronogram. He asked her in mock
seriousness: 'And now, how would my darling like to be called
Farkhunda Begum?' She replied with a bow: 'Whatever name my
Lord may give me, I shall only remain his maid.'

'But you are no maid, my love. You are the ruler of the heart of
the ruler.'

'I just want to stay there, My Lord. I don't aspire to anything
beyond that.'

'But I do,' said Quli teasingly and lifted her up in his arms.

'Easy,' warned Bhag kissing his head. 'You can't be playing with
me like that any longer. This might damage some precious cargo I
am carrying here,' and she tapped the gentle swell of her stomach.

'Oh, how exciting,' cried Mohammad. 'So you are going to give
me a human toy to play with, after all!'

'*Insha Allah*, this winter we shall be blessed.'

'What is it? A Prince or a Princess?'

'It is beyond us mortals to know. I only hope it will be a future
King,' said Bhagmati.

'King or Queen, Bhag, it doesn't matter. I love you for that.' And
in spite of her protestations, Quli carried her around but when he
deposited her on the couch, he was gentle. And he recited to her a
couplet of his. 'What I prayed for the city is going to happen to us
now. Bhag, this palace will be full of small children.'

'One at a time,' she smiled teasingly.

'You never know. Twins or triplets ... ,' Quli laughed.

'Oui Ma,' she cried in mock horror. 'My Lord is already thinking of saving on his labours.'

'Haven't we worked hard enough already?' Quli asked her as
he slid down by her side.

Mohammad Quli was 28 now. He had married the daughter of Mir Shah Mir, his father's Prime Minister, to win the throne of Golconda. There was no love or emotion in that alliance. On the other hand, there was some element of coercion and considerable embarrassment. The girl had been engaged to Mohammad's elder brother, Husain Quli. When Sultan Ibrahim died suddenly, a will was manipulated through some court intrigues, according to which he was shown to have nominated Mohammad Quli as his successor. The marriage of convenience was intended to pave Mohammad Quli's way to the throne, and shortly after securing his throne, Mohammad Quli dismissed his father-in-law and dispatched him to Iran. The hapless young girl also went away with her father and nothing was ever heard of her again.

Mohammad Quli's heart was set on Bhagmati and he married her soon thereafter. He was then 16 and Bhagmati was about the same age.

A horoscope had been prepared when Bhagmati was born. She was the first daughter of her parents. All their sons had died one after the other in their infancy. The horoscope predicted that she would be a person of great renown and the astrologer added by way of advice that she should be allowed to do whatever she wanted. Not only that, he also said that Bhagmati's progeny would dominate the affairs of the state for a long time. It was also forecast indirectly that her mother would pass away when Bhagmati would be eight.

The girl showed great aptitude for singing and dancing and the local priest gave her good coaching. But for her mother's early death, Bhagmati would have been married off by the age of ten or so. The astrologer had advised against that. Her father, Lingayya, too needed her presence in the forlorn house. He did not remarry and the father and daughter became good friends.

Twelve years had passed since Mohammad Quli had married Bhagmati but they did not have any child. Mohammad Quli wasn't bothered too much about continuing his 'line'. He harboured a guilty feeling about the way he had deprived the legitimate heir to the throne of his right and often remorsefully unburdened himself to Bhagmati. She tried to cheer him up often: 'You yourself said that either you ascend the throne or get blinded and killed, or rot in prison. That is the custom of royalty.' That was reassurance enough for Quli's troubled conscience which was further numbed by his cup and the beauties at the Qutb Mandir palace.

During her pregnancy, Bhagmati stayed within her palace. She never came out after the fourth month. Now the Sultan used to visit her. Every Friday evening he was there without fail.

The child was a daughter.

'A piece of moon,' the midwife reported jubilantly, and an elated father threw his own necklace into her extended palms. The celebrations on the birth of a girl were always subdued in royal households, as indeed in the families of the common people, too. But Quli had let it be known that the celebrations were to be on a scale observed for a Prince. All the palaces were profusely illuminated for seven days, as was the Charminar and other buildings of note. The nobles vied with each other in expressing their happiness. All the poor people in the city were fed first on behalf of the Sultan and then by each who was seen to be one with the Sultan in his rejoicing.

On the fortieth day there was a big ceremony. The Qazi, after consulting the Quran, requested the Sultan to indicate a name for the child. Quli called her Hayat Bakshi, the giver of life. The title did not denote the Lord, the Supreme Being, but one who had infused life and a peculiar sense of renewal in all who came in contact with her. It stood for supplication to God to spare her life for this purpose. The little imp had brought alive the whole palace and the Sultan gloried in that.

The horoscope of the new baby predicted long life and glory for her. It was then that Bhagmati took out that old paper tucked away in her secret box, her own horoscope which had been prepared over a quarter of a century ago. She showed it to Quli who was surprised to note that the prediction about Bhagmati and her progeny tallied with what was now forecast for Hayat Bakshi. The horoscope also said that the little girl would have no brother or sister.

Mohammad ruminated over that and decided to concentrate all his affections and attention upon her. What if she was a girl? The Sultan would spare no effort to educate her and make her into someone who would make the predictions about her come true.

Ma Saheba

Hayat Bakshi grew into a beautiful girl. One day she looked into the mirror and tarried there longer than before. She looked at herself admiringly and hummed two lines from one of her father's poems—a couplet addressed to a lover:

> *Tuj bin rhya na jave un neer kuch na bhave*
> *Birha kitta satave man seeti man mila de.*

(I can't stay without you; nor bear any other sight.
Separation torments me; O, let us unite.)

Suddenly, at about this time, Bhagmati fell ill. The illness continued for two weeks. The physicians assured the Sultan that there was nothing serious. Since the cause of her illness could not be detected, the physicians said that probably something was weighing on her mind. Quli questioned her one evening. Tears rolled down her eyes and she simply said: 'You know I am not *that*.'

'What *that*?' asked Quli, perplexed.

'What Faizi says about me.'

'Oh, that rascal! But how did you know what he said? And why should it worry you? You know that I know and the whole world knows.'

Faizi was one of the principal courtiers and a great confidant of the Mughal Emperor, Akbar the Great, who ruled from AD 1556 to 1605. Akbar had sent him to Ahmednagar as his regent when the Mughal incursions into the Deccan began. In his regular confidential dispatches about Golconda Faizi talked disparagingly of Mohammad Quli. He did not refer to him as the King of Golconda. The Mughals never conceded that status to the Sultans of the Deccan who were seen as the local overlords, big nobles, but not rulers. Faizi, in his report, had remarked that the Great Lord of Golconda was excessively fond of an old hag, a woman of ill-repute, called Bhagmati. This observation had been deliberately leaked and was circulated by some of the hostile nobles at the court of Golconda to spite Bhagmati and Mohammad Quli.[8]

'If you know, My Lord,' Bhagmati spoke weakly, 'that is enough for me. But I don't want to embarrass you.'

'I don't feel embarrassed. I feel proud. This rumoured report was made only to make Akbar jealous of me,' Quli smiled vainly, as was his wont. Bhagmati too smiled wanly through her tears.

'If it had been Ala-ud-din-Khilji, he would have waged a war to snatch you away from me, as he did for Padmini, the Rajput Queen. But Akbar has better sense.' Quli's remark was intended to restore Bhagmati's pride in her looks.

'Not now, my love,' she wiped her face with her hand, 'now they can only make jibes at me.'

That night Bhagmati died in her sleep. She was not quite forty then and Hayat Bakshi had just turned 14.

The coterie of nobles who were ill at ease with Bhagmati's presence drew comfort from her demise. They started pressurizing the Sultan to change the name of the city also. Their objections were long-standing. The name Bhagnagar was not quite Islamic. Being the capital of a Shia ruler, they argued, it should be named after Hyder, which was another name of Ali, the Prophet's son-in-law and the fountainhead of inspiration for the Shias. The real cause of their objection was that Bhagnagar reminded them of Bhagmati and her relations with the Sultan, of a pagan commoner's hold over a blue blooded, pious Shia. Mohammad Quli said that the city would keep its name, Bhagnagar. And as for his being pious, he simply laughed. It was a travesty of facts. It was flattery, pure and simple. But then he sighed. A Prince is condemned to listen only to flattery, never to the truth.

At long last the coterie succeeded in its relentless campaign and the name of the city was officially changed to Hyderabad. Mohammad Quli, however, always referred to the city as Bhagnagar, and so did the people. And even with the new name, the association with Bhagmati remained. Wasn't she also called *Hyder Mahal*?

The Qutb Shahis voluntarily accepted the theoretical overlordship of the Shah of Iran. The *khutba*—the Friday exordium in the mosques which in Islam is one of the symbols of sovereignty—was read in the name of Shah Abbas I, the ruler of Iran. He too was kindly disposed towards the ruling house of Golconda. In 1604, he sent Mohammad Quli a crown studded with jewels. The emissary, Ughuzlu Khan, who brought the crown and other gifts, also brought an affectionate letter from Shah Abbas. This contained a proposal for the marriage of Hayat Bakshi with one of the Persian Princes.

Hayat Bakshi came to know about the proposal and pleaded with her father not to send her to exile, as she put it. Mohammad Quli too was disinclined to part with his only daughter whom he had brought up so fondly. He had also in mind the prediction in her horoscope about her long life and renown. If she went to Iran, her future would be uncertain. It was not clear which Prince of Iran she was to marry. And in the war of succession that would inevitably follow the Shah's demise, there was no knowing what would happen to her and her husband. On the other hand, if she stayed on in Bhagnagar she would succeed him. The only possible challenge could be from his nephew, Sultan Mirza, son of his younger brother, Mohammad Amin. If the principle of male succession were followed, he would be the obvious choice. And though Hayat Bakshi was a charming and popular Princess, her being the daughter of Bhagmati was a blemish in the eyes of many.

'No,' said Quli, patting his young daughter. 'We shall not send you away. We too shall not be able to bear separation from the apple of our eye.'

'You don't have to worry about my marriage, respected father. I can stay like this with you forever.' Though Hayat said this, Quli knew that the thought of the Prince in the next palace was caressing her mind.

'That would be selfish on our part, my life. If we were immortal, we might have considered that. But not being that, we cannot think of such a course. Rest assured, my daughter. You shall live here. And the prediction of your horoscope has to be made to come true.'

He consulted his trusted Prime Minister, Mir Momin, who had already given thought to this matter. He invited Ughuzlu Khan to his house and after a week, reported to his sovereign that Iran's Emperor could be placated without the Princess being sent there.

That cleared the way for Hayat Bakshi's marriage with Prince Sultan Mirza, Mohammad Quli's nephew.

Ughuzlu Khan was still in Hyderabad when Hayat's wedding was celebrated in 1607. The Shah of Iran, who had been notified earlier, was gracious enough to send special gifts on the occasion. The Sultans of Bijapur, Berar, and Ahmednagar attended the ceremonies. Mohammad Quli distributed 40,000 *khillats*—robes of honour—amongst the nobility and chief officers of the state. He had also some time ago ordered the construction of a new palace for the young couple and they shifted there after the ceremonies.

No two persons were more unlike than Mohammad Quli, and his nephew and son-in-law, Sultan Mirza. The former was given to a life of ease and sensuality. He drank, and sang, and danced, and loved to be surrounded by women. The detailed testimonials given by him to their lovely bodies and the pleasures they gave him are available in his poetic works. He never wore a mask. He declared openly that 'luxury was born for his sake and that he had sworn to do two things in his life—drink and make love'.

Sultan Mirza had seen his uncle as also his father drowned in alcohol and the pleasures of the flesh. He shrank from that 'royal' mode of life and was a quiet person, austere in his ways and drawn to scholarship and religion. He loved the company of scholars and spent hours discoursing with them. He was also a poet and in that respect stood in tremendous awe of his father-in-law.

Being a woman, and the only daughter of the Sultan, Hayat Bakshi had been brought up with great care with an eye on her future. She got more than the normal share of education of a Princess of those days. She was an introvert, somewhat withdrawn and sober. In many ways, she was an ideal match for Sultan Mirza: both had an aversion for the degenerate way of life in the palace and shared a genuine love for scholarship.

Mohammad Quli died four years after Hayat Bakshi's marriage. He was only forty-six then and had ruled for 31 years. People loved him for what he was. Their grief was heartfelt, the mourning genuine.

The cortege was taken to the Fort first. From there it was brought out through the Banjara Gate in a slow procession. Mohammad Quli had, in his own lifetime, built his own resting place in the family necropolis. It is a magnificent building and outshines all others in its size and splendour. His body was given a bath in the royal mortuary. Then the prayers were read and the coffin was gently lowered into the crypt of his mausoleum.

Mohammad Quli, the Prince and poet, lover and builder, the founder and father of the city, was returned to earth. In the long memory of the city, the imprint of his deep and abiding humanity, his love of poetry and beauty, his swashbuckling manner, his vision, is clear and indelible. There will never be another like him, the city sighed to itself.

❖ ❖ ❖

Mohammad Quli had no male issue and had begged his younger brother, Mohammad Amin, to let him adopt his son, Sultan Mirza. Amin did not agree. Then, while the boy was only four, Amin died and the guardianship of Sultan Mirza fell on Mohammad Quli. Amin's widow, Khanam Agha, was a strong woman who exercised a great influence on him throughout his life. He was brought up on strict religious lines and Khanam saw to it that he did not imbibe any of the sybaritic traits of his uncle. Sultan Mirza thus grew into a serious, sober young man with a religious propensity. However he shared with his uncle a love of poetry, and composed poems himself.

Sultan Mirza's accession was smooth. Mohammad Quli had already arranged that in his lifetime, soon after Hayat Bakshi's marriage. He had also secured the acceptance of this proposal from all his principal nobles because he feared some resistance from his brother, Khuda Banda. Mir Momin, as Prime Minister, provided continuity with the previous regime. There was no internal or external disturbance to distract him. He was lucky to have peace at home. The Mughals were at the door step of the Deccan but Malik Amber in Ahmednagar was fighting them.

Sultan Mohammad was an admirer of Mohammad Quli's poetry. One of the first things he did after his accession was to publish a book of his poems to which he appended some of his own poems in Persian. It was a beautiful book with eight illustrations. Only about a hundred copies were published, if we can use that term for something that is handwritten. Hayat Bakshi was immensely pleased with that and treated it as a gift on her birthday. Her husband often teased her by reading some of the erotic poems in their bedchamber so that whenever she saw the book in his hand, she would snatch it and keep it under her pillow. 'Later,' she would say.

Hayat Bakshi noticed that the publication of Quli's poetry had made her husband more romantic and also a better lover.

One evening the young ruler came to the private chambers and started playing with Hayat's hair. Then he said suddenly: 'Begum, today the flowers in our garden had no fragrance.'

'Oh,' Hayat was surprised, 'what happened? There are so many kinds of flowers—and this is the season too.'

'Yes, the Sultan said with mock-innocence, 'but all the fragrance seems to have gone.'

'But why, and where?' Hayat was still nonplussed.

'It all came and got into your hair,' Mohammad said as he sunk his face into her tresses.

Hayat was touched by this compliment.

He proceeded to unbutton her high-neck blouse.

'These pigeons,' he said in awe, as he seemed to be weighing her breasts. 'They are at once pliant and resistant, soft and solid like pigeons. Resting in friendly hands, yet a bit afraid, not sure whether they want to get released and fly off.'

Hayat tried to cover herself as the Sultan's eyes roved downwards. But her resistance was nominal when he pushed aside her hands. 'Ah, these thighs—they are fresh and supple like the trunk of a banana tree.'

Hayat suddenly sprang up and clung to him. She said in a drowsy whisper: 'Nothing is new for you, my love. How come these new similes?'

'Everything appears new today,' replied the Sultan. 'I have been going through the late Sultan's poems today. He gives me new insights.'

'If this is what they do to you, you should read him more often.' But already they were beyond any conversation. No more poetry was quoted. They melted into each other.

Only when he heard the muezzin's call to prayer did the young lover tear himself away from her. He would be hard put trying to concentrate on his prayers today, he thought. His mind was still on the creature, not the Creator!

On another night, Sultan Mohammad mumbled into Hayat's ears as they lay together in a lover's embrace. 'This is the meeting of Ganga and Jamuna,' and he pressed his body close to hers. 'Our legs are entwined like snakes … .'

'Beware Sultan, there may be poison there,' Hayat butted in.

'You are not your father's dutiful, loyal daughter,' teased Sultan Mohammad. 'I have published his *diwan* because it is a manual for lovers. You should read it sometime.'

'It is bad enough that you have read it.'

'Yes, and listen to this … .'

'No,' said Hayat, 'let him not be disturbed in his peace, nor us in our love.'

Seven years after their marriage Hayat Bakshi had her first child. He was named Abdullah. He was born under an inauspicious star. The royal astrologers were at a loss to convey to the Sultan what they read in the child's horoscope.[9]

The signs said that it would not be good for the Sultan and the Prince to see each other's face for 12 years.

The King and Queen both wept when they met. Then the Sultan consoled her and told her to inform him everyday about the progress of the Prince.

It was suggested to the Sultan that if he could construct a mosque, the 'curse' on the Prince might be lifted. Orders were issued immediately for the construction of a big mosque to the northwest of Charminar. The ruler was advised that the sanctity of the mosque should be kept from the day the foundation stone was laid and the work on it should not be interrupted.

In 1617, the plans for the mosque were ready. Mir Faizullah Beg and Rangayya, alias Husaimand Khan, were in charge of the project. On an auspicious day, the Sultan asked all the nobles to gather for a ceremony to lay the foundation stone. It was an early winter morning. The place was abuzz with hundreds of dignitaries of state. The royal crier read a proclamation that the foundation stone of the new house of God would be laid by someone who had never missed the five daily prayers prescribed in Islam. 'By the command of His Majesty, I invite any such person to step forth and perform the ceremony.'

A hush fell over the assembly.

None rose.

Mohammad then got up and declared that since the age of twelve, he had not missed a single daily prayer of his faith. He therefore laid the foundation stone.

The project was ambitious but the progress on the construction was slow. The Sultan could not complete it in his lifetime. It wasn't complete even during the long reign of his successor or even his successor! About 75 years later when the Mughal Emperor, Aurangzeb, entered Hyderabad as a conqueror, the mosque still needed some funds for its completion. Aurangzeb was approached for the sanction of extra funds. In a cynical reply, he recited a couplet in Persian:

> *Kare duniya, kase tamam nakarad*
> *Harche geerad, mukhtasar geerad*
>
> (No one has been able to complete all the tasks that he undertook to do. One should therefore not take upon himself more than one can accomplish.)

Having administered his admonition, he sanctioned the amount and the biggest mosque in South India was thus completed.

Meanwhile, arrangements were made to impart appropriate education to Abdullah. Different tutors were appointed for religious instructions and martial training. Months and years passed and the twelfth year approached. Both the father and son eagerly looked forward to their first meeting.

One night Abdullah had a strange dream. He saw that he had entered a beautiful garden. All sorts of trees were there and in whichever direction he looked, the trees would bend down in respectful salutation. When he walked past them, they swayed as if in ecstatic delight and seemed to offer him felicitations.

The Prince was surprised by such a quaint dream as he awoke unusually refreshed. He sent for his tutor in religious instruction, Maulvi Muazzam and asked him: 'What is the meaning of this dream, respected teacher?'

'Was there anyone else in the garden?'

'No, Sir.'

'How did you feel on waking up?'

'The freshness of the garden in the dream seemed to stay on even after I had awakened.'

'Well, Prince, it is a good omen for you. But I would respectfully urge you not to mention this dream to anyone.'

'Not even to my mother?'

'Especially not to her,' the tutor advised. 'Soon the doors of a new life are going to open for you.'

'Yes, indeed,' said the Prince excitedly. 'I shall soon be seeing my father. Twelve years will be over soon.'[10]

The old tutor smiled blankly. That night he passed away peacefully in his sleep.

The period of separation between him and his father ordained by the stars was almost over. A special session of the court was fixed to mark the joyous occasion of the meeting between father and son. The Prince was to be brought to the Sultan's court in a procession.

But in one careless moment, during the preparation for the great function for the royal union, the retinue of the Sultan crossed the suite of the Prince in a corridor of the palace.

The meeting had taken place before the appointed day, by accidental oversight. But it was taken lightly because it was in the last month of the twelfth year.

Three months passed in great excitement. The Sultan tested out his son in literary attainments and martial accomplishments. To mark the occasion, he made a special gift of two big elephants to his son. The hefty beasts, specially imported from Saigon, were called Moorat and Soorat.

A plan for a picnic and hunt was drawn up. On the appointed day, the Sultan suddenly developed fever. There was no improvement in his condition and on the fourth day his temperature started rising further. At this stage, Indian *hakims* were called for a second opinion to supplement his treatment by Unani—Greco-Arabic—physicians from Iraq. While the Unani group wanted to administer medicine with cold essence, the Indians suggested a heat-generating medication. The Sultan's mother, Khanam Agha, vetoed in favour of the Indian system. There was no abatement in the condition of the Sultan. A week later he went into delirium.

When the Sultan regained consciousness, he told his mother that there were 3,500 hons in a special locker which should be taken out and distributed in charity. She should also make arrangements for the enthronement of Abdullah. Thereafter, he passed away at the age of 33. It was the year 1626.[11]

Hayat Bakshi was not yet 30 when she became a widow. Abdullah's dream was fulfilled, as his mother's was shattered. Her doom came in her prime. Soon Hayat collected herself, put aside her anguish and braced herself for the celebrations of the new accession. From being a Queen, she was now promoted to the role of the Queen mother. Unless she took care, Abdullah might lose the throne and everything that went with it. For Abdullah, his mother was everything. She had supervised his education and training these last 12 years. During that time, his father was a mere name to him, a vague figure never seen even when alive. He grew up in effect fatherless and therefore imbibed none of the qualities of his father.

Abdullah was as much unlike his father as his father had been unlike his. The son of an abstemious, austere, devout father-in-absentia showed great promise and a taste for worldly pleasures.

Abdullah was a minor and Hayat Bakshi also knew about his proclivities. Her husband, Sultan Mohammad, had not appointed a Peshwa after the death of Mir Momin, the wise old statesman whom he had inherited from his predecessor. He chose to become his own Peshwa. But it was widely believed that his wife inspired this decision and in the absence of a Peshwa, it was she who influenced the affairs of the state.[12]

And now it dawned on the young widow that all that had been only a preparation for the role that she was called upon so suddenly to play. She had done her apprenticeship, and her probation, and now came the real tenure. Though Abdullah was installed as the Sultan, she became the real ruler. In the long years ahead, she was to be the power behind the throne. Through her astute handling of affairs, and even later, when she withdrew from active direction, and gave only advice, she won great renown. Fate has strange ways of fulfilling its designs!

Shortly after his accession, on the auspicious day of Id-uz-Zuha, Abdullah, seated on his favourite elephant Moorat, was returning from the Nadi Mahal, a palace on the bank of river Musi, to the fort. The river was in spate and the turbulent waters were splashing against the bridge.

Near the bridge, seeing the angry swirling of the water, Moorat raised his trunk and grunted as if reluctant to proceed further. He resisted all attempts to coax him. When the mahout struck him with the pointed *ankush*, Moorat coiled his trunk around the mahout, brought him down, and trampled upon him. When the escort cavalry tried to subdue the elephant with their spears it became belligerent and bolted out of sight with the young Sultan on his back.

Search parties were assembled and sent in all directions. The day passed, and then the night and there was no trace of the rogue with the young Sultan on his back. Hayat Bakshi ordered that packets of food and skin-bags of water should be strung to the branches of trees in the jungles so that Abdullah could quench his thirst and satisfy his hunger should the elephant pass that way. Prayers were held all over the city. Hayat Bakshi also vowed that if her son returned safe, she would, besides doing unprecedented charities, make chains of forty quintals of gold and distribute them amongst the poor.

On the seventh day, soldiers on horses brought tidings that the elephant had been traced and subdued. The Sultan was safe and was returning to the fort. A huge crowd shouting slogans for the long life of the young monarch followed the elephant.

Hayat Bakshi came running out of her palace, met her son at the gate, embraced him. Then she tied one of the gold chains around his waist, had the red carpet spread to Hussaini Alam, and made Abdullah walk on it barefoot. There, a big feeding programme was organized for the poor and all the gold was distributed.

Since then that area has been called Langar (which means a chain), and till 1918, feeding of the poor was done there on the fifth day of Moharram every year by the government.[13]

The young Abdullah, like Mohammad Quli, was given to celebrating life in its physical aspects as manifest in seasons like the monsoons. He used to spend time mostly in visiting one garden after another. Thanks to his grandfather, there was an abundance of them. He spent a week at the Bagh Lingampalli in the very first year of his reign. Then he went to the Nabat Pahad and spent a number of days in the three-storey pavilion also built by his romantic grandfather. For full two months he stayed at the Koh-e-Toor. Wine from different countries flowed like water there and the best dancers from all over his kingdom entertained him and his nobles.

Though the share of rainfall is somewhat low—about a hundred centimetres in a year—but that is concentrated in about three months and so appears quite substantial. The complexion of the city, which in the blazing heat is brown and barren, transforms into a cool green with the heavy continuous rain. The sprouting of shrubbery and saplings of all sorts from their chinks and crevices break the barren monotony of copper-brown granite rocks. Animal life also emerges in an amazing variety. Insects, glow-worms, and other tiny creatures of earth can be seen as also varieties of birds such as the *koel*.

The famine of 1632 caused an interruption in this merry-making. For three years the rainfall had been significantly below average. The fourth year was completely dry. The crops failed. Normally, a hon could buy 15 quintals. It came down to seven quintals and finally, to only three.

There were numerous starvation deaths. People clamoured for food. Abdullah ordered three days of fasting and special prayers on Friday, which he himself also joined. The faithful gathered in the *maidan* by the side of Nadi Mahal. Qazi Ahsan, who had come from Mecca, led the prayers. Money was distributed to the poor but there was no grain to be had. At places a fistful of coins could be exchanged for an equal measure of rice or wheat. Free kitchens were started at a number of camps in every locality but it did not help much. People died like flies.

Then the government resorted to price control. That was perhaps the first time that this sort of thing was done. The official price fixed was Rs 1 for 12 kilos of rice or four kilos of *ghee*.

Wells were dug in all localities but few yielded water. The spectre of starvation stalked everywhere. The government provided coffins and made arrangements for the last rites of 100,000 men, women and children. It was an unforgettable nightmare.[14]

Hayat Bakshi retired after the celebration of the 18th birthday of Abdullah. But that retirement was not to be. She was once again to be called upon to save her kingdom in the years ahead. For the time being, she devoted herself to prayers and welfare projects including the education of the poor.

In Praise of Bhagnagar

Soon after its establishment, the city started attracting traders, adventurers, and various other types of visitors. Its fame spread far and wide and some commentators wrote about it even without visiting it.

The first to talk about Bhagnagar was a Persian in his middle age. His name was Mohammad Qasim but he is popularly known as Ferishta, which in Persian means an angel. His father, Ghulam Ali Hindu Shah, was a learned man who left his country and reached Ahmednagar during the reign of Murtuza Nizam Shah (ruled AD 1565–88). Hindu Shah became the tutor of Nizam Shah's son and Ferishta, a class-fellow of the Prince. Ferishta was quite young when his father died but, because of the standing of his father at court, he was patronized by the King. In 1587, Prince Meeran deposed his father Nizam Shah, but was himself deposed and murdered a year later. Ferishta was then 17. He left Ahmednagar and proceeded to Bijapur in 1589 and became a military captain under Ibrahim Adil Shah II of the Adil Shahi dynasty (ruled. AD 1580–1627)

It was the avowed ambition of Ferishta to write a history of the conquests of Islam in India, and his patron, Ibrahim Adil Shah, gave him the necessary support both in terms of money and material for that purpose. He claims that he consulted 34 books and other sources for completing his work.

Thus, he did not visit Bhagnagar but wrote his famous history sitting at Bijapur. The city was less than 20 years old when he wrote about it:

As the air of Golconda had become impure and unhealthy, Mohammad Quli built a magnificent city at a distance of eight miles, which he called Bhagnagar, after his favourite mistress; but this city has since received the name of Hyderabad, although one part of it still retains the former name of Bhagnagar. It is ten miles in circumference; and its principal streets, contrary to the other towns in India, are wide and clean: its air is healthy, and running streams are conveyed through some of the principal markets; on each side of which rows of trees are planted, affording a pleasing shade and sight, and the shops are all of solid masonry. The King's palace is described as the most beautiful and extensive in India.[15]

An Englishman, William Methwold, followed him. Born in London in 1590, he came to India in 1616 as a factor in the East India Company and was posted at Machilipatnam on the east coast. After a break of two years at Surat, Methwold stayed at Machilipatnam from 1618–22. When he visited Hyderabad he was in his mid-20s and the city was around 30.

A citie for sweetness of ayre, conveniencie of water, and fertility of soyle, is accounted the best situated in India, not to speake of the King's Palace, which for bigness and sumptuousness, in the judgement of such as have travelled India, exceedeth all belonging to the Mogull or any other Prince: It being twelve miles in circumference, built all of stone, and, within, the most eminent places garnished with massie gold in such things as we commonly use iron, as in barres of windows, bolts, and such like, and in all other points fitted to the majesty of so great a King, who in elephants and jewels is accounted one of the richest Princes of India.[16]

A train of European travellers followed. Prominent amongst them were the Frenchmen—Tavernier, Thevenot, and the Abbe Carre—and an Italian—Manucci. Of these, the first two wrote at considerable length about the city.

Jean Baptist Tavernier was born in 1605 in Paris. He was, from early childhood, seized with a romantic urge to see foreign countries. He set off to see Europe at the age of 15 and by 22 had seen most of it. Then he made six successive voyages to the east, visiting India thrice in his second, fourth, and sixth voyages between 1640 and 1660. He says that he 'made several journeys to Golconda by different routes.' Two of these were made in 1645 and 1653. He was a dealer in diamonds although he posed as a gentleman trader and not a merchant. He was so full of pride that when told by a eunuch at Golconda that the prices he had asked for his pearls and gems were too high, he took offence and left for Surat.

He had a good standing with the rulers of Iran and the nobles of India. On the last occasion, he reached Golconda on the first day of April in 1653 and observed that 'pearls were the best articles of the trade which could be taken to India.'

Aurangzeb heard from Shaista Khan about Tavernier's pearls and gems and he wanted to be the first to see his jewels. After inspecting his wares, Aurangzeb showed him with great pride the famous Koh-i-Noor diamond and other jewellery. He also met the other two famous French travellers, Bernier and Thevenot, both of whom were ardent admirers of the city.

Tavernier was good at socializing and was endowed with an acute sense of observation. He was also very systematic in his approach and kept a good record of the roads by which he travelled, the mode of transport, the cities through which he passed, and the formalities which he had to undergo. This is what he had to say:

Bhagnagar is the name of the capital town of this kingdom, but it is commonly called GOLCONDA, from the name of the fortress, which is only 2 coss distant from it, and is the residence of the King. This fortress is nearly 2 leagues in circuit, and maintains a large garrison. It is, in reality, a town where the King keeps his treasure, having left his residence in BHAG-NAGAR since it was sacked by the army which AURANGZEB sent against it, as I shall relate in due course.

Bhagnagar is then the town which they commonly call GOLCONDA, and it was commenced by the great grandfather of the King who reigns at present, at the request of one of his wives whom he loved passionately, and whose name was NAGAR [sic]. It was previously only a pleasure resort where the King had beautiful gardens, and his wife often telling him that, on account of the river, the spot was suitable for building a palace and a town, he at length caused the foundations to be laid, and desired that it should bear the name of his wife, called it BHAGNAGAR, i.e. the Garden of NAGAR [sic]. This town is in 16o 58' of lat. The neighbouring country is a flat plain, and near the town you see numerous rocks as at FOUNT AINE-BLEAU. A large river bathes the walls of the town on the southwest side, and flows into the Gulf of BENGAL, close to MASULIPATAM. You cross it at

BHAGNAGAR by a grand stone bridge, which is scarcely less beautiful than the PONT NEUF at Paris. The town is nearly the size of ORLEANS well built and well opened out, and there are many fine large streets in it, but not being paved—any more than are those of all the other towns of PERSIA and INDIA—they are full of sand and dust; this is very inconvenient in summer.

Before reaching the bridge you traverse a large suburb called AURANG-ABAD, a *coss* in length. There are in these suburbs two or three beautiful mosques, which serve as CARAVANSARAIS for strangers, and several pago-das are to be seen in the neighbourhood. It is through the same suburb that you go from the town to the fortress of GOLCONDA.

When you have crossed the bridge you straightaway enter a wide street which leads to the King's palace. You see on the right hand the houses of some nobles of the court, and four or five CARAVANSARAIS, hav-ing, two storeys, where there are large halls and chambers, which are cool. At the end of this street you find a large square, upon which stands one of the walls of the palaces, in the middle of which is a balcony where the King seats himself when he wishes to give audience to the people. The principal door of the palace is not in this square, but in another which is close by; and you enter at first into a large court surrounded by PORTI-COES, under which the King's guards are stationed. From this court you pass to another of the same construction, around which there are several beautiful apartments, with a terraced roof; upon which, as upon those of the quarter of the palace where they keep the elephants, there are beauti-ful gardens, and such large trees, that it is a matter for astonishment how these arches are able to carry such a weight; and one may say in general terms that this house has all the appearance of a royal mansion.

It is about fifty years since they began to build a splendid pagoda in the town; it will be the grandest in all India if it should be completed. The size of the stones is a subject for special astonishment, and that of the niche, which is the place for prayer, is an entire rock, of so enormous a size that they spent five years in quarrying it, and they employed 500 or 600 men continually on this work. It required still more time to roll it upon the conveyance by which they brought it to the pagoda; and they told me that it took 1,400 oxen to draw it. I shall explain why the work is incomplete. If it had been finished it would have justly passed for the noblest edifice in the whole of ASIA.

On the other side of the town, from whence one goes to MASULIPA-TAM, there are two large tanks, each of them being about a coss in circuit, upon which you see some decorated boats intended for the pleasure of the King, and along the banks many fine houses which belong to the prin-cipal officers of the court.

At three coss from the town there is a very fine mosque where there are the tombs of the KINGS OF GOLCONDA; and every day at 4 o'clock p.m. bread and PALAO are given to all the poor who present themselves. When you wish to see something really beautiful, you should go to see these tombs on the day of a festival, for then, from morning to evening, they are covered with rich carpets.

This is what I have been able to observe concerning the good order and the police which is maintained in this town. In the first place, when a stranger presents himself at the gates, they search him carefully to see if he has any salt or tobacco, because these yield the principal revenue of the King. Moreover, it is sometimes necessary that the stranger should wait for one or two days before receiving permission to enter. ...

When the King administers justice he comes, as I stated, into the balcony which overlooks the square, and all those who desire to be present stand below, opposite to where he is seated. ... A Secretary of State remains in the square below the balcony to receive petitions, and when he has five or six in hand he places them in a bag, which a eunuch, who is on the balcony by the side of the King, lowers with a cord and draws up afterwards, in order to present them to his Majesty.

It is the principal nobles who mount guard every Monday each in his turn, and they are not relieved before the end of a week. There are some of these nobles who command 5,000 or 6,000 horses and they encamp under their tents around the town. When they mount guard each goes from his home to the RENDEZVOUS but when they leave it they march in good order across the bridge, and from thence by the main street they assemble in the square in front of the balcony. In the van you see ten or twelve elephants marching, more or fewer, according to the rank of him who goes off guard. There are some among them bearing cages (howdahs) which somewhat resemble the body of a small coach, and there are others which only carry their driver, and another man instead of the cage, who holds a sort of banner. ...

You see coming after them the carriages, around which the servants walk on foot, after which the red horses appear, and finally the noble to whom this whole equipment belongs, preceded by ten or twelve courtesans, who await him at the end of the bridge, leaping and dancing before him up to the square. After him the cavalry and infantry follow in good order. And as all that affords a spectacle, and has something of pomp about it, during three or four consecutive months which I have sometimes spent at BHAGNAGAR, my lodging being in the main street, I enjoyed the amusement every week of seeing these fine troops passing, which are more or less numerous according to the rank of the noble who has been on guard in his turn.

The soldiers have for their sole garment but three or four ells of cloths, with which they clothe the middle of the body before and behind. They wear the hair long, and make a great knot of it on the head as women do, having for sole head-dress a scrap of cloth with three corners, one of which rests on the middle of the head, and the other two they tie together on the nape of the neck. They do not have a sabre like the Persians, but they carry a broad sword like the Swiss, with which they both cut and thrust, and they suspend it from a belt. The barrels of their muskets are stronger than ours, and the iron is better and purer; this makes them not liable to burst. As for the cavalry, they have bow and arrow, shield and mace, with helmet and a coat of mail, which hangs behind from the helmet over the shoulders.

There are so many public women in the town, the suburbs and in the fortress which is like another town. It is estimated that there are generally more than 20,000 [*sic*] entered in the Darogha's register, without which it is not allowed to any woman to ply this trade. They pay no tribute to the King, but a certain number of them are obliged to go every Friday with their governess and their music to present themselves in the square in front of the balcony. If the King be there they dance before him, and if he is not, a eunuch signals to them with his hand that they may withdraw.

In the cool of the evening you see them before the doors of their houses, which are for the most part small huts, and when the night comes they place at the doors a candle or a lighted lamp for a signal. It is then, also, that the shops where they sell *tari* [toddy] are opened. It is a drink obtained from a tree, and it is as sweet as our new wines. It is brought from 5 or 6 coss distant in leather bottles, upon horses which carry one on each side and go at a fast trot, and about 500 or 600 of them enter the town daily. The King derives from the tax which he places on this tari a very considerable revenue, and it is principally on this account that they allow so many public women, because they are the cause of the consumption of much tari, those who sell it having for this reason their shops in their neighbourhood. ...

All the people of GOLCONDA, both men and women, are well proportioned, of good stature, and of fair countenances, and it is only the peasantry who are somewhat dark in complexion.[17]

Footloose and consumed by an insatiable thirst for adventure, Tavernier continued to roam around the world right till the end. His nephew squandered the fortunes accumulated by him, and Tavernier died during one of his journeys in far-off Russia in 1689.

The next chronicler was called M. de Thevenot. Born to a good family in 1633, he studied in the University of Paris. After finishing his studies he left home at the age of 19 and visited Italy where he witnessed the coronation of Pope Alexander VII. Then he visited Turkey, Egypt, and Palestine.

In his second voyage, he visited Iran and India, during the course of which he came to Golconda in 1666–7. He has been described as an example of piety, a model of virtue, and a treasury of knowledge. His aptitude for languages was extraordinary and he wrote about the grammar and syntax of the Malabar language. He was driven by curiosity and was an eager and astute observer of men and maners. He even measured the distance between the landmarks of the city and described the difficulties he had to undergo during his travels and stay here. He died shortly after his visit, on his way back in 1667 at the age of 34. This is what he said of Bhagnagar:

The Capital city of this Kingdom is called BAGNAGAR, the Persians call it AIDERA-BAD, it is fourteen or fifteen Leagues from Viziapour, situated in the Latitude of seventeen Degrees ten Minutes, in a very long plain, hemmed in with little Hills, some Cosses distant from the Town, which makes the Air of that Place very wholesome, besides that, the Country of GOLCONDA lies very high. The Houses of the Suburbs, where we arrived, are only built of Earth and thatched with Straw, they are so low and ill contrived, that they can be reckoned no more than Huts. We went from one end to the other of that suburbs [sic], which is very long and stop near the Bridge which is at the farther end of it. There we stayed for a note from the COT-OUAL to enter the Town, because of the Merchants Goods of the Caravan, which were to be carried to the COTOUALS house to be searched. ... At the end of the bridge, we found the Gates of the City, which are no more but Barriers: Being entered, we marched a quarter of an hour through a long Street with Houses on both sides, but as low as those of the Suburbs, and built of the same materials, though they have very lovely Gardens.

We went to a CARAVANSERAY called NIMETULLA, which has its entry from the same Street. Everyone took his lodging there, and I hired two little Chambers, at two rupees a month. The town makes a kind of Cross, much longer than broad, and extends in a straight line, from the Bridge to the four Towers; but beyond these Towers the Street is no longer straight, and whilst in walking I measured the length of the Town, being come to the four Towers, I was obliged to turn to the left, and entered into a MEIDAN, where there is another Street, that led me to the Town-Gate, which I looked for. Having adjusted my measures, I found that BAG-NAGAR was five thousand six hundred and fifty Paces in length, to wit, two thousand four hundred and fifty from the bridge to the Towers, and from thence, through the MEIDAN to the Gate which leads to MASULIPA-TAM, three thousand two hundred Paces. There is also beyond that Gate, a Suburb eleven hundred Paces long.

There are several MEIDANS or places in this Town, but the fairest is that before the King's Palace. ... Balisters go round the Terrass-walks of the place: The Royal Palace is to the North of it, and there is a Portico over against it, where the Musicians come several times a day to play upon their Instruments when the King is in Town.

In the middle of this place, and in sight of the Royal Palace, there is a Wall built, three Foot thick, and six Fathom in height and length, for the fighting of Elephants, and that Wall is betwixt them, when they excite them to fight, but so soon as they are wrought up to a rage, they quickly throw down the Wall.

The Palace which is three hundred and four score Paces in length, takes up not only one of the sides of the Place, but is continued to the four Towers, where it terminates in a very lofty Pavilion. The Walls of it which are built of great Stones, have at certain distances half Towers, and there are many Windows towards the Palace, with an open gallery to see the shews. They say it is very pleasant within and that the Water rises to the highest Apartments: The Reservatory of that Water, which is brought a great way off, is in the top of the four Towers, from whence it is conveyed into the House by Pipes. No man enters into this place but by an express order from the king who grants it but seldom; nay, commonly nobody comes near it, and in the Palace there is a circuit staked out, that must not be passed over. There is another square MEIDAN in this Town, where many great Men have well built Houses. The CARAVANSERAY are generally all handsome, and the most esteemed is that which is called NIMETULLA in the great Street opposite to the King's Garden: It is a spacious square, and the Court of it is adorned with several Trees of different kinds, and a large bason where the MAHOMETANS perform their Ablutions.

That which is called the four Towers, is a square building, of which each face is ten Fathom broad, and about seven high: It is opened in the four sides, by four Arches, four or five Fathom high, and four Fathom wide, and every one of these arches fronts a Street, of the same breadth as the Arch. There are two Galleries in it, one over another, and over all a Terrass that serves for a Roof, bordered with a Stone—Balcony, and at each corner of that Building, a Decagoue Tower about ten Fathom high, and each Tower hath four Galleries, with little Arches on the outside, the whole Building being adorned with Roses and Festoons pretty well-cut: It is vaulted underneath, and appears like a Dome, which has in the inside all round Balisters of Stone, pierced and open as the Galleries in the outside, and there are several Doors in the Walls to enter at. Under this Dome there is a large Table placed upon a Divan, raised seven or eight Foot from the Ground, with steps to go up to it. All the Galleries of the Building serve to make the Water mount up, that so being afterwards conveyed to the Kings Palace, it might reach the highest Apartments. Nothing in that Town seems so lovely as the outside of that Buildings, and nevertheless it is surrounded with ugly shops made of Wood and covered with Straw, where they sell Fruit which spoils the prospect of it. ...

Besides the Indian Merchants that are at BAGNAGAR, there are many PERSIANS and ARMENIANS, but through the weakness of the Government, the OMRAS sometimes squeeze them, and whilst I was there, an OMRA detained in his house a Gentile Banker whom he had sent for, and made him give him five thousand CHEQUINS, upon the report of this Extortion, the Bankers shut up their Offices, but the King Commanded all to be restored to the Gentile, and so the matter was taken up.

The Tradesmen of the Town, and those who cultivate the land, are Natives of the Country. There are many Franks also in the Kingdome, but most of them are PORTUGESE, who have fled thither for Crimes they have committed: However, the ENGLISH and DUTCH have lately settled there and the last make great profits. They established a Factory there, (three years since) where they buy up for the Company, many CHITES and other Cloaths, which they vent elsewhere in the INDIES. They bring from MASULIPATAM upon Oxen, the Goods which they know to be of readiest sale in BAGNAGAR and other Towns of the Kingdome, as Cloves, Pepper, Cinnamon, Silver, Copper, Tin and Lead, and thereby gain very much for they say, they get five and twenty for one, of profit; and I was assured that this profit amounted yearly to eleven or twelve hundred thousand French LIVRES. They are made welcome in that Country, because they make many Presents and a few days before I parted from BAGNAGAR, their Governor began to have Trumpets and Tymbalas and Standard carried before him, by Orders from his Superiors.

Publick Women are allowed in the Kingdom, so that nobody minds it when they see a Man go to their Houses, and they are often at their Doors well drest to draw in Passengers; But they say, most of them are spoiled. The common People give their Wives great Liberty: When a Man is to be Married, the Father and Mother of his Bride, make him promise that he will not take it ill, that his Wife go and walk through the Town, or visit her Neighbours, nay and drink TARY [toddy], a drink that the Indians of GOLCONDA are extremely fond of.

When a Theft is committed at BAGNAGAR, or elsewhere, they punish the Thief by cutting off both his Hands, which is the Custome also in most Countries of the INDIES.[18]

Then there was another Frenchman, Dominus Barthelamy Carre de Chambon. He was born around 1639 and not much is known about his life or the year of his death. He was a priest and so is generally known as the Abbe Carre.

He visited Bhagnagar on 14 March 1673. He talks of the two towns of Golconda and Bhagnagar. During his visit to the latter, he stayed in the fort with a Portuguese priest whose church was in the suburb called Millepore. He recorded in his journal:

I also visited the large town of Bhagnagar, where I went about more freely as it is a very spacious town, situated in a flat country, watered by a fine river. It is full of strangers and merchants that trade is carried on by for-eigners and others without any or particular business. There is such a concourse of every kind of people, merchandise and riches, that the place seems to be the centre of all trade in the East.[19]

A Venetian, Niccolao Manucci, followed the Frenchmen. He was born in 1639 and ran away from home at the young age of 14. Serving as an artilleryman with the Mughal Emperor Shah Jahan's son, Dara Shikoh, and later Jai Singh, he became a physician and joined Shah Alam when the latter was appointed Governor of the Deccan in 1678. He later joined the last Sultan of Golconda, Tana Shah, and was sought by Shah Alam for desertion. His escape and pursuit by Shah Alam reads like a thriller. His account is noteworthy because of his description of how he was helped by fellow Christians and Europeans in his flight and how he masqueraded successfully as a physician. He described the story himself:

> Nor must I omit to mention how some Christians in the service of the Gulkandah King aware that I was seeking to escape from Shah Alam, came out to meet me and escort me, so as to take my side in case any of the Gulkandah troops attempted to interfere with me. ...
>
> Thus the king heard of my arrival. As his European physician, a Frenchman named Monsieur Destremon, was dead, the king sent for me to his presence. There, after some conversation, he directed me to go and bleed a woman in his harem, much cherished by him, because she knew where the treasures of the King of Gulkandah Cotobxa (Qutb Shah) were concealed. She was Georgian and so extremely stout, and the fat covered the veins so much, that blood could not be drawn from her except from the capillary veins.[20]

He did such a good job of it that the Sultan, Abdullah Qutb Shah, also wanted the same treatment for himself. However, he suspected that Manucci might be Shah Alam's agent and so might harm him. When the Sultan was pressurized to surrender Manucci to Shah Alam, a deal was worked out between the two.

> The information reached me when I was at cards, and suppressing my tribulation, I went on for some time with the game. I then went out and betook myself to the house of the Dutch envoy, who was then Lorenco Pit, and begged his assistance in this delicate situation. After that I sent for the Father Vicar of Gulkandah, named Frey Francisco, of the order of St Augustin and most earnestly entreated him to see Rustam Rao and procure leave to remove to Machilipatnam a brother of his called Ausgustinho, who had fallen ill.[21]

There were many others like William Finch, who had accompanied Hawkins in 1608 but did not visit Bhagnagar.[22] They acknowledged the city even if they did not pay it any compliment. Its reputation as a well-planned city had grown all over the country.

Abdullah's Humiliation

We go back to that Boy-King Abdullah. Given to luxury, he loved rituals and ceremonies that provided occasion for indulgence. He scaled up the observance of Moharram which is really not a celebration but mourning. It is observed in the memory of the brutal killing of Husain, the grandson of Mohammad, the Prophet of Islam.

During this month the royal palaces were draped in black. Eating of meat, chewing of *pan*, and smoking were banned. Even massage and haircutting were not allowed. A few thousand black robes, green batons, and black ebony staves which signify mourning were distributed by the government amongst the nobility and courtiers. For the first ten days, rituals were observed with slight variations but unfailing adherence to detail. On each day, the Sultan used to witness the mourners' procession from his different palaces. He himself used to join the procession on the last day. He would lead it from his palace to the Mecca mosque covering the distance of 3,000 paces on foot. After attending the congregation at the mosque, he would listen to the moving account of the Karbala by the professional narrator and offer prayers before repairing to the Doulat Mahal palace. After that *nan* and *halwa* were distributed amongst the poor, two children of *sayyad*s were given fineries so that the Sultan would earn merit in the next world for having provided succour to orphans.

During the reign of Mohammad Quli, the birthday of Prophet Mohammad was celebrated regularly. But after his death, his successor, Sultan Mohammad, had stopped the practice. The money thus saved was distributed amongst the learned, pious, and holy men of the kingdom.

Abdullah not only revived the celebration, but also enlarged its scope. The festivities used to last for 12 days. Exhibitions of the arts and crafts of the country were organized in the grounds near the Charminar. Dancers came from different parts of India for entertainment. Eating, drinking, and merry-making culminating in a royal saturnalia marked these celebrations. Thirty thousand hons (approximately Rs 135,000) were spent annually on that festival.[23]

Ahmednagar had for long held the advance of the Mughals into the Deccan in check. But with the assassination of Chand Bibi, and later the death of Malik Ambar, the Negro general, Ahmednagar fell and that buffer was removed. Berar was next to go and that brought the Mughals into direct confrontation with Golconda. Earlier Shah Jahan—then the rebel Prince Khurram—had been granted not only safe passage but also help by Mohammad Qutb Shah. Now that he had become Emperor he pressed for Golconda to submit to him. He issued a decree that listed the alleged 'lapses' of the Sultan. These included recitation of the names of the 12 Shia imams followed by that of the Shah of Iran in the Friday exordium—khutba—in mosques, default in the payment of annual tribute to the Mughals, and the pursuit of a foreign policy detrimental to the interests of the Mughal empire. In 1636, Abdullah capitulated on all these points and signed a 'deed of submission' to the Mughal Emperor.

The khutba started reciting the name of the four Caliphs (in accordance with the Sunni practice) and was read in the name of the Mughal Emperor. New coins were also struck in the name of the Mughal Emperor and mutual friendship in foreign affairs was affirmed. For all this Abdullah earned a pat on the back from Shah Jahan. Three days later, Aurangzeb was appointed Viceroy of the Deccan. It is interesting to note that while Abdullah was losing ground to the Mughals, he was able, perhaps because of that, to extend the boundaries of his kingdom in the south. In 1642, he sent his army to attack Karnataka. The Commander-in-Chief of this army was a noble called Mohammad Saeed. His advance was swift. He captured Udayagiri, Cuddapah, Chennai, Tirupati, and Chandragiri. Virtually wiping out the remnant of the Vijayanagar Empire, he proceeded to occupy San Thome and Chengalput or modern Chennai. Abdullah expressed his appreciation of his noble by promoting him to the post of Mir Jumla, or the Prime Minister. After a brief confrontation between the Golconda and Bijapur forces, it was agreed to divide the conquered territories between the two—one-third going to Golconda and two-thirds to Bijapur.

This conquest of Karnataka by Mir Jumla proved to be a curse disguised as a blessing for Golconda. The campaign brought not only glory and promotion to Mir Jumla, it also made him enormously rich. This spurred his ambitions and he recruited a private army in addition to the official army which he commanded. He set up his headquarters at Gandikota in Cuddapah and started behaving like an independent ruler. He also established contacts with Aurangzeb to strengthen himself against his master, Abdullah.

Mir Jumla's pride was perhaps natural but the arrogance of the members of his family was quite unwarranted. One day his son, Mohammad Amin, galloped up to the royal palace in a drunken state. He abused the guards when they tried to stop him and sat on the throne, where he vomited. This enraged Abdullah and he ordered Mir Jumla to appear before him. To ensure compliance with his orders, he held his son captive and confiscated his property.

Mir Jumla knew that his fate was sealed in Golconda. He was conscious of his enormous wealth and military talent. They would be of great importance to the Mughals in the realization of their objectives in the Deccan. Through the good offices of Aurangzeb, Mir Jumla obtained an audience with the Mughal Emperor, Shah Jahan.

After making his obeisance, Mir Jumla laid an enormous packet before Shah Jahan. The entire hall dazzled with the light emanating from it. Shah Jahan looked at it agape and asked Mir Jumla what it was.

'A humble offering from His Majesty's slave', he said.

'We have never seen such a big and luminous diamond!'

'I have brought it where it should properly belong—in the crown of the Emperor of Hindustan.'

Shah Jahan bent forward and touched it. 'God be praised. I am sure there is none other like this anywhere,' he exclaimed.

'Your Majesty is right. It has no peer, no equal.'

'But where did you get it from?'

'From the fabled mines of Golconda, My Lord. It is called Koh-i-Noor, the Mountain of Light.'

'Ah Koh-i-Noor! We had heard about it but thought that it was only a legend.'

'We, in our opulence and glory, are pleased,' said Shah Jahan with the accustomed condescension of an Emperor and then beaming, he declared: 'We grant you the command of five thousand troops.'

Mir Jumla made seven deep bows. 'This slave shall shed his last drop of blood in the service of the Emperor of the World.'

'You shall henceforth be known as Muazzam Khan. Now tell us, our friend, how matters stand in the territory of Qutb-ul-Mulk?'

'Your Majesty has disciplined the Sultan, but not sufficiently. He still feels he can stand before the Master of Hindustan and even defy him. Though he has released my son, he is still holding his property.'

'We shall see to that, Muazzam Khan.'

An order was sent to Abdullah to release Mir Jumla's son and to restore his property which he had confiscated. The Viceroy of the Deccan, Shah Jahan's son, Aurangzeb, was ordered to march to Golconda to ensure compliance with this order and to subdue Abdullah. Another reason for this action was default in the payment of the annual tribute by Abdullah.

Aurangzeb sent his son, Prince Mohammad Sultan at the head of an army to Golconda in 1656. Abdullah was in no mood to fight. He adopted a very conciliatory attitude and sent valuable presents to the Prince. Alongside, he sent abject petitions to Shah Jahan and promised to do whatever he was commanded to. Meanwhile, not taking any chances, he left the city and fled to the safety of the fort. The invading army marched into the city without any opposition. Advancing further, it encircled the fort with trenches and began tightening the noose around the citadel. Aurangzeb himself joined his son ten days after the latter's arrival at Bhagnagar.

Abdullah kept sending a stream of entreaties to Shah Jahan. In these he addressed him with such obsequious epithets that first Shah Jahan felt flattered, then amused, and ultimately even irked. In one petition Abdullah addressed him as 'Adorner of the Realm of Justice; Exhibitor of the Virtue of the Crown of Majesty; Imparter of Glory to the Crown of Suleiman; Brightener of the Crown of the Manual of Governing the World; Alexander with the Wisdom of Plato; Emperor Who Adorns the World; Royal Victorious Hero Against the Infidels, of the Rank and Station of Suleiman; Caliph of the Merciful God.'[24] When the court reader was reading the petition and the string of epithets went on end-lessly, Shah Jahan lost his patience and said brusquely to him: 'Is there anything more than a list of titles in this? Stop this blabber.'

However, partly in pity and partly in sheer exasperation, Shah Jahan relented. He felt that the Sultan had been humiliated enough. He issued a decree pardoning him. But that decree was to be routed through Aurangzeb. He was in no mood to let his quarry off so easily.

It was then that some nobles approached Hayat Bakshi Begum, the Queen mother, to intercede with Aurangzeb on behalf of the sultanate. After waiting for a response to an appointment sought in vain for four days, she ordered her palanquin and asked for a contingent of bodyguards to accompany her.

Meanwhile his nobles had prevailed upon Aurangzeb to per-mit the issue of a safe passage to Ma Saheba.

The besieging Mughal soldiers saw a curious spectacle. The Banjara Gate of the Fort was opened. A charger with a white flag emerged, followed by ten more mounts and a blue and gold palanquin with a hundred footmen in train. Nobody obstructed the forward march of the procession. The guard had instructions that the lady should be escorted to General Shaista Khan's tent. He escorted her to Prince Mohammad Sultan. She presented him with two horses and said she would like to meet the Viceroy urgently.

The meeting took place on 8 March 1656. An old usher led her in. Aurangzeb got up as his royal visitor entered the tent. He was then 39; his visitor about twice his age. The two figures stood opposite each other presenting a contrast in every way. He, a straight sprightly figure; she, plump with a slight stoop. His eyes shone with power; hers, drowsy with meditation. He was resplendent in his long coat with his viceregal turban studded with jewels; she was clad in white, her head covered, but her face bare.

She greeted him first and then presented him a thousand gold mohurs. He acknowledged the greetings and offered her a seat.

'Noble Prince,' she opened, 'I do not know how to begin … . What is your objective?'

'You have taken the trouble to come to me. You must tell me what you came to seek.'

'I see no justification for this … ,' she fumbled for a word. She wanted to say 'harassment'. But that would probably offend him. She quickly amended her unuttered statement, 'the situation,' is what she actually said. 'The Sultan has done everything which the Emperor of Hindustan wanted him to do. Then why this siege, Prince?'

'There have been lapses on the, part of Qutb-ul-Mulk, Lady,' the Viceroy said coldly. 'And no doubt you know about them.'

'I shall be grateful to be enlightened specifically about them, Your Royal Highness.'

There was an implicit admission in this mode of address. Aurangzeb did not like to be addressed as just a Prince. He was more than a mere son of an Emperor. He was also the Viceroy of the Deccan and he wanted that to be acknowledged. He also took care to drive home the status of the supplicant before him. He did not concede her the status of a Queen mother. She was merely the mother of a regional satrap, one of the Mughal tributaries, who had come to plead for her errant son. He showed her the same courtesy which he would show to an old woman of the nobility.

'We are not going to list out charges, Madam. My officials have done this. But … ,' his stern visage seemed to relax a bit, 'since a lady has undertaken such an arduous trip, I may mention that your son defaulted on the payment of the annual *peshkush* ...'

'I can assure you that there was no malafide intention … .' Aurangzeb interrupted her just to underline that he didn't like her interruption when he was talking.

'Moreover, he has imprisoned our noble Muazzam Khan's son and confiscated his property.'

'But Your Royal Highness will recall that the one whom you call Muazzam Khan was our Mir Jumla earlier. He cheated his master and his son insulted us.'

There was now more ice in the Viceroy's tone. 'We don't go into the past. Abdullah's action was against a person who is now our friend and we do not like that.'

'As you rightly say, we can't go on digging up the past. Now if Your Highness will be so kind as to say how peace can be restored here … .'

'We did not come here for peace, Lady, the Emperor's orders are to bring about a finality to the situation in Golconda.'

'But Sire, we understand that the benign Emperor has already excused whatever sins of omission or commission are attributable to Abdullah.'

There was a note of asperity in Aurangzeb's reply: 'The imperial orders come first to the Viceroy. I don't have to learn from you, Madam, what the Emperor has ordered.'

'Surely that is so, Your Royal Highness,' said Hayat Bakshi with an added tone of submission. 'If you would be pleased to state your terms we shall do our utmost to comply with them.'

Aurangzeb beamed. He had won the battle without firing a single shot. 'Our terms are simple, Madam. As I said our aim is to end the uncertainty in our relationship. To that end we would like Abdullah's eldest daughter to be married to our son, Prince Mohammad Sultan. Ramgir will be her dowry. In due course, the Prince will succeed Abdullah to the throne of Golconda.' And as she was trying to absorb the terms Aurangzeb added, 'Lastly, an indemnity of Rs 4.5 million must be paid to us in three installments—the first to be paid now, before we go any further.'

Hayat Bakshi's face fell. Just to let the Viceroy know the harshness of terms, she asked, 'Anything else, Your Royal Highness?'

'That will do, Madam.'

In her long life, Hayat Bakshi had never struck such a poor bargain. But Abdullah and his advisers were happy even at this capitulation.

The first installment of the indemnity was paid forthwith. The siege was lifted for the marriage of the Qutb Shahi Princess with the Mughal Prince. It was performed on 4 April 1656—a month after the signing of the treaty. Abdullah sent about Rs 1 million worth of gems and other articles by way of dowry. His mother accompanied the bride to the pavilion erected near the Viceroy's. The next day Aurangzeb forwarded to Abdullah the decree which had been issued by Shah Jahan earlier pardoning the 'sins' of Abdullah, along with the robe of honour. The Sultan relapsed into his unabashed indulgences as if nothing had happened.

It seems that no humiliation was deep enough for Abdullah. After the abject surrender to Aurangzeb in 1656, he struck a coin which carried the legend: *Khatm bi'l khair-o-saadat*—'the whole thing has ended well and peacefully.'

Aurangzeb withdrew from the Deccan in 1656 in order to fight for a bigger prize—the Mughal throne of India. Two years later Aurangzeb, having succeeded in the war of succession, became the Emperor of India in 1658, though his formal enthronement took place a year later. This brought relief to the hard-pressed sultanate of Golconda for nearly three decades.

During this respite, Abdullah was able to assert his authority over the Dutch and English factories in the south. He appointed Riza Quli Beg with the title of Neknam Khan as Governor of Karnataka in 1662. The Governor forced the English to agree to the Qutb Shahi officials establishing a warehouse at Madras and collecting customs duties. To enforce this he had to lay a siege to the British fortress of St George for a month. Later in 1672, an agreement was arrived at under which the Governor was entitled to half the duties relating to Chennaipatnam, while Madras was left to the full control of the British forever.[25]

Ma Saheba Hayat Bakshi Begum passed away peacefully in 1667. No woman, before or since, has played so dominant a role in Golconda or its successor state. She was the daughter, wife, and mother respectively of three successive Sultans. As the wife of a reserved, reclusive and peace-loving Sultan and the mother of a fun-loving and somewhat irresponsible ruler, she influenced the affairs of the state for over half a century. But for her, the Golconda Sultanate might have become extinct earlier.

Mendicant to Sultan

Abdullah had three daughters and no male issue. The eldest daughter was married to Aurangzeb's son, Prince Mohammad Sultan. The second was married to one Nizamuddin Ahmed of Mecca. The youngest was engaged to Syed Sultan of Najaf. The Golconda–Mughal Treaty of 1656 stipulated that Prince Mohammad Sultan would succeed Abdullah. Mohammad Sultan had sided with Aurangzeb's brother, Shujah, in the war of succession following Shah Jahan's illness. As a punishment for that Aurangzeb imprisoned Mohammad Sultan where he died. That brought up the issue of the succession at Golconda.

As a son-in-law, Nizamuddin Ahmed had established himself both in the family and in the court. It was Nizamuddin Ahmed who had introduced Syed Ahmad to the court and had suggested that an alliance be made between him and the youngest daughter of the Sultan. When this protégée did not pay him due deference, Nizamuddin, who had a say in all state and household matters, raised opposition to the proposed marriage. He even threatened to join the Mughals if this event took place. When the Princess—influenced by Sultana, the Queen, and Fatima Khanam, who was married to Nizamuddin—threatened suicide, Abdullah was unnerved.

He made straight for the hospice of his Sufi preceptor, Shah Raju. He had always done that whenever he had an intractable problem.

When Mohammad Tughlaq came to the Deccan and made Daulatabad his capital in 1327, a large number of people followed in his train. One of them was Sayyad Yousuf, a Sufi saint. He died at Khuldabad in 1331. His son was Sadruddin Mohammad Hussaini, commonly called Khwaja Gesu Daraz Bande Nawaz on account of his long locks. He was born in Delhi in 1331 and was a disciple of Shaikh Naseeruddin Chiragh of Delhi. His mentor sent him to Gulbarga in 1399 when he was already very old. A large number of disciples also came with him. The Bahmani Sultan Feroz received him with honour and even gave his family preference over the previously favoured family of Shaikh Sirajuddin. He was treated as the supreme saint and granted many towns and villages as jagirs together with a college and a monastery. Subsequently, however, there was a quarrel between the Sultan and the saint, and many people attributed Feroz's subsequent misfortune to this dispute. However, Feroz's successor, Ahmad Shah I, gave due deference to Gesu Daraz and took full advantage of his moral and spiritual influence. Both Hindus and Muslims revered the saint and his tomb is still a pilgrim centre attracting a large number of people from all over the country. He died in 1422.

Eighth in the line of Saint Gesu Daraz was Shah Raju. He came to Bhagnagar and set up his monastery on the west side of the Fateh Darwaza of the walled city. He was also greatly revered and was popularly known as Shah Raju Qattal. He was believed to possess great spiritual powers and was an influential teacher of the Sufi doctrine.[26]

Abdullah became his disciple at a fairly early age. Shah Raju also had a soft corner for Abdullah.

Meanwhile there was also a young boy named Abul Hasan in the royal household who was taken as a distant relation of the Sultan and so accorded the treatment due to a Minor Prince. At a young age, he became a champion drunkard and one day misbehaved with no less a person than the Queen. For that he was instantly expelled from the palace and told to fend for himself. Having spent his infancy and adolescence as a parasite, without having acquired the wherewithal to earn a living, this lad of 14 could not do a thing in the world to support himself. On a friend's advice, he made for the hospice of Shah Raju Qattal.

The Sufi saint ran a free kitchen open to all and there was no objection to anyone hanging around so long as he didn't indulge in any objectionable activity.

Shah Raju took pity on the royal castaway and took him on as a novitiate. Abul Hasan became his errand boy and was constantly in and out of the dark hallowed cell in which Shah Raju spent most of his time in meditation. In the evening, Shah Raju would sit in a big verandah. His adherents would come and just sit there respectfully to imbibe something from his mere presence. If those present were lucky, sometimes a question would trigger a discourse. Occasionally, the Sufi mystic would, on his own, give a sermon that the disciples would lap up eagerly and talk about for months afterwards.

Abul Hasan had a good voice and he sang well. He had also a certain innocence about him. Shah Raju gave him the nickname of 'Tana Shah' meaning a child saint. Having been brought up in the palace, he was also of delicate build and was often seen lost in reverie.

One evening, Shah Raju opened his eyes from a long meditation and saw Abul Hasan crouched in a corner, and he was moved.

'Eh Tana Shah, What were you thinking, young lad?'

'Nothing, Sir, nothing.'

'Girls?' intoned the saint. 'You were thinking of your marriage'

He was, but how did the saint know? Yes, the master knew everything that was going on in the disciples' minds. That was his greatness. He knew everything that had happened and was yet to happen to them. That's why people adored him, revered him. He was the only living all-knowing being. Tana Shah's awe of his master increased.

Shah Raju himself demystified his omniscience. 'All boys of your age think of that. Even girls.' And he laughed a mild, forgiving laugh, which trailed off in a faint cough.

Abul Hasan felt relieved. He could manage a shame-faced grin in admission.

'Well. We shall have you married. In good time. With a good rich girl. Whom do you want to marry?'

There was no answer from the shy boy but his thoughts went to the palace. Someone from there, he said to himself. After all he was himself also a Prince. What if he had come to this pass! Every

Prince was like that. Was it too much to aspire for a match from the palace? Alas, the Junior Princess had already been betrothed to Syed Sultan, that upstart from Najaf. It was too late to hope for her hand. She was beyond him. But someone from the vast royal family with pretensions to blue blood would do. This train of thought was broken by the saint's gentle call.

'All right, now go and prepare a smoke for me.'

Abul Hasan scampered off to the backyard on his errand.

At the hermitage, the disciples of Shah Raju had gathered for his daily evening *jalwa*. Suddenly a boy came running nervously and announced the arrival of the Sultan of Golconda. Shah Raju coolly asked him to be brought in. The gathering of plebeians, out of regard for their King, vacated the verandah so that the hermit and the Sultan could have privacy.

Abdullah sat at the feet of his preceptor. He did not open his mouth. Shah Raju gave him a knowing smile.

Encouraged, the Sultan said, 'Respected Murshid, I have a problem.'

'I know,' replied the saint. And teased him: 'Why else will the ruler of the state think of a poor mendicant like me!'

The Sultan tried to mutter an explanation but the saint rescued him from the embarrassment. 'That is all right. You must attend to the affairs of state.' And then turning to what was on Abdullah's mind, he reassured him: 'You are lucky. This will be your last problem. This too shall be solved. Don't worry.'

'Come back to me after three days. You will get the solution.'

'Meanwhile ... ?'

'Let things go on their course. Let all customs and formalities be observed. Don't stop anything. We shall wrap it all up after three days.'

Abdullah felt relieved. He got up, took his leave, and made for the door. Seeing him depart, people returned to the master. When they had taken their seats, Abul Hasan suddenly came rushing in.

Looking at him, Shah Raju exclaimed: 'Lo, one king goeth and another cometh!'

The gathering laughed at the seeming crack at Abul Hasan. He did not know where to hide himself. He sank into the nearest vacant space on the carpet.

A little later, the hermit called Tana Shah to his room. Tana Shah lay prostrate before him. He did this always the first time in the morning and the last thing at night. He had not broken this routine in the years that he had been there.

'Get up, Tana Shah.'

The young man obeyed and waited for the next command. 'You wanted to marry. We shall marry you to the Princess.' Tana Shah's mouth opened and stayed that way in utter disbelief. Like an idiot he stood rooted there.

'My respected Peer ji, you joke with me.'

'No, my son', replied Shah Raju, 'your time has come now.'

The saint walked up to him and gave him a gentle pat on the shoulder. 'The wedding ceremonies are going on for the bride. Let us also observe the ceremonies prescribed for the groom. This is the time for *sachak*. They are putting henna on the palms and feet of the bride. Let me also apply some to you.'

Saying this he picked up a fistful of mud from the channel flowing by his room and rubbed it on his acolyte's palms and feet. There was no mockery in this. The exercise was completed in utter solemnity. Having finished it, he kissed Tana Shah on the forehead and said, '*Alhamdullillah*. Tomorrow we shall have your sachak procession.'

The next morning ten of the inhabitants of the monastery went through a mock sachak procession. After that Shah Raju told Tana Shah: 'My son, from now on all the ceremonies in the palace would be concerned only with your marriage.'

On the third day, a messenger from the palace came to ask the saint whether the Sultan could visit him in the evening, as had been suggested by the former earlier.

'Yes,' he replied. 'And ask him to bring some appropriate dresses for the bridegroom too.'

Abdullah arrived before sunset. Some nobles accompanied him in his train. There was also a spare horse, richly caparisoned, following the distinguished procession.

Abdullah made his bow to Shah Raju. The saint blessed him by raising his right hand. Then, pushing Abul Hasan towards him, said: 'This is the groom. Take him as your son-in-law.'

Abul Hasan, still in a sort of trance, made his obeisance to the Sultan. Abdullah stepped forward and embraced the future husband of his youngest daughter.

Tana Shah was taken to the palace, given a good scrubbing and bath, doused in scents, bedecked with jewellery, and in no time was made into a royal groom. The transformation was as sudden as it looked incredible. All the preparations for the wedding had been made. Only a last minute change of groom was made.

Syed Sultan too was ready in his finery waiting eagerly for the message to come to proceed for the palace. The auspicious moment passed without any signal. Then he saw fireworks in the distance. A little later guns boomed. A member of his retinue explained the meaning of the firing of the cannons. This was a salute to the new couple. Obviously, the wedding had been performed. But with whom?

Soon the news came. The drama was over. Syed Sultan fretted and fumed, but there was nothing he could do now. A hurried counsel was held with his advisors. He took off his bridal finery, changed into battle dress, and along with his faithful companions, stole out of the city the same night because he knew that it would not be safe for him to stay there any longer.

A fortnight later the rejected groom of Golconda had reached Aurangabad. There he was granted an audience by the Mughal Emperor. Aurangzeb heard his tale of woe and even that taciturn monarch couldn't help laughing at the tragi-comedy. He commiserated with Syed Sultan: 'Never mind. Everything is for the better. We will have you married to the daughter of Mir Jumla. It will be better than marrying the daughter of the doddering old Qutb-ul-Mulk of a tottering principality.'

That was in the year 1660. Time passed and the younger son-in-law, with his pleasing manners and easy bearing, ingratiated himself with the Sultan and indeed with the whole household. His extroversion, his love of good things returned to him with a vengeance after the long deprivation at Shah Raju's hermitage. He was generous in his hospitality and loved to mix with people of all sorts. Soon he became popular with the courtiers and nobles. He presented a contrast to Nizamuddin, who used to keep aloof and behaved in a manner as if he was next to the Sultan and also his unquestioned successor. He humiliated the ministers and nobles on every conceivable occasion. His lordly and disdainful bearing earned him many enemies just as Tana Shah's bonhomie and accessibility brought him friends in all places high and low. Everybody called him Tana Shah with affection.

Both men were working towards the same objective—the throne of Golconda. Nizamuddin did that openly. He was already in control of most of the sinews of the state and apparently had but to take a few easy and formal steps to the throne. The court was in awe of him and he mistook it to be reverence for him. His wife was in full charge of the royal palaces. Tana Shah did not take anything for granted, though he had reasons to believe that the Sultan was partial towards him. But Abdullah, if he was indeed partial to Abul Hasan, did not have the courage to declare his preference. In addition to the general goodwill that he earned so quickly, he proceeded to raise mercenaries and for this purpose he made use of the jewellery and the generous dowry of his wife. Though comparatively weak in physical and material resources, he had one great spiritual source of strength—his mentor, the Sufi saint, Shah Raju. This factor alone would see him through, he believed.

In April 1672, Abdullah fell ill. On the morning of 21 April, Tana Shah came to enquire after his health. Nizamuddin's lackeys tried to bar his entry to the palace. In the melee that followed, Tana Shah's steed was injured by one of Nizamuddin's men. Tana Shah complained about this to the Commander of the Army, Sayyad Muzaffar, who was a sympathizer of Tana Shah. The Royal Chamberlain, Moosa Khan, was also on Tana Shah's side.

Sayyad Muzaffar moved with lightning speed and took control of all the vital centres of civil and military power. He also struck at the mansion of Nizamuddin and placed him and his wife under arrest.

While Abdullah lay dying, the bitter but brief struggle for succession was raging in the palace—and in the streets. Unaware of that, he expired the same afternoon. Two days later, Abul Hasan was proclaimed the Sultan of Golconda. As he gave a shoulder to the coffin of his predecessor on the way to the royal necropolis by the side of the fort, Tana Shah suddenly recalled the jesting remark of Shah Raju 12 years ago that evening on the departure of Abdullah from the monastery and his own nervous entry into the presence of Shah Raju: 'Lo, one king goeth and the other cometh.' Shah Raju had told him he never made a joke that hurt anyone. The Sufi's apparent jest was in fact a prophecy, made, characteristically, in the lighter vein.

Kuchipudi, Ramadas, and Madanna

Abul Hasan Tana Shah became Sultan on 21 April 1672.

The first thing he did was assign 14 jagirs to the monastery of Shah Raju for its upkeep. Shah Raju advised him to be a good ruler to his people.

Tana Shah also had to repay the good offices of those who had put the crown on his head. The first amongst those was the Commander of the Army, Sayyad Muzaffar, who was made Mir Jumla, the Prime Minister. Moosa Khan, the Royal Chamberlain, was promoted to Commander-in-Chief of the Army. Neknam Khan was confirmed as the Governor of Karnataka.

Sayyad Muzaffar believed that, having made Tana Shah the Sultan, he must continue to guide him. He therefore became somewhat overbearing in his behaviour with Tana Shah. Occasionally, Tana Shah would tick him off but Sayyad Muzaffar did not take the hint.

Mir Jumla had two very able young men in his office, who were brothers. The elder one, Madanna, was his personal secretary and the younger one, Akkanna, was *peshkar* or his deputy. Sayyad Muzaffar depended on them a great deal and they were largely responsible for his good reputation. Every one, including the Sultan, knew this and there were occasions for Tana Shah to notice these young brothers. Madanna, starting his career at the lowest level, had made rapid strides and anyone who came in contact with him could not but be impressed by his shrewdness. When Sayyad Muzaffar was designated Mir Jumla, Madanna was promoted as *Majmuadar*, or Revenue Minister. That brought him into more frequent and direct contact with the Sultan.

Meanwhile the simmering jealousy between Mir Jumla and Moosa Khan grew.

Things came to such a pass that Moosa Khan attacked the mansion of Sayyad Muzaffar at Golconda. Sayyad Muzaffar appealed to the Sultan for help. For such insolent and rebellious conduct, Tana Shah sacked Moosa Khan. This added to Sayyad Muzaffar's arrogance.

Then Tana Shah turned his attention to Sayyad Muzaffar. He had noted that Sayyad Muzaffar had not bothered to inform the Sultan about the siege of Pulicat by the French and its subsequent surrender and the return of San Thome to the French. The Sultan decided to teach his Mir Jumla a lesson. But he was powerful and well entrenched. Tana Shah therefore started warily by weaning away some of his protégés. This was accomplished through Madanna and Akkanna.

Having prepared himself fully, Tana Shah called an open darbar on 16 June 1674. There, to the surprise of everyone present, he got up and made a speech. In it, he accused Mir Jumla of sedition. However, he added that in view of his past services, he wanted to be lenient with him. Mir Jumla was transferred to the post of Governor of a remote district.[27]

Madanna was appointed in his place with the title of 'Surya Prakash Rao'. Simultaneously, Madanna's younger brother was promoted to the post of Revenue Minister.

❖ ❖ ❖

Madanna set off on his long tenure as Mir Jumla with earnestness and devotion. He was deeply beholden both to God and the Sultan for his good luck and decided to prove equal to the task entrusted to him.

Madanna instituted some reforms to reduce government expenditure, increase revenues and improve efficiency. Some of the mines in the state, that had been closed for some time, were reopened. Many deserted villages were rehabilitated and new ones settled. No land revenue was collected from new villages for a period of nine years. After that there was a gradual increase every year till it reached the normal level. Madanna also abolished the practice of an annual auction of villages to Revenue Collectors. Instead, village officers were appointed for the purpose of collecting revenue and discharging other duties. These posts were made hereditary and agricultural land was assigned to them to compensate for their services. He also subjected all religious and charitable endowments to tax. Periodical transfers of officers were also introduced to prevent emergence of vested interests.[28]

Madanna exerted himself to assert the authority of the Qutb Shahi government on the foreign powers in the south, particularly in the case of the recalcitrant British. They were averse to following the procedures of the government at Golconda, that is, to going through the offices having jurisdiction over Madras, or the Governor of Karnataka. They repeatedly submitted petitions for permission to mint their own currency, and to have their own judicial system in the areas leased to them. They also wanted some more villages leased to them. These requests were firmly rejected. Due to the contumacy and insolence of the English, the local Commander, Linganna, also had to lay siege to Madras for some weeks. This brought the English to heel.[29]

Given the long coastline of the Qutb Shahi Sultanate, the additions to it with the conquest of Karnataka and the naval presence of the European powers there were factors that underlined the need to reinforce the navy. Accordingly, Madanna proceeded to modernize and strengthen both the merchant and the defense navy. There was an instance when the Emperor of Siam (now Thailand) had impounded some Qutb Shahi vessels in 1686. A successful expedition was sent to rescue them. This campaign established the reputation of the Qutb Shahi navy, which, incidentally, employed some English gunners.

Madanna further fortified the outposts at Bhuvangiri, Khammam, Warangal, Kondapalle, and Kondavidu. He had in mind the possible transfer of the seat of government to Kondapalle in case of an attack on Golconda by the Mughals, since he thought that the kingdom could be better defended from there.

Another significant contribution by Madanna consisted of the reforms in the organization of the army. He abolished the feudal contingents and converted them into a crown force. Their salary was paid regularly and generally in the presence of the Sultan. He also increased the proportion of cavalry to infantry, thus making the force a cohesive fighting machine. In addition, he persuaded Tana Shah to have a personal contingent of 40,000, and he added to those 30,000 troops under his own command. All this was done to face the Mughal threat which was looming large on the horizon. The strength of the standing army was raised to 600,000.

By doing this he earned considerable popularity amongst the people at large. At the same time he also earned the hostility of some important sections of the bureaucracy and nobility. For many orthodox Muslims, the presence of an infidel, at the helm of affairs of a Muslim sultanate, was an anathema. The Mughals, who were keen to annex the sultanate, fanned this sentiment.

Like his predecessor, Tana Shah also undertook a tour of the east coast lasting about two and a half months. During this trip a halt was made near the village of Kuchipudi, about 60 kilometres away from Vijayawada.

Late one evening the Sultan heard a distant drumbeat and the jingle of dancing bells.

Madanna explained that it was the traditional Kuchipudi dance local dance, and with Tana Shah's permission, organized a performance the next evening.

The troupe gave a performance of *Bhamakalapam*, a dance form created and choreographed by Siddhendra Yogi. It is based on an episode involving Lord Krishna and his junior wife, Satyabhama.

The legend has it that Krishna had two wives. Rukmini, the senior one, was broad-minded and tolerant of his flirtation with other women. The junior wife, Satyabhama, on the other hand, was jealously possessive of him. One day in a playful mood Krishna asked Satyabhama:

'Tell me Satyabhama, who is more beautiful—you or I?'

Satyabhama asked coquettishly, 'You want to know the truth? Do you have any doubt about it?'

'No,' the Lord said, 'but I want an affirmation from you.'

'Of course, I am more beautiful. There is no comparison.' Krishna, like all lovers, wanted to hear something else. His vanity was hurt and he got up and walked away in a huff from her to Rukmini's abode. There he was sure he could hear what he wanted to.

Satyabhama didn't expect such a reaction from her lover. Suddenly, she felt abandoned, dejected, and forlorn. She tried to call him back, but the divine lover was gone.

Unable to bear the pangs of separation, she unburdened herself to her companion. This dance is based on the dialogue between the two female friends. It described through exquisite *mudras*—gestures—the dark moods of a woman abandoned by her lover.

Madanna explained the fine points of the story and of the gesture to his monarch. Tana Shah, who had seen only the Kathak form of dance so far, was very impressed by this new form. He told Madanna: 'This dance is full of grace and rhythm.'

'Indeed, Your Majesty is right. It depicts stories from the life of Lord Krishna. It evokes reverence. It lifts one above one's senses.'

'No doubt, Surya Prakash Rao Bahadur, I am very pleased.' Then, turning to the leader of the troupe, Vedantam, he asked: 'Tell me, young man, why is that all your dancers are men. Are there no women in this place?' and he smiled at what he thought was an embarrassing query.

'There is a reason for this, respected Sultan,' replied Vedantam. 'The songs of this dance are full of sensuous love. The *devadasis*—the women consecrated to the temples—were already adept at such gestures. The Guru, Siddhendra Yogi, thought that if they were to present this dance with their lewd approach, they would corrupt society further. He therefore forbade women from taking part in the dance. Instead, he induced good-looking young Brahmin boys to learn Bhamakalapam. The Brahmins never danced. Traditionally, they were teachers. They would be excommunicated if they took to dancing. Siddhendra promised them a special exemption from the Udupi Math. He also promised them salvation. The Brahmin boys had to observe strict discipline and study the Vedas, the Sastras and the foremost treatise in aesthetics, the *Natya Sastra*.'

Pleased, Tana Shah asked Vedantam if he could do anything for him.

Emboldened by this offer, Vedantam stepped forward with folded hands and submitted:

'Sire, this classical dance-form is now on the brink of extinction. There is only one family left to practise it. There is no financial support for the artistes. They do it as an act of worship. We do not know how long the dance will survive. But if our Sovereign, in his generosity, could grant us some permanent relief, this great heritage of ours can be saved from extinction.'

Tana Shah thereupon granted the village of Kuchipudi as a jagir to Vedantam for the support of the languishing dance form.

That is how the Kuchipudi dance form was saved from extinction.[30]

❖ ❖ ❖

Madanna had a nephew called Gopanna, who was appointed the Revenue Officer of Husnabad pargana, which included the area of Bhadrachalam. At an early age he was inspired by Pothana's *Bhagavatham* and came to revere Lord Rama both as an ideal human being and as *Paramatma* ('Supreme Soul') pervading the universe. Gopanna adopted Rama as his family deity and called himself his servant—Ramadas.

In Bhadrachalam, a tribal woman called Pokala Dommakka had heard the legend of Sabari and Lord Rama. According to that, Sabari had offered some berries to Rama when he had passed that way during his exile. In order to make sure that the berries were sweet Sabari ate a part of each berry before offering it to Rama. Dommakka imagined herself to be Sabari and became a great devotee of Rama. One night, the story goes, Rama appeared in her dream and told her that there were three idols—of himself, Sita, and Lakshamana—hidden somewhere in the nearby hillock. He also told her that in course of time a devotee of his would come and construct a proper abode for them. Dommakka searched for the idols and found them. The local people constructed a shed for them.

On hearing about the story and seeing the idols, Gopanna took upon himself the task of building a temple dedicated to Lord Rama on the bank of the river Godavari at Bhadrachalam. First, he started with his own savings. Then he collected donations. The project become more and more ambitious and so he started dipping into the public treasury in his custody. Soon he was arrested for misappropriation of public funds and was lodged in the jail in the Golconda Fort. In the cell Ramadas was as if in a trance. He would go on singing devotional songs and keep the walls of his cell reverberating with the name of Rama. The warders of the jail seldom checked on him in their inspection rounds. His melodious chanting of the *kirtans*—devotional songs composed by himself— certified his presence there.

Ramadas spent 12 years in jail and wrote 125 songs in all, mostly kirtans. These songs reveal his varied moods: from the ecstasy of devotion when nothing mattered, to the depths of despondency when he bemoaned his fate and chided his deity for letting him down. In one of his sarcastic moods he lambasts Rama:

> *Kaliki turai melukuga cheisthi Ramachandra*
> *Neevu kulukuchu thirigedavu. evarabba sommani Ramachandra?*
> *Nee thandri Dasaratha maharaju pettena. Ramachandra.*
> *Leka nee mama a Janaka maharaju … pampena. Ramachandra?*

(With great devotion and love I got the aigrette made for you. At whose expense are you wearing it and strutting about? … Did your father, Dasaratha, provide it to you or did your father-in-law, Janaka, give it to you?)

Then he suddenly realizes that he has overstepped his bounds. He is then overtaken by remorse and entreats his Lord:

> *Abba thittithinani, aayasapadavaddu. Ramachandra.*
> *Ee debbalakorvaka, abba. thittithinayya Ramachandra!*[31]

(Do not take amiss what I said. I said all that because I could not bear the torture in the jail. I burst out in pain and scolded you.)

In another song, he rebukes Lord Rama and asks him to see that his debt is repaid. In yet another song he tries to enlist the support of Sita to intercede with Lord Rama on his behalf. He tells her that when her Lord is engaged in love-play with her, she should take the opportunity to plead his case. In one complaint to Sita, Ramadas has the temerity to allege that Rama is *Dharmaheena*, that is, devoid of righteousness.[32]

And thus for 12 long years, he carried on singing his frenzied kirtans in his cell.

One night, according to the legend, two young handsome men, with long hair, armed with bow and arrow, came to his cell. Ramadas was dazed, but he did not stop his recitations till he heard his name. It was Lord Rama calling him: 'Ramadas, I have come. I am here on your summons,' the dark one said with his charming smile, 'it is all over now,' and disappeared.

The next day there was a furore in the Fort. The Sultan was visiting the jail himself. He made straight for the cell in which Ramadas was lodged. He took the key from the Superintendent and ordered the removal of shackles from the prisoner's body.

'Ramadas, you have suffered enough punishment. Your dues have been discharged. You are free to go now.'

'But Your Majesty … ,' Ramadas faltered, 'I haven't … .'

'Somebody paid for you,' smiled the Sultan.

Ramadas was incredulous. 'But who could it be, My Lord?'

'I do not know,' replied the Sultan. 'Last night two young and handsome men came to my chambers. One was slightly dark. He placed a bag near my feet and said: 'Here is what Ramadas owed you. Let him be released now.'[33]

'My Lord, my God,' cried Ramadas. 'So you have seen them too. My penance is over.'

'You can resume your duties now,' said the Sultan in a gesture of forgiveness.

'My duties are now in the temple where my deity lives,' Ramadas folded his hands and made a bow to the Sultan.

This happened sometime in 1683. Tana Shah, to make up for the years of confinement, granted Ramadas a jagir of three villages—Sankaragiripaui, Palvancha, and Bhadrachalam—for the maintenance of the temple. Ramadas spent the few remaining years of his life looking after the temple and composing and singing devotional songs.

Ramadas had good knowledge of tradition and his verses are replete with devotional sentiment. Unlike the great Thyagaraja, who followed him two centuries later and whom he influenced greatly, his compositions could be sung by common folks without any formal training in music. He therefore, became a people's composer and has remained popular till today.

❖ ❖ ❖

Shivaji was born the son of a Maratha chief of Bijapur in 1627. By bold and ambitious campaigns, first against Bijapur, and then against the Mughals, Shivaji soon became a formidable force and was crowned King of the Marathas in 1674. Both Bijapur and the Mughals accepted his claim and concluded peace with him after suffering defeat at his hands in 1675.

Shivaji had a half-brother called Venkoji, who was the chief of Ginjee fort which was then part of Karnataka (the present-day Tamil Nadu). Shivaji wanted to wrest this fort from him and also claim ancestral property and jewellery in the possession of Venkoji. Now that he had dealt successfully with Bijapur and the Mughals and had some respite, he turned his attention towards this problem. In order to move against Venkoji, Shivaji had to pass through the Golconda territory. He also needed financial and military assistance for the campaign.

The government at Golconda knew that the Marathas could be quite a nuisance as they had been in the past in 1672. Now that they were free from engagements with the Bijapur sultanate and the Mughals, their potential for mischief in Golconda became all the greater. The conditions in the Karnataka area also were not good and it was felt that Shivaji's march through that territory as an agent and ally of Golconda could help assert the latter's authority in establishing law and order there. It would save the government considerable expense and exertion. Also, an alliance with Shivaji would signal to the Mughals that Tana Shah was not alone and so should be treated with caution. So, a treaty of friendship between Shivaji and Tana Shah seemed to be in the interest of both the parties. To provide a cover for this expedition, the Marathas announced that their ruler, Shivaji, would undertake a pilgrimage to Srisailam. For this pilgrimage, 30,000 cavalry and 40,000 infantry accompanied him.

On his arrival at Golconda in February 1677, Shivaji was given a royal welcome by Tana Shah. During his month-long stay, a treaty was concluded between the two rulers. Tana Shah was to pay to Shivaji 100,000 hons annually to finance his expedition. In addition, an amount of 3,000 hons per day would be paid to cover his expenditure for the duration of his stay in Karnataka. Further, 5,000 soldiers and a contingent of artillery was to be provided to him. Shivaji would recover his parental territories from his half-brother. Other territories conquered by him would be divided between Shivaji and Tana Shah. The Qutb Shahi officers and administration were given instructions to render all the necessary help to the Marathas.

Shivaji went via Cuddapah and Madras and occupied the Ginjee fort without resistance. Thence he went to Vellore, Kolar, Arani, and Sira. Proceeding further, he invested Bellary and occupied it. Then he plundered some Mughal territories between the Krishna and Bheema rivers. His campaign accomplished more than it had set out to.

But when it came to dividing the conquered territories Shivaji did not keep his part of the treaty. He suddenly turned towards Bijapur without informing Golconda. Misunderstanding developed between Shivaji and Tana Shah because of that, and Madanna, having been instrumental in the conclusion of the treaty, became somewhat suspect in Tana Shah's eyes.

Madanna's Fall

While Golconda had become a vassal state of the Mughals in 1636, it had concluded separate treaties of friendship and mutual assistance with Bijapur and the Marathas.

When Aurangzeb proceeded to attack Bijapur in 1686, he warned Tana Shah not to extend any help to Sikandar Adil Shah, the ruler of Bijapur. Tana Shah acknowledged this message and sent to Aurangzeb his respects and tribute money besides 15 war-elephants, stallions, and some quintals of gold. Simultaneously, however, he sent a secret message to Mohammad Masoom and Mohammad Jaffer, his representatives in the camp of Aurangzeb, that he was dispatching a contingent to help his friend, the ruler of Bijapur. He told them that while Sambhaji, the Maratha chief, would send help from one side, he would send an army of 40,000 to help the young Prince of Bijapur to frustrate Aurangzeb's designs.

The message was intercepted by the Mughal intelligence and brought to the notice of the Mughal Emperor. He was furious at this double-dealing by Tana Shah and decided to teach him a lesson. He therefore diverted part of his army under the command of his son, Muazzam Shah Alam, and sent it to attack Golconda.

The Qutb Shahi forces under the command of Rustam Rao and Sheikh Minhaj met the Mughal army and effectively halted its advance at Malkhed. Mohammad Ibrahim, the Commander-in-Chief of the Golconda army, encircled the Mughal army under Kokaltash. When the Qutb Shahi army had almost won the day, the Mughals made a ferocious war elephant drunk, tied an iron chain weighing about three quintals to its trunk and let it loose amongst the enemy ranks. The beast wrought havoc in the Qutb Shahi ranks killing and mauling a large number of soldiers. Not able to face such an assault, the Golconda army took to its heels.

The Mughals were too fatigued to press their advantage. So the Golconda forces were able to escape and regroup. When the news of this slackness on the part of the Mughal command reached Aurangzeb, he was very annoyed with his son and the Commander, Kokaltash. In the imperial commendation conveyed to the lower Commanders, the Prince and Kokaltash were deliberately left out. This was Aurangzeb's way of conveying his displeasure.

The sulking Mughal Prince was persuaded by his advisors to mount another attack on the Qutb Shahi forces to wipe out the earlier blot on his reputation.

The second battle of Malkhed ensued. The engagement lasted several days. The Golconda army seemed to have an upper hand at one point but then, suddenly, without any apparent reason, it withdrew. The Mughals pursued it. However, the Mughal Prince stayed action for some time to enable the ladies of the Qutb Shahi forces to be shifted to safer places.

Since the Bahmani days, there had been two factions at the court. The local elements, called the Deccanis, were outnumbered by the foreign elements (gharib or afaqi). Naturally, the rulers, themselves being of foreign origin, relied more upon the latter. The 'foreign' elements occupied important positions in both civil and military fields, leading to jealousy and animosity between the two elements.

This feeling erupted suddenly at Malkhed and as a result, the Golconda army packed up at night and retreated to its capital. The next morning, a surprised Mughal Prince saw the ground clear before him. He ordered the beating of drums to announce the Mughal victory.

On returning home the retreating army met the Sultan and complained of the betrayal by its Commander, Mohammad

Ibrahim. He had been harbouring a grudge against the Sultan since 1682. In that year, some territories in Karnataka, belonging to the Golconda sultanate, had been occupied by some Maratha chiefs due to the negligence of Mohammad Ibrahim who was the Commander-in-Chief of the Golconda army. As a punishment for that act of negligence the Sultan had reduced his rank and salary. He was also relieved of the post of Majmuadar. Later, on the intervention of Madanna, he was reinstated as Commander-in-Chief of the army. But the humiliation rankled. Many suspected that Ibrahim retreated in a battle in which the chances of beating the enemy were fair.

In hot pursuit of the fleeing Golconda army, Prince Muazzam reached the outskirts of Bhagnagar in October 1685. At this stage, Mohammad Ibrahim defected to the Mughals, setting in train many desertions from the Golconda side. Tana Shah was upset and unnerved by this. Tale-carriers exploited this opportunity to poison his ears against some of his advisors, in particular against the Prime Minister, Madanna. Wasn't it he who had interceded on Ibrahim's behalf when the latter had let the Maratha chiefs usurp Golconda territories? Madanna, it was alleged, had connived with Shivaji too, as mentioned earlier. It was Madanna and his brother Akkanna who were a danger to the polity. The whispering campaign grew and the foreigners and some ladies in the harem lent support to it.

And when Prince Muazzam was knocking at the gate of Bhagnagar, Tana Shah decided to move to the safety of the Golconda Fort. Madanna pleaded with him not to do so. But the Sultan did not listen to him.

Immediately upon the Sultan's desertion of the city, hordes of thieves, looters, and ruffians descended upon it. They helped themselves to all they could lay their hands on. From the city gates to the fort, a distance of eight kilometres, was one unending stream of people with carts, camels, horses, and cattle carrying their loot from the city.[34]

Fifty million hons in cash was looted. Articles, worth many more times that amount, were carried away. Having restored some semblance of law and order, he offered peace to Tana Shah on the following terms: (1) Madanna and Akkanna should be dismissed from their posts and imprisoned since they were the cause of all trouble; (2) The arrears of tribute amounting to three million hons should be cleared; (3) In future, 200,000 hons should be paid annually as tribute; (4) Sedam fort and adjoining territories should be ceded to the Mughals; and (5) Finally, an apology should be tendered to the Mughal Emperor.[35] Tana Shah was ready to agree to all except the first condition. Ultimately, however, he succembed and signed the treaty. But he did not take any action against Madanna and Akkanna.

Tana Shah carried the problem to his private chambers. The adversaries of Madanna had prepared the ground there already. The Queen also advised acceptance of the terms.

The next morning Madanna appeared before Tana Shah. 'We shall go away, if it serves Your Majesty's interests,' Madanna offered, 'or if you like to confine us, we are prepared for that too. After all, what can be a better test of our loyalty to Your Majesty than this?'

'No, Mir Jumla,' Tana Shah remonstrated. 'Even kings should have a conscience. And you know that in spite of what your enemies have been saying, I trust you. I trust you and value you … .'

'That is enough for us, revered Sultan. The time has come for the final sacrifice. And you will not find us wanting.'

'No, no, Madanna. No. I will never do that,' and he waved his hand in exasperation.

Meanwhile a plot was hatched in the royal harem. Sheikh Minhaj, the Army Commander, some disgruntled nobles, and the Queen hatched a plan. A slave named Jamsheed was commissioned to murder the two brothers. The bodyguards of Madanna and Akkanna were won over by heavy bribes. In the evening when Madanna and Akkanna came out of the office, the assassins pounced upon them. Their beheaded bodies were hung upside down. The whole job was done in a matter of a few minutes.[36]

Tana Shah was waiting for Madanna in his palace. A messenger conveyed the news of the murder to him. He held his head with both his hands and grieved over the death of so wise and devoted a minister who had served him ably for 13 years. A few minutes later he got up and clapped his hands.

'Call the dabir,' he ordered the slave peremptorily.

The dabir had been waiting to join Madanna for a discussion with the Sultan. The response to the offer of a peace treaty by the Mughal Prince was the agenda for discussion.

'What is there to discuss now? The impossible term has been fulfilled by providence. I shall sign the treaty.'

The severed heads of Madanna and Akkanna were sent to Prince Muazzam by the Queen of Golconda in a tray. He, in turn, sent them to his father, Emperor Aurangzeb, who was camping at Sholapur.

Aurangzeb assembled all his nobles and courtiers in an open darbar. An elephant raised one of its feet and crushed the two heads.

The darbar was dismissed.

The Fall of Golconda

Aurangzeb reached Golconda on 8 January 1687. He was not happy with the treaty and wanted to press for Golconda's total surrender. Three weeks later he laid siege to the fort of Golconda. Tana Shah made one last desperate bid for peace. Aurangzeb, in a *firman*, recounted his 'misdeeds', as he termed them. The Sultan, for one, had entrusted the affairs of his state to 'an infidel, a scoundrel, and a tyrant' and had also assisted another 'scoundrel', Sambhaji, the Maratha. 'You do not deserve sympathy from man or God. The arrow has left now. None can take it back.'

A contemporary chronicler, Mohammad Hashim, better known as Khafi Khan, in his Persian account of the reign of Aurangzeb, *Muntakhib-ul-Lubab*, gives graphic details of the siege. We recount some of them here.[37]

Aurangzeb wanted a swift victory, and to that end, he concentrated all his forces and his best generals at Golconda. Not only that, he also went about engineering defections from the top echeleons of the Golconda army. General Mohammad Ibrahim had already crossed over to the Mughals after the second battle of Malkhed. Khalilullah Khan was the next to join them. Shaikh Minhaj followed suit. Then came Sharza Khan. Golconda was now left with Abdullah Khan Panni and Abdur Razzaq Lari. Finally, it was only Lari who was to remain loyal till the end.

But with all that, it was no cakewalk for the Mughals. At times Golconda seemed impregnable. Aurangzeb had staked every-thing on it and he led the besieging forces, while living in a tent and offering his prayers in a small mosque built specially for him by the side of the tomb of Hayat Bakshi Begum.

It was three months into the siege and yet no advance could be made by the Mughals. Aurangzeb was getting restless and he taunted his generals for the delay. Smarting under his bit-ing comments, one night Feroz Jung planned a daring sortie on the fort. Calculating that the guards on the ramparts of the Fort would be asleep, he led some of his soldiers close to them. While he stood below, the soldiers started scaling the walls with lassoes and rope ladders. When the first two soldiers reached the top of the wall, a pariah dog that was sniffing for carrion noticed them. It started barking and that woke up the garrison. The defenders beheaded the soldiers and cut off their lassoes. As a result of that a number of the invading Mughal soldiers fell to their death. Back in the Fort, Tana Shah rewarded the dog with a gold collar and chain and a silk coat[38] and made it sit by the side of his throne.

The stalemate in the siege had gone on for far too long and everyone was looking for some break. As soon as the first Mughal soldiers had reached the top of the wall, the Mughal general, Haji Mehrab, thought that the Fort had been captured. In his eagerness to be the first to break the tidings to the Emperor, he rushed to the imperial tent. The whole camp was abuzz with excitement. Aurangzeb was then at his early morning prayers. When he heard the report, he lay prostrate in gratitude to his Creator. Then he signalled for victory drums to be beaten and asked for his formal dress and mount. But soon it was found that the attempt at break-ing the Fort had been defeated.

Inside the Fort, the event was celebrated with justifiable relief and merriment.

Aurangzeb had tried to secure religious sanction for his attack on Bijapur and Golconda. His Qazi, Shaikh-ul-Islam, was a man known for his piety and integrity. He was the eldest son of the late Abdul Wahab and had been specially prevailed upon to accept the post of Qazi after his father's death. The Qazi said that an attack by a believer on another follower of the faith without any provocation was not justified under the laws of Islam.

Aurangzeb was stunned. The Qazi resigned his job and proceeded to perform the Haj.

Aurangzeb appointed Abdullah to succeed Shaikh-ul-Islam. Bitten once, he never broached the subject again with the new Qazi. But Abdullah was waiting to be asked. When it didn't happen, some of the nobles urged him to volunteer his advice. 'This war is against the Faith and the spilling of the blood of the faithful is contrary to the laws of Islam.' Not stopping here, the Qazi proceeded further: 'My Sovereign, since it is the responsibility of this humble servant to advise, it is respectfully submitted that the crimes of Abul Hasan, who is indeed sin incarnate, and the uncommitted sins of the royal servants, be graciously forgiven. He was sent back to the rear guard of the army.

The first problem faced by the imperial army at the time of laying siege to the Fort was that of food grains for the men and forage for the cattle. There had been a drought the previous year. Because of this, coupled with the unsettled conditions caused by the movement of forces and lack of rains, crops were not sown in time or in large enough areas. This problem was further compounded by the Maratha guerillas, which under Sambhaji had come to the aid of Abul Hasan and had encircled the Mughal army and cut off its supplies. These *bergis* as they were called, specialized in hit-and-run tactics. This led to the outbreak of an epidemic that claimed many lives and in turn caused considerable disaffection in the Mughal army. Hunger and disease drove some of them to the Fort which had adequate stocks of grain and forage to last a long time.

Seeing these conditions, Aurangzeb realized that the siege was likely to be protracted.

The monsoon broke out while the siege was in its fourth month. Once, it poured in full fury for three days on end. The depression adjoining the fort became a vast lake. The hillocks around it contributed small rapid streams which helped to swell the level in no time. Trenches dug by the Mughals were submerged in the vast sheet of water. Their tents began to float like bubbles. Cannons, which dotted the fields, sank under water. There was mud and slush everywhere and any movement became impossible. The army's beasts of burden became a burden themselves.

The hosts were at home with this season. They were comfortably lodged in the fort. They were waiting for such an opportunity to add to the discomfiture of the invaders. They mounted a sortie. Utter confusion descended on the Mughals. Salim Khan, the Abyssinian who reckoned himself a great hero, fought for a while but when he found the going tough, crept into a cave. Amongst the Imperial Army, Saf Shikan Khan was foremost amongst those who entertained the ambition of conquering the Fort, but Lari's men defeated him. He was injured and hid himself in the piles of the dead and the injured. Covered with mud, he lay there with bated breath feigning death and thus saved his life. Another Commander, Jamsheed, took to his heels.

Aurangzeb ordered the Superintendent of the Stables, Hayat Khan, to take about 80 elephants to the scene of action to rescue his officers. Hayat Khan spent the night trying to reach the spot but could not. Elephants, so indomitable in the dry season, began to sink in the slush under their own weight. They stood there, helplessly rooted to the slush. Occasionally, in impotent rage they would let out a grunt, which only demoralized the Mughal soldiery further.

The Golconda forces took the captives to the Fort and presented the distinguished 'guests' to their Sultan, Abul Hasan. Ghairat Khan kept on feigning unconsciousness till a detonator was applied to his forehead and someone threatened to blow him up. Then he suddenly became alive. The Mughal prisoners of war were kept as the guests of the Sultan for three days. They were shown the stocks of food and ammunition in the Fort so that they could disabuse the mind of the Emperor if he had any false notion that the Fort could be starved into submission.

Abul Hasan embarrassed them by his hospitality and when he sent them back to their camp, he gave a robe of honour and a horse each to Ghairat Khan and Sarbrah Khan. Along with these gifts, he gave them a message to be delivered to the Emperor. When these hapless officers reached their camp, Aurangzeb was not amused. He punished some by demoting them and others by sending them away in disgrace.

Abul Hasan in his submission had craved the Emperor's pardon for his sins of commission and omission since he had suffered adequately. He also made a request that, in case Aurangzeb was victorious in the campaign, he might consider appointing Abul Hasan his agent since anybody else would have to resort to new taxation in order to meet the expenses of the new dispensation. For the new man to restore order would also not be easy. If his submission was accepted, Abul Hasan offered to pay ten million hons as reparation. Another amount of the same order would be paid for every stage of the return journey of the imperial forces up to the border of Golconda. 'I am suggesting this so that Muslim blood is not shed needlessly anymore and the royal soldiers are reunited with their families.'

The setback suffered by the Mughal forces was offset by the abject submission of Abul Hasan Tana Shah even at the moment of his triumph. Psychologically, Tana Shah had lost the war even when the Mughal forces were worrying about the impregnability of the fort. Aurangzeb now settled down to renew his offensive. He ordered that a large number of bags, two yards by one yard, be procured from the province of Berar. These should be used to fill up the moat of the Fort to facilitate an attack. 'And', he declared decisively, 'I shall myself stitch the first bag to be used in the project.'

The Mughals had started laying mines to blow up the bastions of the fort right from the beginning. Now three of them were ready. Enormous quantities of gunpowder had gone into their making. On 1 July 1687, the Emperor was informed that the mines were all ready and his orders were awaited to detonate them. He ordered that some troops should raise an alarm so that the besieged soldiers might come out on the ramparts of the Fort. The mine should be detonated at that time so that the maximum damage could be inflicted on the enemy.

The garrison in Golconda however, had intelligence about the mines. Their miners and sappers had quietly been digging tunnels from within the Fort to join these mines. Having established a passage to each of the mines, they removed most of the gun-powder and detonators from one of the mines. The direction of some of the detonators was turned towards the Mughal forces. From the other two mines they removed a considerable quantity of gun-powder and then so filled them up with water that they became damp squibs.

After making deafening noises to draw the defending soldiers on to the walls of the Fort, as planned, the Mughals detonated the first mine. It turned out to be a big flop. Only a part of the bastion was blown up and most of the masonry fell on the Mughals who were standing close to the ramparts. It killed many soldiers and created havoc amongst the survivors. The infantry, which was waiting to attack the Fort after the explosion, also suffered damages in the resulting confusion. The Golconda troops took advantage of the situation, and in accordance with a prior plan, fell upon the enemy and inflicted heavy casualties on them. They even occupied the Mughal trenches after killing the soldiers there.

When informed about the fiasco, the Emperor ordered a fierce attack to be mounted on the Golconda army. Reinforcements were sent, but as they took up their positions, the Golconda engineers detonated the second mine, the direction of which had been turned towards the Mughals. This explosion inflicted further damage on the attackers. It was estimated that the loss of men in the second explosion was ten times that in the first. The number of those killed was obtained by the numerical value of the chronogram Ghogha,[39] which in Persian means 'clamour'. As a chronogram, it yielded the figure 2007. Many soldiers suffered injuries. Stones flew everywhere. One of the soldiers with a sense of humour remarked that they had come to Golconda in the hope of getting precious stones, but not the rough, heavy stones from the wall of the Fort!

Availing of this confusion in the ranks of the enemy, the defending army mounted another sortie. They destroyed the planks made by the Mughals to scale the walls and captured some of their guns. Feroz Jung entered the fray with a large reinforcement, but could not retrieve the situation. The Mughal losses were yielded by the chronogram, Hashrgah[40] or 'the place of resurrection on the day of judgment'. It stood for the figure 534.

On hearing about this rout of his troops, Aurangzeb himself rode out towards the theatre of action. This boosted the sagging morale of the Mughals and they began to repulse the Golconda forces.

Then a sudden cloudburst occurred. The skies thundered and it began to pour so mercilessly that everything was either submerged under water or floating on it. The Golconda forces once again swooped down on the enemy. The Mughals retreated. The Qutb Shahi army collected a huge booty of heavy guns, ordnance, bags of sand, and a large quantity of timber which had been brought to lay planks across the moat. They used this material to repair the breaches in the walls and ramparts of the Fort.

The siege was getting prolonged beyond all expectations. Abul Hasan was exhibiting a strange and surprising mixture of defiant belligerence and abject humility. Corralled in the Fort, he was putting up a heroic resistance. Yet he showed no lack of chivalry. Once one of his marksmen sighted Aurangzeb and took aim at him. Tana Shah patted him on the back and pulled him up: 'Don't you see that the man is at prayer?' Aurangzeb wondered at the code of the man, Tana Shah. He wondered whether by such curious conduct he was mocking the might of the Mughals.

The Mughal nobles consoled the Emperor and advised that the sultanate of Golconda was virtually under the Mughal control. Abul Hasan was now only the Sultan of the Fort of Golconda. While he lay holed up there, the Emperor could proclaim his authority in the rest of the kingdom and bring the city under the imperial administration. This by itself would weaken Tana Shah's authority and demoralize his men, many of whom had their families staying outside the Fort.

Accordingly, Aurangzeb gave appointments to various officers to run the affairs of the city. Abdul Rahim Khan was appointed the Governor of the city and he was ordered to cleanse it of all pagan practices and customs promulgated by Abul Hasan. All places of pagan worship were to be replaced by mosques.[41]

The siege had now entered its eighth month and still there was no sign of the resistance weakening. Aurangzeb was becoming increasingly impatient and irritable with his generals. They met in a conclave and decided to purchase Abul Hasan's key men by offering them fabulous rewards and high ranks in the Mughal army. General Abdullah Khan Panni, who had held out so far, succumbed. On the fateful night of 21 September 1687, he opened the western gate of the Fort. General Ruhulla Khan and his men entered through the main gate and various breaches in the walls of the Fort. Prince Azam also reached the gate with his force and set up a tent there.

Now there was no stopping the avalanche of Mughal hordes pouring into the Fort. The defenders, taken unawares, were cut down like blades of grass.

General Abdul Razzaq Lari, lying exhausted in his camp-cot in full battle dress, heard the commotion. He jumped from his bed straight on to the bare back of his horse. With a sword in one hand and shield in the other, he galloped his steed to meet the marauders. A dozen of his faithful soldiers also followed him. They stemmed the tide with surprising valour. All his soldiers were killed and he was drenched in blood from head to foot. He suffered over 70 wounds, 12 of them on his face alone. His left eyebrow hung precariously over his eye but he kept on fighting. Even when he became unconscious he held on to the horse. The steed took him to the shade of a coconut tree in the Nagina Bagh in the palace area of the fort. Lari could barely manage to clutch at the trunk of the tree and slide down to the ground. Then he lost consciousness. The next morning he was noticed and recognized by Hussaini Beg's men. He was taken to his house and nursed there. When Aurangzeb came to hear about his bravery and loyalty and his grievous injuries, he sent his personal physician to treat him.

When Lari recovered to some extent, the Emperor offered him and his sons employment under him. Lari replied that one who had served Abul Hasan with his heart and soul could not bring himself to serve the Mughal Emperor. Aurangzeb was hurt at this rebuff but was also impressed by Lari's loyalty. He told General Ruhullah Khan that if Abul Hasan had only one more Lari with him, it would have taken much longer for the Fort to be reduced. A year later, when Lari had made complete recovery, he was produced before the Emperor again. Lari begged to be excused and requested that he be allowed to go for Haj where he could pray for the long life and prosperity of the Emperor. This time Aurangzeb felt slighted and ordered that Lari be arrested and produced before him for appropriate punishment. The Mughal Commander-in-Chief intervened and saved Lari. He called Lari and kept him at his house. A year later he was given the rank of 4,000 horses and persuaded to enter the service of the Mughal Emperor.

After Lari's resistance was overcome, the Abyssinian colony near the palace area put up a stiff fight and the progress of the

Mughals was halted there for quite some time. Finally, General Ruhullah Khan, with his guards, rode up to the Bala Hisar, the high palace where the Sultan was staying. The ladies of the harem started wailing at the approaching doom, but Abul Hasan was composed and he consoled them. Then he turned to offer his prayers. When the victorious Commander's arrival was announced, the Sultan was yet at prayer. He took his time to finish his prayers and then went and sat on his throne. The General with his entourage marched up to him. Abul Hasan came out to receive the party and invited them to join him for breakfast. Ruhulla Khan was surprised at his cool. After his breakfast, he bade his wailing ladies good bye, sent for his horse, and accompanied his captors out of the fort. After a few days, he was taken to the Daulatabad Fort to live out his last span of 13 years in captivity.

Tana Shah's life was most unusual and had more drama packed into it than in the lives of all his predecessors put together. In spite of his dissipated life as a Sultan, he showed rare courage and dignity in his last hours on the throne of Golconda.

Having reduced the Fort, Aurangzeb left for Aurangabad. And while going, he and his men loaded their beasts of burden with all the wealth which had taken centuries to accumulate in Bhagnagar. Ferishta, Tavernier, Thevenot, Methwold, Bernier—men of different nationalities—had sung praises of the city. Now poets wrote elegies on its downfall. One such man was Nimat Khan who wrote the poem titled *Qissa-e Shehar-e-Ashob*—'The Story of the City of Misfortune.' Here is a part of his lament:

> The land is ruined and wasted,
> Supports its people no more;
> Dust have the cultured lasted,
> Treasured in graves galore;
> And people deprived are pasted,
> The learned have meaning no more.
> Even soldier's swords produce
> No water or food in mud;
> Wish Golconda's sighs induce
> God's cleansing, Noah's floods.

❖ ❖ ❖

The Qutb Shahi Dynasty
(1518–1687)

			Ruled
1	Sultan Quli, Qutb-ul-Mulk	—	1518–43
2	Jamsheed Quli, Qutb Shah	—	1543–50
3	Subhan Quli, Qutb Shah	(b. 1543)	1550–50
4	Ibrahim Quli, Qutb Shah	(b. 1530)	1550–80
5	Muhammad Quli, Qutb Shah	(b. 1566)	1580–1612
6	Muhammad Qutb Shah	(b. 1593)	1612–26
7	Abdullah Qutb Shah	(b. 1614)	1626–72
8	Abul Hasan, Tana Shah*	—	1672–99

Note: * Deposed in 1687 by Aurangzeb.

Two: A Change of Guard

A New Titan

Feroz Jung had led the Mughal forces of Aurangzeb against Golconda and had died in action in 1687. His son, Ghazi-ud-din, also served Aurangzeb in many campaigns. He became blind due to smallpox. Despite that, out of sheer regard for him, Aurangzeb retained him in his service.

In 1671, he had a son named Qamaruddin. At the age of 20, he was given the rank of 4,000 horses. He participated in a number of campaigns for Aurangzeb. At the time of Aurangzeb's death in 1707 he was the *Subedar* of Bijapur. He traced his ancestry 34 generations back to the first Caliph, Abu Bakr.

During the struggles for succession that followed the death of Aurangzeb, Qamaruddin remained neutral. The new Emperor, Shah Alam Bahadur Shah, appointed him the Subedar of Awadh but entertained some reservations about him. Due to this, and the changed circumstances in the court, Qamaruddin resigned and started living the life of a recluse at Delhi. The Emperor tried to make up with him but the self-respecting noble did not respond. He declined the offer of appointment from the next Emperor, Jahandar Shah, too. In 1712, when Farrukh Siyar ascended the Mughal throne, Qamaruddin was given the title of Nizam-ul-Mulk Fateh Jung (Nizam, for short). Along with this came the rank of 7,000 and the Governorship of the Deccan. After three years, his Governorship of the Deccan was exchanged for that of Muradabad.

From the day of the accession of Farrukh Siyar, the notorious Sayyad brothers started their intrigues and arrogated to themselves the role of kingmakers. Farrukh Siyar sought Nizam-ul-Mulk's help to get free of their stranglehold. The latter offered to subdue them if he was made the Prime Minister and was given an amount of Rs 400,000 for meeting the expenses of his troops. The Emperor preferred the cheaper and meaner method of assassinating one of the Sayyads. When Nizam-ul-Mulk declined to adopt this course, he was relieved of the Governorship of Muradabad. Thereupon, he again retreated into seclusion. A year later, in 1719, he was offered the Governorship of Bihar, but he declined it and stayed on in Delhi and watched the intrigues and machinations of the court in silent agony.

Farrukh Siyar was blinded, deposed, and then murdered by the Sayyad brothers in 1719. For a while they even entertained the hope of usurping the throne, but the conflicting ambitions of the two brothers made this impossible. They, therefore, had to be content with a quick succession of two effeminate, consumptive young Princes who died within a span of nine months.

In 1719, Mohammad Shah was installed in Delhi as a puppet Emperor. With sheer courage and superior military strategy, Nizam-ul-Mulk helped him get rid of the Sayyad brothers. Mohammad Shah thus became the ruler of India in his own right. In 1722, Mohammad Shah made him his Prime Minister.

Mohammad Shah was given to sybaritic ways. He was rightly nicknamed *Rangeela*, the 'merry monarch,' by his subjects. He did not bother about the deteriorating administration, nor did he allow the Premier to do anything to improve matters. The discipline and security in the court was very lax. The self-seeking courtiers of Mohammad Shah were hostile to the Nizam-ul-Mulk and made fun of his old-world values and manners. They ridiculed even his traditional court dress. Finally, in sheer disgust, he withdrew to Malwa. On the instigation of some of his courtiers, the double-dealing Emperor appointed Mubariz Khan as Governor of the Deccan in the place of the Nizam. Thereupon, the latter proceeded towards Aurangabad and attacked and killed Mubariz Khan at Shakarkhed in 1724. He assumed the Governorship of the Deccan but acted as if he was carrying out the orders of the Emperor and had merely removed an interloper. The year marks the virtual independence of the Nizam. He began to issue assignments of land revenue, bestow offices, make promotions, and confer titles at his will and pleasure. He, however, refrained from formally declaring his independence and from assuming the usual attributes of sovereignty.[42]

The Mughal Emperor had now no option but to accept the *fait accompli* of the Nizam. He too kept up the same pretence and tried to cover his humiliation with as much grace as possible. He acclaimed the victory of the Nizam and conferred the title of 'Asaf Jah' on him.[43] Asaf was the mythical Prime Minister of the Biblical ruler Solomon and the title therefore signified wisdom of a high order.

The Mughal empire was tottering. The Marathas were giving it daily jolts. They would even gallop into the streets of Delhi and collect their tribute from the populace unhindered. Mohammad Shah summoned Asaf Jah to come to his rescue. Master of the situation in the Deccan, and acknowledged leader of the nobles at Delhi, the Nizam decided to respond to the royal command for help. Entrusting the Governorship of the Deccan to his son, Nasir Jung, the Nizam proceeded to Delhi to a tumultuous reception.

In 1739, when Nadir Shah attacked India, the Nizam was near Bhopal negotiating a settlement with the Marathas. He rushed to Delhi and joined the Mughal Emperor in his battle with Nadir Shah near Karnal. Nadir Shah won an easy victory against the Mughals and the Nizam was nominated to settle terms with him. Nadir Shah accepted the offer made by the Nizam and agreed to return to his country on payment of an indemnity of Rs 5 million. However, the Governor of Awadh, Saadat Khan, who was jealous of the Nizam, advised the invader that he was accepting too little; there was much more wealth to be had in Delhi. Nadir Shah thereupon repudiated the treaty and marched to Delhi as a conqueror with the Mughal Emperor in his train. Due to a rumour in Delhi that the conqueror had died, the people of Delhi killed some of the soldiers of Nadir Shah. In reprisal, Nadir Shah ordered a general massacre of the city. When it became too much, the Nizam presented himself before Nadir Shah bareheaded with a sword hanging around his neck and appealed to him to stop the carnage[44] by reciting a Persian couplet:

Kase namand keh deegar beh tegh-e-naz kashi,
Magar keh zinda kani khalq ra wa baz kashi

(The roar of your anger has killed so many men. If you want to kill some more, bring the dead back to life again.)

Nadir Shah stopped the massacre saying, 'I grant pardon to these rascals because of your white beard.'

At the time of leaving Delhi, Nadir Shah summoned Nizam-ul-Mulk to his presence and told him, 'You, and not Mohammad Shah, deserve the empire. I want to make you the Emperor of India. I will leave with you 10,000 of my intrepid soldiers who will peel the skin of anyone who might refuse to acknowledge you.'

Nizam-ul-Mulk made a deep bow and replied, 'Sire, to be an Emperor such qualities of greatness are required as I, your humble servant, do not possess.'

'What do you mean?' Nadir Shah asked in disbelief.

The old noble replied humbly: 'Your Majesty, my ancestors have served the King of Delhi for long. I too am a faithful servant of my Sovereign. I would not like to be untrue to my salt and thus acquire the stigma of a traitor.[45]

Nadir Shah was impressed with the integrity and courage of the noble who stood before him.

While the Nizam was in Delhi, his son, Nasir Jung, who officiated for him as the Nizam, declared his independence. Nizam-ul-Mulk cautioned him against such an imprudent course but Nasir Jung was in no mood to listen. The battle between the old warrior and his delinquent son was joined near Daulatabad in 1741. The young man fought bravely but many nobles deserted him and he was easily routed. He was brought as a captive into the presence of his father. The father forgave the son, but kept him under close watch for some time.

When the Nizam was returning to the Deccan, on one of his hunting expeditions, he lost his way. Thirsty and hungry, he approached a hermit for succour. All that the saint could offer him was dry, baked bread called *kulcha*, and plain water. The exhausted noble had his fill. The hermit counted the remaining loaves in his basket and said, 'My son, you have eaten seven loaves. Your family will rule for seven generations. God bless you.' Legend has it that because of that incident the kulcha was incorporated in the

Asaf Jahi flag. The Nizam, however, tried to correct this impression. One day he told his nobles:

I remember events since the age of three. At that age I put the mark of the moon on the standard of my army. My name was Qamaruddin, which means the 'moon of my faith'. Though the mark on the standard represented the moon, people thought that it represented a round piece of bread. This has been continuing from the time of my grandfather, the late Abid Khan, and my father, Feroz Jung. This legend about the representation of bread on the flag is not true, though commonly believed.[46]

The region over which the Nizam ruled in the Deccan covered the whole of peninsular India, south of the river Tapti with the exception of a narrow strip of the country in the western coast which belonged to the Marathas. It reached down to Trichinapalle and probably up to Madura. The Nizam appointed the Nawab of Arcot. On the east coast, from Srikakulam down, his sovereignty was acknowledged and the rajahs and zamindars paid tribute to him. A Governor was stationed at Rajahmundry to collect tributes from them. The revenue from such a vast territory was enormous and the court of the Nizam was the most splendid in India after that of Delhi.

The last summons came from his Mughal overlord in 1747. Ahmed Shah Abdali, ruler of Kabul in Afghanistan, had invaded Delhi. The indefatigable warrior-statesman, then 76, once again set off on his march from Aurangabad. On the way at Burhanpur, he heard that Abdali had been defeated and had fled. Then he received the news that Mohammad Shah too had passed away.

When the Nizam realized that his time had come, he called his official scribe and, in his frail but measured voice, started dictating his will and testament. Surrounding his deathbed were his son, Nasir Jung, the Head of Religious Endowments, his Superintendent of Post, and his Chief Secretary, Lala Mansaram. The 17 articles of this document distilled the essence of his experience and the wisdom of decades spent in struggle and strife, on horseback and in tents. From Aurangzeb to Mohammad Shah, he had seen the reign of eight Mughal Emperors and had actively served four. He had seen the zenith of the glory of the empire under Aurangzeb and its nadir under Mohammad Shah when the territories had shrunk to the area from Delhi to Palam. He had taken part in 87 battles and covered himself with glory in each one of them.

'Beware of the Marathas,' the dying patriarch warned his son in his will and testament. 'Trust not the people of Gujarat and Bijapur; nor the Pathans and Kashmiris. Be grateful for the office and honour conferred upon you by the Mughal Emperor and always remember to remain subservient to him. Otherwise you'd stand condemned before God.'

A veteran of many campaigns, Asaf Jah had evolved his own norms for judging people. There were obvious advantages in professing nominal allegiance to an established but waning authority as the Nizam did. Behind it lay the same consideration that made the early Sultans of Delhi get their accession sanctified by the Caliph at Baghdad. It legitimized their authority and thus made the task of governance easy. The Nizam appeased the Marathas at the cost of his nominal master at Delhi, ceding the territories held by the Emperor while consolidating his own and making them compact.

He was a brilliant military leader, an accomplished diplomat, and a shrewd statesman. He was very proud of the fact the he had learned etiquette and proper conduct at the court of Emperor Aurangzeb who was a stickler for rules and correct manners. Mohammad Shah often tested him in these matters and never found him wanting.

Asaf Jah used to narrate some of the incidents of his life himself and also made observations on men and matters, when he held his court in the interludes of peace in a life packed with action. Lala Mansaram, compiled 94 such anecdotes. They show Asaf Jah's maturity, his analytical mind, and the range of his interests, including aesthetics. He had a good sense of humour and admired repartee from his nobles.

He stood head and shoulders above the other nobles in the Mughal court and did not join their petty intrigues. He knew his abilities and let others know them and stand in awe of him. He was sought out by the Emperor as a saviour and he proved more than equal to the tasks entrusted to him. He was undoubtedly the most outstanding leader in eighteenth century India. It was not for nothing that Nadir Shah offered him the crown of the Empire. He was indeed a titan, a giant amongst nobles, the first and the most outstanding of the dynasty founded by him.

He was also given to the royal pastime of composing poetry. He wrote in Persian and sported the pen name of Shakir, 'the content'. He was the archetypal founder of a dynasty, a soldier, a statesman, and a poet—'a master of sword and of pen'.

Qamaruddin laid no claim to royalty. He sat on no throne. He wore no crown, but wielded more power than the nominal Mughal Emperor.

Dissipation of the Legacy

The Portuguese explorer Vasco da Gama discovered the sea route to India and landed in Kozhikode on the west coast of India in 1498. In 1510, the Portuguese Governor Albuquerque annexed Goa from the Sultan of Bijapur.

In the seventeenth century the Dutch, the Danes, the British, and the French followed them and set up their trading centres in India.

At the time of the death of the first Nizam in 1748, the French and the British were the main parties vying for influence to promote their commerce. The Nizam held the key to it all.

The Nizam's eldest son, Ghazi-ud-Din, was the *Mir Bakshi* (minister for army) under the Mughal Emperor at Delhi. His second son, Nasir Jung, declared himself the Nizam. His grandson from his daughter, Muzaffar Jung, was Governor of Bijapur. Having been a favourite of his grandfather, he aspired to be the Nizam.

The Nawab of Carnatic used to be appointed by the Nizam, though he was practically independent. After the assassination of the Nawab in 1742, the first Nizam had temporarily appointed Anwar-ud-Din as the Nawab. Chanda Saheb, a son-in-law of the earlier Nawab, had been the Governor of Tiruchirappalli. In 1741, the Marathas defeated him and took him into their custody against payment of ransom. He claimed legal right of succession to the Nawabship of Arcot.

The French Governor of Pondicherry, M. Dupleix, was a very able and shrewd person. He believed that if he could gain influence over the Nizam and the Nawab of Carnatic, it would help the French power in India against the British. He therefore conspired with Muzaffar Jung and Chanda Saheb and offered them military help for the realization of their respective ambitions. Thereafter, Dupleix got Chanda Saheb released form the Marathas. The two then joined together and, along with a French military contingent, attacked Carnatic. They won their first victory at Ambur fort in which Anwar-ud-din was killed. His son Mohammed Ali escaped and fled to seek refuge with the British at Chennai.

Muzaffar Jung promptly proclaimed himself the Nizam.

Nasir Jung proceeded to crush the rebellion with a formidable army of 300,000. The Marathas also joined him. Since the French had allied themselves with Muzaffar Jung and Chand Saheb, the British naturally joined the opposite group of Nasir Jung and Mohammed Ali. They, therefore, also sent a small force to help Nasir Jung.

Partly due to his being overwhelmed by such a large force and partly due to the promise of pardon he received from Nasir Jung, Muzaffar Jung gave himself up. However, as soon as he surrendered, he was put in chains by Nasir Jung.

This act of bad faith caused acute disgust amongst the three Nawabs of Kurnool, Kadapa, and Savanur. Dupleix was quick to take advantage of their discontent. So, while negotiating terms of peace with Nasir Jung, he also entered into a conspiracy with the Nawabs against Nasir Jung.

After such an easy victory, Nasir Jung sent away most of his troops and two generals to Hyderabad and started enjoying himself. The British contingent had also left him and withdrawn to Chennai. Taking advantage of this, Dupleix asked his Commander, Bussy, to attack the fort at Gingee.

Instead of laying siege to the fort that was known for its strong defensive layout, Bussy made a sudden and daring attack on the fort at night. Taken aback by the swiftness of the attack, the garrison capitulated.

Nasir Jung was roused by Bussy's feat and proceeded to Gingee to crush him. However, due to rains his progress was slow.

When Nasir Jung was camping about 16 miles away from Gingee, Dupleix ordered Bussy to come out of the fort and attacked Nasir Jung's depleted forces.

The Nawabs, according to a prior secret understanding with Dupleix, did not move to face the attack. Thereupon, Nasir Jung came forward and rebuked the Nawab of Kadapa as a coward for not advancing to fight the enemy. The provoked Nawab shot Nasir Jung down, released Muzaffar Jung from confinement, and proclaimed him Nizam in 1750.

In gratitude, Muzaffar Jung made Dupleix the Nawab of the whole territory from the south of the river Krishna to Kanyakumari, including Mysore and Karnataka, bestowing upon him the title of Nawab Zafar Jung. He also conferred upon him a personal rank of 7,000 and a jagir of Rs 100,000 a year. Dupleix was invited to sit next to the new Nizam to signify equality between the two. Dupleix did not accept all of this lest it should incite jealousy amongst the Nizam's nobles. On his recommendation, Chanda Saheb was appointed Nawab of Carnatic, but real power rested with Dupleix.

Muzaffar Jung then proceeded to Hyderabad and, on his request, Dupleix sent a small force along with Bussy as his body-guard to accompany him.

The Nawabs of Kurnool, Kadapa, and Savanur felt cheated as they had not gotten the expected reward from the new Nizam. On 3 February 1751, the Nawab of Kurnool killed Muzaffar Jung. He had ruled for barely six weeks. Thereupon, Bussy proclaimed Salabat Jung, the third son of the first Nizam, as the next Nizam.

Salabat Jung's gratitude to the French was even greater than that of Muzaffar Jung. He not only confirmed all the earlier privileges to the French but also gave them the east-coast district of Srikakulam and the port town of Machilipatnam. Dupleix's protégé Chanda Saheb was the Nawab of Karnataka. Mohammad Ali, the acolyte of the British, was holed up in Tiruchirappalli besieged by Chanda Saheb and the French.

The French power was now at its zenith. Salabat Jung was in dire need of French help since his eldest brother, Ghazi-ud-Din, had declared his intention to march from Delhi to the Deccan to claim the Nizamate. The Marathas too joined him. However, on his way, at Aurangabad, Ghazi-ud-Din died of poisoning by his stepmother.

In 1751, Robert Clive turned the tables on the French in Carnatic. He broke the French siege of Tiruchirappalli. Chanda Saheb was taken prisoner and turned over to the Marathas, who executed him. Anwar-ud-din's son, Mohammed Ali, was appointed as the Nawab of Carnatic.

Despite this setback, the French influence and hold over Salabat Jung increased. He left everything to Bussy and drowned himself in luxuries. Bussy kept things under control for the Nizam with his small yet highly disciplined force. But the situation was changing fast. The directors of the French East India Company did not approve of the policy of territorial acquisitions adopted by Dupleix. In 1754, Dupleix was recalled to France where he died in poverty and disgrace.

In order to ensure payment of regular salaries to his troops, Bussy secured from Nizam Salabat Jung the grant of a jagir comprising coastal districts from Srikakulam to Machilipatnam. They covered about 750 kilometres of coastline and included some semi-independent Zamindaris such as Vizianagaram and Bobbili. The arrangement yielded an annual revenue of Rs 400,000. Bussy's troops demonstrated the superiority of a small, well-equipped, and trained force over a large rabble for whose upkeep vast jagirs had been given to nobles. This system weakened the ruler and strengthened his feudal lords. Bussy's success raised apprehension amongst the nobles that their jagirs might be taken away. They, therefore, started plotting against him. However, the Nizam continued to depend upon Bussy. Displaying rare pluck and loyalty, Bussy saved the Nizam not only from his external enemies but also from the intrigues and machinations of his own court and his brothers, Nizam Ali and Basalat Jung.

In 1758, Bussy was recalled by the French Governor to Pondicherry. Leaving behind a small force at Machilipatnam for the protection of the coastal districts under the French, Bussy departed and left Salabat Jung without any protection from his enemies.

Happy at the departure of Bussy, the Raja of Vizianagaram, Anand Raj, requested Clive in Bengal to join him in throwing the French out of the east coast. Clive dispatched a force under Colonel Forde.

The British and the Vizianagaram troops quickly overran the east coast up to Machilipatnam. The French garrison there asked Salabat Jung for help. However, before he could reach there, Colonel Forde defeated the French garrison at Machilipatnam on 8 April 1759.

Meanwhile, taking advantage of the absence of Salabat Jung from his capital, the British encouraged his brother, Nizam Ali Khan, to rise against him. Salabat Jung rushed back to control the situation. In his panic, he entered into a treaty with the British in May 1759. According to that, he transferred the cession of *circar*s (districts) of Machilipatnam and Nizampatnam on the east coast from the French to the British. He also undertook to drive the French out of his territories within a fortnight.

However, with British help, Nizam Ali Khan had become very strong and Salabat Jung had to appoint him as his Diwan. He was also forced to send away his other brother, Basalat Jung, to his jagir in Guntur-Adoni.

In 1762, Nizam Ali Khan deposed and imprisoned Salabat Jung and proclaimed himself the Nizam.

Raymond and Kirkpatrick

At this point, Basalat Jung began to plot with the French to become the Nawab of Carnatic by adding the east coast circars and Kadapa to his jagir of Adoni and Guntur. Bussy left behind some of his troops under the command of Michael Joachim Marie Raymond with Basalat Jung. Nizam Ali Khan also came to terms with Basalat Jung and left his jagirs to him, hoping to shut him off from any further mischief.

In 1763, Nizam Ali Khan shifted his capital from Aurangabad to Hyderabad. This infused new life into the city after a neglect of 75 years, since the sack of Golconda by Aurangzeb.

In 1761, Pondicherry was captured by the British. Comte de Lally was taken prisoner and sent to Europe. That marked the end of the French power and the emergence of the British.

In 1765, Clive obtained the grant of the five coastal circars from Mughal Emperor Shah Alam without the knowledge of the Nizam. This enraged the Nizam and he threatened to assert his authority by the use of force. To avoid that, the British entered into a treaty with him in 1766. According to the treaty, the Nizam agreed to make a grant of five coastal circars to the British. As a consideration for the grant, the British agreed to pay the Nizam staggered amounts according to the date of taking possession of different circars, totalling Rs 900,000 annually. That amount was not to be paid whenever the Nizam availed of the assistance of

British troops. The Nizam also was to assist the British East India Company with his troops whenever required.

In 1767, the Nizam joined with the British and the Marathas for an attack against Carnatic under Hyder Ali of Mysore. The latter first bought off the Marathas, and then induced Nizam Ali to desert the British and join him in his invasion of the Carnatic. The British defeated Hyder Ali and advanced upon Hyderabad. A panicked Nizam was driven to enter into a tripartite alliance with the British and the Nawab of the Carnatic in 1768. This treaty reduced the amount to be paid by the British to the Nizam for the grant of the circars. The Nizam had to accept the independence of Mohammed Ali, the new Nawab of Carnatic. The British agreed to provide two battalions and six guns to the Nizam on payment whenever he required them, subject to the exigencies of the British.

Basalat Jung had been given the jagir of Guntur for life. He retained the French officers and troops. In 1779, Hyder Ali of Mysore advanced upon Kadapa, which was part of Basalat Jung's jagir. The latter sought help from the British. Under the treaty entered into between the two, Basalat Jung ceded his jagir to the East India Company on payment of a pension equivalent to the annual revenue from his jagir. He also dismissed Raymond and his French troops. The Nizam promptly took those troops into his service. That gave a new lease of life to the French in the court of the Nizam.

The British protested to the Nizam that his employment of the dismissed troops of Basalat Jung amounted to a violation of the treaty of 1768. The latter explained that the treaty barred him from employing foreign troops but not from keeping a native force officered by the French.

Raymond expanded and strengthened his corps and by 1795 it had grown into an army of 15,000 men formed into 20 battalions officered by 124 Europeans. Raymond was given a jagir in Medak for regular maintenance of his corps. Raymond made it self-sufficient in every respect. He established a gun foundry at Hyderabad to manufacture his own guns. Its ruins can still be seen in the locality with the same name near Fateh Maidan.

The Nizam depended heavily on this force and with it by his side he was confident of tackling the Marathas, who were a constant source of harassment to him. The battle with the Marathas took place in 1795, midway between the forts of Parenda and Khadla, near the river Manjira. The Marathas also had French contingents commanded by famous generals such as de Boigne and Dudrence. Although the British Residents at the courts of the Nizam and the Marathas accompanied their respective hosts to the front, they remained strictly neutral in accordance with the British treaties of friendship with the Nizam and the Marathas.

A small skirmish took place in which Raymond made some advance initially but was repulsed. The Nizam, noticing the disorder in his cavalry, fled and compelled Raymond to follow him. Raymond retreated in an orderly manner and prepared for an attack the next day. At night, a patrol of the Marathas looking for water for their horses chanced upon a party of the Nizam's troops on a stream. Exchange of fire ensued. Alarmed by the confusion, the Nizam tried to escape and took shelter in the fort of Khadla. The Marathas surrounded him and he was confined there for three days. The Nizam had to purchase his release by submitting to the most humiliating terms. He ceded to the Marathas territories including Daulatabad, Ahmednagar, and Sholapur, which were yielding an annual revenue of Rs 55 million as well as an indemnity of Rs 30 million to ensure the fulfilment of the terms of the treaty. The Nizam's Diwan, Arastu Jah (also known as Azim-ul-Umrah) was kept as a hostage by the Marathas.

The Nizam was very sore with the British for not helping him in this battle. He therefore asked them to withdraw their contingent. After that the Nizam's reliance on Raymond grew even more. He was assigned new jagirs to maintain a larger force. The British protested against this accretion of French influence, and when Raymond was sent to take charge of Khammam and Kadapa, the two districts that were the Nizam's share of the booty from the third Mysore War in 1792, he was threatened with military action. Then in 1795, Nizam's eldest son, Ali Jah, fled to Bidar and raised the banner of rebellion. He achieved some measure of success initially. The Nizam dispatched Raymond to subdue his delinquent son. In order to fill the vacuum created by the dispatch of Raymond's forces, the Nizam recalled the two English battalions that had been dismissed by him earlier. Raymond captured the rebel Prince easily and the Diwan, Mir Alam, was sent to bring him home. He was brought on an elephant but the *Diwan* had the howdah of the elephant covered, a practice adopted only in the case of women. Unable to stand the indignity, Ali Jah committed suicide on the way.

Providence helped the British. When Raymond was at the height of his powers, he suddenly died on 25 March 1798 at the young age of forty-three. Piron, a man who had none of Raymond's qualities, succeeded him.

Lord Wellesley arrived as the new Governor General of the East India Company in 1798. His aim was to put an end to French influence in Indian courts. He began by asking the Nizam to disband the French contingent. He allayed the latter's fears of Marathas by offering to increase the number of English battalions at his disposal from two to six. The Nizam was brought around to accept the proposal through the persuasion of Mir Alam, who was Nizam's vakil and representative at Calcutta and was entirely with the British. The crucial Treaty of Subsidiary Alliance was signed between the Company and the Nizam on 1 September 1798. The Nizam thus surrendered his sovereignty to the East India Company and paid for its financial implications.

The Nizam was asked to disband the French Corps immediately. It was no mean task since it provided well-paid jobs to 15,000 families directly and many more indirectly. However, the task was completed with great tact and by the next evening Raymond's legendary 'paltan' (platoon) was replaced by the British contingent. The French sun had finally set in India.

Raymond had become a legend in his own lifetime. He was beloved alike by the ruler and his subjects. He was revered by his soldiers of all faiths because he drilled them, marched them, made men out of the rabble, paid them regularly, and led them to victories. Even the mercenaries of the British were drawn towards him because he paid them Rs 1 more per month. Malleson said about him that no adventurer in India ever stood higher than he did. His ambition was to advance the cause espoused by men such as Dupleix and Lally. But he was cheated by fate. His name 'Monsieur Raymond' was corrupted by its sheer popularity. Muslims called him Moosa Rahim and Hindus Moosa Ram. Till about 1970, an annual *urs* (celebration on a death anniversary) was held at his grave in Asmangarh. Lamps were lighted, flowers offered, and tributes paid by the descendants of his soldiers. His memory is preserved by a locality named after him—'Moosaram Bagh'.

❖ ❖ ❖

The first English Resident to the Nizam's court, J. Holland, was appointed by the government of the Madras Presidency in 1779. A dispute arose about his conduct between the Governor of Madras and the Governor General at Calcutta. Thereupon, the East India Company decided that the power to appoint Residents would be vested in the Governor General.[47]

James Kirkpatrick was the sixth Resident and served for seven years at Hyderabad from 1798 to 1805. Till then, all the Residents had been staying in a garden-house of one of the Nizam's noblemen. Emphasizing the expanding and crucial role of the British agent at the court of the Nizam, Kirkpatrick decided to build an official residence for himself. He sounded out the Diwan, Mir Alam, about the allotment of a suitable piece of land for the purpose. Mir Alam asked the Resident to locate a piece and get a plan of the site prepared so that the Nizam's approval could be obtained. Ignorant of the principle of scale, the Nizam took one look at it and threw it away in horror. Kirkpatrick was crestfallen. He asked Mir Alam the reason for this summary rejection. Mir Alam laughed and chided Kirkpatrick for making the plan on a paper so big that it seemed to the Nizam equal in size to his state. Another audience was then sought with the Nizam. This time Kirkpatrick reduced the scale and got the original plan for the 64-acre piece of land redrawn on a piece of paper the size of a visiting card.[48] This time the Nizam readily agreed. Kirkpatrick then took up the project of building the Residency to the north of the river Musi. It was so grand that on a visit to Hyderabad in 1817, Sir John Malcolm remarked that it was better than the Government House of Madras, and in splendour next only to the Governor General's house in Calcutta.[49] The furniture for the Residency came from Carlton House in London, which was the residence of the Prince Regent. The Nizam, who maintained the

Residency at his expense, also paid for the furniture. Kirkpatrick enjoyed his new abode.

The Nizam conferred the title of 'Hashmat Jung Bahadur' on Kirkpatrick. He had a mistress who stayed not far from the Residency. One late evening, as he entered the verandah of her house, he noticed a dark object lying across the doorway, blocking his passage. Heavily drunk, he could not make out what the object was. Moving closer, he peered at it and found that it was a human being.

'Who are you?' he asked.

Getting no reply, he shouted, 'Who are you? What do you want?' A figure arose and, coming close to touch his feet, mumbled, 'Huzur ... Saheb ... .' It was a woman, a very young woman. A girl, in fact. 'Yes, what do you want, lady?'

'Sir, I am Khairu ... Khairunissa Begum.'

'Yes.'

'Daughter of Mehdi Yar Jung ... .' That name sounded familiar. Kirkpatrick knew the man. He was the son-in-law of Aqeel-ud-Dowlah and a relation of Mir Alam. The inebriated Resident was not slow in working out the relationship. She was a noblewoman, not a pariah. But what was she doing there?

'It was too hot in my house next door. So, I came to lie here for some fresh air and breeze and then dozed off. I am sorry, Saheb ... .' Khairunissa made a gesture of getting up and in doing so her face brushed Kirkpatrick's shoulder. Kirkpatrick saw her fair and moon-like face. She was fresh as a flower. 'All right, stay on here if you like.' He passed through the door into the waiting arms of his paramour. The next evening again he found Khairunissa at the same place. Seeing him, she got up. Kirkpatrick gave a gentle pat on her face as he moved past her. A few more days passed with similar encounters. Then, one day he thought he heard her sob as she got up to make way for him. Kirkpatrick paused. He looked at the round moon-like face for a while and noticed tears in her eyes. 'Are you crying, Khairu?' asked Kirkpatrick with some concern. 'Lad saheb,' she implored him, 'help me, help me.'

'What is the matter?'

'They are marrying me to an old rascal.'

'Old rascal?' the Resident asked in surprise. 'You are very young. You must get a young groom.'

'Help me, saheb,' sobbed Khairunissa.

'Are you in love with someone, Khairu?' She nodded bashfully. 'Who is he?' Kirkpatrick asked mischievously. The young woman paused awhile, looked up at him with her big innocent eyes, took a step towards him, and then all of a sudden put her index finger on the young Resident's lips. Kirkpatrick, bewildered, took her in his strong arms and planted a kiss on her lips. Just across the threshold, his mistress was waiting. Her waiting was never to end. Kirkpatrick did not cross the verge that night, nor ever thereafter.

Soon the city was agog with gossip about the Resident's new discovery. The girl's father came to see Kirkpatrick about it. 'We are men of honour, Sir,' he protested. Kirkpatrick surprised him by asking him to make arrangements for a proper nikah.

In his turban and *sehra* (ceremonial wedding headset) the Resident looked a perfect Muslim groom. He built an annex to the main building of the Residency, called it Rang Mahal, lodged his new bride there, and settled down for a happy conjugal life.[50]

The Diwan, Arastu Jah, instigated Mir Alam to complain about the marriage to the Governor General. Mir Alam complied reluctantly and warned the Governor General of the unhappy consequences of such a marriage for both the British and the Nizam.

Upset with Kirkpatrick for his indiscretion, Lord Wellesley sent Captain John Malcolm as the inquiry officer and authorized him to supersede the Resident if he found it necessary. John Malcolm had at one time served as the first assistant to Kirkpatrick. The latter wrote him a private letter underscoring the embarrassment the proposed inquiry could cause him and the authority of the Company which he represented, adding that he could not suffer the humiliation of an inquiry by someone who had worked under him. To strengthen the substance of his case, he enclosed a letter from Khairunissa's mother testifying that the marriage was performed with her consent and blessing. The Nizam also issued a statement in favour of the Resident. The complainants not only withdrew the complaints but also tendered their apologies. Kirkpatrick, having prepared his case fully, sent the commandant of the Resident's personal escort, Captain Hemming, to meet Malcolm at the port of Machilipatnam and to prevent his coming to Hyderabad. Malcolm too felt embarrassed, having known Kirkpatrick earlier. After going through all the papers, he expressed himself satisfied and returned to Calcutta. On his recommendation, the inquiry was dropped. Khairunissa gave birth to two lovely children, first a boy and then a girl. In 1803, both were sent to England for education. The boy, William George, died there but the girl, Catherine, grew up and married into a good English family. She became known for her beauty and wit and was the first sweetheart of the great writer Carlyle, who portrayed her as Blumhilde in his novel *Sartor Resartus*.

In 1805, Kirkpatrick was suddenly taken ill. He was advised a change of air and some rest. He left for Calcutta for consultations with the Governor General. When his boat reached Calcutta, his health took a turn for the worse.

He died on 15 October 1805. He was barely forty-one and his marriage had lasted only six years. Khairunissa's happy days were over so soon. Her children had been sent to England and she was a widow at the age of 19.

Thus passed into history a flamboyant character who strengthened the foundation of the British Empire in India. Like Raymond, people in Hyderabad remember Kirkpatrick too. His Residency now houses the University College for Women. His ballroom is used for meetings of the general body of the students. Till the end of the twentieth century, on one of the walls of the building hung the pictures of his two children, William George and Catherine. Khairunissa's Rang Mahal has been altered and made into a physics laboratory. The original area of 64 acres has now shrunk to 34 acres, the remaining area having been given to the Osmania Medical College for its hostel. It stands as an oasis in the vast concrete jungle of the city—a patch of green sprinkled with a bevy of young women? Close by is the bazaar known after Kirkpatrick's Indian title—'Hashmat Ganj'.

Kirkpatrick represents a milestone in the career of the British in India. Their Treaty of Subsidiary Alliance with the Nizam in 1798 set a pattern to be imposed on other native states one after another.

The Resident came to not only control the levers of real power but also set the tone in manners and in social behaviour.

The city was now divided into two parts. On the south bank of the Musi stood the original, quintessential part of it, the seat of dwindling power. Across the river emerged a new township with the Residency at its centre. The city had begun to change and expand. People looked towards the north of Musi to note the direction in which the wind was blowing.

The Hyderabad Contingent

Mir Akbar Ali Khan became the Nizam in 1803 with the title of Sikander Jah, Asaf Jah III. Mir Alam, a favourite of the English, was appointed Diwan in 1804. He was an inept administrator. He appointed Chandulal as his Peshkar, who exercised the real powers of the Diwan. On the death of Mir Alam in 1808, his son-in-law, Munir-ul-Mulk, was appointed his successor with the backing of the British. He was made to take Chandulal as his deputy, who was the virtual Diwan till 1832 when he was formally appointed to that post. He held the post till 1842.

Indian states such as Hyderabad kept large armies whose efficiency was not commensurate with the expenses incurred on them. The French and the British had shown the value of a small and efficient body of troops who could defeat hordes. After the Mysore and Maratha Wars, there was comparative peace and there seemed to be little need of large armies sustained by extensive jagirs given to nobles. The Paigah family in Hyderabad alone had a jagir yielding Rs 5.2 million annually for providing a force to protect the Nizam. Because of the involvement of powerful vested interests in the system, retrenchment of forces in the improved circumstances could not be contemplated. Of course, the Nizam was required to provide 15,000 troops under the Treaty of 1800 but he had an army of 70,000 men—mostly of irregular and disorderly description. A good part of these forces was stationed at Berar, while some were in Aurangabad, from where the Nizam feared the most danger.

Henry Russell, who became the Resident at Hyderabad in 1811, took stock of the situation and decided to reform and reorganize a portion of this riff-raff. The primary requirement of discipline was payment of regular salaries to the troops. In the princely states of India, this rule was always observed in its breach. Meadows Taylor, author of *The Confessions of a Thug*, who was an official in the Nizam's service, complained in 1825 that his salary had not been paid for the last six months 'and there was no such thing as getting it.'[51] He, like others, borrowed perpetually at rates of interest varying between 24 to 35 per cent. Soldiers were often so much in arrears of payment that they had to periodically threaten physical action against their officers to get their dues.

In 1812, the troops mutinied and murdered their Commandant, Major Garden. They were about to blow up his successor and brother as well when their demands were conceded. But then it was found that there wasn't adequate money in the Nizam's treasury to fulfill the demand. The Resident came forward and saved the situation by advancing the required amount. He adjusted the amount from the annual *peshkush* of Rs 900,000 which was paid by the Company to the Nizam for the grant of five east coast circars. Then the Resident reorganized the troops into a brigade of about 2,000 men with the necessary train of guns and other equipment to be kept in Hyderabad. This force was nicknamed Russell's Brigade. But formally, it was known as the Hyderabad Contingent and was stationed on the northern boundary of the state of Hyderabad.

Meanwhile, one William Palmer, along with some other Englishmen, set up a firm called Palmer and Company. The members included a relation of the Governor General, Lord Hastings; one of the sons of Rumbold, a former Governor of Madras; and the Residency surgeon. A local Gujarati merchant, Bunkety Das, was the Indian partner of this firm. This company engaged itself in the timber trade on the river Godavari and the production and manufacture of cotton in Berar. It also started banking activities.

When Russell's reform of the army was extended to the troops stationed at Aurangabad and Berar, there was naturally an increase in expenditure which the Nizam was unable to meet, and which exceeded the amount of the peshkush against which Russell had set off the expenses of the initial force established at Hyderabad. The firm entered into an arrangement with the Nizam's government to guarantee regular payment to the troops and to be reimbursed either in cash from time to time or by grant of jagirs. The firm was to be paid an interest at the rate of 24 per cent for outstandings. By entering into such an arrangement with a government, the partners of the firm not only became rich but also very influential. By getting free access to the palace, they came to overshadow the Residency.

The dues to the firm kept on mounting and in course of time the Nizam's government was caught in a debt trap. The Company offered to write off the staggering figure of the loan on payment of Rs 6 million plus Rs 800,000 as commission.

Russell was succeeded by Metcalfe as Resident in 1820. He did not approve of Palmer and Company's involvement with the government of Hyderabad. He was also peeved at the status enjoyed by the Company's partners politically and socially, which completely sidelined the Resident. He suggested to the Governor General that the Nizam's government be granted a loan on reasonable terms to payoff the firm. Metcalfe also wasn't happy with the Hyderabad Contingent which was the cause of the whole trouble, since it was to finance this force that the Nizam's government had become indebted to Palmer and Company.

Initially, the Governor General did not approve of Metcalfe's proposal but later accepted it. A loan was arranged by the British Government to pay off Palmer and Company. In order to meet the loan amount of Rs 6 million, the annual peshkush of Rs 900,000 was abolished. Reluctanctly, Palmer and Company went bankrupt.

Thus, the circars of the east coast, which first had been granted to the French and then to the English in 1759, fell into the lap of the British permanently and without any financial obligation in 1823.

The Hyderabad Contingent was created to secure the Nizam from his enemies. Long after the purpose had been served, the Contingent stayed on. The expenditure on its maintenance continued to grow and the Nizam became unable to meet it. To increase the revenues, Metcalfe tried to reform the system of revenue collection in the state. The prevalent system was to auction the responsibility for the collection of revenue of the highest bidder. But the 'deal' was never sealed. In many cases, after having 'auctioned' a district, a higher bidder was appointed and so there was perpetual uncertainty about the lease. The holders of the lease also tried to recoup their 'investment' in the shortest time possible.

There was a popular joke at that time in Hyderabad that when an appointee to a district went to assume his charge, he rode with his face towards the tail of the horse to see if he was being followed by his successor! In such a situation it was the cultivator who suffered, and many farmers fled the land to escape merciless exactions. Cultivation, thus, suffered and with that the revenue collection. Metcalfe devised a plan to change it by appointing English Collectors who would 'settle' the demand and collect it regularly and humanely. But this amounted to the Resident's taking over of the district administration and was therefore resented by the Nizam. The experiment had to be given up in spite of the increase in the revenue that it brought about.

Meanwhile, the financial situation of the Nizam continued to deteriorate under the weight of the expenditure on the Hyderabad Contingent, which was to be met by the Nizam. Successive Residents—Fraser, Lowe, and men like Law-Lushington—expressed themselves against the continuance of the Contingent to no effect. A proposal by Diwan Chandulal for the cession of territories yielding a revenue of Rs 1.75 million for a loan of Rs 10 million was accepted by the Governor General, provided the administration of the whole state of Hyderabad was made over to the British authorities. Unable to find a way out of the increasing mess, Chandulal submitted his resignation. The Nizam then took out Rs 10 million in cash and jewels worth Rs 800,000 from his private treasures kept in the Golconda Fort. This proved only a temporary expedient because by now the Contingent was costing

Rs 4 million annually, over 20 per cent of the total revenue of the state.

In 1847, when Diwan Siraj-ul-Mulk, tried to disband some 6,000 troops to reduce the expenditure, there was a mutiny that lasted seven days and had to be quelled with the help of the Madras Infantry. That put a stop to any further attempt at reduction of the force.

By 1849, the arrears of payment on account of the regiment had mounted to Rs 6.4 million. Dalhousie sent an ultimatum to clear the arrears by the end of 1850 or else face severe consequences. The Nizam once again dipped into his private kitty and arranged to pay half the arrears, promising to clear the balance after three months. The promise could not be kept and the dues kept on mounting. Then some accountants in the Nizam's government dug up a claim to be paid by the English. For forty years, the British had not paid excise duty on liquor due to the Nizam from the English cantonments. At the rate of Rs 100,000 a year, the amount worked out to Rs 4 million. The Resident refused to accept this point. He said the dues should be paid first. The Nizam's claims could be looked into later.[52]

Finally, the British proposed that if the Nizam assigned certain districts in Berar to them in perpetuity, the outstanding debt would be cancelled and they would thereafter maintain the Contingent. Threatened with the use of force, the Nizam capitulated.[53]

A treaty was drawn up in 1853. According to that, the territories in Berar and Raichur were ceded to discharge the loan of Rs 4 million and to meet the future expenses of the Contingent. After deducting the cost of administration of these territories, the balance if any, was to be refunded to the Nizam.

Immediately after the takeover of territories a reduction in the cost of maintenance of the Contingent was effected and in two years the expenditure came down from Rs 4 million to Rs 2.4 million. On the other hand, the revenue yield from the area kept on increasing. Yet no amount was refunded to the Nizam out of the surplus till 1874, when the accumulated balance in his favour had amounted to Rs 5 million.

However, it weighed on the conscience of the English rulers and they paid off the debt not as a part of an honest bargain, but as a reward of the services rendered by the Nizam to the English in the uprising of 1857, which practically saved the English from being wiped out from India. The British government remitted the Nizam's debt of Rs 5 million. Further, out of the ceded territories, areas in the Raichur, Doab, and Dharasoa were returned to the Nizam. Only Berar was retained with the English. The issue continued to agitate the Nizam and remained an irritant between the two for a long time.

A Parade of Diwans

Hyderabad had attracted people of all sorts right from the beginning. After 1763, when it became the capital city once again after a gap of 76 years, people from all parts of India started flocking here. Its name too had changed from Bhagnagar to Hyderabad. This name was now widely used, although old and poor people, especially amongst the Hindus, continued to call it by its original name of Bhagnagar. Not only Indians, but foreigners too came and settled down here. The French came in the wake of Bussy and Raymond in their brief period of power and glory. The English followed them for a prolonged stay. A colony of English people surrounded by the lesser mortals—Anglo-Indians and Eurasians—sprang up around the Residency in what came to be called the Chaderghat area. Missionaries did not lag behind. Church buildings arose in the vicinity. In the early nineteenth century Arabs in large numbers sought service here and they soon became strong and unruly enough to disturb the peace of the city. Adventurous Rohillas and Afghans from the northwest also gravitated to the Deccan during this period. Raja Chandulal, a Punjabi Khatri and the real power in the state for over 30 years, attracted a large number of Sikhs from the Punjab. With all these accretions, Hyderabad became a truly cosmopolitan city. Meadows Taylor described the city of the 1820s through the mouth of the Thug, Amir Ali, in his novel, *Confessions of a Thug*:

We passed the village of Ulwal, its white pagoda peeping from among groves of tamarind and mango trees, and its large tank now glistening in the rays of the sun; and pursuing our way, we saw, on passing a ridge of rocks, the camp of the army at the far-famed Hussain Sagar, or, as it is more often called, Secunderabad. The tents of the English force glittered in the bright sun, and behind them lay a vast sheet of blue water.

We had heard much of this lake from many persons on our journey, and as we passed it a strong breeze had arisen, and the surface was curled into a thousand waves, whose white crests as they broke: sparkled like diamonds, and threw their spray into our faces as they dashed against the stonework of the embankment. We stood a long time gazing upon the beautiful prospect, so new to us all, and wondering whether the sea, of which we had heard so much, could be anything like what was before us. I have since then, Sahib, twice seen the sea; I need not attempt to describe it, for you have sailed over it; but when I saw it [Hussain Sagar] first, methought I could have fallen down and worshipped it, it appeared so illimitable, its edge touching as it were the heavens, and spread out into an expanse which the utmost stretch of my imagination could not compass—a fit type, Hyderabad thought, of the God of all people, whom every one thinks on; while the hoarse roar of the waves as they rolled on, mountain after mountain, and broke in angry fury against the shore, seemed to be a voice of Omnipotence which could not fail to awaken emotions of awe and dread in the most callous and unobservant! ...

My horse slackened his pace when he reached the top, and allowing him to go on a few steps, Hyderabad opened my eyes, and glorious indeed was the prospect before me.

Beneath lay Hyderabad, the object of many a conjecture, of many an ardent desire to reach it—the first city of the Dukhun, justly celebrated throughout the countries I had passed. Hyderabad had imagined it, like every other Hyderabad had seen, to be in the midst of a plain, and that all that would be visible of it would be here and there a minaret rising out of large groves of trees: but Hyderabad presented a different aspect.

Hyderabad stood on the crest of a gentle slope, which to my right hand was broken at some distance by rude, rocky hills, and to the left appeared gradually to descend into a plain, which stretched away almost uninterruptedly to the horizon. Before me, on the gentle rise of the valley, and beyond where Hyderabad supposed the river to be, lay the city, its white terraced houses gleaming brightly in the sunlight from amidst what seemed to me at the distance almost a forest of trees.

The Char Minar and Mecca Musjid rose proudly from the masses of buildings by which they were surrounded; and here and there a white dome, with its bright gift spire, marked the tomb of some favourite or holy saint, while smaller mosques, I might say in hundreds, were known by their slender white minarets.

Beyond the city rose another connected chain of rocky hills, which ran along until they met those on the right hand, and shut in the valley on that side. The city seemed to be of immense extent; but I thought from the number of trees that it was composed principally of gardens and inclosures, and was much surprised afterwards, when I entered it, to find its streets so filled with houses, and the whole so thickly peopled.

It was altogether a most lovely scene: the freshness of the morning, the pureness of the air, and the glittering effect of the city and its buildings caused an impression which can never be effaced from my memory. I have seen it since, and thought it is ever truly beautiful, it never struck me as it did that day. ...

Crossing over an old but massive bridge, below which ran the river, now a shallow stream, we entered by the gate at the head of it, and inquiring our way went direct to the chowke, or market-place, where we trusted we should find goods exposed for sale similar to our own. The streets were narrow and dirty, and the interior of the city certainly did not answer the expectations we had formed from its outside and distant appearance; still there were evident tokens of its wealth in the numbers of elephants, on the backs of which, in canopied umbaras, sat noblemen or gentlemen, attended by their armed retainers. ...

And here that noble building, the Char Minar, burst at once upon our view. 'How grand!' I exclaimed, stopping my horse and looking up to the huge minarets, which seemed to pierce the clouds; 'to see this alone is worth a journey from Delhi.'

The minarets formed the four corners of the building, and from them sprang immense arches which supported a roof, upon the top of which a small mosque was built. It did not look capable of supporting the immense weight of the whole, and yet it had stood for centuries, and the fabric was unimpaired. ...

And passing by the Char Minar, we turned up a street to our right, and stopped our horses at the gate of the mosque.

A feeling of awe mingled with admiration came over me as we entered the courtyard and advanced along a raised causeway to the foot of a flight of steps which led up to the interior. On either side of us were the graves of Princes and Nobles, many of them of elegant forms and richly carved; but the building itself engrossed my entire admiration. Five lofty and wide arches opened to view the interior of the edifice, where an equal number appeared in depth; and where the arches met, the eye was perplexed by the innumerable points and ornaments, which, running into each other, completed a roof of exquisite design and workmanship. To add to its beauty, the whole was of stone, carefully smoothed; whereas the Char Minar and the other buildings I had as yet seen were, of stucco.[54]

Ameer Ali was perhaps the only one among the city's numerous admirers who visited the necropolis of the Qutb Shahi rulers.

He had a rendezvous with a woman, Azima, there. She had fallen in love with him after she had just a glimpse of him when he, unaware of her, happened to pass below the balcony of her house. So inflamed was she by the sight of the handsome young bandit, that the same evening she sent her maid Kallu beseeching him to 'rescue' her. A most beautiful young woman herself, she had been married to a much older and very cruel man. Ameer Ali and Azima agreed to meet the next morning at the *durgah* of Hazrat Shah Wali from where they were to elope.

The durgah was near the necropolis and since Azima was late in coming, the thug spent some time going round the monuments. He was 'astonished at their size and magnificence'. Inside the compound, 'the silence and desolation were oppressive and we scarcely made a remark to each other, as we traversed one by one the interiors of the noble edifices—some of them dark and gloomy and filled with bats and wild pigeons whose cooing re-echoed within the lofty domes—and others whose wide arches admitted the light of the day, and we were more cheerful in appearance.'[55]

The Kayasths were the trusted and prominent civil servants of the Nizams. They had come with the first Nizam from the north and settled down in Hyderabad. They adopted the ways of the ruling elite and served as a bridge between the rulers and the subjects in all matters. They made good careers and some of them rose to high civil and military positions and even to the ranks of the nobility. One such person who rose to nobility in the nineteenth century was Bhavani Pershad. He was in charge of the salaries of the employees of the royal palaces. When he became prosperous, and was given the title of Raja, he decided to celebrate it by constructing a temple dedicated to Rama. It was constructed near Attapur about 15 kilometres from the city.

The story goes that the idol of Rama installed there was originally commissioned by Raja Som Bhopal of Gadwal for his own temple. Gadwal was a Hindu tributary estate in Raichur district of the Hyderabad state, which it predated. It consisted of the town

Gadwal and 214 villages spread over an area of 1,384 sq. kilometres. While the idol was being sculpted, the Raja had a dream in
which he was told to retrieve an idol from the bottom of a well and
install it in the temple. At the same time, Raja Bhavani Pershad
also dreamt of the idol commissioned by Raja Som Bhopal. He
told the latter about his dream and made a request for the gift
of the idol for his temple. Som Bhopal readily obliged since in
his own temple, he had installed the idol which he had retrieved
form the bottom of the well. When the temple was ready, Raja
Bhavani Pershad invited the third Nizam, Nawab Sikandar Jah, to
perform the ceremony of the installation of the idols of Rama, Sita,
and Lakshamana. The Nizam agreed and the ceremony was performed in 1812. Not only that, the Nizam also granted a jagir for
the maintenance of the temple and sanctioned regular payment
for persons who looked after the temple.[56]

By the end of the eighteenth century, the English Governor
General came to exercise an influence in the appointment of the
Diwan. After the dismissal of Mir Alam as the envoy of the Nizam
to the East India Company, the Diwan, Arastu Jah, in 1797 took
over that function also. The office of the Diwan became therefore,
doubly important for the English. Accordingly, in the decades
that followed there was a rapid turnover of Diwans. The English
forced Mir Alam on the Nizam as Diwan in 1894. His successor,
Munir-ul-Mulk, was accepted by the English as a dummy Diwan
in 1809. His Peshkar, Chandulal, and a favourite of the English,
exercised the real power. He himself became the Diwan in 1832
and remained in that position for ten years. The Diwans, being the
appointees of the Resident, were beholden to him and they saw to
it that the British interests were fully protected.

Sikandar Jah died in 1829 and Nasir-ud-Dowlah succeeded him
as the fifth Nizam. He was 33.

Between 1842 and 1853, there was a period of comparative freedom for the Nizam in the appointment of the Diwan. But he could
not make up his mind. During that period as many as six Diwans
were appointed—three of them for periods ranging between two
to five months. Pushed again by the English, the Nizam appointed
Siraj-ul-Mulk in 1851. He was a man of great learning and did not
seek the office. It was during his incumbency that Berar was ceded

to the English in 1853. Three days later he died, some say because of the tension caused by the cession of Berar.

The Nizam was again called upon to undertake the onerous task of filling the vacancy. For a while he thought of becoming the Diwan himself. But the English did not like it.

In darbars, power and influence seldom flow in the official, pre-scribed channels. Some persons, who have no position in the for-mal power structure whatsoever, worm their way into the ruler's favours. Those, who have regular and uninterrupted access to the source of all patronage, exercise varying degrees of power and influence. A hint thrown at the right time, a suggestion dropped at a receptive moment, an insinuation made at a weak juncture can settle appointments, fix transfers and promotions, and even secure dismissals.

One such person was Burhanuddin, an attendant of the fourth and fifth Nizams. It was he who decided whom the Nizam would see and when. Even the Diwan had to be admitted through him. They also used to obtain approval of most of their proposals through the good offices of this flunkey. Chandulal, the longest serving and the most powerful Diwan early in the century, often complained to the Resident about his difficulties with the Nizam because of Burhanuddin.

Another person was Mama Jamila, a maid-in-waiting. Mamas were an institution by themselves. They were often wet nurses to the royal children, or simply maids to the royal ladies. The Princes and Princesses grew up under their tutelage and could seldom outgrow their influence. In Mughal history, and later with the Asaf Jahs, they came to play a crucial role in palace affairs.[57] Mama Jamila became a notable figure in the nineteenth century court intrigues.

Lala Bahadur, a *daftardar* of the state, also belonged to the set. If these three got together and decided on any course of action nothing could ever stop it. Mama Jamila would often emerge from the darbar and announce to the crowd of expectant supplicants outside what the Nizam had decided on their submission. She would even announce the allotment of a jagir to a particular per-son and the cancellation of another. The machinery of the state had then to move quickly to initiate action to legalize these verbal announcements. Not infrequently, the officials would be put in a quandary because of the contradictory announcements of the Mama. The two rival beneficiaries would then seek arbitration either from her or from the government. The Mama's word could not be ascertained or cross-checked because whereas every other official including the Diwan met the Nizam by appointment, which took weeks to get, the Mama was there on her way from room to room and even in almost every private situation. She was the one whom he, perforce, saw a number of times a day. Often she was the last one he saw before he retired to bed, and so hers was, literally, the last word.

So various persons and coteries were at work to get the most powerful office in the state filled up by one of their men. The palace coterie—comprising the triumvirate of Burhanuddin, Mama Jamila, and Lala Bahadur—decided to support the candidature of Mir Turab Ali Khan, the nephew of the late Diwan, Siraj-ul-Mulk. He was barely 24 then.

Burhanuddin first broached the subject with the Nizam. One evening as he handed him a peg of his favourite drink, he bowed and said, 'Your Highness, if the life of this slave is spared, he would venture to commit an act of insolence ... .'

'Speak up,' the Nizam said in mock abruptness. 'But before that fill up my glass because you are excessively voluble and I shall die of thirst.' The slave noticed an element of receptivity in this banter. He poured the liquid, waited for his master to have a draught and then resumed: 'I am too small a man to open my mouth on the affairs of the state, but ... .'

The Nizam tried to look up with his drooping eyes. He gave a faint smile which meant that Burhanuddin was exceeding his limit, but never mind.

'My Lord, my father, and mother, as your faithful servant I have only your interest and welfare at heart and hence this temerity ... .'

'What is the matter Burhan?' the Sovereign's smile was broader than usual. 'You want to be my Diwan?'

'*Tauba, tauba*,' exclaimed the scandalized doorman, 'how can I even dream of entertaining such blasphemous thoughts, My Lord? For me the devoted service of my Master and the Sovereign of this kingdom are more than ample. My ambitions cannot go beyond his feet. May God give my Master a long life!'

Nasir-ud-Dowlah seemed to enjoy this exchange. He knew that very soon he would ascend to a level where no male company, however obsequious, would be of any interest to him. Burhan also knew that he didn't have much time. But the Nizam was still in a bantering mood.

'Why not, Burhan? None of my Diwans have better manners than you. And you are so faithful! What better qualities could one ask for in a Diwan?' The Nizam teased him. Perhaps he was serious in his specifications for the qualifications for his minister.

'That is my duty and my privilege, Sire. This creature made of dirt came into being to serve My Lord and my anxiety is only that this be done in the best manner possible.'

'Then what is it?'

'Would His Highness be pleased to consider the name of Mir Turab Ali Khan?'

The man waited with trepidation. The Nizam put his empty glass on the teapoy beside him. A trace of irritation passed over his flabby face.

'Turab? That boy ... Why him?'

Burhan was once again filling his glass. He pretended not to be over-interested in the topic. He gave out that he had discharged his duty by mentioning the name. The rest was up to the master. But when the Sovereign asked him the reason for proposing that name, he was duty bound to advance his submission.

'My Master, My Sovereign, the kingdom stands at crossroads. My Lord needs an able adviser. The Mir is descended from Diwans on both his father's and mother's side ... .'

'Is Diwani an inheritance, my man?'

'No Sire, it is entirely a gift in the hands of My Sovereign. Only his eyes will spot the best talent. This humble servant took the courage of suggesting the name because of his great family and the merit of the noble himself. '

'Family ... Ha!' The ruler snorted. Don't forget his uncle was the one who gave away Berar to the English ... .'

Then he waived off Burhan and clapped. He was now ready for some diversion. A young lass of 20 appeared and made a bow.

The Nizam beckoned her to help him get up and then, leaning on her slender shoulders, Nasir-ud-Dowlah passed into his private quarters to sample the latest addition to the harem. He himself was 59 then.

Two days later Mama Jamila broached the subject again while she was pressing his legs. 'Huzur,' she whispered, 'do children have to suffer for the sins of their ancestors?'

The Nizam did not expect such a profound query from an unlettered maid. 'Someone has been teaching you philosophy, old woman.'

'All this worthless creature has learnt is from the wisdom of my Master,' submitted the middle-aged matron.

'Yes, sometime we do suffer for our parents' acts of omission or commission. That is life.' The Nizam's reply was entirely unexpected. This closed her opening gambit. But the query bothered the Nizam because of the unusual source from which it sprang.

'Whose children are you worried about any way, Mama?'

'No one in particular, Sire,' replied the maid. 'But it is heard that His Highness is angry with Turab Ali because of what his uncle did.' 'Oh, now you too want to recommend a Diwan for me, Madam!'

The matron bent double and salaamed a number of times by way of apology. 'All this is beyond this humble, unlettered, worthless creature, My Lord. But please, it is not fair to judge Nawab Saheb by what his uncle did.'

The Nizam withdrew his leg and proffered the other. The Mama noted that she hadn't been snubbed.

Now it was the turn of Lala Bahadur to pursue the case further. He knew that the Nizam was in deep debt and nothing would please him more than hard cash.

'Highness,' he said, 'five cart loads of coins will be presented to Your Honour.'

The Nizam kept quiet as if calculating the capacity of each cart-load. Lala helped. 'Rs 13 lakh in two monthly installments would be placed at the honoured feet of my Master.'

The Nizam remained quiet. The rumour of the offer gained currency in the city. Even a newspaper suggested that a monetary deal had been struck.

Mir Turab Ali Khan was appointed Diwan on 31 May 1853. He was given the title of Salar Jung.

Mir Turab Ali Khan was a grandson of Munir-ul-Mulk and a great grandson of Mir Alam, both of whom had been Diwans. He was thus descended from Diwans on both sides of his parents. Turab's father had died when he was very young and so his uncle, Siraj-ul-Mulk brought him up. Siraj was Diwan for two terms, once during 1846–8 and later during 1851–3. Appointed in 1853, Turab was to remain in that post for full 30 years, longer than anyone in the history of the state.

When the young Diwan entered service, the government was in deep debt to all sorts of creditors. They were the *sahukars* (merchant moneylenders) who gave loans to the government on extortionate rates. Because of the cession of Berar to the English, people who had held jagirs there made claims on the government for compensation. These ranged from Rs 0.5 million to Rs 3 million. The salaries of the Nizam's relatives and *mansabdars* could not be paid for want of resources. On top of that, the Nizam himself was pressing for the release of his jewels, which had been pledged in England to repay part of the state debt. The total debt of the state amounted to Rs 27 million.

Land revenue was the most important source of income for the state. Its collection was farmed out to people on a commission basis. Both agriculture and the collection of land revenue suffered under this system.

Another pernicious aspect of the system was the collection of revenue in kind. The *batai* system, as it was called, was also injurious to the interest both of the cultivator as well as the state. It was a disincentive for any improvement in cultivation to increase the yield. The cultivators were not allowed to harvest the crop until the yield had been checked and security for payment obtained. This system offered great scope for the officials to harass the cultivators.

The nobles supported their own establishments. There were varied ranks of nobility here. At the bottom was the 'Jung' of which there was a large number. The next rank was that of 'Dowlah'. Then came 'Mulk' followed by 'Umra'. At the apex was 'Jah', which was part of the title of the Nizam and of only one other family—the Paigah. 'Paigah' means the stabling place and is derived from the functions of the family—the cavalry guard of the Nizam. The proximity was further reinforced by the practice of the marriage of the females of the ruling family only into this family. These nobles did nothing except live off the land and the people. They had vast jagirs and were subject to no law. They had their own system of law enforcement and their jagirs were states within the state.

That was not all. The Arab, the Rohilla, and the Sikh mercenary armed bands constituted other power centres. The Arabs settled their disputes themselves and acknowledged the jurisdiction of no local civil or criminal law or authority. They were engaged by various nobles to enforce their claims against different groups of people. The Arab jamedars held about half the revenue of the state and nearly all its power. Their men guarded the houses of their debtors lest the debtors should escape. Often they were imprisoned in the houses of Arab jamedars where they were starved into payment. If a debtor died, his body was not allowed to be removed for burial till the debt was discharged. Often the members of respectable families kept the death in the family a secret till they had quietly buried the body in the darkness of night.

The state did not do anything to impart education or to provide public health. Whatever schools existed were private, mostly denominational. Their medium of instruction was mostly Persian and what was taught centered mostly around theology and writing of the script. This 'education' did nothing to liberate one's mind from orthodoxy. Instead, it forged chains for it.

Commerce and banking was controlled by the sahukars. For the realization of their dues they took the help of Arab, Rohilla, or Sikh mercenaries.

As a young man, when his uncle was Diwan, Salar Jung had served as the *Talukdar* (Collector) of Khammam, which was a part of the estate of the family which had been restored after a period of confiscation for non-payment of debts. This district was one of those that for a short time had been administered by English Collectors. They had 'settled' the land revenue and brought about improvements in the system of collection of revenue and other aspects of administration. This, in turn, had brought about prosperity to the cultivators and improved the land-revenue yield. The system was later discontinued, and on the accession of Nasir-ud-Dowlah, the English Collectors were withdrawn and substituted by the Indian Collectors who reverted to the old system of collecting the revenue on a commission basis.

But Salar Jung, during his brief tenure at Khammam, had noticed the scope for improvement and when he became the Diwan he decided to reform the existing system on English lines. But changing the status quo meant an attack on the vested interests and that included the Nizam himself. He therefore thought it safe to take the specific permission of the Nizam before launching on his programme of reforms. While promising regular monthly payments to the Nizam and his dependants, he secured the authority to remove inefficient and corrupt officials.

The first thing he did was to forbid the presentation of *nazrana*— a gift to the appointing authority, including the Nizam—for a job. This he declared to be a corrupt practice. Then, in an attempt to set an example, he married a widow. The marriage was celebrated in a very simple manner and Salar Jung refused to accept any gifts on the occasion.

His next step was drastic even by today's standards. First, he made a voluntary cut in his salary. The monthly remuneration of the Diwan was Rs 25,000. Considering the financial crisis in which the state stood, and the need for economy, Salar Jung reduced his own salary to Rs 15,000 a month. The Peshkar's salary was reduced by 30 per cent—to Rs 10,000 a month. Then he ordered a similar cut across the board for all employees.

The salaries of employees were never paid regularly. The arrears sometimes went into years and people had to incur debts at exorbitant rates to tide over the prolonged 'dry' periods. But due to the uncertainty of the payments, and high rates of interest, they could seldom get out of debts. This held good for all employees including the Diwan, and not infrequently the Nizam himself.

Salar Jung's reduction of the salaries was accompanied by a declaration promising regular monthly disbursement of salaries provided the employees gave up their claim to arrears. There was a howl of protest against this reduction in salaries and the writing-off of arrears but the gravity in the state of affairs can be judged from the fact that the employees ultimately fell in line with the proposal. Jamedar Junaid Khan provided the lead in this respect. He said many of his colleagues had died waiting for as long as 54 to 55 months to receive their salaries which never came. So why not accept this?

The result of this one reform was astounding. Apart from the savings it effected for the government, it released employees from the clutches of the creditors and made it possible for them to plan their family budgets on a monthly basis. Families looked forward to the beginning of the month to make their purchases. The market became buoyant, credit was contracted, and the inflationary trend was curtailed. This earned for the young minister the gratitude not only of the salaried class but also of the petty traders. People talked appreciatively about the miracle wrought by him.

The Mutiny and Hyderabad

Nasir-ud-Dowlah passed away on 17 May 1857, unaware of the outbreak of rebellion of the Indian soldiery against the British in Meerut only a week before. His son, Tahniyat Ali Khan, ascended the masnad the next day with the title of Afzal-ud-Dowlah. The pace of reforms undertaken by Salar Jung was interrupted by that event.

In an age when no license was required for arms, it was considered a mark of distinction to bear them. Captain Hastings Fraser estimated that 26,000 persons out of a population of about 300,000 were armed, some to the teeth. He said that he could raise 75,000 armed men from the city without any difficulty.

With so much of the citizenry armed, the law and order situation was bound to be lax. The nobles were a law unto themselves by custom and law; many others too enforced their authority on the strength of their arms.

Amongst the official armed forces operating in the middle of the nineteenth century were the Subsidiary Force, the Hyderabad Contingent, and the irregular troops of the Nizam. The last were by themselves a menace. They were largely under the command of Rohilla or Arab chiefs who held considerable areas as jagirs either for the maintenance of troops or repayment of loans, which the government had taken from them. But the soldiers being always in arrears of pay, the discipline was poor and the morale low. The Hyderabad Contingent, consisting of 9,397 native ranks and 84 European officers, was distributed in the border areas in the west and north.[58] The Subsidiary Force was stationed at Secunderabad. It consisted of a better mix of the English and the Indians, the battery being entirely under the command of the English.

The British were aware of the unrest which prevailed in the state and in its neighbourhood. One redeeming feature was the antipathy of the people of Hyderabad to the Maratha leadership. Because of the traditional animosity between the Nizam and the Marathas, the insurrectionary movement in the Maratha states was not viewed with favour in Hyderabad. After the suppression of the Wahabi movement the disaffected people were lying low. The news of the early reverses of the English in the north boosted the morale of those harbouring anti-English feelings. On 13 June 1857, inflammatory placards appeared all over the city. They urged the people, and Muslims in particular, to rise in the name of God and his Prophet. They ridiculed the Nizam for not coming forward and tauntingly asked him to wear bangles. They warned him and his Diwan, Salar Jung, that if they did not join the movement, within a year or so they would be working like labourers on the roads. They exhorted moulvis to issue edicts in favour of the *jihad* or else 'their seven generations would be cursed'. Another placard called upon Muslims to kill Christian *kafirs* if they were not to be called the 'descendants of the pariah caste of a pig and of a dog'. The Nizam was urged to march to Delhi after doing away with the heathens in Hyderabad.[59]

The new Resident, Colonel Davidson, was a friendly person and was popular amongst the nobility of the city. Some of them conveyed warnings to him, while others urged him to leave the Residency and take refuge in the cantonment at Bolarum. Davidson waved them aside. He said that the Nizam would be held responsible if any harm came to him. He strengthened the defences of the Residency after sending reinforcements to the Governor of Bombay, and to General Whitelock.

In the month of June 1857, intelligence reported seditious tampering with the Indian soldiers of the Hyderabad Contingent stationed at Secunderabad. A mendicant was found coaxing the soldiers to rise against the English. He was apprehended. A moulvi preaching the doctrine of jihad was also caught hold of by the Diwan and brought before the Nizam who pulled him up and warned him against such utterances. More serious trouble occurred at Aurangabad when on 11 June, the First Cavalry of the Hyderabad Contingent was moved from Mominabad to Aurangabad. That was overcome with great tact and courage on the part of Captain Abbot and a number of soldiers were taken into prison and were court martialled. Of these, two were blown from guns, seven shot, four cut down in charges, and several hanged. About 40 were transported, 100 disbanded, and some 60 flogged or otherwise punished.

About 13 soldiers under Jamedar Cheeda Khan deserted and returned to the city. They were promptly arrested by the government and sent to the Residency for trial. That caused great resentment and commotion in the city and a delegation of four moulvis waited upon the Nizam on 17 June 1857 to plead for their release. They threatened that in case the Nizam refused, the Residency would be sacked.

Earlier, on 18 June, the Resident, Colonel Davidson, had recorded in his letter to the Secretary of the Foreign Department of the Government of India that cavalry and infantry sepoys from the Hyderabad Subsidiary Force had of late been visiting the city without taking any leave of absence from their officers. They were preaching to their comrades and people at large that the time had come to rise and make a common cause against the firangies—the foreigners. All that was missing for a full-scale uprising was a leader and an opportunity. Some soldiers declared that in the event of an uprising they would not march against the city but they would defend their own camp, meaning their own houses, since their families stayed in the lines. This was the extent of their loyalty—but even of that Davidson was not very sure.[60]

During the Friday prayers at the Mecca Masjid that day, when the Imam rose to deliver his khutba, some members of the congregation heckled him. A voice taunted him and asked him not to babble like a woman but speak like a man and exhort the people to raise the standard of revolt against the British. Someone raised a staff through the gathering and cries of 'Deen, Deen' (faith) rent the air.[61] The crowd was about to break into a riot but the kotwal, who was present, had the ringleaders seized. The Imam and the kotwal made good their escape in the melee. Salar Jung sent a body of Arabs to disperse the mob and for a while peace was restored. The storm seemed to have blown over.

A relieved Diwan sent a message to the Resident that the crisis had ended and the report received by the Resident earlier that jihad had been proclaimed was evidently false.

The euphoria was not to last the day. Hardly had the Resident sat for his high tea when a panting messenger brought Salar Jung's verbal intimation that a crowd of about 500 Rohillas had broken loose from the walled city. It was led by Moulvi Ala-ud-Din and Turrebaz Khan and was followed by a large mob. The Diwan asked the Resident to defend himself till he could assemble a force to help him. The time was 5.45 p.m. and the Resident had already done all that he thought was necessary to convert the splendid building into a virtual fort.

Turrebaz Khan led his Rohilla band towards the Residency. Ala-ud-Din was the standard-bearer. The infuriated mob following them converged at Sultan Bazar. There they occupied two buildings near the Residency belonging to two merchants—Jaigopal Das and Akbar Sahib. They thus faced the gate of the Residency on the Pulti Bowli side. From the houses, they asked the Indian guards at the gate of the Residency to deliver Jamedar Cheeda Khan and his associates to them. One of the Indian *risaldar*s, Ismail Khan, came forward to talk them out of their foolhardy venture. The insurgents had expected the Indian soldiers to join them, so the risaldar's loyalty to his foreign masters surprised and annoyed them. They fired at him but Ismail Khan was able to trot back to safety.

The strategy of the Residency Commander, Major S.C. Briggs, was not to take the offensive against the insurgents that night. A contingent of Arab guards sent by Salar Jung was made to encircle the houses occupied by the insurrectionists. The Rohillas launched a fierce attack on the Residency by tearing down the wall of the house adjoining the one they were occupying. The sally brought down the Putli Bowli Gate and a hail of fire was let loose on the

Residency for about half an hour. Briggs responded with cannon fire, and, once started, he kept pounding at them without interruption till dawn. Not able to face this unexpected volley, the Rohillas withdrew under cover of darkness. They left behind four dead but carried away all their wounded comrades. That was the end of the uprising so far as the city was concerned.

The leaders of the rabble—Turrebaz Khan and Maulvi Ala-ud-Din—were declared offenders. A prize of Rs 5,000 each was announced for their capture. Turrebaz Khan was soon apprehended while trying to flee the city. He was tried and sentenced to transportation for life. Once again he escaped but was captured near Toopran. A scuffle ensued in which he was shot dead by the English soldiers. His body was brought to the city and was hung by chains in a public place to serve as a deterrent to the people at large.

Moulvi Ala-ud-Din was captured at Bangalore. He was brought back, tried, and in 1859, sentenced to transportation for life to the Andaman Islands. He died there in 1884.

From the testimony of the two at their trials, it appeared that there wasn't much of a conspiracy or any organization behind the uprising. It seems to have been a spontaneous upsurge. Also, though a fairly large mob gathered, the number of actual participants was very small. Even among those, only a few were adequately armed. Most of them carried *lathis*, and when the English cannon was sighted, some of the mob attacked it with sticks. When the cannon was fired, the rabble took to its heels.

Turrebaz Khan, in his examination, emerged as a man fully in control of himself and proud of his mission. He did not squeal or reveal the names of the other plotters. He did not implicate even Moulvi Ala-ud-Din. From his testimony also, the uprising appeared to be a sporadic affair without any plot. He said that while the number of rioters was about 2,000 to 3,000, only about 10 or 12 persons gathered in Abban Sahib's house. In his second deposition he said stoically: 'I do not like to blame anyone.'

Hyderabad was indeed the bulwark of the British presence in India in 1857. It saved them. As the Governor of Bombay said to the Resident in his nervous telegram: 'If Hyderabad goes, everything goes.' The Nizam was unquestioningly with the British. He did not want to stake anything for anything. His Diwan was even more loyal to the British. The attack on the Residency was a flash in the pan, a tragic footnote to the history of the freedom movement in India.

The disaffection against the English manifested itself in other places too. There is the tragic story of the rebellion of Raja Venkatappa Naik of Shorapur in which the astrological prediction about the death of the Raja at 24 years made to Meadows Taylor when he was Regent at Shorapur confidentially 20 years before the event found its fulfillment. The Raja's tribe of Beydurs attacked a small force of the English sent to reinforce Captain Campbell's garrison. This attack was repulsed and thereupon the Raja fled to Hyderabad. For his part in the rebellion, the Raja was sentenced to death.

On Meadows Taylor's appeal, the Resident, in the maximum exercise of his authority, commuted it to confinement for four years. However, the Raja, after only one day's journey towards his destination, shot himself dead.

The uprising flopped because it lacked competent leadership, unity and organization and because the Nizam and Salar Jung sided with the British. The British did not forget that. First, in expressing their gratitude, they returned the districts of Raichur, Doab, and Naldurg to the Nizam which were taken from him in 1853 for the maintenance of the Hyderabad Contingent, retaining only Berar. The estate of Sholapur was also given to the Nizam. In addition, a debt of Rs 5 million due to the British was written off. A new treaty incorporating these modifications to the original arrangement was executed in 1860.

Presents worth £10,000 sterling were given to the Nizam, and £3,000 sterling worth to Salar Jung. The Nizam, not to be outdone in show of largesse, sent presents worth £15,000 to the Governor General.

The Mutiny was crushed. The Mughal Empire, that had nominally continued so far, came finally to an end. The last Mughal Emperor was exiled to Burma. The Nizam, in theory still the deputy of the Mughal Emperor, was advised by the Governor General to discard the Mughal coins and strike new ones in his own name. The Nizam was reluctant, but had to submit.

In 1858, new coins were struck for the first time in the name of 'Nizam-ul-Mulk Asaf Jah Bahadur'. Also, the Friday khutba began to be read in the name of the Nizam. It was indeed ironical that the Nizam came to adopt these two symbols of Islamic sovereignty at a time when he had all but lost whatever freedom he had enjoyed.

The sovereignty of the Mughals was hollow; the new one of the Nizam was a farce. The British had been nominally subservient to the former; they were overlords of the latter. What the first Nizam never dreamt of doing—proclaiming his independence—the fifth Nizam was forced to do. In 1724 it meant a lot, in 1858 it was devoid of any meaning. He accepted the honour without any enthusiasm.

The Great Diwan

Salar Jung's support of the British in 1857 earned him their gratitude. He therefore, felt free to continue his unfinished business of the reform of the medieval oligarchy that was Hyderabad.

To begin with land revenue, he abolished the system of farming out the collection of and payment in kind. Instead, he adopted the pattern of the Bombay Presidency according to which the 'settlement' was fixed for 30 years. During this period no improvement in the yield from land attracted additional levy. If new wells were constructed, the assessment continued to be made as for dry rates. While abolishing some of the petty and vexing sources of taxation he introduced new sources like stamp duty, excise, customs, cess, road tax, postal receipts, etc.

Turning to the state debt, he had the claims of sahukars closely scrutinized. This resulted in a reduction of their claims by Rs 8 million. He paid off the Arab and Pathan jamedars as much as was possible from the exchequer. For the balance, the sahukars, noting the earnestness of the Diwan, agreed to offer loans to him. He then proceeded to resume jagirs held by Arab and Pathan jamedars, and in the very first years of his office, jagirs worth Rs 1.5 million were resumed. By the following year he had resumed another Rs 2.5 million worth of jagirs. Then he proceeded to put down the armed might of these gang leaders. Two thousand Arabs and an equal number of Pathans, Rohillas, and others were disbanded.

The second most powerful Arab jamedar, Abdullah Bin Ali, was brought round by Salar Jung to surrender the mortgaged jagirs and some of his retainers. This enabled him to tackle the others.

The Arab recalcitrance was further broken when Salar Jung suggested to them that they agree to submit themselves to the common courts. 'No,' said the leading Jamedar, Umar Bin Aud, defiantly, 'we have our own Panchayats. They will deal with our cases.'

'All right', Salar Jung smiled benignly, 'take one of our officers as one of the panchs.'

'No,' replied the Arab. 'Only Arabs will decide our cases.'

Salar Jung smiled. 'Surprising,' he said, 'you don't know your own people.'

He almost broke into a laugh, 'I am one of you, we are descended from Sheikh Ovais Karani ... .'

The icy visage of Bin Aud melted into a smile. 'Sheikh Karani of Medina?' he asked in wonder.

'Yes,' said Salar Jung triumphantly. 'I am thirty-third in line from him.' Bin Aud got up and embraced the Diwan. 'Alhamadulliah,' he exclaimed. 'We have a distinguished brother. Sir, you will head our Panchayat from now on.'

That was the thin end of Salar Jung's wedge. Gradually, he withdrew himself but the Arabs had by then fallen in with the system. Whatever little resistance was exhibited, was overcome by force.

The Pathans were also tackled effectively and respect for the law was instilled into their rebellious minds by a combination of tact and a show of strength.

The Rohillas were brought down with the help of Arab jamedars who hated them. The English also joined in operations against them both within the state and outside. In all these measures, he had the backing of the Resident, who supported him warmly and discreetly. Sometimes he did this by referring to Salar Jung's achievements approvingly in the presence of the Nizam.

All these basic reforms were completed in the first decade of his administration. By 1864, his strenuous reforms had increased the state revenue by three times and brought down the state debt.

His second phase of reforms was implemented during 1864–6. In this period, the districts in the state were reorganized. A Collector was appointed in each district with revenue, civil, and magisterial powers. Earlier there was only one treasury in Hyderabad. Now treasuries were established in each district. Departments of police, health, and education were also set up at the district level. During this period, a Board of Revenue was established. Some departments of the secretariat were also brought into being as also the office of the Accountant General.

In the next phase beginning 1867, the state was divided into five divisions and districts. It is interesting to note that the Diwan himself was not permitted to leave the walls of the city without the express permission of the Nizam. He could not, therefore, take up any inspection himself. For this purpose Divisional Commissioners were found useful. Then to assist himself, he created the posts of four ministers. They were called *sadr-ul-mahams* and they were chosen from the nobility.

Salar Jung also established regular courts of justice. He made the judiciary virtually independent and, to demonstrate that the Rule of Law was supreme, he himself appeared in a court once in response to summons. In a case of bribery, one of the highest judicial officers of the state was convicted and sentenced to two years' imprisonment. Two judges were dismissed from service. He also proposed to separate the civil from the criminal courts.

Then he turned towards education. In 1878, he set up a school for the education of the nobles' children including his own sons. This was called the *Madarsa-e-Aliya* ('The Exalted School'). A number of schools were established all over the state. There were 162 schools at the time of his death. In 105 of these, the medium of instruction was Persian while in the rest it was Kannada, Marathi, or Telugu depending upon their location. He encouraged female education and had his daughters educated on western lines.

By 1856, a communication revolution had taken place in the state. The electric telegraph system had been introduced for official purposes. A regular postal system was established by 1862. Then came the railways. The Government of India had laid a line to connect Bombay and Madras which passed through Sholapur. A proposal to extend the line from Wadi in Sholapur to Hyderabad, a distance of 113 miles, was made in 1863. To begin with, the Nizam was opposed to the idea because it would break the insularity of the state and threaten its orthodoxy with the attendant dangers. The Government of India favoured it for strategic and commercial considerations. Salar Jung was pressurized to bring the Nizam round to accepting the idea. The rail connection was finally established in 1847.

His last and most important administrative reforms were promulgated in 1882. Recapitulating all the previous reforms implemented in different areas of administration, he issued orders for the creation of five ministries with a total of forty-four departments under them. The ministries were assisted by a regular secretariat. To fill up some of the important posts in government at various levels, with people having adequate education and experience in British India, he invited a number of persons from the north and from Madras. In the selection of suitable persons, he took the advice of Sir Sayyad Ahmed, who was active in modernizing the Muslim community in British India, particularly in the north.

He also introduced the system of performance assessment for employees in government service and the principle of promotion by merit.

The magnitude of the achievements of Salar Jung cannot be adequately appreciated without having an idea of the odds he had to fight against. He had to deal with his detractors on three fronts. These antagonists attacked him from all sides.

His first adversary was the Nizam. Nasir-ud-Dowlah had succumbed to the pressure of the Resident reinforced by the zenana and the palace. Nasir Jung had appointed Salar Jung as Diwan, much against his original inclination. Some of the reforms initiated by Salar Jung affected the Nizam's position adversely. For example, the ban on the presentation of nazars meant loss of considerable income for the ruler. Nasir-ud-Dowlah often complained that the young Diwan was upsetting the old Mughlai ways. He ordered that Salar Jung should come to the court only when summoned while his rival nobles and chiefs had comparatively free access to the ruler. A lot of backbiting against him was done by his detractors whereas he had no opportunity to effectively counter it.

In his tiffs with Nasir-ud-Dowlah, the young Diwan also got support from the ladies of the palace simply due to his one solid reform—regular payment of allowances every month.

Nasir-ud-Dowlah's successor, Afzal-ud-Dowlah, the new Nizam, was also jealous of Salar Jung because the English gave him credit for saving them in the revolt of 1857. He insulted his Diwan in the open court. Salar Jung thereupon submitted his resignation to the Nizam. The latter expressed regret and so Salar Jung came out of the incident more powerful. The Resident made it clear to the Nizam that he could not remove the Diwan without the permission of the viceroy. The struggle between the Nizam and the Diwan ended with the death of Afzul-ud-Dowlah in 1869.

The new Nizam was a child of less than three years of age; Salar Jung and the Paigah noble Rafiuddin were appointed his co-regents. The gentle old paigah did not covet Salar Jung's power.

But after Rafiuddin's death in 1877, Rasheeduddin Khan was appointed co-regent. The boy-Nizam was his nephew through his wife.

Rasheeduddin was jealous of Salar Jung and gave him a lot of trouble for the four years that he lived. For a suspected case of conspiracy against the Resident, his name was removed from the Resident's social register. The Paigah noble blamed Salar Jung for that.[62]

Strangely, Salar Jung's third adversary was the very British that had supported him so much. Differences between Salar Jung and the Resident arose on the installation of the child-Nizam, Mahboob Ali Khan. There was also an acute difference of opinion about the type of education to be given to the young Nizam. But more than anything else it was Salar Jung's persistent pursuit of the return of Berar to the Nizam that soured their relations.

He annoyed the English government, and in particular, the Resident, sufficiently to be called the 'only irreconcilable opponent' of the British in native India. Salar Jung threatened to resign, but he gathered his intelligence that in the event of his resignation the Resident had prepared a contingency plan to arrest him and to deport him to Madras. Matters came to such a pass that the Governor General, Lytton, wrote to Salisbury, the Secretary of state, on 24 September 1877 that Salar Jung was 'the most dangerous man in all India; and like a horse, or a woman that had once turned vicious, thoroughly irreclaimable.'[63]

❖ ❖ ❖

Mirza Agha Beg, a grandson of the famous Urdu poet, Ghalib, was brought from the north by Salar Jung as a tutor to the young Nizam, Mahboob Ali Khan. Subsequently, he rose to become Nawab Server-ul-Mulk. In his memoirs, he described the routine of the great Diwan and his darbar.

Salar Jung rose early and after his ablutions and morning prayers, he would make his appearance on the balcony of his palace which was called the Diwan Deodhi ('the mansion of the Diwan'). By that time the servants, guards, and officials of his palace were lined up below. The *chobdar*—mace-bearer—would announce the appearance of His Highness and all the men below would bow their heads and salaam him. After this the Diwan would go to his garden where Tippu Khan, the master of the stables, would be ready with some horses, each held by its syce. Some of the favourite companions of the Diwan in formal dress would be present there. His two sons also joined him off and on. This was the time when some supplicants would be cleverly allowed to submit a petition or make a submission. Now and then Salar Jung would go for a ride towards Saroor Nagar but would always be back at sunrise. On returning, he would sit on his masnad. The court was then open and a stream of officials, nobles, petitioners, and others would be presented, most of them by prior appointment. The chief usher was a black old man, called Fakir Mohammad. He wore a turban and held a staff in his hand that he did not hesitate to use in order to correct a waiting visitor's posture or any other breach of manner of which he was the sole judge.

Many visitors resented the overbearing attitude of the chief macebearer. But he enjoyed the absolute confidence of the Premier. When Salar Jung went out of his mansion to the royal court, or to meet the Resident or call on one of the nobles, he went in a regular procession. The convoy was led by eight to ten camel-riders in red uniforms. The cavalry unit in red livery with a pennant and a band followed them. Behind them was white uniformed cavalry. About a dozen drummers and hundreds of Arabs, in turn, followed them, with muskets on their shoulders. Then came the Diwan's close companions like Mir Tehwwar Ali, Junaid Khan Jamedar and some other dignitaries mounted on steeds flanked and followed by men with silver lances and matchlocks. If the Diwan sat on an elephant, spear-bearing livery covered both his flanks.

Salar Jung was tall, and of broad build. He shaved his head but sported a long moustache. He used to wear a sherwani with pajamas. He wore a double-chained watch and a gold-embroidered cap. If he was visiting the Resident or the nobles he would wear a turban. When he went to the Nizam's court he wore neem jama which was the court dress.

Salar Jung was punctilious about court etiquette, and even before the child-Nizam, could never be faulted in his manners. He never sat before him unless specifically commanded to do so.

The Diwan was also a lavish entertainer. At his dinner parties, there used to be separate arrangements for the English guests and Indian invitees. The *baradari* was tastefully illuminated with lamps of different colours. Being a connoisseur of food, his chef served English, Mughlai, Hindustani, and Dakhini dishes. When the time came for the guests to depart, he would stand near the exit door and offer long bottles of Indian scent to them as parting gifts. The number of bottles given to each guest varied from one to a dozen depending upon his importance.[64]

The thought of death seemed always to be present in Salar Jung's mind. Whenever he proceeded on a longish trip, he always carried with him the paraphernalia required for a funeral, should he pass away during the course of his journey. In the event, he died at home. Sir Salar was interested in astrology and *rummal*. He had some retainers who were competent in these. One of them was Pandit Mohan Lal. The latter had an appointment to meet the Diwan on the evening of 8 February 1883. After finishing his work for the day the Diwan summoned the Pandit. He asked him to draw his horoscope at that time. The astrologer indicated prosperity and success in store for him. The Prime Minister examined the horoscope, smiled and then asked the expert mischievously: 'But *Pandit ji*, the house meant for life is empty.' The Pandit tried to explain away the matter and after a while was allowed to depart.

The astrologer came running to Server-ul-Mulk, his godfather, woke him up and told him the whole story. Server-ul-Mulk was annoyed with him that he had disturbed him for such a small matter. The astrologer said that he hoped his horoscope was wrongly cast.

That very night Sir Salar Jung passed away.[65] The verdict was death due to cholera but his French governess swore that he was poisoned.

The Toddler Nizam

When the fifth Nizam, Afzal-ud-Dowlah, died in 1869, his son Mahboob Ali Khan was two-and-a-half years old. Salar Jung, in consultation with the Paigah and the other nobles, proclaimed him as the new ruler. The Resident objected that prior clearance for that had not been obtained from the English government. Salar Jung rightly replied that it was not required either by treaty or precedent. Piqued the Resident said that he and his party would attend the installation with their shoes on and would sit on chairs. Hitherto, in consonance with the custom of the Mughal court, they used to come to the court bare-foot and sit on the floor.[66] After much wrangling, the Resident's point was conceded and a change in the style of the darbar and the dress worn there was permitted. The Indian nobles of the court still sat on white-sheets spread on the floor. However, in order to keep the level of the floor even with the chairs, the floor was raised by placing wooden planks on it. Gradually this led to change of dress amongst the Indian nobles too. They started wearing trousers and sherwani or long buttoned-up coats with shoes instead of the traditional neem-jama.

Mahboob was too much in the care of the women of the household and the Resident and the English government were concerned about his proper upbringing. He was, therefore, shifted to Sulaiman Jahi's Haveli.

Further, while Salar Jung and the Indian nobles wanted an Indian tutor to educate him in the traditional way, the English wanted him to be given a 'liberal and sound' education under the supervision of an Englishman. After much discussion, the Resident's view prevailed. An Englishman, Captain Clerk, was appointed as the Superintendent of Education with Mirza Agha Beg as his assistant along with some other Indian tutors. A special class was set up in Sulaiman Jahi's palace, consisting the sons of Salar Jung, the Paigahs, the Peshkar, and of some other nobles.

Nawab Mustaqim Jung, one of the Indian teachers, would go to the palace and request his royal pupil with folded hands to come to the class. Like most children of his age, Mahboob did not relish going to school. The teacher had to cajole him. Sometimes, at the sight of his teacher, Mahboob would start running towards the ladies' quarters. The old teacher followed with folded hands. If the student entered the ladies' quarters, the teacher had to stop there and wait for his ward to be brought out. If ever the royal student committed an infraction, some other student was punished. One of the teachers would then whisper respectfully to Mahboob that his tutor was in a bad mood and he should note what happened to the students who did not observe discipline.[67]

When he was eight, almost to a day, on Saturday, 1 August 1874, a state visit was arranged for him to the Residency. The Resident, Saunders, sent out some 400 invitations printed in letters of gold both to Europeans and Indians to attend the reception.

There was great excitement in the city about the visit and the entire route from Purani Haveli to the Residency was full of people. The Nizam's procession was almost two kilometres in length, being composed of his household troops consisting of the infantry and cavalry, camels and elephants with scarlet howdahs, state palanquins, and the royal studs. All the animals were covered with silk drapes called *jhools*. His soldiers wore coats which must originally have been red in colour but were 'now so faded that they assumed the most varied tints, from the hue of brick-dust to a faded bluish purple.' Some of the weapons and daggers they carried were rusted and the shields looked like lids of cooking pots. The lances, which some of the horsemen carried, were made of long and thin bamboos most of which were curved towards the end.

This weird military formation was followed by a number of carts carrying tigers, leopards, and cheetahs, all securely tied by chains and kept in carts, which were also draped, in white silk. Then there was a group of half-naked stonecutters carrying their instruments of trade like pick-axes and crowbars. Last, in this bizarre procession, was a fierce-looking executioner with a bare sword in his hand.

To complete the comic touch, this veritable riot of noise and colour, marched to the tune of 'I am leaving thee in sorrow, Annie,' which was played by the Nizam's brass band.

The procession took over two hours to reach the Residency, which was decked up for a formal reception. Compared to the general chaos on the route, comparative order prevailed in the precincts of the Residency. Entry was strictly by invitation and the invitation cards were subjected to close scrutiny. The invited officials, and the advance party of the Nizam, started arriving from 10.30 a.m. onwards in all modes of transport. The nurse of the young Prince arrived in a sedan chair completely draped in royal yellow and carried by women. The noblemen of different communities kept arriving, wearing the court dress which consisted generally of white muslin and white satin. Every noble wore a jewelled belt from which was suspended a sword with a handle of pure gold. The sheath of the sword was set with gems.

The young Nizam came riding a huge elephant. Behind him, separated by a wooden partition, sat the two regents, Sir Salar Jung and Rafiuddin, the Paigah noble. The elephant was covered with yellow cloth which fringed the howdah as well. The elephant entered the compound of the Residency with a gun salute and stopped in front of the steps. On a command from the mahout it sat down while a ladder was placed promptly against it. The two regents got down hurriedly and joined the Resident at the foot of the Residency steps to form the reception committee. Mahboob, mustering as much dignity as was possible for an overdressed boy of eight, clambered down. He was led up the steps escorted by Sir Salar Jung and the Resident. On seeing him, the excited crowd surged forward but was kept at bay. The boy-ruler's large innocent eyes betrayed his age through his unnaturally dignified bearing. He wore white which seemed to flow down in crinkles down to his knees. The bosom of his dress seemed to be thickly sewn with diamonds. Many strings of diamonds and pearls hung around his neck and he sported a white turban. Entering the glittering hall, he walked up confidently to the masnad—three feet square and two feet high—covered with purple velvet and richly trimmed with gold. Overhead the Asaf Jahi and the British flags crossed.

After the 'little fellow', as the *Times of India* irreverently referred to the Nizam, sat down on the masnad, his nobles, led by Salar Jung took their seats on his right. On the left were ranged his hosts led by the Resident. An exchange of expressions of friendship and goodwill ensued between the juvenescent ruler and the Resident. This was followed by an exchange of gifts. Overhead in the gallery, European ladies in their best finery watched the ceremony with bated breath. Strictly speaking, it was a breach of etiquette because women were not allowed to be present at a darbar. But since it was on a 'foreign' piece of land, it was condoned. They had been advised to observe complete silence.

After a while the Nizam returned to his room to rest. Members of the retinue were entertained to a sumptuous lunch. The Nizam rose from his siesta at about 4 p.m. Once again the darbar sitting was repeated, and after a short while *pan supari* was served to the guests. This meant that the darbar was over. Soon the Prince of the Deccan, on a coded signal from some courtier, got up, stood erect to his full height of three-and-a-half feet, and looked around in a gesture of farewell. The Diwan and the Resident stepped forward, held him by the hand on either side and proceeded to the exit. There was a mild twitter of excitement in the gallery overhead.

The booming of the gun could be heard in the distance as a salute for the departing guest as the Prince left the Residency.

It was time for the guests to depart too and the Indian guests started taking leave of the hosts at the appropriate level and made for their carriages which were called as the dignitary was sighted on top of the steps.

But the Europeans lingered on awhile. A conspiracy had been hatched amongst the ladies that full advantage should be taken of this rare occasion. Such a visit would not take place again in their tenure here—or perhaps even their lifetime. It was too early to withdraw to the dull routine of the 'lines'. Margaret, the wife of General Blake, Commander of the British forces, had been won over to the proposition that though it was a little early, there should be a dance. Everything was there—Mumm's champagne, Bass's beer bottled by Stone, Moselle cup and sherry, a fair quantity of which had been imbibed by everyone. And there were the bands too both from the cantonment and the city. And what a gathering of men! No, this opportunity should not be lost. Margaret whispered to the General. He smiled yieldingly and said something to Resident Saunders. He, in turn, beckoned Captain Tweedie. There was clapping of hands and the minions got into action. Soon the place was cleared and the ball started. The sedate waltz and fox trot were soon overtaken by the vigorous Scottish dances. For full two hours the dancing went on. And then, all of a sudden, the band struck the national anthem. It was a polite hint that the party was over.[68]

Mahboob's penchant for the cup and for women had become a cause of concern when he attained puberty. That was why he was shifted to Sulaiman Jahi's Haveli.

A high wall separated the bachelors' quarters from the ladies' quarters in the Purani Haveli. Besides Mahboob, his companions— Laik Ali Khan and Saadat Ali Khan, the two sons of Salar Jung; Kishen Pershad; and some other sons of nobles—inhabited the bachelors' quarters. Mahboob was allowed to spend a night in the ladies' quarters once a week.

One evening Mahboob wanted to spend an extra night in the female quarters. That was no easy matter since special permission was required for that and the quarters were closely guarded. Mahboob asked Kishen Pershad to get hold of a ladder. That was placed against the wall adjoining the female quarters. Then Laik Ali, who was the strongest of all the boys, was asked to scale the wall and pull out one of the maids from the other side.

The guard brought the matter discreetly to the notice of Salar Jung. He sent a note to Raja Narender whose grandson, Kishen

Pershad, was found guilty of procuring the ladder. Kishen Pershad explained that he was duty-bound to carry out the orders of his ruler. It was Laik Ali who had used the ladder for the impugned act. Raja Narender agreed with the explanation given by his grandson and told Salar Jung that he would have done likewise if he had received such orders from his sovereign. Nothing came out of the inquiry, but Mahboob did not like the fuss made about the incident, and it rankled.

The Viceroy, Lord Ripon, came to Hyderabad to formally install Mahboob Ali Khan on the masnad on 5 February 1884. On the same day, Mahboob also chose Laik Ali as his Diwan. He was the son of the first Salar Jung, a class fellow, and a bosom friend of Mahboob.

The first Salar Jung had somehow kept things under his control for three decades. But his son was unable to carry forward the legacy. He introduced changes but they were of a superficial kind aimed at modernizing only some of the procedures. The office of *arzbegee*—an official who received petitions in the Nizam's court— was replaced by an ADC (aide-de-camp). The daily court circular, *Siahah*, was virtually abolished. The ADC issued all invitations to the darbar. Urgent matters or important correspondence with the Residency was seldom brought to the notice of the Nizam and even when it was, it was only for information. The language of the court and administration was changed from Persian to Urdu—a 'reform' which the first Salar Jung had resisted, because to him Persian 'symbolized the victory of Islam in India.'

No relationship between a ruler and his premier started with greater warmth than that between Mahboob and Laik Ali. Before his installation, Mahboob sent an effusive note to Laik Ali Khan in which he quoted a couplet from the poet Roomi in Persian:

> *Mun too shudam too mun shudi; mun tan shudam too jan shudi*
> *Ta kas no goyad bad azin mun deegram too deegri*

> (I am you and you are me, like body and soul united Now no body can say that you are you and I am I).

This couplet is supposed to denote the essence of Sufism. Two separate entities merge indistinguishably into one. No subject could expect a greater compliment from a ruler.

The Diwan lost no time in dissipating his advantage—not in driblets but by the barrel. Thanks to the inept breach of traditional court etiquette by him and the efforts of the tale-carriers, the relationship began to sour soon and it was not long after, that Mahboob found no language harsh enough to criticize his Prime Minister.

The suspicion of the Nizam seems to have been aroused by a small incident. On 5 March 1884, Mahboob was taken down with cholera. The Diwan immediately went into a conference with the Amir-e-Kabir to prepare a contingency plan, just in case. But the Nizam recovered and just to cover himself up, Laik Ali told the Nizam that the Paigah and his tutor had met the Resident to make plans for the succession of Zaffar Jung, a cousin of the Nizam. This was contradicted by both of them. The Nizam's tutor told him the real facts.

But the reasons given by the Nizam for his displeasure with his Diwan concerned only the glaring breach of etiquette. In a secret midnight meeting with the Paigah noble and his tutor at the Saroornagar Palace, he recounted his grouses to them.

See the attitude Laik Ali Khan has taken up in respect to himself. For instance, without my permission and knowledge, he does what he likes in important matters. He will sit on a chair, with legs straightened out, while I stand; he will take out cigarette and smoke without hesitation in my presence; and in spite of strict orders, he wears whatever dress he likes at Court functions, and will sit with his back towards me, laughing and joking with others. He did not consider me equal in rank, but lower.[69]Laik Ali's father had warned him about the gulf that separated a Prince from a commoner, however high. He had emphasized the importance of correct etiquette and manners in one's behaviour with a ruler and the infallibility of the latter. The young premier ignored the lesson and so lost his office in less than three years despite all the support from the Resident and the Viceroy.

By the end of the nineteenth century, the anglicization of the Nizam and his court was almost complete. The attitudes, household furniture, the dress, the cuisine—in all matters it became a mark of distinction to be westernized. The restrictions on social intercourse between the Indians and the Europeans were a thing of the past. People learnt English and travelled to Europe if they could afford it. The government also evolved a scheme of giving scholarships to selected deserving students. English games and sports like polo, cricket, and horseracing became popular amongst the wealthy classes. European brands of liquor replaced the indigenous wines. The motorcar made its appearance in the last decade of the century and of course Mahboob Ali Khan was the first to acquire one. Mahboob was a vain, narcissistic young man fond of dressing well. He was the first Nizam to start wearing the western dress. But he never wore the same dress twice. The result was that he came to have the largest wardrobe in the world. One full wing of his residence, the Purani Haveli—with a length of 240 feet (73.15 m)—was full of clothes and shoes, and other accoutrements. It took 124 cupboards to accommodate them. Most of the clothes were given away to make room for new ones. In 1990, one top hat in a box, two pairs of riding boots, pair of pumps, and one pair of straw slippers were all that were left of that formidable collection. One could see from the sole of the shoes that they could not have been worn more than once. Their brand name was intact.

Mahboob had no illusions about his position *vis-à-vis* the mighty British. He accepted their supremacy and, within the set framework, did whatever he liked. Beneath his western veneer, there was the orthodox oriental core. Like the rulers of old, he liked to go around incognito at night just to see how the people lived, what they thought and said of him. Sometimes he would pick up a derelict old starving woman and fill her empty bowl with gold coins. People began to see in him a benign ruler, a holy spirit, of the sort about whom they had only heard stories. He encouraged such fairy-tales about himself.

A legend grew that he could cure victims of snakebite and it was widely believed that he had given instructions that whatever the time of the day or night, no victim of snakebite should be turned away from his door. And even today, nearly a century after his death, if one goes to the Mecca Masjid, in the courtyard of which he lies buried in a simple grave by the side of his ancestors, one is likely to run into some person from some remote village who has come to thank her late ruler for curing some one in the family of snakebite by a mere invocation of his name: *Mahboob Ali Pasha ki duhai.* ('Mercy of King Mahboob Ali!'). Two bitter neem leaves were to be chewed after the incantation. People loved his medieval, benevolent style. Muslims thanked God for giving them a spiritual saint as a ruler. His Hindu subjects too revered him as an incarnation of Manik Prabhu, the saint of Humnabad.

In an age when people did not expect anything from a ruler except a concession to run the normal course of their lives, Mahboob sometimes stepped out of his dream world and shared their sorrows. They said that Mahboob, of all their rulers, was appropriately named. He was really *Mahboob*—the beloved!

Paigah's Fancy Dress Party

After the tumult of the mutiny of 1857, things began to settle down. Hyderabad had stayed loyal to the British and had saved them from doom. That was duly acknowledged by the British, and so normalcy returned to Hyderabad sooner than elsewhere in India. Mahboob was the right type of ruler for good times. The nobles soon took to their old ways. They threw lavish parties. Those hosted by Sir Asman Jah were simply fabulous. The European army officers stationed at the Bolarum cantonment keenly looked forward to them.

One such memorable party was held at his Bashir Bagh palace in the city on Monday, 17 February 1890. The instruction on the card both in English and Urdu said it was compulsory to wear a fancy dress for the party. The invitations went out three weeks in advance. Those who were excluded in the first list of invitees wrangled invitations through their contacts because, apart from being a matter of prestige, it would be a memorable occasion with infinite possibilities for fun and flirtation.

The Bashir Bagh mansion looked resplendent. Preparations had been made for the party well in advance. The generally trim garden was spruced up even further. Some of the tapestry was washed, some replenished. Carpets were changed. New chairs were purchased. Ten thousand lamps were placed in different parts of the palace, though some people put the number at 50,000.

All the fountains were switched on and the evening breeze wafted water vapour beyond the cisterns. Three bands played softly in different corners of the garden. One played in the corner of the ballroom. In yet another corner, a *mujra*, the Indian nautch, was organized in which beautiful girls danced to the accompaniment of an orchestra and the singing of ghazals.

The latter was for the benefit of those who had no taste for ballroom dancing or those who wanted to savour something typically Indian. Six young men from the staff were detailed for receiving guests and ushering them in. Three wore black jackets and bows in the western style and three sported the traditional Hyderabadi dress. Against the normal practice of announcing the guests on arrival, this time it was to be a guessing game. What would be the fun of the fancy dress if the identity of the invitee was known in advance?

Everybody came in an unusual dress and make-up. The Indians were a little careful in donning their disguises because after all they were going to the house of the Prime Minister. One senior official contented himself by merely putting on a three-piece suit and saying that he was a Mr John Fox. Another dyed his beard gray and put on the dress of a Muslim holy man. Another came as a Hindu astrologer. Yet another came as a beggar.

Some dressed as Rohilla chiefs, some as Arab *jamedar*s, some as moneylenders. At the approach of a group of moneylenders, for once, a shiver ran down the spine of the host. Maybe, he thought, some group had decided to embarrass him on that occasion. He was heavily in debt and could see no way of cutting down his expenses or managing his affairs prudently. He heaved a sigh of relief when the fake moneylenders made their respectful bow to him and filed past to where alcohol was being served. Hindu moneylenders never drank, not in public, not even at other people's expense. It was one of the cardinal pillars of their belief that Lakshmi, the goddess of wealth, did not visit, far less stayed with, those whose mouth emitted the foul smell of alcohol.

It was the Europeans who really took the dress regulation on the invitation card literally and exercised a lot of imagination and care in putting on disguises.

The first English couple arrived as a tiger and tigress led by a hunter. A pair of fine horses led by an Arab followed that. One English woman came as a nautch girl, dancing to the tune of the duff beaten by her husband. She made straight for the mujra where the real dancing girl stopped wonderstruck in her tracks. The whole gathering broke into laughter and applause when it was discovered that the comely new nautch girl was a guest. One army major came dressed like a buxom begum. Another came as Santa Claus with a bag of charcoal on his back. A young subaltern, who was a proficient gymnast, came as a necromancer and jumped past the ushers to their great astonishment. One couple came as night and day: the man in tight-fitting black vest and stockings and the woman in a fluffy white long shirt, white sleeves, and a white hat. She had painted her face a pale yellow, indicating sunrise.

Nearly 200 men and women attended the party that evening. They drank and danced, and danced and drank. Others sat watching the dancing girl and threw silver and gold coins at her in the Indian fashion. Some held small bags of coins in their hands and jingled them to attract the dancer's attention. She would come to them dancing and gesticulating tantalizingly, almost within their grasp. And then with one swirl of her shapely body and the mischievous words of a song to match, she would pick up the bag and retreat. Some of the Englishmen too joined this group. Some gallant Indian guests, who were glad to have the opportunity of dancing with white women, took them eagerly to the wooden floor.

While this was going on, the sky was suddenly lit as if by 10,000 incandescent lamps. People in the garden looked up. Those inside rushed out to see what was happening. It was the inauguration of fireworks, which went on for over half an hour. There were giant sparklers, 'fountains', 'trees', and finally rockets that went up and then broke up and disappeared from view. Indians heaved sighs of exclamation at every item while the Europeans clapped lustily.

At the stroke of midnight, dinner was announced. Each guest had their seat marked. For every two guests there was a menu card and a waiter. The hall glittered with glass, china, and gold cutlery. Eleven courses were served. There was a choice of continental and

Mughlai dishes. Amongst the five desserts, the most popular was Nimsh. It was the fluff of boiled milk mixed with sugar and kept in small earthen pots overnight under the open sky so that it could absorb the dew.

The guests started departing at half past two in the morning. The old Diwan and his son stood on the steps of the portico to say goodbye. Every guest was given two or three bottles of Indian scent. Some important guests were given more, even up to a dozen.

Before the departure of the guests, all their attendants and coachmen had been fed. Someone saw to it that no one missed the hospitality of the premier.

Mahboob's Camelot

Mahboob embarked upon the new century with a new Diwan.

In 1900, he appointed Kishen Pershad as the new Diwan. He was the grandson of Raja Narender who, in turn, was the grandson of Chandulal who had ruled the roost first as Peshkar and then as Diwan for nearly forty years in the first half of the nineteenth century. Chandulal himself traced his ancestry to Todar Mall, the celebrated Revenue Minister of the Great Mughal, Akbar.

Kishen Pershad was a contemporary of Mahboob and the two sons of Sir Salar Jung, and because he had lost his father at a very young age, Sir Salar had taken him under his protective care and educated him along with his sons and other young nobles.

Kishen Pershad grew into a well groomed, highly cultured young man. He turned out to be a perfect courtier. For long on the fringes of power, and once even disinherited by his own grandfather in favour of his younger brother, Kishen Pershad found an ingenious way of ingratiating himself with the Nizam. The normal rewards expected by any boon companion of the Nizam had eluded him and he continued to suffer comparative adversity. One day he applied for discipleship of the Nizam in poetry through his tutor, Mirza Agha, and also presented a nazar in token of that. It was indeed very flattering for the Nizam, who himself had engaged a teacher for correcting his poetic compositions, to be asked to accept a pupil. This subtle move worked.

This was followed by his appointment as Minister for Military Affairs under the new dispensation introduced at the behest of Mirza Agha. Kishen Pershad also started a journal called *Mahboob al Kalam* which carried the poems of Mahboob as the opening piece followed by his own poem and those of a handful of others. It circulated in the right quarters and the courtiers' praise of the poems of the Nizam redounded to the credit of Kishen Pershad.

He was also given the very flattering title of *Yamin-us-Saltanat*—the right hand of the sultanate—and the prefix of Raja was elevated to that of Maharaja.

The Nizam and the new Prime Minister were alike in so many ways. They shared many common interests—from hunting to composing poetry. And Kishen Pershad was the great exponent of the theory of the divine right of the ruler. For him the Nizam could never be wrong, never in need of advice. He had merely to be obeyed. He anticipated his wishes, echoed his sentiments, and implemented his orders even before they were fully given. Kishen Pershad knew Arabic, Persian, Urdu, English, Sanskrit, and Punjabi. His versatility covered a surprising range—from the manly pastimes of hunting, shooting, and composing poetry in Persian and Urdu to the feminine arts of painting and cooking.

In a Hindu-majority state ruled by a Muslim, he had tremendous advantages. By birth and belief a Hindu, he was virtually a Muslim in his way of living and manners. As if to underline his secularism, he married three Hindu and four Muslim women. They bore him 30 children. His children through Muslim wives had Muslim names. Each wife and her children followed their own religion. Himself a polygamist, towards the end of his life, he advised his sons about the virtues of monogamy.

Extravagance was a part of the feudal way of life even if it meant incurring debts. Kishen Pershad was no exception. He never left his home without a bagful of coins which he would throw around as his elephant, and later his car, drove through the streets. He loved the sight of the scramble it caused amongst children and beggars of all ages. His one time ADC, Colonel Bilgrami, recalled that before getting into the car he always made sure that the bag of coins was there —and that it was full. He was affectionately called *Bachon Ka Raja*—'Children's Raja'.

He was a generous man and the philosophy of *noblesse oblige* often manifested itself in his whimsical acts of generosity. If a man approached him saying that he was poor and could not afford to marry off his daughter, Kishen Pershad, like many of his contemporaries, would take on the entire financial burden and declare that the girl in question was his daughter. One such act fostered many legends.

He wore his humility on his sleeve and referred to himself as a mendicant. He was a patron of the learned and himself sported the pen name *Shad* (the 'happy one') for his poetry. His palace became renowned for its mushairas (Urdu poetic gatherings) and the best poets of India recited their compositions there. His were the only poetic assemblies in which the poems composed by the Nizam could be recited. The mushairas used to begin with the 'auspicious' poem of the Nizam recited by a messenger and every line in it was so vociferously lauded as if the poet himself was present. Kishen Pershad used to receive the Nizam's poems reverentially by touching them with his forehead and eyes. He would give it to the messenger to recite. People still remember the elaborate ritual and grand scale of those events. All in all, he was a man for all seasons.[70]

In the first decade of the twentieth century, the city became a virtual Camelot. God was in his heaven, the Nizam on his masnad and everything was all right in the beautiful city of Hyderabad.

❖ ❖ ❖

And then came the Great Flood of 1908.

The river Musi is named after Moses, the Hebrew prophet. It has a tributary, which is called the Isi or Isa, meaning Christ. The two rivers join each other near the Golconda Fort.

Today people mock the river. There is only a trickle of water and some stagnant pools made up of the sewerage flowing in from various localities.

But it has not always been like that. Once it was a normal river, full of water. That's why Mohammad Quli chose a spot on its bank to build the city. He even constructed one of his palaces on its right bank and called it *Nadi Mahal*. A public hospital was also established on its bank to provide fresh air to hasten the recovery of patients.

There is a legend that Mohammad Quli as a juvenile Prince galloped his horse into the flooded river one evening in order to meet his beloved Bhagmati who used to live across it. His father, coming to know of this dare-devilry, had a bridge built across the river. It was the first bridge on the river. Constructed in 1578, it is still in use. It is called the Purana Pul or the old bridge.

The Musi also used to flood off and on.

Since the foundation of Hyderabad, the local chroniclers have recorded the occurrence of 12 major floods in the Musi.

The first great flood occurred in 1631. At that time the old bridge was overtopped and several populous quarters of the new city were swept away. This was regarded by the people of that time as the worst flood on record. Another flood occurred in 1831 and it was attended with considerable loss of life. The Chaderghat Bridge, which was then under construction, was seriously damaged by it. Again in 1903 there was a flood of moderate intensity in which over 1,400 houses were destroyed. After that the government discouraged rebuilding of the destroyed houses and no permission was given for construction of new houses on the bank of the river.

The worst flood on record is the deluge of 1908. It occurred on Monday, the 28 September 1908, and was caused by a cyclonic storm in the Bay of Bengal. It had rained throughout Sunday. A cloudburst developed at midnight over an extensive area. Rain descended in sheets flooding small tanks and overburdening their weirs. As a result one tank after another gave way.

The flood rose about 16 feet in less than three-and-a-half hours. All the four bridges were overtopped and their parapet walls were carried away. The approaches to the oldest bridge, the Purana Pul, were damaged but the bridge itself did not suffer any damage. The latest, the Afzal Jung Bridge or the Naya Pul, suffered the most.

The houses in Kalsovadi, along with the river, began to collapse on Sunday night and continued falling till ten the next morning. Yadgar Hussain Kunta, Shaheed Gunj, Char Mahal, Badri Aiawa, and Anjee Bagh were the worst sufferers. Darul Shifa was also damaged extensively. Three thousand people were perched on the city wall near Petla Burj, which was washed away.

More than two-and-a-half kilometres of thickly populated area was devastated on the north bank and about half of that on the south bank. Nearly 19,000 houses collapsed and about 80,000 people, representing roughly one quarter of the entire population of the city, were left homeless. About 15,000 lives were lost and property worth Rs 30 million was destroyed.[71]

Many eyewitness accounts have been written about the devastation caused by the Flood, mostly by those who suffered loss of property and some members of their family. One of them, Sayyad Ahmed Husain 'Amjad', the well-known poet, narrates the tragedy as it befell him:

Since evening (on Sunday) the Musi was rising furiously. By 8 p.m. water was knee-deep in our house which was in Ghansi Mian Bazar. We urged our mother that we should leave but she replied that if our end had arrived then it was better to die in our own house. By 10 p.m. water had surrounded us like a vengeful enemy. In panic we moved to a nearby house which was strong and which had survived a flood earlier. Many persons had already taken refuge there. We stayed in the sitting room. Soon the west wall collapsed and water started rushing in. We ran to the other side but there too water came gushing in from the courtyard. We put a wooden platform in the middle of the room and stood on top of it. Then we decided to move out of the room into the street. My mother, my wife my little girl and I—all four—clung to each other. Water kept on rising even above the terrace. At 2 a.m., it touched our ankles, then came to our calves, then the knees, then our waist and finally, it reached our necks. We held each other tight so that if we got drowned, we would go down together. One step beyond—and plom—we fell into a ditch. At that time we lost hold of each other and got separated. My mother saw me swirl past her in a swift current. I shouted to her that she should catch hold of a branch of the tree overhead. She said, 'My son I can't. Your daughter is tied to my back and because of her weight I can't pull myself up.' Those were the last words I heard from her. My little daughter had become a millstone around my mother's waist. Both went down together. My wife was nowhere to be seen. I was swept towards the Maternity Hospital. Someone there pulled me up and saved me. Forlorn, naked and shivering, I was saved but there is no use of such escape. I could not even trace the dead bodies of the members of my family.[72]

This was a story which applied to thousands of people. The Nizam, Mahboob Ali Pasha, came out on his elephant to survey the scene. Some one suggested that the flood was caused by the fury of goddess Bhavani. He should placate her by doing an arti for her. A silver plate with five earthen lamps and a sari were produced. He performed the *puja* in all solemnity. People believed that the water started receding because of that.

The government set up refugee camps. Clothes were distributed to all. Five kitchens were opened for Muslims, five for Hindus, and one for the women who observed *purdah*. All government offices were closed for ten days. Employees were given one month's salary by way of advance.

This was the last great gesture of the ruler beloved of the people. It endeared him to them still more. That unprecedented tragedy reinforced the legend of the man.

The memory of this flood is so strong and so fresh that more than nearly a century after the event, people born long after the tragedy refer to it as *Parson ki Tughyani*—the Deluge of the Day-before-Yesterday.

The Great Achievers

It was not as if all life revolved around Purani Haveli; the palaces of the Paigahs, Deodhis, and other nobles; and the Residency. Real life—and a lot of it—pulsated beyond those confines.

A city is primarily people—people of all ages—belonging to different age groups, and to numerous communities. Men and women live in it, eat and drink, sweat and toil, sleep and dream there. Like a river, a city is always in transition, parts of it dying, parts of it renewing every minute. There are cries of children being born, laughter of young persons, groans of old people dying. They make a city.

Hyderabad was also growing through such contrarieties.

As the nineteenth century closed, people in Hyderabad began to receive impulses from beyond the borders of the state which had been drawn artificially and arbitrarily through war and peace, through victories and defeats, through deceit and chicanery, through treaties and their violation. People had travelled freely across these tentative boundaries for ages and had always believed that they belonged to the larger entity of India. The introduction of the telegraph, the railways, and the emergence of the newspapers brought other parts of the country closer to the people in Hyderabad. Now they began to look beyond their usual horizons. It was not only the nobles who travelled to England and to Europe. Their retinues too saw another world. Officials too went and observed the ways of life there and young men of promise were also deputed abroad by the state for higher education. Sir Salar Jung himself had recruited civil servants from British India to modernize the administration in his state.

While most of them became the bulwarks of the status quo, some like Dr Aghornath Chattopadhyay, Mulla Abdul Qayyum, and Mohammad Murtuza became vigorous agents of social and political changes.

Soon after the death of Salar Jung, Persian was replaced by Urdu as the language of administration in 1884. The administration thus came a little closer to the people. It also encouraged the growth of higher education in the state. The extension of the railway line to the mining area of the state opened it up for growth. Hyderabad, now connected to the three principal presidency towns of the British—to Calcutta and Madras through Vijayawada and to Bombay through Wadi—became a part of the larger world. Diverse developments came to affect the pace and quality of life in the city.

With the introduction of the examination for pleaders in 1883, a new articulate and vocal class came into existence. The legal profession also attracted talent from outside the state and men like Ramachandra Pillai and Rudra came to practise in the courts of Hyderabad. Social service organizations like the Young Men's Improvement Society contributed to the shaping of public opinion. A branch of Annie Besant's Theosophical Society was set up at Chaderghat in 1882. This organization, which enjoyed the patronage of some officials, also attracted the elite and became a centre for discussion on religious and cultural matters.

The Hindu Social Club of Chaderghat, under the Presidentship of Raja Murli Manohar Bahadur, was bold enough to protest against the requirement of a good knowledge of Urdu and Persian amongst the candidates for scholarships given by the government to go abroad. It also termed as 'gross injustice', the appointment of a body of orthodox and ill-informed men to decide from the religious point of view whether Hindu students could cross the seas to go to England for higher studies. Both these measures were held as discriminatory against the Hindus.[73]

The latter half of the nineteenth century was characterized by the emergence of vigorous journalistic activity in Hyderabad. A number of newspapers and journals in Urdu, Persian, Telugu, Marathi, and English came into being. Some of them were started only to celebrate the accession of Mir Mahboob Ali Khan and ceased publication soon thereafter. There were about 22 papers and periodicals in the 1890s. Of these, the *Deccan Times*, the *Deccan Standard*, and the *Public Opinion* were in English. One called *Dena Vartam* was a bilingual, bi-weekly in Urdu and English. However in 1901, the number published in Urdu stood at 12 and in Marathi only two. One half of these were newspapers and the other half periodicals.[74]

The early press was vastly different from the one seen today. The press dispatches in English papers were in the form of long stories laced with the comments and observations of their correspondents. The papers from Bombay and Madras in English wrote critically and boldly about a large variety of topics. Those published within the state showed considerable circumspection and their tone was respectful towards the Nizam, the nobility, and the officialdom.

The Urdu press, which was dominant in the state, had no correspondents. Even local news would take a week to get into print. The news was mostly about the activities of the palaces and deodhies. There was no advertisement in the papers and so circulation was the only source of income. The amount of subscription varied according to the status of the subscriber. Thus the Nizam's government paid one rate, the Resident's office another. The nobles paid more than the plebeians.

The papers had to carry something to tickle the ego of the nobles. Above the masthead of every paper was a declaration of loyalty to the Nizam. An Urdu couplet filled the space after that. Most papers carried the firmans (orders) of the Nizam. The *Nizam Gazette* published all orders of the Nizam verbatim, however trivial. It continued to do so even after the seventh Nizam ceased to hold power—right until his death in 1967. Then they were mostly his private decisions or observations, or sometimes only some pathetic advice.

If the Nizam sent in one of his poems, it had to be published on the front page. And it had to be printed as it came; not even a comma could be edited. The corrections and comments of the royal instructor had also to be carried along with the original composition.

There was no settled policy for granting permission to start a paper. Depending upon the territorial jurisdiction, it was the whim of the kotwal or the Resident whether to grant the permission or not.

In 1891, the Government issued a number of restrictions against the press. It advised editors to refrain from publishing anything which might prejudice the public against the Nizam, his government, or his officials. All editors were required to sign an undertaking to that effect. This was objected to generally and one newspaper, *Shoukat-ul-Islam,* not only refused to sign the agreement, but also criticized it in strong terms. Consequently, the paper was proscribed. The action of the kotwal, in calling for the explanation of some of the editors, was also criticized and ridiculed by some papers. Some more Urdu papers and the *Deccan Standard* also shared the fate of *Shoukat-ul-Islam.* Yet, there were others which meekly toed the line. The comments, however, continued to be fairly strident against various acts of commission and omission of the Nizam's government as well as the Governor General's administration which also included the Resident.

Mohib Hussain was one of the pioneers of journalism in Hyderabad. He edited three journals and carried on a campaign for social and educational reforms amongst women. He was also an opponent of the purdah system. This created a furore amongst the orthodox Muslims and the government stepped in to close one of his journals dealing with the problems of women. He raised his voice of protest against the discrimination between the Europeans and Indians by the police and in criminal courts, and like Mulla Abdul Qayyum, criticized the two-nation theory. He described those who talked of Hindus and Muslims as two nations as 'deadly snakes'. In 1906, he suddenly turned away from active social and journalistic work and embraced mysticism and spiritualism. He spent the rest of his life as a recluse.[75]

Gradually, a policy began to be evolved for granting permission for starting newspapers. During the early period of Nizam VII, the editor and publisher of a paper had to fulfill three conditions. He had to be educated; he had to have adequate finances;

and he had to be married.[76] The last condition was put to ensure good behaviour on the part of the prospective journalist—the view being that a married man had more at stake in the status quo than a bachelor—a very ingenious way of ensuring a docile press. But there were journalists who risked even their marital happiness and financial security to publish what they felt was right.

Another event of significance was that the Arya Samaj established its branch in the city in 1892. It stood for reforms in the existing religious practices of the Hindus and so it evoked a strong reaction amongst the orthodox section of that community. The Sanatan Dharma Maha Mandal was established about this time to defend the status quo. The Muslims and Christians were also alarmed at its aggressive defence of Hinduism. The kotwal, fearing disturbance due to the activities of the Arya Samaj, deported two of its preachers and since the others had moved out of his jurisdiction to that of the Resident, he requested the Nizam's government to keep the Resident posted about the objectionable activities of the preachers. The judicial secretary, Nawab Imad Jung, objected to the action of the police in expelling one of the preachers since no charge had been proffered against him.

In another development, the Ganesh Utsav, to celebrate the birthday of the popular Hindu god Ganesh, was started in Maharashtra by the great revolutionary leader, Bal Gangadhar Tilak. The celebrations, which lasted for a week, became popular and served as an effective means of public awakening through the media of songs, lectures, and *melas*. In 1895, for the first time, the Ganesh festival was held at Shah Ali Banda and Chaderghat and it evoked a good response. The festival at Chaderghat was organized entirely by students.

The emergence of the Arya Samaj and the celebration of the Ganesh festivities together proved an effective means for focusing public attention and rousing public opinion on various issues. They also provided a training ground for workers in constructive social action. Men like Koratkar, Satwalekar, and Dr Aghornath Chattopadhyay joined the Arya Samaj and became pioneers of political, social, and educational reforms in the state.

Mulla Abdul Qayyum was an employee of the Survey and Settlement Department. He was reform-minded and so with some of his friends started the *Ikhwan-us-Sufa Society,* which held monthly meetings on social and educational reforms. It also ran a monthly journal. The Mulla became a friend of Dr Aghornath Chattopadhyay. Both were responsible for the agitation against the scheme for the extension of the railway line to Chanda and Vijayawada. For this the venerable doctor was deported and Abdul Qayyum had to go out to Madras for sometime.

On his return, when he was posted as Assistant Director in the Education Department, Abdul Qayyum became a member of the Indian National Congress. He also joined the Swadeshi Movement along with Dr Chattopadhyay. He was an advocate of compulsory education with a technical bias and wrote a pamphlet on the subject. He was responsible for the establishment of the *Diarat-ul-Maarif* in 1891 for the editing and translation of rare Arabic manuscripts. This institution earned considerable international respect for its work but is now in neglect. The Mulla was also instrumental in the establishment of the State Central Library in 1892. For opposing the aggressive and coercive method of the European officers in dealing with the cases of plague, during his term as the Collector of a district, he was driven to premature and compulsory retirement in 1901. He continued to work for bringing about social awakening and was so devoid of any form of communal bias that, at the invitation of Koratkar, he also took keen interest in the Ganesh Utsav celebrations in 1906. He died the same year.[77]

Mohammad Murtuza was another government employee who was a great votary of education through the medium of the mother tongue, which for him meant Urdu. He pleaded for the establishment of a Translation Bureau, an Urdu Library, and for devoting greater attention to technical education. He was the first nationalist Muslim to envisage the establishment of a separate University with Urdu as the medium of instruction. He was instrumental in holding the first Educational Conference in 1915, which led to the establishment of Osmania University in 1918.[78]

The library movement also emerged with the coming of the twentieth century. The Krishna Devaraya Andhra Bhasha Nilayam started the first private library in 1901 in Sultan Bazar. This was ten years before any library came into being in the coastal Andhra areas.

The first private Marathi primary school was founded in 1901 in the Residency Bazar. This grew into the Vivek Vardhini Pathasala. When, in the Musi floods of 1908, the rented premises of the school, along with its furniture and the library, were washed away, the government gave a generous grant of Rs 150 to repair the loss. The school grew into a college later.

Ranga Rao Kaloji started the first Telugu school at Chaderghat in 1904 in memory of his wife. Here girls were given instruction both in Telugu and Marathi.[79]

Given the demographic composition of Hyderabad, some unity of approach was necessary amongst various communities to achieve any worthwhile result. All social and political activities took place at three natural levels. Some enlightened Muslims with social concerns took up the cause of social and educational reform in their community. They would naturally not have countenanced any attempts at that by a member of any other community. Hindus, the dominant majority accounting for about 87 per cent of the population, amongst themselves had a community of interest in general though there were subgroups based on regional and linguistic interests. Telugu was the language of the largest number of people. Marathi and Kannada were the other regional languages.

Urdu was the mother tongue of the ruling elite and the medium of instruction as well as administration. Men from all communities learnt it. These communities had their own movements for renaissance and reform within their own linguistic and regional subdivisions. Though there could be some divergence of interest on the basis of linguistic and regional concerns, the social concerns were common and it was possible to gather together on a common platform. It was on this platform that the question of Hindu-Muslim unity could be raised. Remarkable instances of unity were seen in that context, though divergence of interest also came to be manifested in various forms.

At the turn of the nineteenth century, and well into the twentieth century, there was no class of politicians, as we know them today. The best-educated class was that of government servants. Sir Salar Jung had recruited these men largely from outside the state. Among these officials like Mehdi Hasan, Mushtaq Hasan, Mirza

Agha Beg took interest in social and political reforms. Mulla Abdul Qayyum, Mohammad Murtuza, Dr Aghornath Chattopadhyay were all government officers. But they did not feel restrained from participating in agitations against the government. Some of them suffered. Aghornath—father of Sarojini Naidu and Principal of the Nizam College—was deported and on return after six years had to suffer a reduction in rank. But they were all civil servants as well as politicians. It was much later, in the twentieth century, that the sinister specialization started developing and a separate class of politicians emerged. This is not to say that there were no advocates of social reforms outside the public services. The names of Keshav Rao Koratkar, Komarraju Laxman Rao, and Mohib Hussain are only a few from amongst the public-spirited persons.

Apart from the happenings in the city and the state of Hyderabad, what was taking place across the borders of the state had its repercussions in the state and people responded to calls from national leaders. International events, like the plight of the Arabs, and the First World War, and the deposition of the Caliph of Turkey also had their impact on the imagination of the people and inspired them to action.

It was, however, not mere luxury and intrigue in the Camelot and struggle and politics outside it. Slow, orderly, evolutionary development was taking place in various branches of life as a whole. We will mention the three men and their achievements in science and technology.

The first concerned the use of chloroform as an aid to surgery. It was first used in 1847 by Dr James Simpson at Edinburgh. While hailing its advent, the medical men of London expressed the caution that its use constituted a risk to the heart of the patient. The Edinburgh School, on the other hand, held that it was entirely safe for the heart and that the risk of its use was only for respiration.

In 1885, Edward Lawrie, a surgeon educated at Edinburgh, was appointed the Principal of the Hyderabad Medical School and was also the personal physician to the Nizam. Lawrie persuaded the Nizam to pay for a scientific investigation into the question of the safety of the use of chloroform. A four-man commission was accordingly set up in 1889. It conducted a number of experiments on dogs and confirmed the Edinburgh theory. Lawrie publicized the results enthusiastically.

Lancet, the renowned journal of the British Medical Association, re-buked Lawrie for rushing to conclusions based on inadequate evidence.

Thereupon Lawrie, with the approval of the Nizam, announced the establishment of a Second Commission. He invited the editor of the *Lancet* to nominate an expert of his choice to serve on the Commission. The Nizam gave a grant of a thousand pounds sterling to meet the travel and hospitality expenses of the expert. The *Lancet* nominated Dr T.L. Brunton to serve on the Commission. The Commission conducted 600 experiments on different animals for three months.

The Nizam witnessed the administration of chloroform to a goat, a horse, and a monkey on 29 November 1889.

The Second Commission confirmed the findings of the First Commission that it was the care of respiration and not of the heart that was crucial in the administration of chloroform. These findings were published in the *Lancet*, and in its issue of 21 June 1890, the editor expressed the gratitude of the medical profession to Nizam Mahboob Ali Khan 'for the opportunity of scientific progress which his unbounded liberality has afforded.'

Later, however, Lawrie's theory was proved wrong. But trial and error are the methods of science. Thus, Lawrie with his enthusiasm, and Mahboob with his patronage, advanced the cause of science.[80]

The other event was of far greater significance and the man responsible for that was a multi-faceted genius. He was a poet, a novelist, a musician, a mathematician—and a reluctant man of medicine. And ironically, it was in that last field that he made his great discovery.

Ronald Ross was born in Almora in Uttar Pradesh in 1857. After doing his medicine in England he returned to join the Indian Medical Service in which his father also had served.

While he was posted at Bangalore he became aware of the problem of malaria. The medical theory at that time was that breathing the damp air of the marshes caused malaria. In fact the term 'malaria' means bad air. It was at that time by far the most common disease in tropical countries. It caused the largest number of deaths and those who survived it became permanently enfeebled.

Louis Pasteur, a French chemist, had proved in the mid-nineteenth century that bacteria caused diseases. Robert Koch, a German pathologist, had shown which type of bacteria caused which particular diseases. Another French army doctor in Algeria, Laveran, had discovered that malaria was caused by parasites living on the human blood and they were different in shape from the parasites of other diseases. Yet another French scientist, Dr Beauperthuy, had observed that malaria was caused by mosquitoes.

Ross integrated all these isolated findings to determine the process of transmission of malaria. He concentrated his efforts on the study of the parasite in the mosquito rather than in the patient. Ross was posted at Secunderabad when his research came to fruition. He would try to get mosquitoes to bite patients suffering from malaria and thus get them infected. This he tried to do by letting loose a swarm of mosquitoes into the mosquito net under which the patient was made to sleep. To tempt the mosquitoes, he would wet both the bed and the net with water. He paid Rs 1 each to the volunteers. Then he dissected the infected mosquitoes and after prolonged efforts found that only the female of certain type of mosquito—the Anopheles—contracted the infection.

The parasite was nurtured in its stomach for a week after which it went to its mouth and entered the salivary glands. The mosquito transmitted the germ by his sting to the person. It took about two weeks to incubate in the human blood. The full-cycle was thus established. This great discovery of the process of the transmission of malaria was made on 20 August 1897 at Secunderabad.

It was a discovery of such magnitude that Ross was awarded the Nobel Prize for Medicine in 1902 and was knighted in 1911.

It is worth noting that he carried on his research entirely at his own expense. Instead of help, he often got discouragement from authorities. When the ecstatic moment of discovery arrived, he wrote a poem to his wife which concluded with the observation:

> I know this little thing
> A myriad man will save
> O Death, where is thy sting?
> Thy Victory, O Grave?[81]

The governments of various countries like Egypt, Greece, Cyprus, Spain, and Mauritius sought his advice for the eradication of malaria. The construction of the Panama Canal, which had been abandoned because of large-scale deaths due to yellow fever, was resumed under his advice and completed in 1914.

Laden with international honours, Sir Ronald Ross died in 1932.[82]

Photography was invented in 1838 and within a decade it arrived in India. Many people took to it with great enthusiasm.

Deen Dayal was born in 1846 and after studying engineering, took up the job of a draughtsman in Indore. There his talent for photography was noticed by Sir Lepel Griffin. Deen Dayal accompanied him as an architectural photographer on his tours in 1882 and produced magnificent photographs of the ancient architecture of central India.

In 1885 Deen Dayal came to Hyderabad and was appointed state photographer. In 1895 he was given the title of 'Raja'.

Deen Dayal's studio in Secunderabad employed 50 persons. He outshone his European contemporaries and was honoured internationally.

Deen Dayal's versatility was remarkable. He took many outstanding photographs of monuments. The Archaeological Survey of India took 250 of them from him. Queen Victoria gave him the Royal Warrant of Appointment in 1887. He is considered India's best photographer who raised photography to the level of art. His photographs are treasured by Collectors all over the world. He passed away in full glory in 1905.

A Unique Collection

The sixth Nizam, Mahboob Ali Khan, died on 29 August 1911. Three days earlier, his wife, Ujala Begum, had urged him to change the succession plan. Instead of Osman Ali Khan, she wanted her son, Basalat Jah, to be proclaimed the heir apparent. He was the rightful successor, she insisted. He, not Osman Ali Khan, was his son. Born in 1907, he was 21 years junior to Osman.[83]

Mahboob had dodged the issue every time she raised it. But that day she was adamant.

Driven to the wall, he left for the hilltop Falaknuma palace. There Mahboob bolted the doors and went into a drinking binge for three days. He then slipped into a coma and died without saying a word. He was only forty-five years and had ruled for over forty-two years.

The Begum, instead of gaining the throne for her son, lost her husband.

Osman Ali Khan became the Nizam on 18 September 1911. His succession was proclaimed by the beating of drums from the top of the surviving gates of the city, as had been done five times previously since the city became the capital of the Nizams in 1763.

Some members of the nobility had reservations about the claim of Osman to the masnad. There was also a petition to the Viceroy on the subject of Osman Ali Khan's succession to the *gaddi*. They had treated him with cool aloofness when he was the heir apparent and did not show proper respect even after he became the ruler. Osman mentioned this to Shahab Jung, the Minister of Police. The Minister said he was willing to be made an example if it helped to drive home the point to the other nobles that they had to acknowledge the new ruler. As agreed between the two, the next day Shahab Jung came late to the court. The Nizam was to reprimand him but as he started doing that in mock anger, he lost his temper and expelled him from the court. Shahab Jung, out of disgrace, could not move out of his house thereafter. But the new Nizam's standing amongst his nobles was established and thereafter there was no trouble.[84]

With Osman's accession, the old order gave place to the new. Not only was there was a disparity of age between the ruler who was barely 25 and his premier, Kishen Pershad, who was about twice his age; there was also a new coterie working against Kishen Pershad and intrigues abounded.

An ambitious and unscrupulous police officer had ingratiated himself with the new Nizam and had risen to be the Commissioner of Police. He claimed that, amongst others, Kishen Pershad and Sir Nizamat Jung, the Acting Political Secretary, had plotted to send a memorial to the Viceroy submitting that Osman Ali Khan was not the real heir but a pretender to the masnad of Hyderabad. Sir Nizamat had been approached to turn an approver. He repulsed the offer and had the facts conveyed to the Nizam through Sir Faridoon Mulk. An inquiry was then ordered. A British handwriting expert from Calcutta, Hardless, opined that most of the signatures in the memorial were forged. It was established that it was entirely beyond the Maharaja to indulge in such a treasonable act. But the damage had been done.

Just as the young Mahboob had started his reign with an equally young Prime Minister, Laik Ali, so did now his son choose the deceased Diwan's son, Yusuf Ali Khan, as his Diwan. Upon the selection of the new Diwan in 1912, a poet called Ahsan—playing masterfully upon the legend of Yusuf and Zuleikha and the double meaning of Diwani, (it means both premiership and an insane woman)—wrote a poem, the concluding line of which yielded the chronogram of the assumption of premiership by Yusuf Ali Khan, Salar Jung III:

> *Zuleikha ban ke diwani mere Yusuf ke ghar ayee.*
>
> (Zuleikha, insane with love, came to the house of my Yusuf).

In a repetition of history, Yusuf too, like his father, lost the Prime-Ministership within two years. Unlike his father, however, he did not go out of the state to die broken-hearted in self-imposed exile; he sublimated his will to power and glory by his indulgence in a very unusual hobby.

Brought up without a father who had died before he was one year old, Yusuf was over-protected by his young mother, Zainab Begum. She was very proud of the family and watched over the young boy like a hawk. Yusuf, an introvert and romantic by nature, had wanted to marry a cousin on his father's side when still in his teens. The mother did not approve of the alliance. He turned to another cousin, and thereafter he felt infatuated by the Resident's daughter. Many other women, from other religions also, caught his fancy but none was approved. So, he decided to remain a bachelor all his life.

He had hardly settled in the Prime-Ministership when he was eased out of it in 1917. His mother was alarmed as the same fate of her husband, who had died of a broken heart at the age of 27 on losing the Diwani, seemed to be overtaking her 25-year-old son. Now she was willing to waive her objection to any match of his choice. But he was no longer interested. Yusuf went into a severe depression. She sent for the family physician, Dr Hunt. When the doctor's examination revealed that there was no ailment, she asked him to treat the depression.

Dr Hunt started talking of various matters of interest to the young man.

'Some of the European nobles save themselves from boredom by collecting art objects,' observed the physician neutrally. 'And that is, good business too,' he added with a chuckle.

Yusuf just nodded his head.

The first thing Yusuf did that evening was to take stock of all the family heirlooms and antiques. His grandfather, and later his father, had received many presents from dignitaries from all over the world. Even before his grandfather's time the family had a pretty good collection of antiques and valuables, collected during their trips to Europe. The Veiled Rebecca—a masterpiece by the Italian sculptor, Benzoni—and the double statue of Mephistopheles and Marguerite, which were to become the pride of the collection, were the acquisitions of the first Salar Jung. Then there were books—ranging from oriental manuscripts of the Quran and the illustrated anthology of Mohammad Quli to the works of less well-known authors. He already had a core, he thought, and set about organizing and expanding it.

He asked Guzder, his favourite jeweller from Bombay, to help him evaluate some foreign jewellry. The local auction halls belonging to J. Moosa, Rahim Khan, and Abdul Aziz became his agents for the collection of antiques. The word reached Christies and Sothebys of London and they began to treat him as a valued client. They would regularly send their catalogues to him and inform him in advance about the rare objects being handled by them. He made a lot of purchases during his two trips abroad and crates kept on being unloaded for him for months after his return.

His residence in the city and at Saroornagar became a haunt of antiquarians, art dealers, jewellers, booksellers, and all types of people who had anything they believed would interest him. Sometimes he was duped. Whatever he acquired was first kept on the big round marble table near the statue of the Veiled Rebecca in the hall of his mansion at the Diwan Deodhi so that his friends and visitors could see the exhibits before they were sent to the appropriate warehouse for storage or to one of his rooms for display. One day Abdul Aziz noticed a statuette at the display table and instead of praising it, as he was wont to, he kept a discreet silence. Salar Jung detected disapproval in that silence. 'I know,' he said with a defensive smile, 'the piece is counterfeit. But the man needed money.' He made some purchases just to help some people out of their difficulties. His acquisitions were sometimes also acts of indirect charity.

In course of time, Yusuf came to own a formidable collection. Over 43,000 art objects, 47,000 books, and 9,000 manuscripts comprised a unique one-man collection in the whole world. Once he bought an entire mansion in Poona called the *Glad Hust* just to acquire the glass, porcelain, and other objects which it contained. His collection could now boast of Noor Jahan's dagger, Jahangir's wine cup, and Aurangzeb's sword, to mention only a few items. His European paintings included both originals as well as copies.

Salar Jung had plans to set up a museum either at Khwaja Pahadi near the Mir Alam Tank or at Maula Ali. He even considered Ooty or Poona as possible sites for his project and spent a good deal of money on the blueprints. But before any design could be finalized he was plucked away in March 1949. He was not yet 60. His last purchase—a set of ivory chairs belonging to Tippu Sultan—arrived after his death.

After his death, when it was decided to set up a museum to house his collection, some 114 parties rose to lay claim to his estate including his acquisitions. The government stepped in to effect a compromise and on the renunciation of the claims, a museum was set up in 1951 at the official and hereditary residence of the Salar Jungs—the Diwan Deodhi. It was a sprawling 100-room palace about 250 years old in a setting of the Arabian Nights.

Apart from other things, for dilettantes and connoisseurs, for the discerning and the crank, for the pedant and the scholar, a masterpiece of the collection is a clock made in the likeness of a cottage stood on a raised platform. Every hour, a bird coos and the door of the cottage opens. An old woodcutter, with an axe in his hand, then emerges and strikes the hour. Today, forty years later, the clock still works and remains the chief attraction for visitors of all ages.

The Museum became an institution of national importance by an Act of Parliament enacted in 1961. It moved into a new, typically soul-less government building in 1968. The statue of the Collector stands facing the building, as if keeping a watch over its contents and seeing who comes to see his collection. Some 15,000 visitors of all ages and from all over visit it every day. Yet, no one can see more than one-third of the collection of a lifetime because the rest are not on display. No one's visit to the city is complete without a call on Yusuf's House of Wonder. Later the architectural design of the building has been improved.

❖ ❖ ❖

The floods of 1908 proved a blessing in disguise. When a large part of the old medieval city was destroyed, it was decided to appoint an expert to suggest measures to prevent the recurrence of such a tragedy. The job went to the great engineer-statesman, Sir M. Viswesvarayya of Mysore.

Viswesvarayya submitted his report on 1 October 1909. By the time it was examined, Mir Osman Ali Khan had succeeded as Nizam VII. Viswesvarayya's report prompted a spurt of planned growth under Nizam VII. His recommendations covered not only measures to prevent the recurrence of floods, but also the improvement of the outdated civic amenities.[85] A City Improvement Trust was constituted in 1912 under the Chairmanship of the Junior Prince, Muazzam Jah. The wide Pathargatti Bazar, from the south bank of the Musi to Charminar, with shops on the ground and flats on the first floor was the first to be laid. It remains one of the widest bazaars in the country even today. The next was the Osman Sagar Reservoir constructed on river Musi and its tributary, the Esi in 1920. Another reservoir called Himayat Sagar was constructed in 1927. These lakes prevented the flooding of the river Musi, but also served as reservoirs for drinking water for the city. The building of the State High Court, designed by a Rajasthani architect, Shankar Lal, on the south bank of the river Musi was completed on 31 March 1919. Built in red and white stone in the Saracenic style, it presents a fine specimen of architecture. Opposite the High Court, across the river, the Osmania Hospital was constructed in 1927. The beautiful building houses one of the largest hospitals.

Visveswarayya submitted another report in 1930. This brief 25-page report presaged the Master Plan of Hyderabad, promulgated finally in 1977. It suggested the modern city concepts of outer and inner ring roads, zoning, slum clearance, sewerage and drainage schemes, construction of markets and the like—all at a cost of Rs 44.7 million.[86]

A modern market called the Muazzam Jahi Market with granite stone and a clock tower was constructed in 1935. A wide cement concrete road named Mukarram Jahi Road, after the grandson of the Nizam, led to it from the Public Garden. A number of low-income group houses were constructed along with a separate complex for bachelors. A good number of roads in the city were paved with cement slabs.

The Asafiya Library, established in 1891, was shifted to a new imposing building less than a kilometre away from the Osmania Hospital in 1936. It is now called the State Central Library.

In the Public Garden, laid out in 1864, the Nizam had built a palace for one of his daughters. It was called 'Doll's House'. However, due to a superstition, she did not occupy the palace. In 1930, at the suggestion of the first Director of Archeology, Ghulam Yazdani, it was converted into the State Museum. This museum has the largest collection of coins in the world after the British Museum. These include, besides Indian coins from fifth century BC, some Roman coins also. It is the only museum in the country, which has facsimiles of the Ajanta paintings. They were made by two artists of Hyderabad—Syed Ahmed and Mohammad Jamaluddin—under the guidance of an Italian painter. The museum has a number of sculptures belonging to the Hindu, Buddhist, and Jain periods. It also has an impressive collection of bronzes from as early as the second century BC, the masterpiece being the unusual Nataraja of the tenth century. Its manuscript section includes a copy of the Quran bearing the seal of Emperor Shah Jahan. Another copy of the Quran is in manuscript form by Dara Shikoh in 1664, while a third is by his brother, Aurangzeb.

The Museum has a 3,000–year old mummy of an Egyptian Princess. It is one of the five mummies in India. The arms in the museum include a shield belonging to Shah Jahan and a jewel-studded sword of the Nizam.

The silver jubilee of Nizam VII was held in 1937—a year later than due because of the death of King George V in 1936. To commemorate it, the beautiful Jubilee Hall with appurtenant buildings was constructed in the Public Gardens.

The first Industrial Exhibition was held in the Public Garden in 1938. Later it was shifted to the present Exhibition Grounds and became an annual feature.

The Osmania University, named after the seventh Nizam, was established in 1919. It was located temporarily in rented premises in the city while action was initiated to construct a building for it. Sir Patrick Geddes selected an area of 1,400 acres for setting up the complex. In 1930, two eminent architects of Hyderabad—Nawab Zain Yar Jung and Syed Ali Raza—were sent abroad to study the architecture of various Universities of the world. On their recommendation, a Belgian expert, Jasper, was entrusted with the task of preparing the design of the new building. Engaged in 1933, Jasper visited various places in India including Bidar, Golconda, Charminar, Ajanta and Ellora caves, and Delhi to study the features of Indian architecture. The first building of the University, the Arts College, was inaugurated in 1938. An imposing granite structure, it combines the dominant characteristics of the Hindu style with that of the Saracenic. In this unique form are also beautifully blended medieval Muslim, Arab, Moorish, and even Gothic forms of architecture. The building stands majestically amidst neatly laid out gardens. It is indeed a jewel in the architectural crown of the Nizam.

It was unique in that it was the first University in India with an Indian language as the medium of instruction. A Bureau of Translation was established in the University to translate important books from European languages into Urdu. From 1918 to 1948, when the medium of instruction was changed to English, it translated 380 books at a cost of Rs 400,000. It recruited staff largely from outside the state. C. Rajagopalachari, the renowned Indian statesman was so impressed with the use of an Indian language as a medium of instruction that in his convocation address at the university in 1943 he called it a 'national university, the true Vidya Peeth'. Later other buildings and hostels were added to it. The physical amenities provided in the University, as corroborated by professors coming from other Indian Universities, were the best in India. Sibte Hasan, who had come from the north, asked Makhdoom Mohiuddin, who was studying in the University at the time: 'The students live in such luxury here. What will they do after leaving the University?' Makhdoom replied with his typical laugh: 'Become clerks under the government'.[87]

The city thus was revitalized and looked beautiful. Urdu poets and men of letters who were attracted to it from all over the country called it *Uroos-ul-balad*—a bride amongst cities. The Nizam and his subjects were rightly proud of the new-look city. Indeed, no public building constructed after the seventh Nizam matches the grandeur and majesty of those built during his time.

Amongst the social and political reforms carried out during the regime of the seventh Nizam were the abolition of the death penalty, the banning of bonded labour, and separation of judiciary from the executive—all in 1922. Hyderabad was also the first state in India to set up a public sector unit—the Road Transport Department—as a part of the Nizam's State Railways in 1932.

The Masters of Verse

In Islam, traditionally, the ideal ruler should be a master of the pen as well as the sword. It was customary, therefore, that some eminent poet was appointed to teach his royal pupil the art of composing poetry. He also corrected and improved the poems written by the Princes.

Amongst the Qutb Shahi Sultans, Mohammad Quli and his successor, Sultan Mohammad, were poets of great merit. Abdullah also wrote some poems. Amongst the Nizams, the first Nizam and his son, Nasir Jung, wrote poetry in Persian. Later, Mahboob Ali Khan, the sixth Nizam, and Osman Ali Khan, the seventh Nizam, also composed poetry. They also appointed court-poets who also acted as their *ustads*—preceptors.

Mahboob Ali Khan and his nobles also extended patronage to a large number of poets, and after the demise of the Mughal Empire and the disappearance of the Lucknow and the Rampur courts, their patronage became especially important. As a result, Hyderabad became the greatest magnet for Urdu poets. They flocked here from all parts of the country to try their luck. Mushairas were a great feature of the cultural life of the city and five of them became particularly famous which included those held at the residence of Jamedar Muniruddin and Maharaja Kishen Pershad.

Dagh was a poet at the court of the Nawab of Rampur. His employment terminated there after the death of Nawab Kalab Ali

Khan and he came then to Hyderabad in 1887. In a short while, he became very popular but did not succeed in gaining access to the Nizam. When his fame spread, Maharaja Kishen Pershad mentioned his name to Mahboob Ali Khan and praised his accomplishments as a poet. Mahboob sent for him and liked his poetry immensely. After that he was called occasionally and sometimes was asked to join the Nizam for dinner also. But he did not get a job or any other help.

A year passed. One day when Mahboob went for a hunt in the wilderness of the jungle he suddenly thought of Dagh. He asked his Prime Minister to send for the poet. Messengers were rushed and a harried but expectant Dagh presented himself at the camp.

The next evening, the royal horse-trainers were exhibiting their skills with some horses for the amusement of the Nizam. One horse was particularly obstinate but the trainer was equally tenacious. Enjoying the struggle, Mahboob suddenly turned to Dagh and asked, 'Have you ever sat on a horse?'

Dagh folded his hands and replied, 'Yes, My Lord. But it was so long ago in my childhood.'

'Right then,' observed the ruler, 'let us see how you ride,' and he asked that the frisky horse be brought to the hapless poet.

As soon as Dagh mounted the horse, the trainer, on a hint from the Nizam, cracked a whip on the beast. The horse bolted and Dagh fell on the ground. Luckily, he was unhurt. The Nizam broke into uncontrollable laughter at the discomfiture of the poet. When he had finished, he said mockingly: 'You are a good rider. I shall appoint you as officer of my trainers!'

Dagh made salaams in gratefulness though the job did not suit him. Then, as if changing the topic, the Nizam asked him: 'How long have you been here?'

'Ten years, Your Highness.'

The Nizam turned to Kishen Pershad, and said: 'We are pleased to appoint Dagh as our poet-laureate with a salary of Rs 1,000 a month. Retrospectively. Have his salary paid at that rate for the last ten years.'

'As it pleases Your Highness,' said the Maharaja obediently. The next day a number of carts bearing 110,000 silver coins pulled up in front of Dagh's house.[88]

For the rest of his life Dagh did not know any want. He died in February 1905.

Jaleel Manikpuri also came from Rampur in 1900 to seek his fortune in Hyderabad. He had to wait for nine long years before dame luck smiled on him.

Maharaja Kishen Pershad had organized a mushaira on the occasion of the jubilee of Nizam VI in 1905. The Nizam himself attended it and, instead of taking the gilded chair specially provided for him, he sat on the floor along with the others. Amongst the poets present were well-known names like 'Shostri', Abdul Jabbar Khan 'Asafi', Girdhari Lal 'Baqi', Abdul Ali 'Wala', Turk Ali Shah 'Turki', Ghulam Quadir 'Girami', Zahir 'Dehlvi', Sirajuddin 'Sayar', Zia Yar 'Jung', 'Tabatabai', 'Rasa','Azad' Ansari, Nawab Vazir-ud-Dowlah, Nadir Ali 'Bartar', 'Wasafi', 'Alam', Mahboob Raj 'Mahboob', and Abid Ali 'Begum'. The last one was a poet who dressed, wrote, and recited as if he were a woman and so provided the humourous touch in the proceedings. In one mushaira he read a couplet in which he expressed gratitude to his patron, Maharaja Kishen Pershad, who had granted him a monthly stipend. Using a double entendre he said, 'Thanks to the Maharaja, I still get my monthly.' The Maharaja retorted: 'Strange. I have grown old but you still get your monthlies.'

Some nobles also were present at this mushaira. Maulana Hali, the famous poet from the north who happened to be here was also invited.

The poets sat in a semi-circle. Since it was a special jubilee mushaira, only *qasidas*—poems of praise—were to be recited and the length of each poem was restricted to 12 couplets. A tall candle in a gold stand with the personal emblem of Kishen Pershad was brought by a liveried attendant and was kept in the centre. This, when placed in front of a poet, marked his turn for recitation in order of juniority. Overhead hung a giant chandelier. The walls of the hall had life-size mirrors in gilded frames. A portrait of the Nizam stood smiling over the main door. The host said a few words of welcome to his ruler, congratulated him on his silver jubilee, and wished him many more. Then the Master of Ceremonies gave a brief introduction of all the poets. As each poet was introduced, he got up and made seven salaams to the royal guest. Thereafter, the proceedings began. A copy of each poem recited there had been framed earlier and immediately after its recitation, was presented to the Nizam.

Normally, a mushaira is a loud affair and there is no dearth of praise even from rival poets by way of professional courtesy. Encores for a line or a couplet are quite common. But somehow in this session there was no special applause; no shouts for encore. After a while the Nizam who sat impassively reclining against a bolster, whispered to the host, Kishen Pershad. He then broke the order of roll call of the poets and invited the newcomer Jaleel to recite his poem. He was an instant success. The Nizam, who was almost dozing off with boredom, sat up and exclaimed, '*Wah*! Well done'.

The drowsy assembly suddenly woke up at this exclamation. Thereafter Jaleel could not cope with shouts of praise and he had to stop midway at every line to acknowledge the cheers by salaaming many times. He took one hour to complete the recitation of the prescribed 12 couplets.

When the sitting was over at about 4 a.m. and the poets started leaving, the Prime Minister stopped Jaleel at the door. His Highness wanted him back. Jaleel returned excitedly and made his salutation to the Nizam. Mahboob said he wanted to hear the complete poem again. When a search was started for his framed poem, Jaleel said he had a copy with him. The Nizam heard the poem with rapt attention and was loud and generous in his praise.

Some time later Jaleel wrote a book dealing with the gender of 7,000 words in Urdu. He presented a copy of it to the Nizam. The ruler leafed through the book and then said cryptically in Urdu: '*Jaleel-ul-qadr ho saheb tumhari bat kya kehna*' (You are just great; what comment can one make?).

Jaleel was overwhelmed by this compliment. He treated this exclamation as a hemistich and composed a couplet on the spot. The Nizam was pleased. Another year passed. At a ceremony in his palace, for commencing instruction in the Holy Quran to a Prince, Mahboob had composed a poem but wasn't satisfied with it. He asked for Jaleel. When Jaleel came, he said that a particular word bothered him. He wanted to change it but was unable to think of the right word. Jaleel successively suggested different

The Ancient Rocks in Fantastic Shapes are an Important Feature

The First Meeting between Mohammad Quli and Bhagmati

A Replica of Heaven

1 Dad Mahal 2 Khudadad Mahal 4 Lal Mahal
3 Chandan Mahal 5 Saat Mahal 6 Record Office
7 Jamshed Mahal 8 Nadi Mahal 9 Jilan Mahal

10 Jama Masjid

Hyderabad (Bhagnagar). The artist's impression of the
original layout.
Conceived by S.P. Shorey, based on historical accounts
Drawings/colour artwork by Kshara Advertising, Hyderabad
after Shorey's axonometric drawing.
Copyright*

Mir Qamaruddin, Nizam I

SIR RONALD ROSS
1857 — 1932

Sir Ronald Ross, Winner
of the Nobel Prize for
Medicine

Raja Deen Dayal, India's Greatest Photographer

Silver Jubilee of Mir Osman Ali Khan Nizam VII Held in 1937

B. Ramakrishna Rao, the
First Popularly Elected Chief
Minister of Hyderabad in
1952.

N.T. Rama Rao,
a Film Star and
Founder of the TDP
who Became Chief
Minister of Andhra
Pradesh Thrice

HITEC City Towers at Hyderabad Marking the Birth of 'Cyberabad'

K. Chandrasekhar Rao, Chief
Minister of Telangana, 2 June 2014

words. On the fourth attempt, the Nizam jumped up. 'Yes. That's it.' And he made the correction in pencil.

A few days later, in 1909, Jaleel was appointed a successor to Dagh as the royal tutor on a salary of Rs 500 a month. By another order he was also appointed a royal companion. When Mahboob passed away in 1911 and Osman succeeded him, Jaleel's appointment was renewed. So he became the new ruler's tutor and courtier as well.

As the official poet, Jaleel was required to attend the court daily and had to compose at least one poem every day, and sometimes more on various occasions. The Nizam used to send his compositions to Jaleel's house through a special messenger in a sealed cover. They had to be returned after corrections the next day. Sometimes the bearer would wait on till they were corrected. Then the frequency increased. Some days a dozen poems would come one after the other. The ustad had to be available from around 8 a.m. to 10 p.m. because the special courier could come any time.

The seventh Nizam used to write with a pencil, on scraps of paper—and on both sides. Sometimes he wrote on the flap of a cigarette packet if that was the only thing handy at that time. Apart from the needed corrections which had to be made in very respectful terms, Jaleel was required to give his opinion on each couplet and shower all possible praise on those which needed no emendation. Remarks like 'Excellent', 'Congratulations', 'Superb', 'What an idea!' 'One in a million; my humble praise', etc. were made in the margin or below a given word or phrase. In addition, a general assessment had to be given on the poem as a whole, and it had better be positive. While the poem was written in pencil, the amendments were made in red ink.

Osman was possessive about his teacher and did not like him to give instructions to anybody else. Only Kishen Pershad was exempted from that injunction. Jaleel's other pupils had therefore to maintain secrecy about their relationship with him. Once Nawab Qudrat Jung, brother of Osman's wife Dulhan Pasha, showed him a poem of his as corrected by Jaleel. The Nizam was enraged and smudged out the corrections. The ustad was also not allowed to participate in any mushaira. The Nizam himself also never took part in any. His compositions could be recited only in the mushairas of Maharaja Kishen Pershad. They used to be received with due ceremony and someone particularly good at delivery was chosen to recite them. Everyone in the gathering would try to out-shout each other in their exclamations of praise with the knowledge that the 'conduct' of the participants would be reported duly to His Highness.

In the royal sittings, only the Nizam's poetry was recited and the ustad was expected to make instant corrections, if necessary.

Osman's earlier compositions are regarded as superior to his later work because then he used to take corrections regularly. Later, when he felt that he was no longer in need of instruction, the quality of his poems deteriorated.

In Urdu poetry, one of the signs of virtuosity is the composition of chronograms in verse. Osman was not good at it. He would compose something and indicate the date he wanted it to yield. It was then the business of his ustad to make the necessary adjustments. Sometimes he would give a line and the ustad had then to compose one or more poems on the basis of the metre and rhyme of the given line.

The job of the ustad was therefore not easy and required perhaps more than the mastery of prosody, a degree of astuteness to survive. But Jaleel did well and served two Nizams successfully from 1909 till his death in 1946. In due course, his salary was increased from Rs 500 to Rs 1,000 a month. By a strange accounting procedure, the salary was paid from the state exchequer but routed through the *sarf-e-khas*—personal estate office—of the Nizam. Once, as a measure of economy, the salaries of all sarf-e-khas employees were reduced by half. Jaleel too suffered the cut. Then, some auditor pointed out that the cut could not apply to Jaleel because he was being paid by the state. The Sarf-e-khas was only a disbursing agency and all the while it was receiving the full amount from the state exchequer. Thereupon, the full salary was restored but the arrears were not paid. The Nizam, Osman Ali Khan, told Jaleel not to worry; the arrears, about Rs 100,000, were intact; they were with him in trust, and would be paid to him whenever he needed them. Jaleel never got the amount.[89]

Poetry and royalty cannot go together easily. Most lyrical poetry is born out of poverty of means, of frustration, of a feeling of deprivation, and of injustice. By the sheer surfeit of power and affluence, these impulses are denied to rulers. Their lyrical poetry therefore lacks the authentic touch; it has a false ring about it. Most of the poetry becomes a matter of craftsmanship in the hands of ruler-poets. Osman Ali Khan was no exception to this rule. Notice his yearning for yearning:

> *She would not hear the story.*
> *Of yearning love and pain.*
> *No word she let me utter*
> *All efforts were in vain.*

But there are some good couplets in which he describes the beauty of his beloved or praises his own poetry—a traditional foible of Urdu poets.

There is one couplet in the style of one of his celebrated predecessors—four centuries and a dynasty removed from him—Mohammad Quli Qutb Shah, when he confesses to his hedonism:

> *Mujhe shahid parasti se nahin inkar ai Osman*
> *Na abid hoon, na zahid hoon, na alim hoon, na fazil hoon.*

(Worship of idols I do not deny
Not scholar, believer, nor ascetic am I.)

Such declarations could be made in verse with impunity, not in prose. Once, he wrote:

> *Salatin-e-salf ho gaye nazar-e-ajal Osman*
> *Musalmanon ka teri saltanat se hai nishan baqi*

(Sultans of old, O' Osman, have all died
By your rule are Muslims now identified)[90]

But he wrote profusely and two volumes of his verses were published. Some sycophantic courtiers praised his poetry to the skies and suggested that it ought to be prescribed as a text for the graduate course in the Osmania University. The Nizam approved the idea. Moulvi Abdul Haq, popularly known as the 'Grand old man of Urdu', was the Professor of Urdu at the University and it fell to him to implement the orders. The moulvi was in a fix. If he did not carry out the edict, he would attract the royal ire; on the other hand if he obeyed meekly, he would become the laughing stock amongst the men of letters. He asked for an audience with the Nizam. When he reached the Presence, he saw the Nizam sitting in a rickety chair. Manzoor Jung, Hosh Bilgrami, and Zain Yar Jung were standing in front of him.

'Yes, Moulvi, have you seen our orders?' asked the Nizam as he saw the savant.

'Yes, My Lord,' submitted the professor, 'your compositions are royal amongst verses. What can be a greater honour for me than to expound those to students? But my humble submission is that this worthless creature lacks the necessary depth of scholarship to be able to explain them adequately to students. Your Exalted Highness' slave thought of presenting himself before his master many times in order to obtain an adequate understanding of the subtle points in the royal verses but I couldn't gather enough courage for fear that if, in spite of His Exalted Highness' expostulation, my limited brains could not grasp them, then what would I do?'

The Nizam turned to his favourite acolyte, Hosh Bilgrami: 'Do you hear what he says?' Hosh stepped forward with folded hands. 'Yes, My Lord and Master. The royal composition is indeed royal amongst the common compositions. It is not easy to explain it.'

'You are right,' observed the Nizam, 'if the teacher himself can't understand, how will he explain it to students? That's right. But,' he added after a pause, 'how long do you think it will take for the University to get such teachers who can appreciate my verse adequately?'

'My Gracious Lord,' submitted Hosh, 'it depends not on the verses but on the intelligence of the reader.'

'Right you are. It is the intelligence that matters. I can give them my poems, but I can't give them the intelligence necessary to grasp them. Cancel the orders for teaching my poems in the University. Let them understand them first.' So the 'mad' Moulvi, as the Nizam used to call him, saved the students from the imposition.[91]

Osman patronized other poets too. Amongst them the most celebrated was Josh Malihabadi, who later fell from his grace and was banished from the state. His entry and exit were equally dramatic. He later migrated to Pakistan and died an unhappy man there.

The Princes and other nobles too had their circle of poets who attended their darbars every evening. They were lavishly fed and some of them were even paid a stipend. In return they had to listen to the poetry of those worthies through most of the night, praise them to the skies and return home jaded and pale at the crack of dawn.

Mir Shujjat Ali Khan Muazzam Jah, the second son of Nizam VII, was also a poet. He sported the pen name of Shajeeh (the 'bold one'). He had his own glittering nocturnal court at the Hill Fort Palace, which later housed the Ritz Hotel. 'Fani', Sidq Jaisi, 'Mahir', and 'Najm' Afandi were the leading minstrels of this court, besides many other poetasters and hangers-on. Sidq Jaisi, who spent over two decades in Hyderabad, wrote an interesting account of the nightlife of Muazzam Jah's court and the indignities he and others had to suffer there.

That interesting book in Urdu, *Darbaar-e-Dürbaar* gives an authentic picture of the degenerate life led by the royalty and nobility in a feudal system. It also shows how divorced that life was from the lives of the common people. Wine, woman, and song were the preoccupation of those people whom the accident of birth had provided a golden spoon at the start of their life.[92]

'Shajeeh' was the last of the royal poets. His poems are easy to understand and are still sung at parties. Often, when the composition of the masters are being recited by singers, someone, exhibiting his claim to the knowledge of the 'culture of Hyderabad', asks for a poem by 'Shajeeh'. Ghazals are written even today. Poets recite them in public mushairas where thousands gather to cheer and heckle them. However, the tradition of the mushairas of Hyderabad has lately been in decline.

Chunnu Nawab and the 'Balishter'

After sacking the Prime Minister Salar Jung II in 1914, Mir Osman Ali Khan decided to do away with that office and embarked on direct rule. For five years, therefore, which coincided with the duration of the First World War, he had no Premier. He gave tremendous support to the British in their war effort by way of money and men. In grateful acknowledgement of that help the British promoted him from a simple 'Highness' to 'Exalted Highness'. He was also given the title of the 'Faithful Ally' of the British.

However, they pressed him to end his direct rule and install a ministry. In November 1919, the Nizam announced reforms in the governance of the state. In the place of the earlier Cabinet Council, he introduced the system of an Executive Council. This council consisted of a President, seven ordinary members, and one extraordinary member without portfolio. Those powers, which the Nizam did not reserve to himself, were to be exercised by the council of nine.

Sir Ali Imam—a prominent barrister from Bihar who had served as a member of the Viceroy's Executive Council and who, at the time was a member of the Executive Council of Bihar and Orissa—was appointed President of the new Executive Council— or the Prime Minister in 1919. In his letter of acceptance, Ali Imam noted that to 'have the privilege of serving a Muslim Sovereign is an inestimable distinction to a man of the same faith and it is my conviction that to serve such a Potentate is to serve Islam'.[93]

Ali Imam was no a stranger to Hyderabad. He had made a professional visit to Hyderabad before, when he had come to appear in a case in the High Court there.

On the way down, when his train stopped at Veyjapur station, he saw a huge crowd surrounding a squat, fat, pompous person who was receiving tributes from all sorts of people. Someone would come and make a bow before him and pass on. Another fellow would come and tie an *imam-e-zamin* and hug him or garland him, or present a bouquet of flowers. Liveried servants were rushing into and out of the first-class compartment of the train and loading it with suitcases, trunks, bedrolls, tiffin-carriers, fruit-baskets, bouquets, spittoons, silver tumblers, towels, a small carpet for prayers, and numerous other knick-knacks.

Ali Imam became curious to know what this rush was all about. He asked one of the servants and was told that the local tahsildar—Revenue Officer—Chunnu Nawab, was going to Hyderabad on leave.

The train whistled, Chunnu Nawab bade farewell to the crowd and boarded the train.

'Well, what do you do?' Chunnu Nawab asked Ali Imam after discharging a red streak of saliva into the polished spittoon kept by the side of his berth.

'I am a barrister,' he explained, ' I do *vakalat*.'

'Oh. So you are a vakil,' exclaimed the Nawab. 'I understand. Vakils appear before me also. So far no balishter has appeared in my court, but many vakils have. These balishters are nothing before our vakils!'

With that, the bulky official opened up and there was no stopping him. 'Balishter, you said. How much can you make in a month? Have you bought a car? Have you constructed a house?' Then as if explaining to himself, he said: 'Must be making good money. How else could you be traveling Fus klas!'

Ali Imam said, 'Well, I earn enough to afford *dal* and *roti*.'

'Dal and roti', Chunnu remarked with contempt, 'are for un-enterprising people? The voluble tahsildar, then advised him to get out of 'balishtery'. For a tahsildar like himself a salary of

Rs 200 is 'for pan and *beedi*. The rest depends on your skill. You must have the knack.'

As the barrister's name, Ali Imam, struck no familiar chord, Chunnu Nawab enquired and soon learnt that his companion was headed for Hyderabad High Court to argue a case.

'Oh, the High Court—yes—*adalat-e-aliya*. Great. It is a big court. But some day you must appear in a tahsildar's court. Come to my court and see the glory. You will forget your balishtery.'

Ali Imam smiled, 'Perhaps, some day I will achieve that honour too.'

Then Ali Imam asked: 'What is that knack you were talking about? You mean ability?'

'No *Janab*, not ability, *knack*. The knack to make income from above.'

'From above?' Imam feigned surprise. 'All income is from above,' he said looking towards the ceiling of the compartment and beyond. 'Allah gives us all we have.'

'A real good tahsildar knows what to make and how. You have to control these rascals—these mali patels and police patels. Otherwise they will eat you up. It is his subjects who look after the tahsildar—the people, you know.'

The train slowed down and then it pulled up at a station. A bearer came to take orders for lunch. The Brandon Company used to be the caterer on the Nizam's State Railways.

Ali Imam was about to order his lunch. But Chunnu Nawab waved the bearer aside. 'What lunch? Don't you see what we have?' And then addressing Ali Imam he said, 'Eat with me, Janab. All these things which people in their affection have loaded me with—I can't eat them alone. And then these will be better than the dull tasteless food which you get from these English companies.' Turning to the bearer once again, he said. 'Oh yes, do bring six or seven lemnid and sodas.'

'Why so many lemonades and sodas?' asked Ali Imam in surprise. Chunnu Nawab replied casually: 'It is a matter of status, Janab. A tahsildar can't just order one or two drinks. Whatever is left over will be consumed by the servants.'

Chunnu Nawab pressed Ali Imam to gorge on the delicacies. Having finished, he belched.

Presently the train steamed into the city's main station at Nampally. A number of people had come to receive Chunnu Nawab. Only his client had come to meet Ali Imam.

'Well, you haven't given me your name tahsildar sahib?'

'I am Zain-ul-Abdeen,' he replied briefly. 'But everybody knows me as Chunnu Nawab. You can ask anyone, anywhere. He will know. And, by the way, if you need any help in the city, please let me know. I have friends here in high places.'

Less than a year later, Ali Imam came as President of the Nizam's Executive Council. Soon after settling down, he expressed a wish to see a certain tahsildar, a man called Chunnu Nawab. 'Chunnu Nawab Sahib,' Ali Imam beamed as he got up from his seat and came forward to greet the immobile flunkey standing there. 'How are you?'

'With the kind blessings of the *sarkar*, this particle of dust is doing fine, huzoor. Orders for me?'

Neither his reply nor his features betrayed any hint of recognition.

'You remember our last meeting Chunnu Miyan,' Sir Ali Imam smiled, 'when you were so generous to me.'

'There must be a mistake, sarkar. This slave has not had the good fortune of ever having had the noble sight before.'

'It is a great honour for me to have had an audience with Your Excellency, thanks to some mix-up. I shall forever remember this privilege proudly. Orders for this humble creature?' the expressionless moron repeated.

The Prime Minister understood. After all he was a tahsildar of the old school. If he had tackled those rascals of mali patels and police patels for 30 years, he would certainly know how to dispose of a mere Prime Minister, and a novice at that. Sir Ali Imam gave up. He came forward, patted the bowed official's back and by way of a return of the gesture of last year, he said, 'Good to see you. If I can do anything, do let me know.'

Zain-ul-Abdeen, alias Chunnu Nawab, still had a year or so to go in service. He came home and, on the plea of ill health, asked for pre-mature retirement. Let me leave while the going is good, he thought, why get into trouble after such a long and distinguished service?[94]

Sir Ali was a gracious and dignified man who beamed with self-
-confidence. He believed the administration needed immediate
reform. To the specific task allotted to him by the Nizam, namely,
the return of Berar, he added two more himself. They were the
grant of franchise to the people and the reclamation of wastelands
in the state for colonization. For both of these, he had the Nizam
issue firmans. Three months after he joined, a firman, promising
reforms in the legislative system proclaimed, 'it would achieve the
aspirations of our dear subjects and take them on the path of progress.' A committee, under the Chairmanship of a former judge of
the High Court, Balmukand, was set up to suggest the pattern of
reforms. The committee submitted its proposals after one-and-a-
half years but for one reason or the other they were never implemented.[95] It was alleged that the scheme for colonization intended
to increase the Muslim population of Hyderabad by encouraging
the immigration of Muslims from Bihar and UP. It did not meet
with much success due to malpractices in the initial stages.

However, he was able to introduce one important reform,
namely, the separation of the judiciary from the legislature.
Hyderabad, thus became the first state in India to introduce this
basic principle of separation of powers in 1922.

When Ali Imam came upon the scene, life in Hyderabad was
apparently calm. The demands of the State Reforms Association
also were very modest. However, political stirrings, like the Non-
Cooperation Movement and the Khilafat Movement, had started
in British India and they had begun to be echoed in the state. Even
that alarmed the government and the Police Secretary, in a note to
the Prime Minister, observed that the developments were 'becoming increasingly dangerous'.

Hyderabad was the great centre of a unique type of life style,
heavily oriental with Muslim accent. Everybody, from the Nizam
down to a peon in an office was similarly dressed in a sherwani
and narrow-bottom pajamas in which the ankles showed somewhat awkwardly. Most people wore the Turkish cap with a tassel,
though some Hindus wore a different type of a cap or a turban.

Women wore saris and it was not uncommon for Muslim women to sport a *bindi* (dot) on their forehead. People of different faiths greeted each other on their important festivals. One could not easily make out the religion of the common people from the way they dressed or spoke.

The Nizam used to drive down to the old city every day in the afternoon to pay respects to his old mother who stayed in the Purani Haveli. Thereby he set an example of proper filial behaviour. On that visit, and every time the Nizam drove out in his old car, the roads were cleared of all traffic and men and women hurriedly disappeared into bylanes. Those who could not stood still, bowed, and made their obeisance as the ruler's car passed by. Every Friday he came to the small mosque in the Public Gardens to say his congregational prayers. A handful of selected nobles and officials followed him there. His two daughters also joined him in the front row.

On normal days, the Nizam came out only once, but his first wife, Dulhan Pasha, used to go around the city a great deal. She had moved to Eden Bagh across the street from the King Kothi where she lived alone after Osman had installed his new find, Leila Begum from Gulbarga, at the Nazri Bagh, which was a part of the King Kothi complex. People used to be terrified of Dulhan Pasha because she was very short-tempered. No time or direction of her movements could be anticipated. But the police had to make arrangements for the passage of her car on the same scale and pattern as for the Nizam, though she neither needed such security nor cared for it. Shopkeepers used to dread her visits. She would enter any shop on impulse, and get packed whatever caught her fancy, and have it sent to her residence. The interesting thing was that later she could not recall what shopping she had done and from where. The comptroller of the household used to have most of her shopping returned.

Sibte Hasan, a progressive writer who was then working in the Urdu daily *Payam*, used to come from Hyderguda to Abid Road by a foot-track passing by the side of King Kothi. In a bungalow close by, five or six sons of the Nizam were lodged. They were not allowed to go out of the compound of the house and laze inside all day. In the evening, an open top car used to come and take them for a short drive.

Passing that way I saw them many times sitting on the compound wall and I would always try to pass by without being noticed. One day from a distance I saw these boys eating hot chickpeas bought from a petty vendor. I lowered my eyes so as not to intrude upon their enjoyment. One of the boys called after me. I got frightened. Might be they had taken offence at my unintentional intrusion. I thought, I'd get into a scrape. Anyway, I went near the wall and asked them respectfully what they wanted. One of them said bashfully: 'Could you give us some money? This vendor has to be paid.' I was wonderstruck at this strange request. Anyway I dipped my hand into my pocket and whatever I had, which was about half-a-rupee in small coins, I gave to them. When I came home and narrated this incident to Qazi Abdul Ghaffar, he was not at all surprised. He told me that before their marriage, the Prince of Berar, Azam Jah, and his younger brother, Muazzam Jah, were treated similarly. It was at the suggestion of the viceroy that allowances were fixed for the two Princes. After that they started living in gorgeous mansions and, in spite of their handsome allowances, ran hundreds of thousands of rupees in debts.[96]

By that time, Hyderabad was reckoned a beautiful city by all standards, better than most cities in India. The main roads of the city were made largely not of asphalt but of reinforced cement concrete slabs which gave a smooth ride to every type of vehicle. The roads and streets were properly lit and in the unpaved areas, the municipal lorries sprinkled water daily to settle the dust. The great gun was still fired three times a day to remind people that their life span had been reduced further by so many hours. Greenery still predominated its landscape and, with the onset of monsoon for which the official date was the 7 June, people took out their light woollens. They threw parties in their gardens or on their terraces. Amongst the lower-middle classes there were stag gatherings. The poor people gathered at the *sendhi khanas*—taverns where toddy was sold.

Mushairas were a part of the nightlife of the people. They were held at mansions for the nobles, but every locality had its own mushaira and often it was from there that some of the talent was spotted and brought up. Then there was the red-light area called *Mahboob ki Mehndi*.

Sir Ali Imam had kindled hope amongst the people, but then he left abruptly in a huff. He had a small tiff with one of his ministers and insisted on his removal. When this did not happen he left having completed only three out of the five years of his tenure. The Paigah noble Wali-ud-Dowlah, succeeded him. He had been educated in England from early childhood and so had become thoroughly westernized. After his removal, less than three years later, he suddenly turned religious and went to Madina where he died. He was soon followed by the old faithful, Maharaja Kishen Pershad. But the brief stint of Ali Imam had changed the situation. The Paigah and the Maharaja essentially belonged to the nineteenth century and had merely survived into the twentieth. They did not belong to the new age that was astir with new notions about the relationship between the ruler and the subject. That the Maharaja lasted for a decade is a tribute to his mastery of the art of courtiership. With his exit in 1937, the era of comparative calm ended and the city entered upon the last dramatic and turbulent phase under the old order.

The Troubled Decades

By the 1930s, a perceptible change had come over Hyderabad. Political activity, though generally forbidden, was taking place all around. Such a harmless celebration, as that of Mahatma Gandhi's birthday, was not permitted in 1921. It was, nevertheless, held.

In 1927, a party called the Majlis-e-Ittehad-ul-Musalmeen (the Council of the Union of Muslims) came into being. The Majlis or Ittehad, as it was popularly known, was started as a cultural-religious organization but soon started developing on the lines of the Muslim League in British India.

A public meeting was held at the Victory Playground to celebrate the birthday of Prophet Mohammad in November 1930. Bahadur Khan, a young jagirdar, was moving his audience to tears by his oratory. Midway through his speech, he saw the Nizam arrive unannounced to attend the meeting. The young speaker paused only for a while and then greeted the ruler of Hyderabad, in an emotionally charged manner: 'O crowned slave of the Mohammad of Arabia, come, let me tell thee about the style of governance of that Emperor of both the spiritual and the corporeal worlds.' Osman sat there completely mesmerized and, like thousands amongst the audience, washed by the flood of words coming from that young speaker, began to shed tears. He asked some of the telling sentences to be repeated, just as people shout encores in mushairas.

A week later, on 25 November, the young speaker received a firman from the Nizam: 'The royal personage was delighted to hear your sermon and, on the auspicious occasion of his birthday, is pleased to confer the title of Bahadur Yar Jung on you.'

The new knight rose to be the supreme and unquestioned leader of the Ittehad and imparted a new militancy to it. His oratory helped it strengthen and spread its hold over the Muslims.

The late Sheikh Abdullah, the renowned Kashmiri leader, recalls listening to the speech of Bahadur Yar Jung at the public meeting of the Muslim League in Lahore in 1940. It was at that meeting that the resolution for the creation of Pakistan was passed. Speaking of Kashmir, Bahadur Yar Jung demanded the establishment of a complete responsible government. However, that demand did not apply to Hyderabad because the Muslims had conquered Hyderabad through the sword and would keep it the same way.' When Abdullah asked the next day why the same logic was not applied to both the cases, Ghulam Rasool Mehr replied brusquely, 'We can sacrifice lakhs of Kashmirs for Hyderabad.'[97]

Bahadur Yar Jung noted the peculiar political situation of Hyderabad. It was a state with an overwhelming Hindu population, of about 87 per cent, with a Muslim ruler. In the context of the changing political scene, the talk of democracy, and the demands for responsible government, the control of power was bound to pass from the ruling Muslim minority to the Hindu majority. To perpetuate the status quo, which heavily weighed in favour of the Muslims, Bahadur Yar Jung, in 1918, enunciated the doctrine of *Ani 'l malik*—I am the ruler. According to this theory, sovereignty did not vest in the ruler, but in the Muslim community. The Nizam was merely a symbol of that sovereignty. Every Muslim in the state thus became a participant and a stakeholder in sovereignty. It was, therefore, in the interest of every Muslim to protect his sovereignty and its symbol, the Nizam. It became the official doctrine of the Ittehad and Bahadur Yar Jung insisted that Hyderabad should be declared a Muslim state.

To that end, the demographic balance of the state had to be altered. He therefore undertook a vigorous programme of conversion of Hindus to Islam—particularly those belonging to the 'untouchable' and backward classes in villages. He advised his band of missionary workers to aim not at the conversion of individuals but at whole groups. This work was done with particular zeal for three years and during that period he is credited with the conversion of 24,000 persons. Maulana Ghulam Bheek (Narang), General Secretary of the *All India Jamiat-e-Tabligh* ('Society for the Propagation of Islam'), acknowledged his valuable services in this regard and Maulana Abdul Majid Daryabadi said that this alone, of all his noble deeds, was enough to confer greatness upon him.[98]

Bahadur Yar Jung used to approach various persons of means for funds for stated or unstated purposes. Laik Ali (not Salar Jung II)—an industrialist who became the last Prime Minister of the state in 1948—was one of the main and frequent donors. He testified that Bahadur Yar Jung always rendered accounts of the funds collected by him. In course of time, Bahadur Yar Jung grew too big even for the Nizam.

He had already reduced the Nizam from the personification of sovereignty to its mere symbol. He often said things which caused the Nizam discomfiture in his relations with the Resident. Once when he thundered against the British presence and their direction of administration in the state, the Nizam was compelled by the Resident to censure him, to ask him to shut his mouth and be confined to his house for some time. Thereupon Bahadur Yar Jung surrendered his title in protest. The ban and his defiant reaction added to his popularity.

Bhadur Yar Jung died apparently of a heart attack at a dinner in 1944. The Nizam joined the mammoth funeral procession the next morning.

No mild leader could take on the mantle of the flamboyant Bahadur Yar Jung. One after the other, his two successors, Abul Hasan and Kamil, both men of gentle nature, had to bow out.

In the contest that followed there were three aspirants: Rais, Kasim Razvi, and Anees. The saner elements in the party and their sympathizers outside felt that a balanced and sober leader was needed at that juncture in 1946. Some leading Muslims even issued an appeal to that effect. But Kasim Razvi, who had the support of the hoi polloi, won by a large margin. He hailed from Uttar Pradesh and had a small law practice in Latur in Osmanabad district. He was a highly emotional person and made dramatic gestures. Once he offered his house to Bahadur Yar Jung for use as party office, and even started pulling out his household effects into the street. Razvi's followers were aggressive fanatics and he rejoiced in enthusing them by his wild utterances. He never let them forget that they had conquered India by force and they were born to rule.

Razvi created a paramilitary wing of the party composed of men and women called Razakars ('volunteers'). They were given physical and military training and were organized on the model of the 'brown shirts' of Hitler. A Razakar had to take a pledge that he would be ready to sacrifice his life for the leader and the party and to fight to the last to maintain the Muslim power in the state. Razvi claimed its strength to be 200,000, though the Resident put the number at half of that.

Though created avowedly as 'self-defence' units against the alleged attacks from across the borders by the Congress *jathas* ('groups of volunteers'), the Razakars soon began to terrorize the people all over the state, particularly in the western district. Most of the Razakars were armed with a variety of weapons which included swords, spears, and muzzle-loading guns. Some of them had .303 rifles and revolvers. Their menacing posture in general and their attacks on the Hindu population set in motion an exodus of Hindus from the state. The Razakars had two brigades and Razvi proclaimed himself their Field Marshal and wore a khaki uniform. The army and the police often colluded with the Razakars in their nefarious activities or mostly remained silent spectators.

It was widely believed that Razvi had the blessings of the Nizam, though in the later period, Razvi began to dictate terms even to him. Razvi had his ministers in the government and the last ministry in 1948 was constituted entirely according to his wishes. He thus enjoyed the material and financial support of the government. Some leading industrialists like Laik Ali, Ahmed Aladdin, and Babu Khan gave him liberal financial help.

On the other side was the Hyderabad Political Conference. It was generally composed of nationalist elements, largely Hindu. It was not allowed to hold its sessions within Hyderabad since freedom of association was not permitted in the state. The first conference took place in 1923 at Kakinada in the then Madras province (now in Andhra Pradesh). It passed four resolutions. The first was to place on record its 'continued and devoted loyalty and fidelity to His Exalted Highness'. Then it meekly asked for the implementation of the Nizam's promise of legislative reforms. From there it proceeded to 'respectfully pray' for the removal of restrictions on the freedom of the press and of the Assembly. The second conference was held at Bombay in 1926. The tone of speeches there was aggressive, compared to the first. The practice of nazar was criticized and Muslims were assured that they had a common interest with the Hindus in ending the autocratic misrule in the state.

The tone of the speeches at the third conference held at Pune in 1929 was bolder still. The prevalence of liberties in British India, as compared with the situation in the states, was highlighted. Discrimination against Hindus in the services was criticized, while stressing the convergence of interest between different communities. The criticism of the conditions in the state became more strident at the fourth conference at Akola in 1931. It ended with a respectful prayer for the inauguration of a legislative council on modern lines.

The Karnataka Parishad was started in 1934 as a literary body but soon began to clamour for political freedom.

Parallel and supplementary to this was the Maharashtra Parishad, started in 1937. The Andhra Maha Sabha was yet another body with identical aims and objectives, started in 1936.

The Arya Samaj had been established as early as in 1892, but by 1938, the Nizam's government issued orders that it could not set up *kunds*—fireplace for prayers—without permission. There were communal riots in Gulbarga and at Dhoolpet in Hyderabad in the same year. A large number of members of the Arya Samaj were arrested when they started their *satyagraha* in 1938.

These various streams had their confluence in the Hyderabad State Congress. A provisional committee was established in September 1938 to draft a constitution for the Congress. Its object was the attainment of responsible government under the aegis of the Nizam and the Asaf Jahi dynasty.[99]

The government banned it immediately on the ground that it was constituted with communal and subversive motives and that it would only retard the pace of legislative reforms in the state.

The first meeting of the general body of the Congress was scheduled for 9 September 1938 at the residence of M. Ramachari. On 7 September, the Commissioner of Police called him and told him that if the meeting was held, apart from other action that would be taken, his house might be confiscated. Thereupon, the leaders decided to postpone the meeting.

This was followed by negotiations between the leaders of the provisional committee and the government about the lifting of the ban on the Congress. The government suggested first, that its name should be changed because 'Congress' was suggestive of the Indian National Congress to which the leaders reluctantly agreed. Next, it demanded that the body should have no affiliation with any outside party—meaning of course, again, the Indian National Congress. The leaders assured that it had none. Thereafter, the government repeated its allegation that it was a communal body. The leaders resolutely denied this. They contended that the party had some Muslim members also; the government said they were so few as to be negligible.

The leaders asked by what logic did the government permit patently communal parties like the Arya Samaj, the Hindu Mahasabha, and the Ittehad to function while it banned a broad-based and avowedly secular body like the Congress by dubbing it communal!

On 24 October 1938, the provisional committee, exasperated by the cat-and-mouse game of the government, dissolved itself and set up the Council of Action. It issued a manifesto in which its basic aim was reiterated—responsible government under the aegis of the Nizam. Then it went on to demand fundamental rights for the people. Although it was opposed to communal reservations in principle, it conceded such a reservation for ten years.

The Council of Action had a working committee consisting of Govind Rao, Nanal, Ramkishan Dhoot, Ravi Narayana Reddy, Sreenivas Rao, and Janardhan Rao Desai. Membership of all primary members was suspended so that they stood absolved of any responsibility. A plan for satyagraha was announced. The satyagraha was to be undertaken not by the Party but in one's individual capacity. However, the satyagrahis were required to declare themselves members of Congress and stand by its ideals of responsible government, non-violence, and communal unity. The committee called the public in general, and the youth in particular, to stake everything at the altar of political and civil liberties. Four to five determined and tested political workers were handpicked for each batch with a leader who was called a dictator. Two or three such satyagrahas were organized every week in different localities.

The satyagraha continued for two months. There were 18 batches in all. The selected place was notified in advance.

A crowd would gather there. The 'dictator' of the satyagraha would make a speech, if he could, before his arrest. The members carried the Congress flags, which were promptly snatched away by the police, and the agitators were arrested. The show over, the crowds thereafter melted. The Arya Samaj and the Hindu Mahasabha were also organizing satyagraha at that time and the Congress leaders felt that their satyagraha was thus acquiring a communal tinge. This might lead to the allegation of communalism by the government. So the Congress decided to withdraw the agitation on 24 December 1938.[100]

Around this time Swami Ramananda Tirtha appeared on the scene. His original name was Venkatesh Bhavu Rao Khedgikar. He was born on 3 October 1903 in a jagir village of Gulbarga district. His father led a wandering life as an ascetic and so Venkatesh was educated on the charities of relatives. As a schoolboy he came under the influence of Tilak and, on the day of the latter's death, he resolved to remain celibate and to dedicate his life to the service of the nation. He defied the ban on the wearing of the Gandhi cap in school and left his studies during Mahatma Gandhi's Non-Cooperation Movement. Then he joined the Congress, in the then Bombay state (now Maharashtra), and toured many villages.

Thereafter he joined the Trade Union Movement under the renowned labour leader, N.M. Joshi at Bombay. Thus he acquired first-hand acquaintance with poverty and exploitation, both in rural as well as urban areas. While on a visit to Delhi, in connection with his trade union work in the winter of 1926, he was struck by paraplegia—a disease that afflicts the backbone and paralyses the lower part of the body. It took him 18 months to make a reasonable recovery and regain his body movements.

In 1928, Venkatesh was arrested for the first time on account of his trade union activities in Bombay. After his release he found that his lingering physical disability affected his arduous trade union work. So in 1929, he took Joshi's permission to leave that field, and became the headmaster of a school in Osmanabad. There, as he says in his memoirs, he became aware of the repression of Hindus in the Hyderabad state. The Hindus wanted to start a high school for which the permission of the government was not given. Then somebody found a loophole. No permission was needed to upgrade a middle school that existed there. So donations were collected and, despite opposition from the government, a high school came into being with Venkatesh as the headmaster.

On 14 January 1930, Venkatesh formally took *sanyas* and took the name and appellation of Swami Ramananda Tirtha by which he was known henceforth. He started subsisting only on alms and devoted himself fully to the cause of education.

In 1937, he was invited to the State Educational Conference held at Hyderabad. There he analysed the prevailing political conditions and came to the conclusion that what seemed to be a communal situation was in reality a two-fold phenomenon. It was a combination of feudal autocracy and British imperialism. He found that people in Hyderabad were not yet prepared to wage a battle for freedom. When he was invited to address the students of the Osmania University on the occasion of the birthday of Lord Krishna, he found palpable discontent amongst the Hindu students there.

The same year at the Maharashtra Conference held at Latur he was urged to leave the field of education and join the wider field of politics. He did so on 9 June 1938. The leaders felt the need for a statewide organization but Tirtha did not yet find adequate enthusiasm amongst the city people. The material required for vigorous political activity was available only in the districts. He found the members of the provisional committee of the banned State Congress going round in circles in their fruitless negotiations with the government.

On 27 October, Swami Ramananda Tirtha was appointed the dictator of the second batch of the satyagraha started by the Congress three days earlier. Before embarking on the satyagraha he notified the Commissioner of Police of his intention to do so in the afternoon near the Putli Bowli Police Station. He addressed the Commissioner as 'Dear Sweet Self' and closed his letter with 'In Lord, with best regards'.[101]

He and his colleagues were promptly arrested and sentenced to rigorous imprisonment for 18 months.

Tirtha dominated the political scene in the state thereafter. With all his worldly possessions handy—a bowl, a blanket, a copy of the Gita, and a staff—he was ever ready for arrest and it did not seem to matter to him whether he was inside the jail or outside. He was, in due course, able to achieve all his political and socio-economic goals. After the integration of Hyderabad with India, he fought the communist hold over Telangana and got elected to the Lok Sabha for two terms. He played a pivotal role in the enactment of tenancy and land reform legislation in Hyderabad, and in the establishment of the new state of Andhra Pradesh. Thereafter, he retired to his ashram and devoted himself to education and meditation. He took complete sanyas and settled down in the village of Totapalle. He lived there till 1972 when, having been taken ill, he was brought to Hyderabad where he died.

Sir Akbar Hydari succeeded Maharaja Kishen Pershad as Prime Minister in 1937.

He was born in 1869 to Seth Nazar Ali Hydari, a Suleimani Bohra businessman of Bombay. His mother was the sister of Badruddin Tayabji, a judge of the Bombay High Court, who later became the President of the Indian National Congress at its third session in Chennai in 1887.

After his graduation, Akbar joined the finance department of the Government of India. In 1905 he was deputed to Hyderabad as

Accountant General. Two years later, he was promoted as Finance Secretary. In 1911, he became Home Secretary.

Akbar Hydari was responsible for the establishment of the Osmania University's Department of Archeology.

He became a minister in 1921 and held successively the portfolios of Finance, Home, and Railways. He was knighted in 1928 and made a member of the Privy Council. He represented Hyderabad in three Round Table Conferences in London from 1930 onwards.

He was a simple and kind person who made people feel at ease with him.

Sir Akbar had two interests. He used to have boxing sessions with an American physical instructor, Weber, and the children found it quite amusing to see the burly American with the somewhat puny minister punching each other. His other hobby was collection of miniature paintings. He willed them to the Prince Albert Museum in Bombay, and the State Archaeological Museum at Hyderabad. Those not taken by either of these were given to his children.

A lengthy correspondence regarding political reforms in the state took place between Mahatma Gandhi and Akbar Hydari. In spite of their different political standpoints, which could not be reconciled, their correspondence was polite and charming. In one of his letters Mahatma Gandhi enquired about the health of Lady Hydari. In reply, Sir Akbar informed him that Jagadguru Shankaracharya was treating her. However, no progress took place in the political negotiations and ultimately Gandhi gave up with a sarcastic comment: 'I had been asking for bread, and you gave me stones.' The thread was later picked up by Seth Jamnalal Bajaj, but without success.

It was compulsory to sing the anthem 'God Preserve Osman' in all schools in Hyderabad. One day, instead of that, Hindu students began to sing 'Vande Mataram'.

Then it spread to Hyderabad. The three hostels of the Osmania University had two prayer halls each—one each for the Hindu and Muslim students.

In September 1938, Hindu students started reciting 'Vande Mataram' in their prayer halls. The authorities forbade it saying it was not a religious song and it offended the sensitivity of the

Muslim students. On their refusal to comply with the orders, boarders were expelled from the hostels and were evicted forcibly. Police was posted in the University campus. The next morning, on learning about the expulsion of boarders, the Hindu day scholars went on strike. The also protested against the compulsory official dress for students, which consisted of a sherwani and pajama.

Further, in the ethics class for the Hindus, the books prescribed were written by non-Hindus, while for the Muslim students, the books were written by Muslims. Another grievance was that while there were post-graduate classes in Arabic, Persian, and Urdu, there were none for Sanskrit, Telugu, Marathi, or Kannada. The students also took exception to the derogatory reference to Hindus made by the Professor of Religion, Mazharul Hassan Gilani, on the occasion of the birthday of the Prophet in 1937. When Jinnah addressed the students' union of the University, he opened his speech by saying 'My Muslim Students', when in fact it was mixed gathering.[102]

When a delegation of the expelled students waited upon the Prime Minister, Sir Akbar Hydari, he admitted that there was nothing in the 'Vande Mataram' song that could hurt the Muslims, but advised that the song be sung in social functions and not in the prayer hall. The students did not relent.

The University then rusticated the recalcitrant students. Some colleges, both in the city and the districts, followed suit. In all 850 students were rusticated, of whom 420 belonged to the city.

The vice chancellor of Nagpur University, Justice Kedar, in a bold move, offered to take all the rusticated students into his University. He responded to the criticism of his alleged communal bias reflected in this move, by saying that he would have offered a similar facility to Muslim students if they had been similarly harassed in a Hindu state.[103]

✧ ✧ ✧

One of the students thus rusticated was P.V. Narasimha Rao from Warangal where he was born to a well-to-do agriculturist on 28 June 1921. He also went and joined the Nagpur University where he completed his graduation. Later, he took a degree in law from

Poona. During his stay in Maharashtra, he also acquired a high degree of proficiency in Marathi.

On his return home he joined the struggle against the Nizam and became a member of the Andhra Mahasabha. Finding its policies too militant, he left it and joined the State Congress and became a follower of Swami Ramananda Tirtha. He participated in the border camp of the State Congress at Chanda during the 'Join Indian Union' movement. As a lawyer, he also joined the Pleaders' Protest Committee and boycotted the law courts. He also dabbled in journalism and became known for his crisp, fearless writings.

After the Police Action of 1948, he rose steadily in the Party in the state. In 1957, he was elected to the State Legislative Assembly and continued to be its member for 20 years. The same year he became a minister in the state and held a variety of portfolios for a decade. In 1971, he became the first Chief Minister of Andhra Pradesh from Telangana.

Two years later, he moved to the national scene. There too he made a mark with his keen analytical mind, friendly disposition, and unflinching loyalty to the Congress cause. Indira Gandhi inducted him into her Cabinet and he successively held a number of important portfolios like Home, Education, Defence, and External Affairs. After her death he continued to be a trusted aide of Rajiv Gandhi.

In 1991, after the assassination of Rajiv Gandhi, he was elected the President of the Congress at first and later became the Prime Minister of India, the first from the south.

Narasimha Rao was known to be an introvert given to reading and writing. At home in a number of languages, he translated a major Telugu classic into Hindi and another from Marathi into Telugu (*Sahasra Phan*), besides numerous other writings. His expression, both verbal and written, was marked by its clarity and precision. His autobiographical novel *Insider* became one of the best sellers.

After the defeat of the Congress in 1996, a number of cases were filed against him. His name was however, cleared after a prolonged trial. He expired in December 2004.

❖ ❖ ❖

From 1938 onwards, political activity became acute in Hyderabad. There were statements, slogans, processions, agitations, and bans and arrests. There were also negotiations amongst the moderate elements and there were discussions between political leaders and officials of the government.

The introduction of provincial autonomy in British India under the 1935 Act had generated new hopes and aspirations amongst the people in the Indian states too. If the empire could respond, surely the Indian Princes could not resist for long.

Later, correspondence ensued between Kashinath Rao Vaidya, on behalf of the Congress and Home Secretary, Azhar Hussain, on behalf of the government, on the subject of the removal of the ban on the Congress. That exchange provides rare instances of quibbling, prevarication, and equivocation on the part of the government. There were clear attempts at trying to score a point by giving a twist to an expression here and there, instead of facing the issues. Responding to Vaidya's letter of 2 March 1940, Azhar Hussain observed with reference to the demand for a responsible government:

Since your organization aims at a form of government deriving authority from the majority in the legislature, it is directed against the principle recently made the subject of official pronouncement, that the needs of the people must continue to be determined by the undivided responsibility of the ruler for the welfare of his subjects.[104]

When, in response to the demand of the government, which was allergic to the use of the term 'Congress', the name of the organization was changed from 'Hyderabad State Congress' to 'Hyderabad National Conference', the government proceeded to observe that the body could not be called 'national' since all the communities (really the two major communities), were not represented in it. It was pointed out that the Congress had in fact, members drawn from all communities. Out of a total of 1,000 members, as many as 150 were Muslims. But the government did not consider it adequate.

Vaidya too got disgusted with the twisted interpretations given to words and phrases in his letters. His letter of 6 May 1940 is full of suppressed anger and unbridled anguish. In that he gave a classic definition of what could be considered 'National':

It fills me with shame and sorrow that in order to support an untenable decision you should have seen fit to resort to misrepresentation. I suggest that a packed body cannot be called national. I suggest further that a body which has all the communities represented in it may conceivably be anti-national. The national character of an association can only be determined by its objective. Its behaviour may either confirm or deny the character. The composition of a body is surely the least part of its quality. A body composed entirely of selfless and impartial Muslims may well represent all communities and one composed of all communities who have joined it from selfish motives will hopelessly fail to represent any part of the nation. But it is useless to appeal to reason when considerations outside reason regulate action.[105]

Azhar Hussain said that the government did not feel called upon to reply to the points raised by Vaidya, the tone of which he found impertinent. Thereupon Vaidya, over the objection of the government, released the entire correspondence in the form of a booklet. This was printed outside the state and distributed stealthily before the government could lay its hands on it.

It is interesting to know that the real author of all the letters signed by Vaidya was none other than Mahatma Gandhi. While the ghost was the Mahatma, the courier was Swami Tirtha, who commuted regularly to Sevagram, carried the letter of the government, got a reply drafted by Mahatma Gandhi, and gave it to Vaidya for signature and dispatch. The style of the Mahatma in the letters, and in particular the extract quoted above, is clear and unmistakable.

Sir Akbar Hydari seemed now to have become a spent force in Hyderabad. He was not able to deliver what the Nizam was most interested in, namely, Berar. He was appointed as a member of the Executive Council of the Viceroy. He left Hyderabad reluctantly in 1941 and expired a year later, in 1942.

The Nawab of Chhattari succeeded Hydari in 1941. He was a jagirdar from Uttar Pradesh and knew some of the leading political leaders of India personally. He had served as a minister in the government of the United Province (now Uttar Pradesh) and had also officiated briefly as the Governor of that province before coming to Hyderabad.

Like everybody else before and after him, he was also charmed by the city. On a social plane, he found much greater harmony amongst different communities in Hyderabad than in the north. Irrespective of religion or the position of an individual, he found the people in general better behaved. In Hyderabad the land revenue assessment was lower than in British India and income tax was non-existent. But politically he found things were heating up in the state. The Ittehad had emerged as a strong militant party and it seemed to enjoy more than the mere patronage of the Nizam. It had his open backing. Coming to Hyderabad, he felt 'as if a stranger was walking on a path after sunset'.[106]

On the assumption of his charge, Chhatari met all his colleagues separately and collectively to assess the overall situation.

Sir Theodore Tasker was a member of the Nizam's Executive Council. Chhattari told him that he had experience of administration in British India, but a princely state was something new for him and he would need his help in discharging his duties here. Tasker assured him of his full and faithful support and summarized the position in the state by observing that 'the ministers here are like nurses who have been appointed to protect a child who wants to commit suicide. Our task is to prevent him from taking such a step.'[107]

Nawab Mehdi Yar Jung, another member of the Executive Council, remarked to him 'the Nizam is the permanent leader of the opposition of his own government.' On that Chhatari commented: 'The interesting thing is that while the government has limited powers, the "leader of the opposition" has absolute powers.'[108]

Kazim Yar Jung was the Nizam's Secretary. He later became Minister of the Nizam's Secretariat. He conveyed the Nizam's mandate to the new Prime Minister. He was to get the restrictions on the Nizam's power removed, to get Berar back and to secure for him the title of 'His Majesty'.

Chhatari had other priorities. However, when pressed, he broached the point about the conferment of the title of 'His Majesty' on the Nizam with the Government of India. He was given a homily in reply: such a title is not granted; it is acquired by oneself.

Chhattari's assessment of the situation was that the administrative machinery of the state was not bad. It had some excellent officers. The bane of the system was intrigues, particularly the court intrigues. He also believed that there was autocracy in the administration and the Hindu subjects of the Nizam constituted a predominant 87 per cent majority and had lately become conscious of the discrimination against them. He was in favour of carrying them with the government. An advisory council was proposed as a measure of reform in the government. Hindus and Muslims were proposed to be nominated to it on the basis of parity. But the Ittehad said that the parity would be not as between Hindus and Muslims but as between Muslims on the one side and all non-Muslims on the other. This was not acceptable to any non-Muslim party. Chhattari too felt it was not fair.[109]

In March 1942, Sir Stafford Cripps, a member of the British Cabinet, came to India with a plan to grant freedom to India. It contemplated dominion status for India and a body to draft a constitution after the ongoing Second World War. While its members would be elected by provincial assemblies, the representatives of Indian states would be nominated by the respective rulers. It thus retained the privileged position of the Princes. It also provided for a right for any province not to accept the new constitution and work out a separate arrangement with the British government. That contained the seed of the partition of the country. The Congress Party rejected the plan. Thereupon Mahatma Gandhi gave a call for 'Quit India' in August 1942. The passage of this resolution in the session of the Congress at Bombay marked a radical departure in its policy towards the freedom struggle in Indian states. Earlier, the approach was that these people should fight their own battles. In this resolution the struggle for freedom became an integrated movement and covered the whole country including the princely states. It had thus two aspects: freedom from the British and end of the feudal regimes in the princely states.

Time passed but the ban on the Hyderabad State Congress continued. The charade of negotiations between the Congress and the government—played earlier in 1939—was repeated in 1945. Formerly Vaidya represented the Congress; now it was Ramachari. Earlier Hydari headed the government team; now it was Chhattari. Then the Home Secretary was Azhar Hussain; now it was Ali Yavar Jung. The actors had changed; the act did not. The old demands of the government too were reiterated. This time, however, the Congress was not willing to relent, as it had been earlier. Once again the agitation was resumed. It was followed by large-scale arrests.

The relentless march of time continued—without any advance.

Nazar for the Nizam

The Asaf Jahs brought with them the Mughal practice of payment and acceptance of nazar. It was paid to a superior at an audience, a formal meeting, or on auspicious occasions. Ultimately, it became an established practice to present nazar to the Nizam on the two Ids and his birthday. Special darbars were held for the purpose. Individual nazars were also presented at other special audiences.

The presenter of the nazar came forward, bent low with outstretched palms one above the other. The palm on top was covered with a clean handkerchief or a shimmering piece of embroidered cloth. On that cloth were kept a gold coin called ashrafi and Rs 4. This was the minimum amount; there was no maximum limit and the amount depended on the status of the person making the nazar.

Osman Ali Khan made the practice into a regular source of income. He would pick up coins, put the gold coin in one bag and the rupees in another, kept on either side of his seat for the purpose. Invitations were sent out to nobles and officials on the Ids and his birthday. They were required to file up to the Presence and make the offering. Officers in districts travelled on official accounts to the capital to make the nazar. A register of attendance was kept to see whether everyone had responded to the 'invitation'. After the Jubilee Hall had been constructed, it was used for such occasions. It took hours to go through the ritual but at the end of that the Nizam was richer by hundreds of thousands of rupees. If a person was granted a title, or honoured in some other way, he was expected to present himself at the darbar the next day and make the offering by way of thanks.

Then the Nizam saw greater possibilities in this remunerative practice and refined it further. He would send *khasa*—part of the royal meal—to a selected individual—usually a noble. The items of food were placed in a wooden tray called *khwan*. It had a lid made of cane called *chhiba*. This receptacle was wrapped in a red or yellow cloth secured by the royal seal. The final packet was then covered by a decorative piece of cloth. The packet was carried by an African servant on his head. A liveried retainer preceded him. The whole locality noticed the special honour entailed in the gesture, and the whole city talked about it. The honour was acknowledged by the recepient seeking a personal audience with the Nizam at which a suitable nazar was presented.

Once, Qazi Abdul Gaffar, the editor of the *Payam* daily was unexpectedly honoured with the gift of the khasa. His servant came in running nervously and reported the arrival of the royal bearers. The Qazi smiled and told his wife: 'Begum, the wretch has seen our house. Now we will have to move from here. Come, hurry and give me an ashrafi and four rupees.' She said she had Rs 4 but no ashrafi. Somehow a gold coin was procured from the neighbours and the obligation was discharged. When the package was opened, it contained a stale kulcha and two over ripe mangoes![110]

The Nizam's personal estate had extensive gardens with different types of fruit-bearing trees. Sometimes, the Nizam would send some seasonal fruit, usually a mango each, to some selected persons. They would promptly reciprocate by making their nazar. Mangoes from the Nizam's gardens thus went for Rs 24 a piece. This made them the costliest fruit in the world. Sometimes he would send sweetmeats. It is a pity that the meal or the mangoes paid for like that could not be preserved for long by the recipients as proud mementoes.

Ali Ahmed Jaleeli, the son of the poet-laureate, Jaleel Manikpuri, had the honour of an audience with His Exalted Highness sometime in 1936 at King Kothi. The clearance was obtained through the kotwal of the city. He accompanied his elder brother, Siddiq Ahmed Asar, who was a district judge at that time. Both the brothers went in the formal dress—bugloos and dastar. They walked up to the portico and stood there at the bottom of the three steps which led up to the verandah of Nazri Bagh, the residence of the Nizam. The brothers salaamed and extended their palms respectfully with their respective nazars. The royal instructor and his family had a special exemption: they did not have to include the gold coin in their nazar. They could pay just Rs 22. The Nizam came down one step of the portico and accepted the nazar and spoke to the elder brother while Jaleeli stood by nervously with downcast eyes.

Whatever caught the Nizam's fancy became his through the device of nazar. It was part of the expected behaviour amongst his subjects, particularly his nobles, to offer him anything that he said he fancied. He had thus just to praise a thing, however precious, in order to get it from others. The Falaknuma Palace, built by Viqar-ul-Umra, was thus presented as a nazar to the sixth Nizam. It was his grace that he treated only a part of the palace as a nazar. For the rest he paid an amount to bail the Paigah noble out of his debts incurred in building it. So was the case with King Kothi. Kamal Khan, a noble, built that mansion and invited Nizam VII to visit it. While going around the palace, he expressed his appreciation of the beauty of the building. This was a discreet indication and Kamal Khan immediately bowed and presented the mansion to him. He had his initials K.K. engraved on every door, window and all pieces of furniture. Some intelligent courtier suggested that instead of erasing the initials 'K.K.' that would spoil the beauty of the building, it might be named 'King Kothi'. The Nizam decided to move in there from the Purani Haveli in the old city.

Abid Ali Khan, the founder-editor of the leading Urdu daily, Siasat, had also an opportunity to present a nazar to the Nizam. The occasion was his marriage on 8 May 1942. His father, Nawab Mahmood Ali Khan, a jagirdar, was not on good terms with the Nizam and so he did not invite him for the wedding. The bride's father was Sayyad Mohammad Shah Saber Hussaini, the custodian of the shrine of Shah Khamosh (the 'silent saint'), which is located at Nampally and is now more than 135 years old. He sent an invitation to the Nizam. It was also published in the Urdu papers. The wedding was fixed for the evening. A day prior to that, the Nizam sent a message saying that he, along with the Prime Minister, would attend the wedding at 7 a.m.

This sent the family into a flurry. How could the ceremony be advanced at such a short notice? The whole town had been invited. How were they to inform everyone about the change? But that was the royal wish and there was no way to escape it. So the nikah was performed in the morning in the presence of a small number of family members. After the ceremony, the young groom made his bows and presented his nazar to Mir Osman Ali Khan.

Abid Ali Khan's father-in-law had been given a mansab for looking after the shrine by one of the earlier Nizams. After the marriage, Osman cancelled the mansab. 'Since you have married your daughter into the family of jagirdars,' the Nizam told the bewildered old man, 'you don't need the mansab now.'

The reason for the displeasure of the Nizam could be traced back to the days before Abid Ali Khan was born. The Mughal practice, which the Asaf Jahs had adopted, was that any jagir or mansab given by the ruler was personal to the grantee and was not inheritable. So all the property of the noble reverted to the ruler on the death of the noble. The police effected the recovery often through force, which virtually amounted to a plunder. Three or four such cases occurred during the early years of Osman's rule. This practice was stopped on the intervention of the Residency. One such case was that of Nawab Saulat Jung II, the maternal grandfather of Abid Ali Khan, who died on 2 June 1919. The kot-wal's men landed at the mansion and started taking charge of all the property including even the gems and jewellery worn by the members of the family. The burial of the body had to wait till the completion of the 'loot'.

His younger brother, Nawab Intekhab Jung, who was also the paternal grandfather of Abid Ali Khan, witnessed this brutality and foresaw that the same thing would happen to his family on his death. In anger and disgust he, on his own, surrendered his movable property to the Nizam saying that he did not wish to share the fate of his brother. But he made one fine point. He sur-rendered only such property as, to his knowledge, had accrued to him from the Asaf Jahs. He did not surrender the gems and jewels which the family had got from the Sultans of Bijapur whom his ancestors had served. Amongst these was a book, the complete works of the poet Saeb. The covers of this book and its leaves were of solid gold and the writing was engraved. At that time it was valued at Rs 600,000.

Jealous tale-carriers told the Nizam that the insolent act of returning property by Intekhab Jung was an empty gesture. In fact the Nawab had kept back the jewellery and articles of real value. And they named the book as an example. The Nizam asked for the book but the Nawab refused to surrender it. Intekhab Jung's son, Mahmood Ali Khan, Abid Ali Khan's father, was a childhood companion of Osman. They had studied and played together. As soon as he had passed the middle school examination, Mahmood was appointed a Second Talukdar (Deputy Collector). Now Osman started pestering and harassing him to get that book from his father. He said that he merely wanted to have a look at it. The Nawab persisted in his refusal. For this both the father and the son were dismissed from service. Mahmood Ali Khan was the only surviving son of the Nawab who had lost eight children. Fearing further reprisals against his son, he allowed him to take the book only to be shown to the Nizam. When the book was shown to the Nizam, it was retained by him as a nazar.

The story does not end here. In due course, Abid Ali Khan grew up, and shortly after the Police Action in 1948, he resigned from his job in the Information Department and started the daily newspaper, *Siasat*. It succeeded beyond expectations and for expanding it new machinery was needed. Abid Ali Khan therefore petitioned the Nizam requesting most respectfully for the return of the book or alternatively to grant him an amount of Rs 400,000 to enable him to import new machines for expanding his paper. There being no response, he again reminded him. The Nizam pretended to have forgotten about that acquisition and, when pressed, said that he could not locate the book. A search was mounted but to no avail. Then the Nizam said it must be with Salar Jung III, the founder of the famed museum named after him. 'That rascal was very fond of collecting such things,' he reportedly said to justify his suspicion. The Museum's record did not list any book of that type. Then Jamaluddin, one of the attenders of the Nizam, came forward and asked about the object of their search.

'It is a bulky book—some ten kilos ... .'

'Oh that,' Jamaluddin's quick-mind recalled the incident. 'That is in a box lying under the bed of Ala Hazrat.'

And there it was, in the box full of dust. Inside that the book lay snugly wrapped in a piece of cloth untouched for a quarter of a century.

Seeing the book again, the Nizam's acquisitive instinct was sharpened. He said he would rather pay compensation than return the book. A committee consisting of Deen Yar Jung, former Director General of Police; S.N. Reddy, Commissioner of Police; and Humayun Ali Baig, a senior officer, was appointed to determine the quantum of compensation. Abid Ali Khan contested the committee's statement that the book was a nazar. He pointed out, rightly, that all nazar were entered in a register and signed by the person making the present. There was no such entry for this book. The committee deliberated again and offered a compensation of Rs 12,000. Abid refused to accept it. He said it was a gross undervaluation. Moreover, he had to share the compensation amount with his brothers who also had a claim to it. He would thus hardly get anything out of it. He had asked for Rs 400,000 to modernize his press. He made an appeal to the Nizam and sought an audience with him to make his representation personally.

When two hours passed and he was not called in, the Peshi Secretary, S.N. Reddy, thought he would go and remind the Nizam. Abid heard a thunder of abuses hurled at Reddy by the Nizam. Abid took the hint, apologized to the Secretary for causing him embarrassment and returned.

Meanwhile time passed. In 1964, Prince Barkat Ali Khan, Mukarram Jah, the grandson of the Nizam, was declared his successor, superseding his father. To reclaim his family heirloom, Abid petitioned him again on 17 November 1965. A meeting with him was also arranged through the good offices of Zahir Ahmed who, after his retirement from the civil service, was working as the Prince's secretary.

Mukarram Jah heard the story and then replied: 'I can't do anything during the lifetime of my grandfather. But after him, *Insha Allah,* 1 shall do something.'[111]

Nothing was done. 'I have made many times the value of the book,' Abid Ali Khan used to say with smug satisfaction. His paper and he himself came to be widely respected and he has made many contributions to the social and cultural enrichment of the city.

The practice of nazar was severely criticized by the Resident and, in a letter dated 17 March 1923, he advised the Nizam to stop it. In the second Hyderabad Political Conference at Mumbai in 1926, Y.M. Kale attacked the practice. The Nizam first defended it, and then under pressure from the Resident, issued orders restricting it.[112] In 1945, the young Raja Rameshwar Rao of Wanaparthy, a principality under the Nizam, received a packet of eight mangoes as a present from the Nizam. With that was a note scribbled in Urdu by the Nizam: 'For this no nazar need be presented.'

'Rabbit in a Hutch'

Razvi and his goons made life difficult for Chhattari. When he demitted office of the President of the Executive Council, in 1946, the Nizam invited Sir Mirza Ismail to succeed him. Sir Mirza was a liberal statesman and had served as the Diwan of the Hindu state of Mysore with distinction for a long time. Thereafter, he was appointed the Diwan of Jaipur. His appointment at Hyderabad was opposed by Mohammad Ali Jinnah, the leader of Muslims, and by Kasim Razvi. But the Nizam persisted.

Ismail had an acute aesthetic sense. There was a wall along the road on the tank bund at Hussain Sagar, which shut off the view of the lake from the passers-by. He had it pulled down and replaced by an iron railing. That opened up a magnificent vista to the public. Similarly, he had parts of a wall enclosing the public garden replaced by an artistic iron railing. Many a sharp bend on the road was straightened.

However, he did not show much interest in the representations and demands of the people who had gathered to meet him there.

His penchant for pulling down ugly structures and replacing them with better ones earned him the nickname of *Tod-Phod Mirza*—the Demolisher Mirza.

The suave Mirza had high hopes also to secure a satisfactory political modus vivendi between the Nizam and the Government

of India. But he found that 'the Nizam was bent upon independence. Even more so were the wretched band of foolish Muslims
called the Ittehad-ul-Musalmeen'. Not only that, he found that
'even many senior officers had lost their heads'. He could not
stand the oppressive atmosphere in Hyderabad. In the summer
of 1947, he went on leave to Bangalore—his beloved hometown.
From there he shot off his letter of resignation to the Nizam. It
was an anguished note: ' I have had the misfortune to find myself
opposed at every turn, by a certain section of the local Musalmans
who, in my opinion, are set on a course that is suicidal to the
state.'[113]

After the warning, Mirza concluded with a prayer that 'God in
His Mercy may protect the Asaf Jah Crown from the dangers that
I see looming ahead.'[114]

His warning was to prove prophetic; his prayer, ineffective.

The Nizam tried to get him back. But Mirza had made up his
mind. Having failed to persuade Mirza to return, the Nizam
turned to Chhattari again. He flew in on 9 June 1947, and entered
the murky waters once again.

While clouds were gathering on the horizon and life was becoming difficult in the districts, Hyderabad still retained its charm and
attraction. Philip Mason, of the Indian Civil Service, who visited
the city in March 1947 and stayed here for a few weeks before
leaving India, could not resist describing its cosmopolitan culture
and the even tenor of the life of its people.

It was someone's birthday and the children were playing 'Oranges and
Lemons'. Uncle Yusuf and Aunt Fatima held up their hands to make an
arch; they were enjoying themselves as much as the children and Uncle
Yusuf seemed to have forgotten that he was a member of the Cabinet and
that he was formally addressed by a tremendous title that meant he was
a leader in battle and victorious in war.

'Here comes a chopper to CHOP off his head!' Their hands came down
and they had caught a merry, struggling little urchin who was trying to
escape. 'Oranges or Lemons?' they whispered in his ear and with peals of
laughter he joined the tug-of-war team behind Aunt Fatima.

'Who is that little boy?' I asked my nearest neighbour and she told
me a name I have forgotten, but a name unmistakably Hindu, some Ram
Swarup or Jag Deo.

'But he's wearing the wrong sort of hat!' I exclaimed in astonishment.
He was wearing a Turkish fez, like an inverted red plant pot with a black

silk tassel, which in Northern India was always the sign of a Muslim. 'Oh, here in Hyderabad we do not care for things like that!' said my neighbour gaily. 'It is one of the nice things here that we are so delightfully cosmopolitan.

She was right for the moment and up to a point. None of us knew that it would be only five months till the end of nearly two centuries of stability. It was like the spring of 1789 at Versailles. At the buffet suppers that the grandees of Hyderabad enjoyed so much, the men were elegant in black sherwanis or gorgeous in gold brocade, the ladies wore saris of sapphire or flame-colour or starlit blue; they moved here and there between flowering bushes, enjoying the scented dusk, just cool enough after the heat of the day, clustering like bees round their Queen in the flood-lighted centre of the gathering, or stepping for a moment away from the bright centre to rest the eyes or to look up at the brilliance of the stars. Everyone seemed to be happy and witty and amused; the tables were laden with Persian *pilaos*, Mughal *kebabs*, Indian curries, French salads—dishes to suit every taste. There were Arabs, Persians and Turks as well as a smattering of French and English. And of the Hyderabadis themselves, the people of the state, there would be among the guests some Hindus, the daughter of a high court judge perhaps, with her young banker husband, or there might be the descendant of some Maratha freebooter who, two hundred years ago, had led his cavalry to fight for the Viceroy of the Deccan and had been rewarded with an estate. But nine out of ten would be Muslims, descendants of men who had come into India from Persia or Afghanistan or Central Asia, many of them still pale as ivory, each treasuring a crescent sword from Damascus that was the symbol of his family honour, a reminder that he was really a noble and a warrior even though by day he worked in the Secretariat as a civil servant. It was a state of the same size of population as Spain, Muslim in culture and language. Its ruler maintained that his was the largest Muslim state in the world—but there was one little fact that he did not always remember, that he had fifteen Hindu subjects for every Muslim. ... The Hindus knew better than to raise their heads. They were tolerated; they became judges and vice-chancellors; they made money; they practised their religion; some of them were even invited to parties. They lived quietly. The Muslims did not fear them; they too lived quietly. They had given up their independence and they had tranquility instead. Now it was 1947 and in five more months the British would be saying that all that was over.[115]

The wheels were moving fast now. In March 1947, the new Viceroy of India, Lord Mountbatten, arrived. His mandate was to grant freedom to India by June 1948.

In June 1947, when the shape of the political future of India became known, the Nizam declared that he would join neither of the two proposed dominions—India or Pakistan—but would assume independence. A week before India became independent, a 'Join India Day' was observed in Hyderabad. People who participated in this demonstration were arrested. Many people hoisted the Indian flag on 15 August when India became independent. More arrests were made.

Negotiations between the Nizam and the new Government of India dragged on. Indian leaders wanted the state to accede and pending that the introduction of responsible government. The Nizam wanted independence. Given the past history of the state, its pattern of relationship with the British, and its geographical position, this was an untenable proposition, but Razvi and his shock brigades of Razakars fanned such fanciful notions. Razvi promised him and his own witless followers that 'soon the waters of the Bay of Bengal would be kissing the feet of the Nizam'. He even declared that he would plant the Asafia flag on the ramparts of the Red Fort at Delhi. He exhorted the Razakars to march with sword in one hand and the Quran in the other and annihilate all opposition. By now Razvi was advising the Nizam on all crucial matters.

A Standstill Agreement—ensuring adherence to the status quo for one year—was worked out between the Nizam's delegation and the Government of India. The draft of the documents were brought by the delegation from Delhi for the Nizam's signature on 22 October 1947 and it had been agreed that they would be taken back to Delhi by 26 October. The Nizam referred this draft to his Executive Council which discussed it for three days and at the end recommended its acceptance by six votes to three. When it was submitted to the Nizam on the evening of 25 October, he approved the decision of the Council but deferred signing the agreement till the next day. On the next day he postponed it again. He said he would sign it the next morning when the delegation was to fly to Delhi. On 26 October, around midnight, a mob of around 30,000, comprising largely members of the Ittehad, surrounded the houses of the Prime Minister, Nawab of Chhattari, Sir Walter Monckton, and Sir Sultan Ahmed who were members of the delegation. Their purpose was to prevent the delegation from leaving for Delhi.

Another meeting was held the next day to which surprisingly Razvi had also been invited. Razvi was dissatisfied with the draft agreement and said that better terms could be secured from the Government of India, particularly since India had been embroiled in troubles elsewhere. His allusion was to the invasion of Kashmir by the tribals on 23 October 1947 and the dispatch of Indian troops there on 26 October, which compounded the problems caused by communal riots and the rehabilitation of refugees subsequent to the independence and partition of India. The Nizam was impressed by Razvi's logic. The members of the delegation were not. All of them resigned in protest. The Nizam took this opportunity to drop some members of the delegation by accepting their resignation. From that point on Razvi was the virtual ruler of the state.

Chhattari resigned in disgust and left Hyderabad in early November 1947. The new delegation made many visits to Delhi asking for various changes and amendments in the draft, but the Government of India was now adamant. At last on 29 November, the Standstill Agreement was signed. It was exactly the same document, which had been rejected by the Ittehad earlier. It provided for temporary continuation, as between the Nizam and the Government of India, of 'all agreements and administrative arrangements as to matters of common concern, including External Affairs, Defence, and Communications' existing between Great Britain and the Nizam immediately before 15 August 1947.

In December 1947, Razvi imposed a new government on the Nizam. The new Prime Minister, Mir Laik Ali, had started his life as an Assistant Engineer in the government. Sir Akbar Hydari took a fancy to him and helped him start the Hyderabad Construction Company by giving him government contracts to build. He thus grew into one of the leading industrialists of the state. Just before his appointment, Laik Ali was the representative of Pakistan at the United Nations.

The ministry consisted of the nominees of the Ittehad. Out of 12, 4 ministers were Hindus. They were independent. The Congress was not represented because it had boycotted elections to the Legislative Assembly set up in 1946.

The Standstill Agreement of November 1947 brought a false peace. According to the Agreement, Agents-General were exchanged between India and Hyderabad. Zain Yar Jung, an eminent architect, was stationed in Delhi while K.M. Munshi, a scholar, lawyer, and a politician, was posted at Hyderabad. They supplemented the intelligence on both sides with their own appreciation of the situation. Their status was vague and peculiar. Munshi believed he was the successor of the all-powerful British Resident. The Nizam disabused his mind of any such notion by not allowing him to use the Residency or permitting him any of the trappings suggestive of paramountcy functions. He had to take a military bungalow in Bolaram in the midst of the establishment of the Indian Army which was in the process of departure as a part of the Standstill Agreement. Munshi was somewhat abrupt in his manners. Zain Yar Jung was a suave person who made many friends in Delhi. That stood him in good stead. He was appointed a minister after the Police Action.

Thus began the darkest phase in the modern history of Hyderabad which was fully controlled by Razvi. His handpicked Prime Minister and Cabinet were the marionettes manipulated by him. There was now harmony amongst these centres of power—King Kothi, the abode of the ruler; Shah Manzil, the residence of the Prime Minister; and Dar-us-Salam, the headquarters of the Ittehad. Their objective was common—freedom and sovereignty for the Nizam as the head of an Islamic state. Osman Ali Khan had became 'a rabbit in a hutch', said Philip Mason. A rabbit is so secure in its hutch that it does not know that it is a rabbit.

Dissent and Sanity

Sir Mirza Ismail had said that in Hyderabad many Muslims had lost their heads. As time passed the number increased.

But also there were Muslims who were unhappy at the course of events, who believed that what was happening was wrong, whose heart came out in sympathy with the victims of the loot, arson, and rape committed by the Razakars, and who felt that all this should stop. They were all good Muslims. They drew inspiration from their holy book, the Quran, and the life and teachings of their Prophet, Mohammad. According to Baihaqui, Mohammad had said that the worst form of class prejudice is to support one's community even in tyranny. Tabrani's collection of the sayings of the Prophet quotes him as declaring that 'he who knowingly lends support to tyranny is outside the pale of Islam'. Tirmazi, Abu Dawood, and Ibn-e-Maja quote the Prophet as saying that 'his jehad is best who speaks a just word before a tyrannical authority'. *Sura* 26: 152 of the Quran exhorts the faithful: 'Obey not the bidding of those who commit excesses, who make mischief on the earth and mend not their ways.' What was happening in Hyderabad, therefore, was un-Islamic in spirit, they believed. They saw the writing on the wall which was invisible to men in power.[116]

A majority of those kept quiet. What could they do, they asked themselves in anguish and despair? There were men whose conscience bothered them, who could not see man's inhumanity to man. They were in politics—that was to be expected—but they were also in services, in journalism, in the professions, in all sorts of callings and situations.

However, some men of courage stood up and said they had to do something to stop it. We mention some of them below.

Ghulam Akbar Khan, born in 1876, belonged to a Pathan family settled in Farukhabad district of Uttar Pradesh. In 1893, he came to Hyderabad and, after studying law, began working as a junior to his cousin, Fida Hussain Khan, father of Dr Zakir Hussain who later rose to be the President of India. In course of time he himself became an eminent lawyer. In 1918, he was appointed a judge of the newly established High Court of the state. From 1922 to 1932 he served as Home Secretary, earning the title of Nawab Akbar Yar Jung Bahadur. In between, during 1928–30 and again in 1932, he served as a judge of the High Court.

On 11 August 1936, the Young Men's Kayasth Union organized a function on the occasion of Janamashtami—the birthday of Lord Krishna. It was held in the mansion of Raja Narsing Raj Bahadur Avail at Hussaini Alam and was presided over by Mirza Yar Jung Bahadur, Chief Justice of the state. Nawab Akbar Yar Jung delivered the keynote address entitled—'Shri Krishna: The Prophet of Hind'. In this most brilliant address in Urdu, laced with quotations from Arabic and Persian, he made the bold assertion that Lord Krishna was indeed a prophet like others mentioned in the Holy Book of the Muslims.

The main thrust and argument of his lucid speech, and his interpretations and deductions were based mainly on the Islamic exegesis, namely, the verses of the Quran, the sayings of the Prophet, and commentaries of some of the enlightened and liberal scholars of the faith. His main proposition was based on two verses of the Quran. *Ayat* 7 of *Sura* 13 declares: 'and for every people there has been a guide'. Later, in *Ayat* 40 of *Sura* 78, it is stated that 'certainly we sent apostles before thee; there are some of them that we have mentioned to thee and others whom we have not mentioned.'

From this major premise of the Quran, Akbar Yar Jung postulated that 'if therefore Shri Krishna is not mentioned by name in the Quran, that is no reason to doubt his prophethood. Would you believe that a nation, whose civilization and culture had spread over such a large part of Asia, whose philosophy and learning had influenced Greece and Egypt, was left without a guide and teacher?' Then he affirmed: 'These teachers are styled variously by some as *rishis* and *munis* and by others as *nabis* and *paighambars*, etc. Amongst these there was one holy personage, whose birth we are here to celebrate. I mean Shri Krishna whom, in my religious phraseology, I would call Krishna *alai is salam* ("upon whom be peace!"). I have no hesitation in regarding this great personage, whom the Hindus consider an avatar of God, as nabi ("a prophet of God"). I therefore offer him the salutations due to the prophets.'

Then he went on to underline the doctrine that, according to the teaching of the Quran, a Muslim can make no distinction between the prophets. 'Even as they regard Noah, Abraham, Moses, and Jesus—upon all of whom be peace!—as prophets of God, even so do they regard the prophets of all nations.'[117]

Akbar Yar Jung used a benediction for Krishna—'may peace be upon him'—which the Muslims use only for their acknowledged prophets. This act roused the ire of a section of the orthodox theologians. One, Aini Shah Nizami, wrote in the *Subeh Deccan*, an Urdu daily, in its issue of 19 August 1936, accusing the speaker of an 'innovative flight of imagination', which went beyond the pale of conventional and traditional Muslim beliefs and which, according to him, might not even be acceptable to the orthodox Hindus. On his promptings, the Nizam, Mir Osman Ali Khan, also wrote his personal comments in the same paper on 22 August 1936 adding an admonition that government officials should refrain from making public speeches on controversial themes, religious or political, that might upset the prevailing peace and harmony. He also warned editors of newspapers against printing such controversial speeches or articles.

It was rumoured that the Nizam was being pressurized to banish Akbar Yar Jung from the state for his heretical utterances. However, both the Nizam and the Prime Minister, Maharaja Kishen Pershad, held him in high regard and were not inclined to

take any extreme step to penalize him. Indeed, such was his reputation that within four months of that speech, when he reached the
age of superannuation, he was given an extraordinary extension
of two years as Judge of the High Court, and was also nominated
as a member of the Legislative Council, which he served from
1936 to 1940.

Mir Akbar Ali Khan was the son of a minor jagirdar in Bidar. He
was born in 1899 and went to the Aligarh Muslim University for
his education. In 1919, while a student of the last year of BA, he
gave up his studies and joined the Non-Cooperation Movement
started by Mahatma Gandhi. Later, he completed his graduation from Osmania University. In 1922, he went to England
and studied law at the London University. Thereafter, he was
called to the bar from Middle Temple, London. He returned from
London in 1927 and set up his practice. In 1929, reacting against
the communal policies of the Nizam's government, along with
some others, like Padmaja Naidu, B. Ramakrishna Rao, Baqar
Ali Mirza, M. Narsing Rao, Ali Yavar Jung, M. Ramchander Rao,
M. H. Jafari, and Fazlur Rahman he set up a body called 'Society
of Union and Progress'. The members signed a pledge affirming
their belief in responsible government. No person belonging to
any communal organization was taken as a member. It was a
moderate body with limited membership. Akbar Ali Khan was
elected Mayor of Hyderabad and a Member of the Legislative
Council. He met the Nizam many times. The Nizam listened to
him but did not react.

He believed the state was conservative but not communal until
after the advent of the Ittehad and in particular, of Razvi. There
were a number of non-communal people, he found, but they
were not ready to make the necessary sacrifice for correcting the
situation. He found Razvi crude and insensitive but capable of
rousing mass hysteria. Razvi offered him the Prime-Ministership
after the departure of Chhattari in 1946. But there was one condition: Akbar should become a member of the Ittehad party. Akbar
declined the offer. In 1948, on the assassination of Mahatma

Gandhi, he organized a public condolence meeting. Razvi disrupted the meeting and Akbar Ali Khan was assaulted by the Razakars.

For his protests against the atrocities of Razakars, he was harassed. Every night a band of hooligans used to come and chant *murdabad* ('death to him') slogans outside his residence at Saifabad. But he remained firm in his belief.

❖ ❖ ❖

Another man unhappy with the prevalent situation was Mirza Ali Yar Khan. Born in 1905, in a family of scholars and administrators, he was sent for higher studies to Oxford and Paris. On his return, in 1927, he was appointed a Reader and, later, Professor in Modern History in the Osmania University. He continued to teach till 1935. Simultaneously, he was also President of the Society of Union and Progress and the editor of the magazine, *Onward*. In 1935, he was appointed Director of Information. During 1936–42, as Secretary, Constitutional Affairs and Broadcasting, he represented the state in the Constitutional and Reorganization Committee of the Chamber of Princes. In 1942, he became Secretary for Home, Judicial, and Constitutional Affairs and occupied that post for three years. In that capacity he continued the negotiations with the representatives of the Hyderabad State Congress for lifting the ban on its establishment.

In 1946, he became the Police Minister in the Chhattari government and earned the title of Ali Yavar Jung by which he was known thereafter. As Police Minister his attitude towards the State Congress was considered by the Ittehad to be soft. Its organ, the *Rahbar-e-Deccan*, published distorted versions of the speeches of Congress leaders and made loud demands for their arrest, particularly, of the President, Swami Ramananda Tirtha, and the General Secretary, Madapati Ramachander Rao. Ali Yavar Jung found that no case could be made out against them and so did not oblige the Ittehad extremists.

The Ittehad made two more demands. The old muzzle-loading guns used by the police had been replaced by modern rifles. The Ittehad leaders asked the Police Minister to give them the

discarded weapons for distribution to their members and sympathizers. The second demand was that the police should not search
vehicles bringing firearms from across the borders of the state.
At this time Razakars were being recruited in large numbers and
they needed arms. Ali Yavar Jung did not concede these demands.
Thereupon, the portfolio of police was transferred from him to a
minister under the control of the Ittehad. This development trig-
gered an exodus of Hindus from Secunderabad.

Ali Yavar Jung was a member of the state delegation which conducted negotiations with the Government of India regarding the
Standstill Agreement. In 1947, a note on the state's independence
and the introduction of constitutional reforms was prepared and
was presented to the Nizam by Nawab of Chhattari, Ali Yavar
Jung, and Walter Monckton in a meeting on the 19 August 1947.
When the Nizam saw the note on reforms, he lost his temper with
Nawab Ali Yavar Jung. Monckton tried to clarify that the draft
was prepared in consultation with him, but the Nizam would not
relent. The Nizam also remarked angrily that the Muslims had no
confidence in him.

He was harassed a great deal after his resignation. He was
dubbed as an agent of the Government of India. He had to lie low
until after the Police Action.

Another dissenting voice was that of a liberal who hailed from the
north. Qazi Mohammad Abdul Ghaffar was born in a well-to-do
family of Muradabad in Uttar Pradesh in 1889. His ancestors were
Qazis under the Mughals. In 1857, his grandfather gave refuge to
a Mughal Prince. For that, he was executed by the British and his
property was confiscated. Later, he was exonerated posthumously
and his property was returned to the family. 'Qazi' was thus an
inherited title. His father had good relations with the British and
earned the title of Khan Bahadur. But Abdul Ghaffar did not like
the British.

He took a job, fought with his British superior, and resigned it.
Then he took to import-export business and having lost money
in it, turned to journalism. In 1931, he came to Hyderabad and

two years later started the Urdu daily, *Payam*. It was a progressive paper and was opposed to the communal policies of the Ittehad and the feudal system prevalent in the state. He earned the deep enmity of the com-munal elements in the state because of his writings. But he stood firm.

When Sir Mirza Ismail became the Prime Minister of the state in 1946, Abdul Ghaffar was appointed Director of Information. But soon after Mirza's departure, the Qazi was also dismissed from service. He left Hyderabad in 1947. At the time of his departure he sent the Nizam a letter running into 21 foolscap pages. In this he warned him against 'the dictatorship of the political charlatans' who, under the guise of protecting the rights of their co-religionists, were in fact trying to establish a fascist domination over the Nizam, whom they were using as a pawn in their game of power politics. He told him about his corrupt bureaucracy which had aligned itself with communal elements and said that everything that was happening had his alleged backing and support. He recalled that he had pleaded in vain with the Nizam for a fair and just form of government. If he favoured one community, it would lead to a civil war. Nothing less than responsible government could save the Nizam's position and his refusal to do so 'will always mean utter disregard of public welfare'.

Referring to the 'fire-eating' Razvi and his threats he said that his

constant provocation drenched in angry threats and dripping with humiliating ridicule and contempt has served as nothing else could have done to rouse the complaisant Hindu. I may not be accused of exaggeration if I say that apart from the outside influence, the Hindu majority of this state has been goaded into action by constant pinpricks and reckless shouting of the Majlis leaders who, encouraged by Your Exalted Highness's support and much advertised patronage and the deplorable inactivity of the Government, have gone too far to recede.

He deplored the treatment meted out successively to Sir Akbar Hydari, the Nawab of Chhattari, and Sir Mirza Ismail and prophesied 'that the final outcome of the negotiations with the Union Government is not going to be much different from what Sir Mirza envisages.'

He concluded his brilliant and forceful analysis by suggesting the adoption of the 'self-evident maxim that no ruler can rule without the support of the public opinion representing the majority of his subjects.'[118]

It is idle to guess what Mir Osman Ali Khan would have done to the author of such an impertinent letter but it was so arranged that by the time the letter was delivered, Qazi Abdul Ghaffar had already gone beyond the jurisdiction of the Nizam. His warning proved prophetic.

❖ ❖ ❖

Mehdi Ali was another man cast in the same mould. Born in 1917, he was educated at Aligarh, and was selected in the elite Hyderabad Civil Service in 1941.

In 1948, he was Deputy Collector at Madhira in the present-day Khammam district. The Razakars were all over the district at the time and even the administration was afraid of them. They would enter trains, search passengers, and confiscate whatever they liked. Once they detained a group of Marwaris and accused them of smuggling gold in their jars. When a search was made, it was found that the jars contained only pickles. But the Deputy Collector could not do anything to help them. The Razakars and the police defied him and allowed the hapless Marwaris to go only after harassing them for 12 hours.

The Commissioner of Warangal, under whose jurisdiction Mehdi Ali worked, was an Arab, Habeeb Mohammad. Habeeb Mohammad had earned a good reputation as an officer and as a person earlier but changed completely when he took charge of Warangal. There he became a rabid communalist and a fanatic Razakar. He used to say that he would mix the blood of Hindus with the waters of the Bay of Bengal. Naturally, Mehdi Ali could not like him, but he was his subordinate.

According to Mehdi Ali, 80 per cent of the Hindus had fled Madhira across the border into British India.

Under the Nizam, the Arabs guarded all treasuries and they discharged their duties with great devotion. On the night of 7 September 1945, the Arabs attacked Dindkur village, about five kilometres from Madhira. They indulged in loot, rape, and arson. They even removed the *mangalasutras*—necklaces denoting married status—held sacred by every married Hindu woman. At 8.30 a.m. the following day, a procession of woe-begone women from that village came to Mehdi Ali's house. They were dumb and panic-stricken. The sub inspector of police, Habeebullah, was with Mehdi Ali and the police station was just opposite his house.

Mehdi Ali's orders to the police to apprehend the Arabs were not obeyed. The hooligans lounged around and waited on the platform of the railway station. When the train came, they boarded it with all the loot. Mehdi Ali's blood boiled at this rank lawlessness and the collusion of the police with the goons. More than anything, he felt humiliated at his own helplessness. He wrote to the Commissioner protesting about the incident. Habeeb Mohammad was enraged at the temerity of Mehdi Ali in complaining against his brethren of the faith and wrote to the government to transfer him immediately.

Earlier, Razvi also had written to Mehdi Ali saying that he was unnecessarily harassing his Razakars and threatened him that if he did not mend his ways, he would face dire consequences. Razvi's letter also added that he would soon 'see Warangal'. Mehdi Ali did not understand the meaning of this expression. He learnt later that this was a vulgar colloquialism, which meant that he would be sodomized.

Mehdi Ali was promptly transferred but luckily for him the Police Action took place soon thereafter and he was saved from the dire consequences threatened by the Razakar leader.[119]

❖ ❖ ❖

Fareed Mirza's story is even more dramatic. Born in 1918, he was in college in 1938–9 when he came under the influence of Mahatma Gandhi and Nehru. Someone had suggested that he should read their autobiographies if he wanted to improve his English and when he did that, he was fired with the spirit of nationalism.

Early in 1948, when he was Tahsildar of Khandar in Nanded District, a group of Pathans attacked and looted the houses of Hindus in a village called Loha and committed rape and arson on a large scale. He reached there and saw the carnage. The police did not cooperate with him in his attempts to provide relief and succour to the victims. When he reported this to Collector Nawab Shahabuddin Khan, the latter replied that army personnel were being sent there. But the reason given by the Collector for taking this action was that the Ittehad President, Akhlaq Hussain, had informed him that some Hindus were making bombs there to attack the Muslims. Fareed Mirza met the Collector and told him what had happened and what he himself had seen. At that time, the distinct head of the Ittehad, Akhlaq Hussain, was sitting with the Collector. The Collector paid no attention to that. Instead he pulled up Fareed and said that several instances of his non-cooperation with the Razakars had been reported to him. It was also alleged that he had shown disrespect to the state flag. Finally, he told Fareed that it had been decided to place him under suspension.

After the departure of the District Chief of Ittehad, Mirza asked the Collector to order his suspension. The Collector said that he had to placate the Ittehad Chief and advised him to be more discreet in his conduct in future to stay out of trouble. In another instance, the Collector advised that the *taccavi* loans to be distributed to villagers, should be given only to Muslims or only to those who were loyal to the state. Fareed Mirza could not understand how to make the discrimination when Hindus too would apply.

Later, at a district meeting of officials, the Collector publically told him, again in the presence of Akhlaq Hussain, that the Government had decided to suspend him because of his political ideas. In private, however, he again told him to be more circumspect and said that, since the Razakars were against him, he would only recommend his transfer. Harassed and disgusted, Mirza decided to resign.

After some time some Hindu pleaders of Khandar came to him in panic. Mirza advised them to keep their valuables in the bank at the district headquarters at Nanded. Accordingly, one prominent lawyer, Gangadhar Rao, took his cash and valuables by the bus which was also taking the surplus cash from the sub-treasury to the district treasury. Fareed Mirza and his colleague, Ghulam Abbas, were there at the bus stand. Mirza told the guard to provide security to Gangadhar Rao and to help him deposit his jewellery safely in the State Bank at Nanded. The police sent a distorted report about this incident and alleged that the two officers had helped a Hindu carry gold and jewellery outside the state thus violating the orders of the government banning export of gold and jewellery from the state. Mirza's explanation was called for. He said that the cash and jewellery had not been sent out of the state but to the district head-quarters. He had merely discharged his duty in providing protection to a citizen. He also added that, in any case, he had resigned from service and owed no explanation to the government. Ghulam Abbas was suspended on the basis of this false allegation.

In his letter of resignation, Mirza criticized the collusion between the government and the Ittehad, and advised the government to bring about peace in the state and to come to an agreement with India.

After resigning he went to Hyderabad. There he met Mulla Abdul Basith, who was the son of Mulla Abdul Qayyum, a reformer in the early part of the century already mentioned above. Mulla Abdul Basith was at that time editing the Urdu paper, *Payam*, which advocated a union with India. The Mirza found that the Ittehad and Razakars had led a large section of the Muslim community astray. The Urdu press fed their prejudices by giving a distorted version of events and concocting false stories. Many Muslims felt that the Ittehad's policy and approach were wrong but they were afraid to come out openly to oppose it.

Mirza contacted many like-minded people amongst the Muslims. Some of them decided to issue a joint statement appealing to the social conscience of the community. The statement criticized the prevailing situation, emphasized the need for cordiality amongst communities, advocated the disbandment of the Razakars, and suggested the introduction of a responsible government and accession to India. The statement was published in *Payam* on 13 August 1948.

Fareed Mirza; Mulla Abdul Basith, a retired District Judge and editor of *Khadim* Weekly, which was proscribed; and Baker Ali Mirza, a trade union leader, drafted the original statement. Ahmed Mirza, a retired Chief Engineer; Mohammad Hussain Jafferi, a retired Director of Public Instruction; Hussain Abdul Muneem, a retired Accountant General; and Nawab Manzoor Jung, a former Collector and a close friend of the Nizam also signed the statement. Some others who were in government service or in the University were willing to sign but were advised out of discretion not to do so.[120]

Shoebullah Khan, editor of the Urdu daily, *Imroz*, was upset that the statement was not given to him for publication in his paper. But it was explained to him that his paper was subject to pre-censorship and if sent to him, the statement would have been killed before publication.

The statement created a sensation. The issue of the *Payam* sold like hot cakes and at four times its normal price.

There was a howl of condemnation and protest in the Urdu press over it. *The Nizam Gazette* dubbed the signatories as traitors. Eighteen Urdu writers severely criticized the statement and attributed dishonourable and treasonable motives to the signatories. Mohammad Hussain Jafferi's son issued a statement condemning his father and others severely. He said that their conduct was reminiscent of Mir Jaffar and Mir Sadiq. One retired judge demanded capital punishment for the 'Seven Mirzas' as they were pejoratively called—though only three out of seven had the surname of Mirza. It was an insinuation against Sir Mirza Ismail also. The Ittehad supremo, Razvi, also referred to the statement in his speech four days later. He said that these people and some others like them would not be tolerated. He declared that any hand that was raised against the honour and the self-respect of Muslims would be cut off.

Later, one of the signatories of the statement, Ahmed Mirza, recanted. He said he had signed without reading it. In a letter, the Nizam pressurized Nawab Manzoor Jung to issue a contradiction. He received the Nizam's letter with due respect by touching it with his eyes and kissing it, but said he would not change even a comma in his statement. All the signatories and their families were harassed and lived under abuses and constant threat to their lives. Luckily the situation did not last long. But it lasted long enough to claim another victim.

❖ ❖ ❖

Shoebullah Khan was a handsome young man born in 1920. He was an opponent of communal fanaticism. He had successively worked in the *Taj* weekly and the *Rayyat* daily, both of which were banned for championing the cause of responsible government in Hyderabad. Then he founded a daily, *Imroz*, through which he exposed the atrocities of the Razakars and the police. Through his bold writings, he maintained the tempo of popular struggle against the Nizam's government and earned the ire of the Ittehad. On 21 August 1948, he wrote an editorial criticizing the stand of the Ittehad and advocating the state's accession to India. That midnight he, along with his brother-in-law Ismail Khan, was set upon by the Razakars when they were going home from the office of *Imroz* located at the house of B. Ramakrishna Rao. While two persons engaged Shoebullah in a conversation the third man shot him from behind with a revolver. Ismail was attacked with swords. Shoebullah fell on the ground. Then, as if to fulfill Razvi's threat, delivered in his speech on 19 August literally, that every hand raised against the honour of Muslims would be cut off, Shoeb's hand was cut off from his body. The cup of Razakars' atrocities was filling to the brim.

Shoebullah Khan fell a martyr to the cause of communal amity; Akbar Ali Khan, Mehdi Ali, and Fareed Mirza survived, and we will meet them later.

Kabaddi, Polo, and Caterpillar

There were pockets of Indian territory inside the Nizam's domain while portions of the Nizam's state lay inside the Indian territory. It had always been an informal border but with changing conditions and attitudes the 'defence' of borders was made strict. Incidents and border skirmishes began to occur regularly.

Razvi kept on fanning the fires of communalism. He made a call for volunteers to swell the ranks of his Razakars and their number went up, according to Razvi, to 200,000. Military training was imparted even to women. When he met V.P. Menon in Delhi, and the latter suggested a plebiscite to settle the future of the state, Razvi replied haughtily that the final arbiter would be the sword. A 'Weapons Week' was celebrated from 31 March 1948. In his inaugural speech on the occasion, Razvi urged his followers not to sheathe their swords until their goal of Islamic supremacy had been achieved. He also declared that in case of a showdown, forty-five million Muslims of India would act as their fifth columnists.[121]

Now at last, the city also began to be affected.

In 1947, the total strength of the Nizam's armed forces was 31,660. Of these, 10,000 belonged to the Subsidiary Force and 7,000 to the Hyderabad Contingent, both of which were under British control. Since the last two forces were being withdrawn, the Nizam's government argued that in the new situation it needed an armed force twice the original total strength. It also needed to equip it with modern weaponry besides refurbishing the old arms. It asked the Government of India to supply the required arms and equipment and, since there was a delay, proceeded to meet its requirements through imports. Its Army Chief, General El Edroos, was sent to England to shop for arms. But, land-locked as the state was, the import could not take place without the permission of the Government of India. An Australian gunrunner, Sydney Cotton, was therefore engaged to smuggle arms into Hyderabad in his aeroplanes. The Nizam sanctioned £ 1 million sterling for the import. Besides, manufacture of small arms and ammunition was also started in the state. To meet the shortage of petrol, alcohol plants in the state were converted to produce synthetic gasoline. The need for arms and equipment was not only felt by the armed forces and police but also for the Razakars. These were organized as a para-military force called *askar* with a strength of 43,824 men. This was in addition to the volunteers, who were armed with *lathis* and crude swords. There was also one brigade composed entirely of the Muslim refugees, who had come to the state from other parts of India following the riots sparked off at the time of the partition of India.

The Hyderabad army was almost entirely manned by members of one community, as were most of the police and the civil services. The officers of the army cut a fine figure in their impressive uniforms and with their impeccable manners. But, except for a handful, who had gone in aid of the British in the Second World War, they had never seen any action in living memory. Their experience was mostly confined to police work and ceremonial duties. They had no equipment necessary even for training and mock exercises.

In December 1947, the Nizam issued two orders. One banned the export of precious metals from the state into India and the other declared that the Indian currency was no longer legal tender in the state. Then it became known that the Nizam had sanctioned a loan of Rs 200 million to Pakistan. These were taken as hostile acts in breach of the Standstill Agreement. The Government of India asked for the cancellation of these orders and on its part tightened the economic blockade of the state. There were also border raids, both from and into Hyderabad. These increased in frequency and depredation as the months went by.[122]

The Razakars started attacking Indian trains passing through the state. After some incidents, particularly on 22 May 1948, the trains passing through the state were provided with armed guards. On 24 July, a company of Indian infantry passing through a strip of the Nizam's territory to an Indian enclave, was ambushed by Razakars at a village called Nanaj killing six and injuring an equal number. The Indian soldiers retaliated and killed the ambushers and occupied the village.

Irritants such as this were occurring daily. The Indian leadership had come to the conclusion that the Nizam would neither accede to India nor introduce responsible government in the state. A physical intervention would probably be inevitable sooner or later. The army was therefore asked to make an appreciation of the situation with that objective in view. Lieutenant General Goddard, Chief of the Southern Command, did this. His appreciation is interesting:

An ageing, headstrong, ill-advised, and anachronous ruler is at the head of an autocratic and worn-out administration, on which the various political agitations and trends are exercising an ever increasing, weakening influence. Behind this crumbling administrative edifice stands the Ittehad-ul-Musalmeen, fanatic, unrealistic and devoid of men skilled in public affairs. Engaged in a tussle with the administration and Ittehadis are the Communists who are in a semi-open revolt in the eastern districts of the state, and the satyagraha movements.[123]

While the strategy for a future attack was being worked out, the Indian police wanted the help of the army to check the depredations of the Razakars along the borders because they were causing panic and tension. It was then decided that the army would not stop at the border after the marauding Razakars had retreated to the safety of the state borders but would follow the doctrine of 'hot pursuit' and chase them across the border up to a limit which was extended up to 15 miles by July 1948. This operation was code-named 'Kabaddi'—after the popular Indian game of the same name which permits limited forays into the 'enemy' territory. The overall plan was named 'Operation Polo'. In July, it was feared that this code name had leaked out and so a new code-name 'Operation Caterpillar' was given to it on 19 July 1948.

The plan was to make two main thrusts into the state. One from Sholapur in the west at a distance of 299 kilometres from Hyderabad and the other from Vijayawada in the east—a distance of 287 kilometres. Subsidiary thrusts were to be made from the south and north from three places. The Air Force was to support the army and, if necessary, to bombard the airports to render them unfit for any flights. Hakimpet was the principal and Warangal and Bidar subsidiary airports. Major General J.N. Choudhuri was the man in overall charge of the operations. He started intensive exercises of his men at Pune.

At the political level negotiations continued. Lord Mountbatten and Walter Monckton tried their best to arrive at a settlement before Mountbatten left India in June 1948, but he was not destined to add this feather to his cap. Though, on an average, the state's delegation made one visit every three weeks to Delhi, no sub-stantial progress was made. Sardar Patel's attitude also stiffened after Mountbatten's departure. He had succumbed to the latter's charms and conceded a great deal but when even Mountbatten failed, all hope was lost in Delhi.

On 17 August 1948, Laik Ali informed Nehru, the Prime Minister of India, that his government was approaching the United Nations to resolve the dispute between Hyderabad and India. Delhi replied that, this being an internal matter of India, the United Nations had no locus standi. The facilities for the flight of the Hyderabad delegation to the United Nations were therefore refused. However, the delegation led by Nawab Moin Nawaz Jung, Foreign Minister of Hyderabad, went to Pakistan and from there flew to Paris to place their case before the Security Council of the United Nations.

The die was now cast and both sides knew that action was immi-nent. The men in power had no doubt about the superior military might of India. The question on either side was not whether the state could ever win in an armed conflict against India. It was sim-ply: how long could it resist it. The Indian military assessment was that it would last three weeks. The versions about Hyderabad's own assessment varied vastly. The Prime Minister, Laik Ali, said that El Edroos gave half of that figure to the Nizam, but his own estimate was that the resistance could last four to six weeks.

During the three days of the discussions of the draft Standstill Agreement between 23–5 October 1947 by the Executive Council, one meeting was held at the King Kothi in the presence of the Nizam. General El Edroos was specially invited to it as the Army Chief. Another special invitee was Raja Bahadur Aravamudu Ayangar, the author of the Nizam's quaint legislative reforms. The Nizam asked each one present there for his opinion on the proposal for the Standstill Agreement.

Ayangar asked El Edroos: 'How long can we hold out against an attack by the Indian Army?'

El Edroos replied: 'Not more than four days.' The Nizam intervened and said: 'Not more than two.' Ayangar then suggested acceptance of the Standstill Agreement. What happened subsequently has already been described.[124]

In early September, Laik Ali flew secretly to Pakistan in Sydney Cotton's aeroplane. He was to meet the founder of Pakistan and its Governor General, M.A. Jinnah. The purpose was to seek Jinnah's counsel and also to ascertain what sort of support Pakistan could lend to Hyderabad in case of an attack by India. Jinnah was on his deathbed and Laik Ali could not meet him. No one else could give an authoritative reply to Laik Ali's query. There he was told that the Pakistan intelligence expected an attack by India on 23 September. This tallied with Laik Ali's own intelligence.

The Indian Army headquarters wanted some more time to mount an attack. It was told firmly on 9 September 1948 that the attack should be launched on the morning of 13 September. But the Nizam and his confidants seemed to have got the intelligence that the fateful day was 15 September 1948. They prepared themselves for that.

The main thrust of the attack was to come from the west. On that front, the first obstacle for the Indian Army was Naldurg, some 19 kilometres inside the border. It was feared that the Nizam's army would have blown up the narrow bridge on the Bori River. The advancing army could not believe its luck when it found the bridge intact. The capture of the strategic fort and town of Naldurg cost the Indian Army only two shots!

The next point where the advancing army could be very vulnerable was Talmud, where for about 18 kilometres the road passed through a narrow winding valley. The hillocks on either side had a lot of jungle growth and thus presented an excellent vantage point for an ambush. The Indian Army therefore approached this place very cautiously. An air strike had been made earlier. Here too, to their utter surprise, the advancing column found the place abandoned. After that it was a straight road and all the elaborate strategies worked out by the Indian Army seemed to have been a waste of effort.

The advancing column at Bidar also met no resistance and when General Choudhuri landed there in a Dakota plane on 17 September, he found Indian flags flying all over and citizens gathered in clusters to greet him. The only thing that slowed the march of the Indian Army was the report that the roads had been mined but those also seemed to be exaggerated. In any case now there were the captured officers and men of the state's army to guide and lead them.

Hyderabad was now in the midst of hectic activity. There were frantic consultations and a great deal of excitement and tension. Busloads of Razakars roamed the streets shouting slogans declaring their loyalty to the Nizam and Razvi and reiterating their resolve for fighting a holy war and, if necessary, to drink the cup of martyrdom.

The first thing that the State Government did was to move K.M. Munshi from his official residence in the cantonment and place him under protective custody at the Lake View Guest House next to the Shah Manzil, the official residence of the Prime Minister, (present Raj Bhavan). Munshi had already burnt all the important documents. He had taken care earlier to send his diaries, the manuscript of the novel that he was writing, and other state papers in a sealed cover to Buch who was a Joint Secretary in the Defence Ministry. They were to be passed on to his wife, Leelavati Munshi, should anything happen to Munshi.

The Prime Minister of Hyderabad had just returned after a conference with his Commander in the control room when a signal was received that the tanks and armoured cars of the Indian Army were moving on the Kalyani-Bidar road. Laik Ali looked up at the map on the wall. Then he peered hard but found no road linking the two towns. He rang up the Chief Engineer of roads and buildings to check if there was any road between the two towns. The Chief Engineer replied proudly that a first-class road had been laid and opened only a few days ago. But the army maps did not show that.

Kasim Razvi dropped in at that time. To Laik Ali, in his depressed mood, the bearded Field Marshal of the Razakar force looked better than his Army Chief. Laik Ali asked him whether he could spare some men to go to the front. He said yes of course but they would have to be provided with arms. Then he left saying he would be back soon. He appeared three hours later and said four battalions of Razakars were ready to go anywhere.[125]

Some of them were dispatched, mostly armed with rough homemade spears, and were transported in the buses of the Road Transport Department because there was such an acute dearth of military vehicles.

The columns of the Indian Army, advancing without meeting any resistance on the eastern front, had reached Suryapet. Major Dhanarajulu Naidu, leading his column of armoured cars, saw boys in their teens shouting slogans like *Allah-ho-Akbar* and *Shah Osman Zindabad* rushing to attack the armoured cars. Naidu thought of his own son who was in a college at Madras. And, as he would with him, he shouted at them, 'Go home, boys. Don't be mad.' Most obeyed, as his son would have. Some persisted. A hail of bullets issued from one of the cars. Three boys fell in a heap. The rest ran back in a few minutes. Then the column resumed its onward march.[126]

While the state forces were retreating as fast as they could, the Urdu papers and the Deccan Radio were reporting victories and heroic resistance by the state forces everywhere.

The Urdu press, by and large, had ranged itself on the side of the government and Razvi—if there was any difference between the two now. Razvi, without any position in the government, toured the districts often accompanied by ministers, and made speeches exhorting the people to rise as one man against India.

The *Nizam Gazette*, an Urdu paper and virtually an official organ, referred to Hindustan as 'Hindu Asthan', thus splitting one noun into two words to paste a religious label on a secular state. The *Rehbar-e-Deccan*, the Ittehad paper, invariably called Indian Union 'Hindu Union' and referred to All India Radio as Patel Radio (Patel was the Home Minister of India). In its issue of 27 July 1948, it quoted Razvi as saying that if Hyderabad was attacked, Hindus would be destroyed because they had money, and trade, and everything. Muslims had nothing to lose. He concluded by warning that in case of attack, he would not be responsible for the safety of the Red Fort!

These papers exulted in India's discomfiture in Kashmir. They extolled and exaggerated the achievements, real or imaginary, of the 'Azad' Kashmir government and adopted its cause as their own. Between the 7–11 September 1948 the statements of solidarity with the Nizam by the students of Baluchistan, the Pathan Jirgah, and of Shah Farooq of Egypt were highlighted in all papers. On the 9 September, the *Rehabar-e-Deccan* declared that Hyderabad was far more powerful than India and asked whether Pandit Nehru could survive a collision with it.

On 14 September, the *Meezan* reported that India had invaded the state but the attack on Naldurg and Nalgonda had proved ineffective. In another column it reported that the Nizam's forces had retaken Talmud. There was a declaration in London by some Muslim leaders that the entire Muslim world would unite in favour of the Nizam.

On 15 September, stiff resistance by the Hyderabad forces was reported at Jalna and Hangoli. The advance at Talmud had been checked.

A dispatch stated: 'By God's grace, the enemy was beaten back at Jalna and Raichur. There was a surprising demonstration of courage and bravery by the state forces.'

On the day of the announcement of a cease-fire by the Nizam, that is, 17 September, the *Meezan* carried a news item datelined London that eight tanks of Baldev Singh—the Defence Minister of India—were destroyed and the brave soldiers of Hyderabad were massacring the Indian Army.

It was a propaganda war by a committed press. To the official handouts they added their own wishful thinking. The Urdu press was living in a fool's paradise and was inviting its readers to do likewise.

The Information Department of the State Government had put up a poster at the General Post Office showing the Red Fort in the background. In the foreground, the Nizam was shown with a slipper in his hand, giving a thrashing to Nehru and Patel.

The Deccan Radio was also extolling the courage and bravery of its soldiers. Most of the material, used by the papers and the radio, was the same and emanated from a common source. The retreat of the Hyderabad army was described as tactical withdrawal, the resistance was always praised as heroic. On the third day, a captain of the state army came to the radio station and said that a major of the Indian Army had been captured and the authorities would like his confessions to be broadcast. Mirza Zafarul Hasan, the Assistant Director of the Station, took a wire-recorder with him to the Fateh Maidan, where the captain was supposed to have been lodged. There he was told sheepishly that no Indian Army officer in fact had been captured. 'One of our own officers will pose as one and narrate his story.'

Zafarul Hasan advised against the broadcast saying the public would see through it. His advice was accepted.[127]

While the Deccan Radio was still boasting news of the courage and bravery of its soldiers, Aurangabad fell and people tuned in to the Indian radio heard the announcement: 'This is All India Radio, Aurangabad.' That demoralized even the staff of the Deccan Radio.

By 15 September, soldiers and Razakars had started returning home, deserting some of the fronts. When a bus full of Razakars passed through Afzul Ganj, some passers-by shouted: 'Shah Osman Zindabad', 'Azad Hyderabad *Payandabad*'—the usual slogans of Razakars popular those days. Contrary to the normal practice, there were no answering slogans from the bus.

Some people were insisting that the Deccan radio should declare that Hyderabad was a Muslim state. Zafarul Hasan asked for orders from the Controller of Broadcasting, Hameedudin Ahmed. The latter did not reply. He left the station quietly and did not return.

On 16 September, Deen Yar Jung, Director-General of Police summoned Zafarul Hasan, who was by now virtually the Controller of the Deccan Radio. Deen Yar Jung told Zafar-ul-Hasan to stop all programmes and play only music.

He told Zafar that the Indian Army was about 25 miles from the city.

Zafar said defiantly: 'We will revive the memories of Stalingrad.'

'Baba,' the Nawab reprimanded Zafar, 'the time for slogans has passed. Now just play music.'

Zafar said, 'On hearing the first disc, people's hearts will break.'

At the radio station his colleagues, Majid, Virasat Mirza, and Rizwan were awaiting his return anxiously. They told him that they had been told by Salim Bin Sayeed to stop broadcasting slogans and to start playing music. In a frenzy, Zafar led them all into the studio and shouted into the microphone: 'We were independent. We are independent. We will remain independent.' That was the last act of bravado of the employees of the Deccan Radio.

On the morning of 17 September, Kasim Razvi rang up Zafar at the radio station to say that there were rumours that he had fled Hyderabad in Sydney Cotton's aeroplane to Pakistan. He wanted to dispel these rumours by making a broadcast. Zafar told him that he could come at 10.30 a.m.

Razvi started by saying that the Indian beasts had committed an act of aggression and were advancing towards the capital. But then he changed his tone and added: 'The rumours about my having fled to Pakistan are incorrect. I have lived with you and shall die with you. I have drawn the first drop of blood from you but I shall not take the last. I appeal to you to bear whatever misfortune befalls us with courage and fortitude. This was perhaps written in our fate; God willed it that way.'[128]

This was the soberest speech he had ever made. This was also his last. Next time he was to open his mouth would be only in a court at his trial.

Then he came out from the studio. Some members of the staff of the radio station embraced him and wept. As he reached his car, he looked back at the building and saw the state flag fluttering on top. He saluted it in military style, turned back and sped.

Inside the studio, after Razvi's speech, Badar Rizvan played a disc which sang Saqib Lakhnavi's famous lines:

Zamana bade shouk se sun raha tha
Hameen so gaye dastan kehte kehte

(All were listening with eyes so bright
Only I dozed off while narrating my plight)

The Debacle

During the Police Action, Laik Ali used to meet the Nizam every morning. On 16 September he had two meetings in the forenoon. In the second meeting, Laik Ali felt that the Nizam had a distant look in his eyes.

In the afternoon there were summons from the King Kothi for another meeting. This time the Nizam had a concentrated look. The Nizam told Laik Ali that all his calculations had gone wrong. 'Pakistan has remained a silent spectator. No Muslim country has made a move in our favour. Your army has put up a hopeless show. The Security Council is yet to meet. The Indian Army is racing towards the city from all directions.' The Nizam demanded his resignation by 9 a.m. the next day. Laik Ali felt that the Nizam was at that time concerned for his own safety and that the hour for final decision for him had arrived.[129]

Laik Ali wanted some time for himself to think over the Nizam's ultimatum to him. But he got a message that the Nizam wanted him immediately. There was nothing that either one had to convey to the other. As the two sat facing each other in silence, they heard the drone of some aeroplanes flying over the King Kothi. That was followed by the clatter of anti-aircraft guns which had been installed at the palace.

'Whose planes were they?' asked the Nizam nervously. Laik Ali knew as little. Someone rushed out to find out. Must be the enemy's, otherwise why had the guns been fired? All was guess-work. Laik Ali felt that already he was not with his ruler, that he was not the Prime Minister. The two sat silent, distant, each lost in his own world. It was better to be at the control room, thought Laik Ali and he got up and took the Nizam's leave.

Early in the morning the Railway Chief rang up Laik Ali to say that he had received a message from Bibinagar that heavy shelling was heard there. Bibinagar was only forty-five kilometres away from the city.

General EI Edroos came a little later and said he'd just returned from the western front. 'Our boys are so fatigued and worn out that they can't hold out any longer.'

Laik Ali looked over the shoulders of the woe-begone Commander and asked: 'Any news from Paris?'

Some one answered from behind Edroos, 'No Sir, but we have lots of messages from Pakistan.' He summarized them for the Premier's benefit. 'The Security Council had met at 4.00 p.m. yes-terday. It had decided to take our case on the agenda. The hearing will begin on 20 September.' The Commander said that was three days away. He would be surprised if they could hold out for more than three hours.

On the morning of 17 September 1948, Laik Ali drove to the King Kothi and submitted his resignation to the Nizam. He also advised him to burn all the important papers. He did likewise in his own office.

Abdul Rahim, Minister for Railways, came in a rush and said, 'Sir, I have a request to make. We know we'd all be shot dead. But Razvi Saheb will be tortured; his body will be cut into pieces and fed to vultures. Can you have him flown out to Pakistan or any other country where he would be safe?'

Laik Ali saw the point. He phoned El Edroos and asked if he could arrange that. 'Impossible, Sir,' the General said. 'Even if we made the attempt there are too many enemy planes covering the skies. The plane will be brought down.[130]

About noon of the same day, a messenger brought a note from the Nizam to K.M. Munshi asking him whether he could see him at 4.00 p.m.

A desolate Nizam greeted him at the King Kothi. He said: 'The vultures have resigned. I don't know what to do.' He handed over Laik Ali's letter of resignation. His hands were shaking. He had had this problem for some time which became pronounced when he was tense or angry.

After a brief discussion, Munshi suggested that the Nizam should make a broadcast welcoming the Police Action and withdrawing his complaint to the Security Council.

'But how does one broadcast?' asked the Nizam innocently.

'Very simple,' said Munshi, 'you speak into a tube.'

'All right,' the Nizam agreed. 'But then you should also do likewise.' It was the Nizam's first visit to the radio station. He was nervous, as all broadcasters are when they first enter the studio and face the microphone. The gravity of the occasion and the text of the broadcast added to that. It was only natural that his voice should tremble and he should fumble for words.[131] He addressed Munshi as 'K.M. *ji*, Munshi ji' instead of 'Munshi ji'.

At the radio station, no red carpet was spread for the Nizam, no formalities were observed. No music, no anthem was played before or after the broadcast. The speech was in English. Nobody bothered to translate it into Urdu. At that moment an era ended. While the Indian Army was yet to arrive a day later, the old order had already collapsed.

After the broadcast the Nizam drove to King Kothi, and Munshi, to Bolarum. Osman Ali Khan made his short journey quietly and went to brood in his room. Munshi found the streets full of excited crowds shouting national slogans. There were knots of people and processions everywhere. Munshi was mobbed and had to address groups of people here and there. There was a general release of tension and a new, quivering anticipation. That night the city changed a great deal. Many khaki uniforms were discarded, many beards, shaved. The shouting, rampaging crowds of Razakars disappeared magically.

The citizens emerged from their houses. People of all ages came out in throngs waving the tricolours of India. Suddenly, where there was fear and panic amongst people, there was life and laughter.

Considering the slow pace of advance of the Indian Army, it was agreed that the surrender ceremony would take place eight kilometres out of the city at 4.00 p.m.

General Edroos was waiting at the appointed place with one aide. General Choudhuri reached the spot exactly on time. His accompanying team had had a wash a little earlier and looked spick and span in their ceremonial uniforms. El Edroos saluted. Choudhuri returned it and then spoke gravely.

'I have been ordered by Lt General Maharaj Rajendrasinhji, General Officer Commanding-in-Chief, Southern Command, to take the surrender of your army.'

'You have it.'

'You understand that this surrender is unconditional.'

'Yes, I understand.'[132]

Choudhuri's grim visage melted into a smile. He stretched his hand and shook El Edroos by the hand. Then he opened his cigarette case and offered El Edroos a smoke. Edroos proffered a lighter. Choudhuri's team joined them. Crowds had begun to gather at the corner of the Parade Ground in Secunderabad since morning to greet the Indian Army.

It was a sea of humanity—heads, bare and covered. Men and women, ten, twenty deep, children on shoulders, on heads of adults, unattached young people perched on the railings, on treetops, even on telephone poles. It was a riot of colours, dresses of all types in all the colours of rainbow, only deeper, like a field of flowers of different hues. And then tricolours— thousands of them, each hand holding one or two green, white, and ochre—fluttering joyously were seen all around. Had all the people been stitching these flags all these days? Flags made of cloth, and of paper quivered in the gentle breeze. They reflected the frisson of the hands holding them. There was clapping and wild cheering, shouting and shrieking. People threw flower- petals at soldiers sitting on top of armoured cars and waving to crowds. Garlands were flung onto the army vehicles. Throngs of people were shouting slogans that could not be uttered till the previous day.

'*Qaumi nara*,' a shrill lone voice shouted. And the mob shouted back in unison, in a loud abandon, '*Jai Hind*'. This was taken up and repeated by different groups. 'Mahatma Gandhi' cried one voice—'*Ki Jai*' came the chorus. Pandit Nehru—*Zindabad!* Sardar Patel—*Zindabad!* General Choudhuri—*Zindabad!* Hindustani Fauj—*Zindabad!* Bharat Mata—*ki jai.*

Somebody suddenly shouted 'Razakar' and the crowd roared back *'Murdabad'*. But that was a discordant note. The cheerleaders brought them back to the cycle of recitation of *zindabads*. It was a sacred, positive moment. Let it not be marred by negative, profane outbursts.

There was no order, no sequence but one slogan followed another without any interruption.

Soon there was quiet everywhere. Silence and knowledge of security, such as the city had not felt for the last many months, overcame it. A feeling of peace wrapped it, like a snug coverlet. It too slid into sleep, exhausted and relieved.

Tomorrow would be a new dawn.

B.P.R.Vithal, an IAS officer who retired as Principal Secretary and then served as a member of the 10th Finance Commission was, at the time of Police Action, a young man of 21, studying at Madras. His father, Ram Narsu, was an Assistant Professor in the Nizam College. He was an outspoken non-conformist and did not hesitate to utilize his lectures on British history to underline the justification of the aspiration for freedom amongst Indians. The Principal, an Englishman called Turner, did not like him and terminated his services one day on the plea that the post had ceased to exist. Narsu's wife was a friend of the adopted daughter of Sir Akbar Hyadari, the Prime Minister. Narsu was re-instated through Sir Akbar's intercessions.

Vithal, meanwhile, had finished his schooling at the Aliya and had joined the Nizam College. A keen, sensitive student, Vithal became interested in politics and took part in the Quit India Movement of 1942. He also used to wear khadi. The new Principal of the college, Khader Hussain Khan, did not approve of his conduct. He called Narsu and told him about his son's activities and then gave him an ultimatum: 'One of you will have to leave the college—you or your son.' So Vithal went and joined the Christian College at Madras. He found comparatively greater freedom to indulge in his juvenile politics there. Like some sensitive young people, Vithal started maintaining a private journal.

In and around the city, tension had started mounting in 1948. Ram Narsu asked a student of his, Makhdoom Ali Khan, who had by then become the Treasurer of the Ittehad, to keep his jewellery and valuables in safe custody, just in case ... .

'Don't worry, Sir,' replied Makhdoom respectfully, as he took the packet, 'Insha Allah everything will be all right.'

From the newspapers in Madras in September 1948, Vithal gathered that something serious was in the offing. He took the train from Madras on 11 September and reached home on the evening of 12 September to the mild surprise of his family.

The Indian forces moved into the state early next morning. His was the last train to have been permitted to enter the state. On 17 September, when the Nizam read his surrender speech over the radio, Vithal noted that he tried to sound innocent as if he had been misled. The next day Vithal went to the telegraph office to send a telegram to his relatives in Vijayawada to inform them that the family was safe. As he stood in a queue, a Muslim youth walked in nonchalantly and stood at the head of the line. Vithal told him that there was a queue and that he should not break it. The young man quietly came back and stood behind Vithal.

That night Vithal recorded the incident in his journal and added a comment—'Can you imagine my doing such a thing a few days ago!'

The same afternoon Makhdoom Ali Khan came to Ram Narsu. He returned the packet of jewellery which had been in his safe-keeping. Then he handed Ram Narsu another packet.

'What is this?' the teacher asked.

'Sir, now it is my turn to request you to keep our jewellery in safe custody with you. If you don't mind'

The gentle teacher's voice choked as he accepted the packet, patted the young man and said, 'Don't worry. With God's grace things will be all right.'

THREE: End of an Order

Hope, Despair, Hope

The Government of India had prepared itself fully for the takeover of the administration in the state. A civil team had been selected in advance and kept ready. While General Choudhuri was the Military Governor, D.S. Bakhle of ICS was appointed the Chief Civil Administrator. A team of five, including Choudhuri and Zain Yar Jung, who had been the Agent General of Hyderabad at Delhi, constituted the new ministry. A Civil Administrator was posted in each of the 16 districts. These arrangements came into effect on 19 September 1948.

Laik Ali, his ministers, General EI Edroos, Razvi, and some others were placed under house arrest. Later, Razvi was taken to the military jail at Trimulgherry, and some others were moved to the Central Jail at Chanchalguda.

All officials of the state, especially Muslims, were subjected to a quick screening. Some were removed, some were reduced in rank, and some were put in jail, pending investigations. On 26 October 1948, Choudhuri summoned all secretaries and heads of departments of the government at the Bolarum Residency. He wanted to talk with some of them individually and make his own assessment on the basis of the dossiers which had been prepared on various officers and given to him.

Rai Janaki Pershad was then acting as Director of Information and Public Relations.

He went in his sherwani and fez cap, which he had always worn outside his house. The ADC to the Military Governor, Captain Pyare Lal, called officials one by one. He would peep into the waiting hall and call the name politely, as nurses do in clinics.

'Mr Rai Janaki Pershad,' the ADC called softly, not knowing that the prefix of 'Mr' was superfluous with Rai

The gentleman got up and made for the door. The ADC stopped him. 'Not you, yet.' And he waited. Nobody else got up. The ADC looked at the list and called the next name. Habeebur Rehman went in.

The ADC came out again as Rehman emerged from his interview.

'Mr Rai Janaki Pershad,' he called.

Janaki Pershad got up and began to make for the door with all the dignity at his command. The ADC said sharply, 'Not you Mr,' he said brusquely. 'I want Mr Rai Janaki Pershad.'

'I *am* Rai Janaki Pershad,' said the Acting Head of the Information Department in an offended tone.

'Oh!' Captain Pyare Lal observed. 'Then why are you dressed like a Muslim?'

'This is the way we dress here,' replied Janaki Pershad coolly. The ADC smiled in embarrassment and ushered the officer in.

Rai Dilsukh Ram was a law graduate and had done his articles from London. He was a Joint Secretary in the Finance Department of the Secretariat and was currently on deputation as Head of the Income Tax Department.

He did not respond to the summons of General Choudhuri for the interview. When his explanation was called, he replied that he was a highly educated person, an England-returned chartered accountant, and therefore, could not be summoned by a Military Officer who was not even a graduate. He was then in his 50s. Unlike most of his other colleagues, he was not promoted to the IAS. He did not care. A colony named after him, Dilsukh Nagar, later sprang up on the road to Vijayawada.

Later, General Choudhuri visited the Board of Revenue. Syed Kalimullah Qadri was a member of the Board. He was very orthodox and a strict observer of his faith and used to give away all but Rs 300 of his monthly salary of Rs 2,250 in charities. He did not come for the group photograph saying that photography was prohibited in Islam. This was taken as an affront to the Military Governor but was allowed to pass. He was then transferred and posted as Commissioner of Excise. Qadri did not accept the posting on the plea that this subject too was repugnant to the 'spirit' of Islam since it dealt with alcohol, which was taboo in his religion. Later, he was asked to appear for an interview for consideration for appointment to the IAS. He declined to do so, saying that the Hyderabad Civil Service (HCS) was equivalent to ICS and he was at a level at which one holds interviews, not appears for them. He was transferred to Aurangabad as Collector and retired from that post in due course.

The Civil Administrators in the district, all ICS officers specially selected from the Bombay and Madras provinces, were placed above the respective District Collectors. They tackled the situations according to their own judgment. Pimputkar was a gruff, no-nonsense ICS officer from Bombay. He was given the charge of Bir district. On his arrival, he put all district officers including the Civil Judge, Srinivas Rao, in the district jail. Three days later, when he thought they must have been suitably demoralized, he sent for Srinivas Rao and confidentially asked his opinion about the Muslim officers. Rao replied they were all right. This omnibus clean chit made Pimputkar suspicious of Rao. He thought that either Rao was partial to his colleagues or had not applied his mind. He therefore extended his detention also.[133]

Habeeb Mohammad, the fanatic Commissioner of Warangal, about whom we have written earlier, was arrested. From his grand official mansion, he was marched to the local jail in prisoner's clothes. Not many commiserated with him.

Mehmood Ali, a tahsildar in Warangal district, was arrested and imprisoned for two-and-a-half years. It was then discovered that, during the period of his alleged delinquencies, he was not there at that time. On that alibi he was released, reinstated, and promoted.

Mir Vilayat Ali, a Superintendent in the Board of Revenue, had written articles and pamphlets against the Razakars when their menace was rising. However, after the Police Action, he was asked to proceed on retirement, or to face charges. He chose the latter course.

More notable than that was the retaliation against the Razakars. It was easy to dub any Muslim as one. The victims of the Razakars—and the relations and friends of those who had suffered at their hands—were now out to avenge themselves. They identified the alleged culprits to the advancing army who often dispensed summary justice to them. More than the army, it was their camp followers and the aggrieved people themselves who could now settle scores with the officials, with the local leaders, and other lumpen elements who had earlier perpetrated atrocities on them. The reprisals were generally severe in the western district of the state which had suffered the most at the hands of the Razakars. In some villages, men, women, and children were killed, and houses burnt. In some cases women were raped. Muslims from villages flocked to towns for safety and in many cases even fled from there to the safety of the city. The Razakars, who only weeks earlier had strutted about in their beards and uniforms, shed them both and either burnt them or dumped them in wells. Many wells were flushed out even in Secunderabad and dumped uniforms and lethal weapons were recovered from them.

Some Muslim families, even from Secunderabad, moved to the older parts of the city to seek safety in their numbers. There was tension in Hyderabad but no disturbance. Social workers like Padmaja Naidu, Jaisoorya, Gyan Kumari Heda, Subbiah, and Motilal Patny went round the city pacifying the Hindus and infusing confidence in the terrified minority.

On top of that came the announcement that all refugee camps for the Hindus who had fled from Hyderabad to Berar, Chanda, and the Central Provinces would be closed by 21 October 1948. On 25 September, the *Deccan Chronicle* reported that 200,000 Hindu refugees were returning to the state on the closure of these camps.

The city of Hyderabad was, therefore, subjected to intense pressure. Memories of the recent past haunted people. How the people had changed, how they had turned against each other and how men of straw had come to direct the lives and affairs of the citizens. It was strange to hear perpetrators of injustice complain now of injustice to them. What had happened was no ordinary occurrence. It was a drastic reversal of established order.

Slowly, normalcy began to return. For the man in the street, the old pace resumed. The borders, the invisible barriers between the state and the rest of the country, disappeared. General Choudhuri, and the members of the new government, mixed freely with the local people. Soon the outsiders were overwhelmed by the charm, the polite manners, and generous hospitality of the local populace. The local aristocrats, industrialists, and influence peddlers lost no time in ingratiating themselves with the new men in power.

The new administration found that the levers of power were predominantly in the hands of one community. In a state where they constituted about 12 per cent of the population, Muslims held every senior appointment. Bakhle, the Chief Civil Administrator, asked for the civil list of 1948, the latest available. As he sat flipping through its pages, he was surprised. He found the situation in the field the same as in the Secretariat. Of the 16 secretaries, only one, L.N. Gupta, was a non-Muslim. The officers in the Secretariat, down to Chief Superintendents and Registrars, numbered 118. Out of them there were only 13 Hindus and four Christians. Out of 51 heads of departments, ten were Hindus, two Parsees, and one Christian. The total non-Muslim representation in the senior levels worked out to less than 15 per cent The redressal of this glaring imbalance had been one of the points in the representations of various political associations like the Hyderabad Political Conference and the State Congress.

Amongst the terms offered to the Nizam on 23 June 1948, the Government of India had proposed that the communal composition of the proposed Constituent Assembly and the services between non-Muslims and Muslims would be changed to 60:40 by 1 January 1954, that is, over a period of six years. The Nizam summarily rejected this. 'Leave it to my judgment,' he had replied. Now the judgment had passed on to the hands of the other party. There was pressure for change from the underdogs of yesteryears.

Here we return to our heroes: those who had dissented and spoke with sanity, men of faith and courage, men who stood up and suffered.

Nawab Akbar Yar Jung, who had put Lord Krishna in the galaxy of prophets, was lucky. Perhaps the timing of his pronouncement had turned out to be opportune. In the middle of the 1930s there was still some sanity. A decade later perhaps it would have earned him a severe, summary, and even a capital disposal. As it turned out, he lived to see his people suffer the consequences of criticizing his sober interpretation of the holy book of his faith. He passed away peacefully in 1957.

Nawab Mir Akbar Ali Khan formally joined the Congress after the Police Action. He became the Vice-President of the reception committee of the State Congress when its session was held in Hyderabad in 1949. Later, for three terms, spanning 18 years, he was a Member of the Rajya Sabha, the upper house of the Indian Parliament, out of that, for 11 years, he was its Vice-Chairman. This was followed by Governorship of two states successively, Uttar Pradesh and Orissa. As Governor of Orissa, in April 1976, he invited his old friend and socialist leader, Jaya Prakash Narayan for dinner. J.P. had by then become an arch political enemy of the then Prime Minister, Indira Gandhi. A phone call came to Mir Akbar Ali Khan from Delhi advising him to cancel the dinner. He replied that it was a private dinner for an old friend and he could not bring himself to call it off. He was told that the Prime Minister was not happy about it. 'I note that,' he replied. Later that evening the two friends met and had dinner together. The next morning he sent his resignation and returned to Hyderabad. There he took up cultural causes, worked for communal harmony, and was respected as an elder statesman. He passed away in 1994.

Nawab Ali Yavar Jung emerged from his brief eclipse and resumed his meteoric rise. He became Vice-Chancellor successively of the Osmania and Aligarh Muslim Universities, and then held a string of ambassadorial assignments in Argentina, Egypt, Yugoslavia, Greece, France, and the United States of America. Finally, in 1976, he died of a heart attack in harness as the Governor of Maharashtra.

Mehdi Ali, who had protested against the ravages of the Razakars as Deputy Collector of Madhira, was on leave when the Police Action took place. He resumed duty after the change-over. When in 1949, his turn came for promotion as Collector, he found that his name was missing from the list of eight who had been promoted. There was no Muslim name in the list. Mehdi Ali

contacted Mulla Abdul Basith, who was one of the famous seven
Mirzas. Basith met Nehru and complained about the discrimination under the new dispensation. Nehru did not believe it. Basith
gave him a copy of the order. Nehru was shocked. He rang up the
Chief Civil Administrator. 'Bakhle,' he said, 'what is happening?'

Bakhle was a little surprised at the call. Nothing particular
had happened which should occasion an inquiry from the Prime
Minister. 'Nothing, Sir, everything is all right.'

'You have promoted some officers as Collectors?'

'Yes, Sir.'

'How is it that there is no Muslim in the list?'

'We have done some screening. And also we are trying to
redress the heavy imbalance in favour of ... .'

'This is too much and too sudden. Go slow. Let them not feel
that we are discriminating ... .'

'Yes, Sir, I shall have another look at it.'

The list was revised. Three Muslims were included in the new
list. Mehdi Ali got his due.

But Mehdi Ali did not advance beyond the Collectorship. Some
years later when his turn came for promotion, he was overlooked.
At Delhi, Vohra, an ICS officer who had been trained along with
him, told him that some superior officer had recorded in his confidential roll that 'his loyalties are divided'.

Loyalties divided? In an officer who at the height of communalism had protested against it and suffered! A man who could
have gone away to Pakistan as thousands had, but did not. There
was no point in appealing, in agitating. How could he fight such
an allegation? How can any Muslim in India fight such haunting
shadows?

However, Mehdi Ali did not exhibit bitterness even if he felt
any. Prejudice will never be eradicated from humanity.

Fareed Mirza's struggle and his agony did not end with the
Police Action. Just as he had tried to stem the atrocities of the
Razakars, now he struggled to oppose reprisals. He toured the
state along with other leaders like Basith to help the authorities
restore order and confidence amongst the terror-stricken minority.
He crusaded for justice. The government soon offered to take him
back in service at the level at which he had left it. He represented

that since his resignation, his juniors had been promoted as Deputy Collectors. After reconsideration he too was promoted after one year of uncertainty.

He joined the team of Pandit Sunder Lal and Qazi Abdul Ghaffar which toured parts of the state to conduct an inquiry into the 'atrocities' committed against Muslims as reprisals for the *zoolum* (violence) of the Razakars. He wrote to the authorities about the sad plight of the Muslims and issued statements. He was also a member of the delegation which met Sardar Patel on 13 April 1949 to apprise him of the situation and request for an end of the military rule. Many friends and politicians asked Fareed Mirza to join politics, but he refused.[134] Omar Khalidi edited a volume entitled, *Hyderabad After the Fall*, in which he has reproduced parts of the Report referred to above, along with an introduction. But, given the demographic composition of the time, the figure of 'at least 200,000 Muslim' causalities mentioned by Khalidi on the basis of the report seems to be a gross exaggeration.[135]

When the report finally became public, the outer limit of casualties was put at 40,000.

On being overlooked when the time came for him to be promoted as Collector, Mirza resigned in 1961. He started a printing press and did some poultry farming till he died in 2001. He too was not bitter.

When Pandit Nehru and Maulana Azad visited Hyderabad after the Police Action, an interesting incident was narrated to Azad as an instance of harassment of the Muslims. Three workers of the Railway Workshop at Lallaguda—two Muslims and one Hindu, all good friends—were having lunch together on the lawn of the workshop. After a hearty meal, one of the Muslims named Shakir belched and as he did that he said: Alhamdullillah (God be praised). The Hindu friend, Shamraj, asked mischievously: 'What do you say when your fart?'

Shakir replied, 'We say, Jai Hind' (Salute India)!

They all laughed at this repartee. The next day Shakir was picked up by the police and detained.

Azad had a hearty laugh, and immediately called Nehru and narrated the incident to him. 'How petty these bureaucrats can get,' said Nehru impatiently.

The man was released the same evening.

Many Muslims migrated to Pakistan—some out of commitment to a cause and others out of fear of the new order. They had dreamt of an Islamic State, of being masters in a theocratic El Dorado. That dream had crashed around them. But there was another piece of the Promised Land not far away—Pakistan.

A stream of emigration started. Some, who had more than devotion and pious aspiration, went further. Those who had some good qualifications went to England, to the United States of America, to Canada. Soon little Hyderabads sprang up on foreign soils. They took with them small plants of their memories. Gardens of nostalgia grew on three continents. Earlier, Hyderabad had known only people coming to it and settling down there. For the first time it saw people were fleeing it. Some of them would soon be disillusioned. Could there be a better place to live in? People who had ever drunk of the water of the Osman Sagar Lake belonged only to Hyderabad. How could they be at peace with themselves anywhere else?

An Escape and a Sentence

On 7 March 1950, the city woke up to a sensational day. The newspapers reported that Laik Ali had escaped from house arrest. All sorts of stories were heard in the country about the manner of his escape. Immediately thereafter, all former ministers and others were transferred to the Central Jail.

The Director of the Intelligence Bureau of the Government of India, Malik, was flown to Hyderabad to investigate the case, and a number of persons including the relatives and friends of Laik Ali were taken into custody. Neither the Inspector General of Police, Jetley, nor the Commissioner of City Police, S.N. Reddy, were able to make any headway in the case.

At last they sent for Khan Fazal Rasool Khan Nagar, the ace detective of Hyderabad. He had risen from a constable to Assistant Commissioner of the City Police. He did not use a table or chair and used to work sitting on a carpet. For his renown in detective work, he came to be known as the Sherlock Holmes of Hyderabad. The top brass had interrogated Laik Ali's sister, Shoukatunnisa Begum, but failed to get anything out of her. His request for talking to her alone and not in the intimidating presence of the boss was conceded reluctantly.

She looked famished and the first thing Nagar did was to order some tea and snacks for her and made her relax. He gained her confidence by telling her that it was understood that, as a sister, she was morally duty-bound to help her brother. However, her interest lay in telling the truth, and if she did so, he would try to see that no harm came to her or to her family.

Shoukatunnisa, thus reassured, agreed to narrate the following sequence of events.

Laik Ali and the detained ministers had expected that with the promulgation of the Constitution of India on 26 January 1950, which made the state a part of the country, they would all be released. When this did not happen, his friend, Abdul Quvi, an advocate, made a number of trips between Pakistan and India according to a plan. He studied minutely what documents were required for Laik Ali to get out of India, and how they were scrutinized at the airports. Towards the end of February 1950 he procured all the necessary documents.

Laik Ali's elder daughter, Alia, then started liaising between her father and his visitors. The security check on the incoming and outgoing persons to Laik Ali's house had by then become fairly lax.

One day, Laik Ali's wife came on her daily visits and winking conspiratorially said loudly to him: 'Saheb, you are not well. You must take some rest.'

From that moment, Laik Ali took to bed and started behaving like a sick man. Mrs Laik Ali began to make many frantic trips to a doctor every day and would come back loaded with bottles of medicines and tablets. Her assumed nervousness and the flurry of activity made the illness known to all including the guards at the gate and in the verandah, and the female sleuth posted at the window. The doors of the car which Mrs Laik Ali used had curtains which was usual those days when Muslim ladies rode in cars. As a matter of discretion, it was never stopped or peeped into. This went on for 10 or 12 days and the pattern became fairly well established. Occasionally, a guard would even inquire after the Saheb's health from the Begum.

Meanwhile, it was announced that a marriage in the house of one of the close relations was about to be celebrated. A lorry was brought and many utensils and other things required on such occasions were taken away from Laik Ali's house. According to custom, many Lambadas would come to dance there daily in celebration of the coming auspicious event. A servant would come and announce loudly that the Saheb had given a tip to the dancers. The guards and attendants also were glad for the diversion provided by the Lambada dancers.

On the appointed day, 3 March 1950, the maid called for the car at the usual time—around 9.30 a.m.—and announced that the Begum was ready and waiting to go to the doctor. When the car pulled in under the portico, Laik Ali quietly slipped into it. His wife hid herself in the upper portion of the house. Laik Ali drove straight to his sister's house. There Laik Ali met his sister and drove away in another car to Abdul Quvi's house. The original car was returned to the bungalow. When it came back, the maid announced casually that the madam had returned with the medicines. Mrs Laik Ali thereupon descended from her hiding-place and went into Laik Ali's room. The intelligence woman cast a routine glance from the window and noticed the usual drill being repeated, though unknown to her the medicines were being administered only to some pillows.

A taxi with curtains was waiting at Abdul Quvi's house in which Quvi was already sitting. Laik Ali also got into it. He was wearing a sherwani and rumi cap. Then, Shoukatunnisa's son, Fasihuddin, also drove in and joined them. The three left in the taxi for Gulbarga. After it got out of the city, the curtains of the taxi were removed. Laik Ali could then have a last look at the green fields of his homeland.

A first-class compartment with four berths had been reserved in the train from Secunderabad to Bombay with instructions that the passengers would get into it at Gulbarga. Although there were only three passengers, all the four berths were reserved to ensure that no one else entered the compartment.

The taxi stopped in front of the shrine at Gulbarga. The party offered their prayers and floral tributes to the saint and then proceeded to the railway station. The train was about half-an-hour late so they sat in the waiting room.

They reached Bombay at six the next morning. A waiting car picked them up at the Victoria Terminus and took them to a friend's house. After a bath and breakfast there, they proceeded to the airport. Laik Ali travelled under the name of Ghulam Ahmed.

On the second day after his escape, Laik Ali's children got ready in their best finery to go to the well-advertised, fictitious wedding. Mrs Laik Ali kept on making her fake trips to the ghost physician and she was noticed devotedly administering medicines to the pillows. Groups of Holi revellers also came to the house and were given tips on behalf of the ailing ex-Prime Minister. Laik Ali's children got into the train at Nampally Station for Bombay with a maid. Abdul Quvi was waiting for them at the other end.

The next day Begum Laik Ali made a number of bundles of currency notes, on each one of which the name of a servant was inscribed along with a note of thanks for the services rendered. She gave them to the old family servant, an Arab, called Khadim Ali-Bin-Ahmed-ba-Ghazzal with instructions that they should be disbursed to the named servants but not before Sunday. She then drove out and went to her brother. From there she proceeded to the Begumpet airport. Less than a kilometre short of the airport, her car broke down. Her nephew took the steering wheel and the driver started pushing the car. Jetley, the Police Chief, was passing that way. Seeing a stalled curtained-car, obviously with a lady in distress, the chivalrous police officer got down and helped push the car to the airport!

From Bombay, Laik Ali took the flight for Karachi. The same afternoon the Begum along with her children, took the boat 'S.S. Sabaramati' to Karachi.[136]

The news of Laik Ali's escape first came from Radio Pakistan in its news bulletin. It casually mentioned the presence of the former Prime Minister of Hyderabad at an important reception.

Laik Ali's sister, his Arab servant, and nine other persons were apprehended and charged under the Hyderabad Public Safety and Public Interest Regulation read with section 77 (B) of the Hyderabad Penal Code for abetting the escape of Laik Ali. The Defence Counsel raised the plea that Laik Ali's detention, being under a regulation of an administration which had ceased to exist after the promulgation of the Constitution of India, was by itself illegal and so the offence of abetting his escape could not sustain.

The lower court dismissed this plea. An appeal was then filed in the High Court. The full bench of the High Court, in its judgment of 11 August 1950, held that the detention of Mir Laik Ali was repugnant to the provisions of Article 22 of the Constitution of India and hence void. Since the detention of Laik Ali beyond 26 January 1950 was held to be illegal, consequently those who had helped him to escape were not guilty of any offence.

All the accused were released.

✤ ✤ ✤

After the escape of Laik Ali, the security for Razvi was further tightened and the processing of the cases against him was expedited. Three charge sheets were filed against him: the Aland Sharif Murder Case; the Shoebullah Khan Murder Case; and the Bibinagar Dacoity Case. There were seven accused in all including Razvi. A special court called Special Tribunal No. IV was constituted for trying them. Pinto, a Christian judge from Mangalore, was appointed as its President. Ahmed Ali Khan and Jagannath Rao, were the other members of the Tribunal.

The government appointed Askar Yar Jung, a retired President of the State Judicial Committee, as the Defence Counsel. This Committee was the Supreme Court of Hyderabad with the difference that its decisions were subject to review by the Nizam. Since Askar did not have any experience in conducting cross-examinations, Baqar Hasan, his cousin, was appointed to assist him in the cross examinations along with Mustafa Hasan who was Askar Khan's son and junior. Askar, being a Shia, accepted only an amount of Rs 99,000 as fees for each case, instead of the full amount offered. Baqar was to be paid a sum of Rs 75,000 per case while the junior's entitlement was Rs 10,000 per case.

When a young advocate, Zahid Ali Kamil, requested Askar to appoint him as his junior as he wanted to write about the case. Askar offered to get him a visitor's pass for attending the court instead. Kamil, who was a good friend of Razvi and on a personal basis was to play an important part in the remaining years of the life of Kasim Razvi in India, declined the offer. Earlier, he had been a member of the Society for Union and Progress and had joined the Ittehad on the eve of the Police Action.

Of the three cases, the Government withdrew the Aland Sharif Murder Case for want of sufficient evidence. When the trial reached the stage of arguments, Razvi petitioned for the removal of his counsels and said he would argue his own case.[137]

The Tribunal, in its judgment delivered on 10 September 1950, awarded Razvi seven years of hard labour in the Bibinagar Dacoity Case and a life sentence in the Shoebullah Murder Case.

Both the prosecution and defence were dissatisfied with the sentences. An appeal was filed in the High Court. The prosecution prayed for the enhancement of the life sentence to a death penalty, while the defence wanted the sentence to be quashed. The High Court upheld the plea of the defence and the life sentence was quashed. It upheld the sentence of seven years' rigorous imprisonment in the Bibinagar Dacoity case. Razvi appealed to the Supreme Court. The appeal was dismissed on 19 January 1953.[138]

Razvi was put in bar-fetters and placed in the Chanchalguda jail in Hyderabad. The Field Marshal of the Razakars was dressed in the striped uniform of criminals, assigned the number 20,063, and given the job of cutting grass in the jail compound.

'You can smuggle anything into a jail, from a needle to an elephant,' said Zahid Ali Kamil. And they made full use of the practice. Generally, letters were inserted in the ink-barrel of old-fashioned fountain pens and Kamil bought a number of these from the Missak Company near the Nampally railway station. A copy of Razvi's strong letter written to Nehru from jail was smuggled out. So was Razvi's protest against the alleged ill treatment meted out to the Razakars, and he threatened to undertake a fast unto death in the jail. The statement was released to the press which puzzled the government. Finally, unable to control this malpractice, the government decided in 1954 to shift Razvi to the Yervada jail in Pune, where he served the rest of his sentence.

He was released on 11 September 1957 on completion of his term. Kamil was the only one amongst the old faithfuls who went to Pune to receive him on his release. He had carried with him a new suit of clothes for Razvi, fruits, snacks, fresh water, tea, and various other things which a man who had spent nine years behind bars, including two years under trial, might need or fancy. Gradually the whole place was filled with vehicles of all types. Three vans of the armed police, and many cars with various officials, and a battery of about 25 pressmen, and photographers crowded the place. At 19 minutes past nine the black postern gate of the jail opened. Two policemen emerged followed by the emaciated figure of Razvi wearing a white kurta and pajama given by the jail authorities and holding two bags in which all his possessions were stuffed. He seemed excited. Kamil stepped forward and embraced the Razakar supremo. Razvi broke into a smile, looked around and saw no crowd of friends and admirers. The jail authorities had given him a ticket for a first-class berth on the train to Secunderabad, but Kamil decided that it would be safer to travel directly by his car. One police van and one official limousine followed Kamil's car to ensure Razvi's safety. In Marathwada, the infamous acts of the Razakars were still fresh in many people's minds and the government did not want to face the allegation that after release Razvi had been bumped off. They encountered not very friendly crowds at Sholapur where they stopped to fill up the tank of the car.

They reached Kamil's house on the morning of 12 September 1957. Soon after sunrise, visitors started coming to see him. The first group was the workers of the Zinda Tilismat Factory. Many of Razvi's old colleagues made themselves scarce. Razvi felt that he had became irrelevant. He called a general body meeting of the Ittehad. Some forty out of 140 members turned up.

He asked a number of leading members to take up the Presidentship of the party. There was no taker. Then, after long discussions, Abdul Khair Siddiqui's name was decided upon. He had been the Secretary of the party and was a leading criminal lawyer.

After the meeting the pressmen had a volley of questions for Razvi. He announced that as an ex-convict he could not practice or support himself. Therefore he said, 'I am going away to Pakistan.'

'Who will be the next President of the Ittehad?'

'Abdul Khair Siddiqui,' said Razvi with an air of his earlier bravado. The press conference was over. The correspondents closed their notebooks and, as they left the hall, they saw Siddiqui drive in.

They congratulated him. He said he had not accepted the offer. Razvi was crestfallen. The realization came to him now that his writ no longer ran as before. Some other members were sent for, one of them was Abdul Wahid Owaisi. Finally, he was nominated.

Razvi left Hyderabad on the morning of 18 September 1957. Kamil flew with him to Bombay.

At the airport in Bombay a pressman recognized Razvi and asked him some questions. On being told that he was leaving for Pakistan the next day, the correspondent rushed to his office with his scoop. A special supplement with Razvi's latest photograph hit the stands in the evening. As Kamil and Razvi waited at the office of the Income Tax Officer of Bombay, Sheikh Abdullah, to obtain the income tax clearance, Kamil found a crowd gathering outside. An armed policeman also appeared from somewhere. Suspecting foul play, Kamil asked Sheikh Abdullah the reason for the crowd. The latter pulled out a copy of the special supplement from his drawer and showed it to Razvi. The whole city knew that Razvi was there.

Kamil took Razvi to a hotel, and locked him in a room with instructions not to open the door to anyone and then went out to see whether all the arrangements were in order. Kamil's worries increased now that Razvi's presence in Bombay and his plans had been publicized. Somebody could shoot him. Somebody could even poison him. So he decided that they would not eat anything at the hotel. His concern was that his ward must reach his destination safely.

The next morning Kamil called a taxi and they left for the airport without taking breakfast. At the airport the Customs Officer called Razvi in earlier than expected. He was frisked; his luggage was thoroughly checked. Razvi came to the enclosure which was separated by a wire-mesh from the visitors' lounge. Some curious people had gathered at that point to see Razvi.

Razvi received no reception in Pakistan, no support, no recognition. He was nobody there. He started his practice amongst the refugees from India. The sap within him had dried. The soil was new and uncongenial. He died unwept and unsung on 15 January 1970 at the age of 67.

Laik Ali expired in New York on 24 October 1970 while he was at his morning prayer. His body was brought to Madina where he was laid to rest.

A Call to Arms

The Hyderabad unit of the Communist Party of India was set up in 1939. The Comrades' Association and the Students' Union were its two wings. The moving spirit behind it all was Makhdoom Mohiuddin, a poet and lecturer in the City College.

In October 1946, the Communists observed 'Anti-Repression Day'. The Government swooped down on its members. Many were arrested; those who could, went underground. From then on, they operated under cover through organizations like the Comrades' Association and the Progressive Writers' Association.

The aims of both the Communists and the leadership of the banned State Congress were common up to a point. Both wanted democracy but the Communists went beyond that and wanted an overthrow of the entire bourgeois system. They found the Congress, with its ideology of non-violence, too mild for the circumstances. On one side was the Ittehad Party with its pernicious theory of *Ana'l Malik* and its armed Razakars with the backing of the police, the army, and the entire state machinery. On the other side was a conglomeration of parties without any specific ideology. The Communists filled in the gap. They galvanized the industrial workers, the students, and the intelligentsia in the urban areas. They organized the peasantry in the countryside and inspired it to stand up against the excesses of the landlords, the Razakars, and the government. They took on the landlords. Some of them submitted, others fled, yet others enlisted the support of the police and even the army, and resisted. The party squads took on the police, attacked and destroyed some of the police stations, and decamped with their arms and ammunitions. They took on the Razakars and taught them many a lesson. By taking up the cause of the rural masses, they identified themselves with them and won their trust, sympathy, admiration, and support. They gave the villagers a new confidence in themselves and hope for a new, roseate dawn in which there would be justice and equity, freedom from exploitation, and a new brotherhood.

Women also participated in the movement. They constituted the auxiliary corps to provide essential services for the squads. They also acted as spies and scouts and, in some cases, they participated in battles in which they overpowered the police and Razakars by throwing potfuls of red-chilli powder in their eyes.

They organized militia squads called *dalams*, each consisting of about forty able-bodied young people. The movement was particularly strong in the Nalgonda and Warangal districts. In 1946 it was claimed that there were 10,000 dalams operating in Telangana.

On 11 November 1947, Ravi Narayana Reddy, Baddam Yella Reddy, and Makhdoom Mohiuddin gave a call to their cadres to intensify the liberation struggle and to take to arms.[139]

They bought arms from wherever they could. People collected donations and subscriptions for purchase of arms. They attacked the landlords, the police, and the army and looted their armouries. Their raids were generally characterized by the element of surprise. In some cases the army itself sold arms to them.

Young people were specially selected and trained in guerilla warfare. First, each recruit was administered an elaborate oath in which he undertook to 'shed blood for blood and take life for life'. If, through cowardice or weakness, he violated the pledge, he undertook to 'die the death of a traitor at the hands of my comrades'.[140]

The squads were of three types. The first consisted of persons who could work full-time. They were the offence groups. Their job was to attack the enemy. The second comprised those who could spare only part of their time. They were constituted into self-defence units for the villages. The third category was entrusted with the task of destroying the communication and transport lines of the army and the Razakars. Ex-army men gave them military training. The squads functioned at the *firka* (a group of villages), *taluka*, and the district level and duplicated broadly the army command structure.

In village after village, people took to arms and put an end to their age-old exploitation. The most notable instances of the success of the struggle were in Vasalamarri, Jagadepuram, and Visnuru.

Vasalamarri, a village in the Nizam's personal estate, was the headquarters of a block of 30 villages with a police station. In response to the Party call, people refused to provide the levy grain. Thereupon the tahsildar came down to Vasalamarri and camped there with a large police force. He collected the levy forcibly from many villages and transported it to Vasalamarri in carts requisitioned from the people. A thousand persons collected from these villages and with red flags marched to Vasalamarri with the object of retrieving the grain. They surrounded the police station in which officials were present and shouted slogans. Around 9 p.m., the police opened fire killing a young man, Mallayya, belonging to Dattayapalli village. The mob, instead of dispersing, removed the top of a hut made of palm tree leaves, set it afire and flung these burning branches at the police station. A policeman, who was firing with a 12-bore gun, was shot dead by an armed comrade. Scared, the tahsildar fled. The guerilla squad members jumped over the burning walls and captured two American rifles, two 12-bore guns, and three muzzleloaders and came out safely. The police station was reduced to ashes.

Collecting their grain-carts the people left for their respective villages. The very next day reinforcements of the Reserve Police arrived from the headquarters. Anticipating the impending repression, people and guerilla squads had taken precautionary measures. Subsequently, the police station at Vasalamarri was disbanded and for quite some time the government could not really get to know of the happenings in these villages. A procession, with the dead body of the martyr Mallayya, was taken out by nearly 2,000 people.

All these incidents, within a span of 14 hours, electrified the atmosphere. The successful attack on the police station brought about a new awareness of their power to the people.[141]

Jagadepuram was a jagir village ruled and controlled by one Abdul Rehman, the deputy of the jagirdar. Abdul Rehman had acquired hundreds of acres of land through forcible eviction of the cultivators and exercised absolute authority in the village. He mobilized the Muslim families from the neighbouring villages, settled them in Jagadepuram, and made it a major Razakar centre. Under his instructions, the Razakars raided a hamlet of Gandamalla village. They burnt haystacks, huts and houses, took away sheep, and killed two persons. Following this act of murder and destruction he sent letters to nearly 25 villages demanding Rs 3,000 to Rs 10,000 each from these people within 24 hours. Failure to comply with this order would lead to destruction of their property and their lives, he threatened.

In response to Abdul Rehman's threat, it was decided that no amount would be paid to him. Instead, an attack on the Razakar centre was planned by the guerilla and village defence squads that had been established. Three thousand inadequately equipped people and guerilla squads from 30 villages started towards Jagadepuram. Not to attack would have been taken as weakness and would have emboldened the oppressor. Two thousand out of these people were armed with spears, daggers, slings and stones, and sticks.[142] Arutla Ramachandra Reddy, the leader, describes this campaign:

We organized four batches; the first batch comprised those with modern weapons like sten gun, bren gun, .303 rifle; the second one had medium range weapons like 12–borerifle; the third was a people's army consisting of two thousand persons. With this organization we moved into battle.

It is inconceivable how three thousand persons continued to sustain themselves for three days. Peerlapalli, a nearby village, was the base from where we operated. Its inhabitants provided all the three thousand persons with cooked rice, vegetables and meat. … They managed to serve everyone with very good food within an hour. There was no dearth of good cooks or food; only modern weapons and ammunition were in short supply.

The battle at Jagadepuram lasted three days. On the first day, beginning at 10 a.m. fighting continued till 4 p.m. While there were no causalities on our side, the razakars did lose a substantial number. However, no exact figures of their loss could be obtained. For every shot from them we replied with two.

On the second day also, the battle began at 10 a.m. The enemy struck at our squads from behind a few trees and rocks; they moved close to our squad on its third flank and opened fire. The Squad Commander ordered a retreat to some distance to enable our forces to counter-attack but the people in the rear with simple arms began to flee. This was fully exploited by the razakars; they fired and killed Pasham Ram Reddy who was not quick on his feet. This Ram Reddy, with a muzzle-loader gun, had joined our forces to teach a lesson to Abdul Rehman with whom he had been friendly at one time. He fought bravely against the razakars and laid down his life. Our squad moved back slowly seeing the advancing enemy force, strayed from their path and attacked them from the rear; since the fourth flank was open they managed to escape. This also enabled our retreating people with simple arms to avoid losses.

It was decided to attack again on the third day and conclude the operations. Failure to do so would have given a false impression of lack of strength and tenacity of purpose on our part. The enemy would consider it as a defeat. After a review of the two-day battle we decided to punish the enemy properly. We attacked his forces and inflicted heavy casualties. As a result of this, police vans were to transport the dead and injured to Hyderabad. I, along with a squad of twelve comrades, went over to the route through which the vans were to pass. We dug trenches and covered them with hay. The plan was that the moment the vehicles fell into the trenches I was to throw bombs on them and other comrades across the road would ambush them with sten guns. We waited from nine in the night to two in the morning but the enemy vehicles did not come. Apparently, they had taken a different route via Kodagondla. The three-day battle proved costly in terms of ammunition. Instead of involving the people's militia, defence squads and guerilla squads in such large numbers, we could have besieged and kept a tight grip over Jagadepuram razakars with four small guerilla squads stationed on four sides of the village.

I sent a detailed report of this experience to the Party leadership. They sent a circular to guerilla squads all over Telangana reviewing the Jagadepuram battle and issued instructions for the formation of smaller guerilla squads and for greater care in the use of ammunition.

As a result of this battle, the razakars in the area around stopped raiding villages and their centre was wound up. The Armed Reserve

Police stepped in and made the village an important centre for their activities.[143]

Ramachandra Reddy (not Arutla), the Deshmukh of Visnuru, ruled over 60 villages in such a tyrannical manner that he was nicknamed Ravana. Through a meticulous organization of the oppressed villagers, a prolonged and heroic resistance was launched, and in the face of the combined onslaught of the goons of the landlord and the police, his authority was successfully challenged. After the Police Action, when the military government tried to restore the oppressive regime of the landlord, the people dragged his son from the train and murdered him.

There were numerous other cases where the down-trodden and exploited peasants were, for the first time, able to stand tall as human beings and refuse to be exploited.

The diary of Raj Bahadur Gour and the memoirs of Arutla Ramachandra Reddy could do credit to a Che Guevara. But Telangana did not turn out to be Cuba. When success seemed so close at hand, other moderate elements, snatched away the fruit. The armed struggle lasted for six years from 1946 to 1952. It had two phases. First, from 1946 to the Police Action in September 1948; second, from early 1949 to the first General Elections in 1952.

At its height, just before the Police Action, over 2,000 villages had been 'liberated'. In these villages far-reaching reforms were introduced. Land in excess of 200 acres was forcibly taken over by the people's militia. One million acres of land was distributed amongst the landless. Wages of agricultural labour were raised. Toddy tappers were given palmyra trees at low cost. People contributed voluntary labour to dig canals, tanks, and wells for irrigation. Wood was made available, free from the government forestland, for making agricultural implements and carts. People's courts were constituted. Widow remarriages were organized. Adult literacy through night schools was propagated. A new political and social consciousness was created amongst the people.

The heroes of this movement were many but three of them stand out.

The first was Ravi Narayan Reddy. Born in 1908 in Bollepalle village of Nalgonda district, he came from a prosperous agricultural family. As a student, while staying at the Reddy Hostel in Sultan Bazar, he took keen interest in sports, scouting, and acting. In 1930, he gave up his studies for the intermediate exam and joined Mahatma Gandhi's Civil Disobedience movement. He set up the Hyderabad State Harijan Sevak Sangh and was its President for six years from 1932. In 1938, he became one of the founder members of the Hyderabad State Congress and, on the government's refusal to lift the ban on it, offered satyagraha in the first batch on 24 October 1938. For that he was imprisoned.

He was also a leading member of the Andhra Mahasabha which started in 1928 as a socio-cultural organization for the Telugu-speaking people of the state. He became its President thrice in 1941, 1944, and 1945. Under his leadership it was transformed into a vigorous political body. He took up social issues like widow remarriage and literacy and distributed 500 acres of his ancestral land to the cultivators, keeping only the prescribed 200 acres for himself. When Mahatma Gandhi visited Hyderabad in 1940, Ravi donated 50 *tolas* of gold for his cause. However, he was influenced in his political life more by Nehru than Gandhi. Finding the approach of the Congress leaders in the state too mild, he joined the Communist Party in 1939 and led the armed struggle of the Telangana peasantry in the state. After the Police Action, Ravi believed that the goal had been achieved and the Communists should give up the armed struggle. However, Ranadive, General Secretary of the Communist Party of India, ordered the continuation of the armed struggle at the Second Congress of the Communist Party at Calcutta in February 1948. There was confusion in the ranks of the party as to the future course of action.

The imposition of the ban on the Communist Party three days after the Police Action, in September 1948, forced the decision for Ravi and his comrades who, on the verge of coming out, were once again driven to their hideouts. They reverted to their previous lifestyle—spending their days either underground or in prison. Released days before the first General Elections of 1952, Ravi contested both for the Parliament as well as the State

Assembly and was elected to both. He polled the highest number of votes for the Parliament in the country; his opponents did not get a single vote.

Ravi was an atheist. He never visited a temple but did not stop his family members from doing so.[144]

He was one of the strong proponents of the movement for an integrated Telugu-speaking state and some of the credit for the formation of Andhra Pradesh must go to him.

A legend during his lifetime, this veteran of the armed struggle passed away at the height of his glory on 7 September 1989.

In his will he said that his wife should not remove her bangles or her bindi, the vermilion mark on her forehead, as widows do customarily. Then—not wanting to lay down the law for her— he clarified that it was only a suggestion and that she should do as she pleased. Such a liberal approach had characterized his attitude to her and to women in general all his life. He however enjoined upon his children not to immerse his ashes in the Ganga or any other river, but to scatter them over the crops in his fields. A *samadhi* might also be constructed in one of the family farms.

Makhdoom Mohiuddin was a blithe spirit, a romantic poet who strayed into politics. He had a vast circle of friends and admirers and he mesmerized his audience by reciting his poetry in a resonant voice.

He was born into poverty and deprivation in a village called Andole in Medak district on 4 February 1908. His father died when he was an infant and his mother remarried and left him with his father's brother. His early upbringing was on strict religious lines. But his uncle was broadminded and used to tell his children stories of the happenings in the world. When the Russian revolution took place, he told them that in Russia everybody had become equal and that all the people ate together. Makhdoom used to wonder about the size of the spread from which a whole nation could eat together! When he came from Medak and joined the Dharamvant High School Hyderabad, he had to sell calendars and pictures of actors and actresses to earn his keep.

He did his MA in Urdu from Osmania University where he became famous for his wit and repartee. He adapted George Bernard Shaw's play *Widowers' Houses* in Urdu and called it *Hosh Ke Nakhun*. It became the first play to be staged at Osmania University. He was the only student to have appeared without the customary formal dress of sherwani and bugloos in the presence of the Nizam when he attended a function at the University. At that gathering, Makhdoom recited his poem: 'The Yellow Shawl'. The Nizam enjoyed it very much and it became a hit.

Religious instruction was compulsory for Muslim students at Osmania. The non-Muslims had the option to take Ethics. Makhdoom failed in religious instruction, whereupon he asked to be transferred to the Ethics class. He supported himself in the University by doing part-time work in newspapers and in the Deccan Radio.

After he completed his MA, he prepared to go to Bangalore for a job. Sarojini Naidu gave him a letter of recommendation. However, he abandoned the plan.

Thereafter, he became a lecturer in the City College and was often caught reciting poetry, sometimes his own compositions, at the insistence of his students. In 1942, he left teaching to become a full-time worker of the Communist Party. From 1946 onwards, he was mostly either in jail or underground. He played an important part in organizing the Trade Union Movement in the state and was an office bearer of a number of unions in various industrial units.

His politics flowed from limitless empathy for the downtrodden. The debates on dialectics in the party did not interest him much. He would have been a communist even without the party ever having existed. But he was a very disciplined worker who followed the party line if the leadership decided that way. After the Police Action he opposed the continuation of the armed struggle after the state had been merged with India. When the party decided to persist, Makhdoom obeyed and resumed his life of vagrancy. By now he had become a legend, a man loved across all barriers of belief, rank, and status. He could now justly indulge his ego and write about himself.

Shehar mein dhoom hai ik shola nawa ki Makhdoom
Tazkare raston mein charche hain pari khanon mein

(The city resounds with the thunder of the one,
Who is the topic on footpaths, and in mansions.)

In 1957, he was elected to the State Legislative Council and remained the leader of this Legislature Party till his death.

In August 1969, he went to Delhi in connection with the election of the President of India. On the morning of 25 August, he woke up Raj Bahadur and said he was feeling uneasy. He was sweating. He was moved to Pant Hospital where he died in the afternoon.

The city has not seen a crowd like the one which gathered to receive the coffin at the Hyderabad airport or to bid him good-bye at his funeral. There were people, masses of men and women, collected to make one vast ocean of heads.[145]

When his body was taken for burial at the cemetery of Hazrat Shah Khamosh, an objection was raised from amongst the orthodox circles that a non-believer like him could not be given that honour. But the people, if they could, would have sent him direct to heaven, The voice of dissent was lost in the uproarious chants of *Makhdoom Zindabad*.

On his grave is inscribed a line from one of his own couplets: 'Before break of dawn, head resting on his instrument, he went to sleep'.

❖ ❖ ❖

Raj Bahadur Gour belonged to a Kayasth family, which had settled in Hyderabad some generations ago. Born in 1918, he was a very bright student who always stood first and earned scholarships in every class. Out of his scholarship money he started a reading room and a library in 1934. In 1939, he joined the Communist Party and the next year he became a Member of the Comrades' Association. In 1941, when he was studying medicine, he was not only elected Vice-President of the Students' Union but also the editor of his college magazine.

In October 1946, Raj Bahadur Gour participated in the Anti-Repression Day and, along with many of his colleagues, was arrested on 15 November 1946.

Restless and impatient, he could not submit to the confines of the prison, so a conspiracy was soon hatched. He and Jawad Razvi started complaining of recurrent fever. Examined by Dr Bankat Chander, who found apparently nothing wrong with them, they were referred to Dr Morris, the dentist. As the equipment could not be brought to the jail, the patients were taken to the clinic on 7 May 1947.

That was the day Jaya Prakash Narayan, the socialist leader, was visiting the city and so most of the police were busy in that connection. A number of comrades in disguise stood in a queue outside the clinic, which was on the ground floor and opened on to Begum Bazar from the back. The two patients were sent inside where the escorting police could not accompany them and after the treatment, they escaped through the back door to Begum Bazar where a car stood waiting for them. They were driven to Asaf Nagar where the car was changed, the two separated and from that day for four years Raj was underground.

On 24 April 1951, while drinking water from a pond in a jungle at Devarkonda, Raj was captured and imprisoned for the next 13 months. During this period he was subjected to torture and was placed in the condemned prisoner's cell. For some time he was in the company of some of the officers of Hyderabad who had been detained in the Central Jail after the Police Action. Raj, with those who were literary-minded, set up a 'Shaw's Corner' in the jail to discuss literary topics.

Raj was also one of those who were in favour of the withdrawal of the armed struggle after the Police Action, but once the Party decided otherwise, he scrupulously followed the line.

It was during the armed struggle that he met and married Brij Rani, who was also a brave worker of the party.

A slum had developed in Chikkadpalli near the big drain. The authorities had planned to evict the squatters when Brij Rani stepped in and stopped it. The grateful people offered one of the huts to Brij Rani and Raj, and that is how they got a roof over their head. In 1982, their daughter, Tamara, built a small *pucca* house there. Raj named it *Chambeli Ka Mandwa* after Makhdoom's famous poem. Once when communal riots broke out, Raj jumped between the two factions and said they could cross that point only over his dead body. Since then no incident has taken place there.

Trade unionism and literature are his two abiding interests. In 1970, he became Vice-President of All India Trade Union Congress. Alongside, he wrote three books of literary criticism in Urdu. He rose to be a member of the politburo of the party and was elected to the Rajya Sabha twice. But he remains rooted to his original slum and his people. Like Makhdoom, he led a very clean political life.

When he was a Member of Parliament, a visitor had come to offer him some money. At that point, Tamara, then a child of eight, came asking for some money. Raj said he did not have any and asked her brusquely to go away. The stranger felt he had found an opening and gave her Rs 1.

'That was the only time,' recollects his daughter Tamara, 'that my father ever slapped me.'

Raj got the Bahadur Shah Zafar Award in 1991 for his outstanding service to the cause of Urdu. He found that it carried a cash award of Rs 25,000 with it.

Discharging his sundry debts, he donated the remaining amount of about Rs 10,000 to the Makhdoom Trust.

Makhdoom, ten years his senior, was his mentor and his bosom friend. They drank and sang and agitated together.

He believed that the Telangana armed struggle was the confluence of three streams: economic, political, and cultural; and it was inevitable in those circumstances for it to come about and for young men and women to join it. Till the end of his life in 2011, Raj remained involved in his mission of ameliorating the conditions of the working class.[146]

❖ ❖ ❖

After the Police Action, two opposing views emerged within the Communist Party regarding the continuance of the armed struggle in Hyderabad. Most of those, who had been in the thick of the struggle, were in favour of giving it up but others led by Ranadive favoured its continuance. While the issue was being debated, the Central Government initiated massive operations against the Communists.

It had been easy to fight the Nizam's outfit; but it was different with the Indian Army. In a matter of three days the Communists lost 200 of their men. It was then decided by the leadership to go underground. Most retreated into the forests of the Godavari and Karimnagar districts.

Meanwhile, the mood of the peasantry had also changed. The Military Governor had abolished the abhorrent jagirdari with an administrative order in August 1949. The civil administration had provided for the protection of the rights of tenants. What was there now to fight for? The new regime seemed to be going on the right lines. When Chandra Rajeshwara Rao, the Communist leader who later rose to be the head of the Communist Party in India, sought refuge in a field of his old hosts, the tribals in Damelakonta in Karimnagar, he perceived a certain lack of warmth on their part. As of old, he plucked some ears of millet and started roasting them to appease his hunger. Suddenly, he noticed that the tribals were looking around with shifty eyes. Instinct told him that he had been betrayed to the army. In fact, the soldiers were closing in on the field. He jumped and bolted and was barely able to escape.[147]

The same villagers who used to welcome the dalams now begged them not to come to them. There was now no protection against the army because the comrades did not stay in the villages as they used to earlier. The police and the military followed their visit. It was then that the saying gained currency in the country-side that the Communists were the 'lords of the night', and the army the 'lords of the day'.

In 1951, the army adopted the ruthless 'Briggs Plan', which had been implemented earlier in Malaysia. They burnt the tribal villages, collected all the tribals, set them up in barbed-wire encampments and, while members of the family were allowed to go to the forest to collect the produce, an adult male member was kept as a hostage to ensure their return. No drinking water source in the jungles was left uncontrolled by the army. Thus, having isolated and trapped the guerillas, they set out to annihilate them. The crunch was acute.

When the party leadership could not settle the issue of the continuance of the armed struggle, a delegation went to Moscow in 1951 to discuss the issue with Stalin, the leader of International Communism. The delegation consisted of four leaders. Dange and Ajoy Ghosh were in favour of the withdrawal. Chandra Rajeshwara Rao and Basavapunniah were against the proposal— or were not quite sure.

They went in different disguises and by different routes. They stayed in Moscow for six months and had a number of meetings with the top leadership. They met Stalin in Kremlin. Molotov, Malenkov, and Suzlov were also present. A stack of documents had been smuggled to Moscow earlier. They had been translated into Russian. Stalin asked for a map of the area in question. A map of India and another of the southern peninsula were spread before him. He lit his pipe and asked:

'Do you manufacture your own weapons?'

'No, Sir.'

'Is there a foreign country close to the area?'

'No.'

'Is there a port from which you can escape?'

'No.'

'Is there any other sanctuary where you can take refuge?'

'No, Sir.'

Stalin took a deep pull at his pipe, pushed the maps away to clear his table and observed: 'In the circumstance it would seem difficult for you to sustain the resistance.'

As a result of this verdict, the party line in India changed. The decision to withdraw the Telangana Armed Struggle was released to the public and press and broadcast on 21 October 1951.[148] But by that time the Government of India had all but crushed the resistance physically.

The 'new order', as envisaged by the Communists, had after all failed to emerge.

But the struggle had not been in vain. Some of its fruits, both physical and psychological, were palpable. The courage to defy authority had been imparted to the long-suffering peasantry. The feudal state of yesterday became a pioneer in rural and agricultural reforms. The jagirdari system was abolished in the state much before anywhere else in the country. Similarly, the enactment of legislaion for the protection of tenants was also undertaken in Hyderabad before any other place in the country. The extent of grazing land, which stood at 15 per cent of the village land before the armed struggle and which had been completely abolished by the people's squads, was reduced by law to 5 per cent by the government headed by B. Ramakrishna Rao, the first elected Chief Minister of Hyderabad. It also appointed a Land Commission that went into the entire question of agrarian reforms. Amongst others, it suggested a ceiling on land holdings. Legislation was enacted subsequently on those lines. All these were plants the seeds of which had been sown during the armed struggle. That uprising had blazed a trail, not only in the state, but also in the whole country.

In the city, life went on pretty well as before.

Jamaluddin was the Wit Laureate of Hyderabad. He was the common source of most jokes. Whatever joke was attributed to Jamaluddin, acquired a local touch and immediate currency.

Jamaluddin was not a fictitious character. He was a real, flesh-and blood person, and a trusted officer of the Nizam. He claimed descent from the family of Tippu Sultan and had come to Hyderabad in the late nineteenth century. Here he became a ward of Dr Aghornath Chattopadhyay, father of Sarojini Naidu. In due course, he married Ghousia Begum, the sister of Nawab Kazim Yar Jung, who was a favourite of the last Nizam and rose to be the minister of his secretariat. Ghousia was a remarkable woman and continued her education even after marriage, becoming one of the first women graduates of the state. She took an interest in education and was one of those who introduced the Montessori System of education for children in the state. She went to England for training in that system.

Because of his relationship with Kazim Yar Jung, Jamaluddin also came close to the Nizam. He was appointed to the horticulture department and rose to be the Director of Public Gardens, which was one of the proud attractions of the city. He was sent to Japan and on returning set up a Japanese section in the Public Garden.

He built a house for himself in the Red Hills and called it 'Fern Villa'. It had a hall built and decorated in the Japanese style. Once when the seventh Nizam visited it, he liked it very much and acquired it with all its furnishings and decorations, for his second son, Prince Muazzam Jah.

At that time if any person visited one Prince or was patronized by him, the other blacklisted him. But Jamaluddin was a favourite of both of them. He was very informal with the Junior Prince and whenever the latter came for riding to the Public Garden, he would have a chat with him and listen to his anecdotes and jokes.

That was Jamaluddin's special talent—his wit. Whatever his contribution to gardening, he was remembered for his jokes. The students of the Osmania University, particularly Makhdoom Mohiuddin, specially built up this reputation for him. A favourite joke of Makhdoom was that Jamaluddin used to wear his head-dress with the front facing backwards. When someone asked him why, he replied: 'Suppose the Nizam suddenly comes from behind.'

Once his servant was trying to fix a nail on the wall. Jamaluddin noticed that the head of the nail was towards the wall while the pointed end was facing the hammer. He pulled up the servant and told him that the nail in his hand was the wrong one. It was meant for the opposite wall.

While on a drive, Jamaluddin noticed that his driver had suddenly applied brakes to the car to slow it down. He asked the driver what the matter was. The driver said that he had noticed a pit on the road in front of him. 'Then why did you not blow the horn?' asked Jamaluddin angrily.

There was no end to the jokes of Jamaluddin. Any joke could be pasted on him. He was ever so obliging. Even after his death in 1942, the legend lived on and he continued to serve the cause of humour even posthumously. Hyderabad was, in due course, to become renowned as the humour capital of the country.[149]

Nizams (Asaf Jahi Dynasty)

			Period of Rule
1	Mir Qamaruddin Khan Asaf Jah I	(b. 1671)	1720–48
2*	Mir Ahmed Ali Khan Nasir Jung Nizam-ud-Dowlah	(b. 1671)	1748–50
3*	Hidayat Mohuddin Khan Muzaffar Jung	–	1750–1
4*	Syed Mohammed Khan Amir ul Mulk Salabat Jung	(b. 1718)	1751–62
5	Nizam Ali Khan Nizam ul Mulk Asaf Jah II	(b. 1734)	1762–1803
6	Mir Akbar Ali Khan Sikander Jah Asaf Jah III	(b. 1768)	1803–29
7	Mir Farkhonda Ali Khan Nasir-ud-Dowlah Asaf Jah IV	(b. 1794)	1829–57
8	Mir Tahniat Ali Khan Afzal-ud-Dowlah Asaf Jah V	(b. 1827)	1857–69
9	Mir Mahboob Ali Khan Asaf Jah VI	(b. 1866)	1869–1911
10	Mir Osman Ali Khan Asaf Jah VII	(b. 1886)	1911–48

Note: * These three rulers are not enumerated in the serial order of the Asaf Jahs mainly because they were not granted the title of Asaf Jah.

Diwans/Prime Ministers/Presidents of the Executive Council of the Nizams

		Period in Office
1	Diyanat Khan	1724–36
2	Anwar Ullah Khan	1736–42
3	Kudabandah Khan	1742–8
4	Shah Nawaz Khan	1748–50
5	Ram Dass alias Raghunath Dass	1750–2
6	Syed Lashker Khan	1752–5
7	Shah Nawaz Khan Shams-ud-Dowlah	1755–8
8	Nawab Basalat Jung	1758–60
9	Raja Pratabwant	1761–3
10	Syed Lashker Khan reappointed with the title of Nawab Rukn-ud-Dowlah	1765–75
11	Nawab Shams-ul-Mulk and Nawab Vikar-ud-Dowlah	1775–8
12	Nawab Azim-ul-Umrah Arastu Jah	1778–95
13	Sham Raj Raja Rai Rayan	1795–7
14	Nawab Arastu Jah, Azim-ul-Umrah	1797–1804
15	Meer Alam (Mir Abul Qasim)	1804–8
16	Nawab Munir-ul-Mulk	1809–32
17	Maharaja Chandulal	1832–42
18	Raja Ram Buksh	1843–6
19	Nawab Siraj-ul-Mulk	1846–8
20	Saif Jung	November–December 1848
21	Nawab Shams-ul-Umrah	January–May 1849
22	Raja Ram Buksh	1849–51

Cont'd

		Period in Office
23	Raja Ganesh Rao	April–June 1851
24	Nawab Siraj-ul-Mulk	1851–3
25	Mir Turab Ali Khan Salar Jung I	1853–83
26	Council of Regency	1883–4
27	Laik Ali Khan Salar Jung II	1884–7
28	Sir Asman Jah	1888–94
29	Sir Vikar-ul-Umrah	1894–1901
30	Maharaja Sir Kishen Pershad	1901–12
31	Yusuf Ali Khan Salar Jung III	1912–14
32	*Nizam's Direct Administration Presidents of Executive Council*	1914–19
33	Sir Ali Imam	1919–22
34	Nawab Sir Faridoon Mulk Bahadur	1922–3
35	Nawab Wali-ud-Dowlah	1923–5
36	Maharaja Sir Kishen Pershad	1926–37
37	Sir Akbar Hydari	1937–41
38	Syed Ahmed Khan, Nawab of Chhattari	1941–6
39	Sir Mirza Ismail	1946–7
40	Syed Ahmed Khan, Nawab of Chhattari	June–November 1947
41	Mir Laik Ali	November 1947–September 1948
42	D.S. Bakhle (Chief Civil Administrator)	1948–9
43	M.K. Vellodi, ICS (Chief Minister)	1949–52

Four: Dawn of Democracy

The Transition

General Choudhuri's was no mere holding operation. Within five months of his marching in, the Nizam's personal estate, the sarf-e-khas, was given up, by a firman issued on 6 February 1949. Its worth was estimated at Rs 25 million. In lieu thereof he was given an annual compensation of Rs 2.5 million for life. Going further, the government announced the take over of all jagirs in August 1949. These comprised 6,536 villages and covered about one third of the entire area of the state. The jagirdars were to be compensated by payment of annuities over a period of five to ten years.

The military government was succeeded by a civil administration in January 1950. An ICS officer, M.K. Vellodi, was appointed as Chief Minister with some Congress leaders of the state as ministers.

On the eve of the inauguration of the new Constitution of India, the Nizam signed an agreement with the Government of India that the new Constitution would also apply to Hyderabad. The next day, 26 January 1950, India became a republic. Hyderabad became one of the states of the new Union, and the Nizam, the Raj Pramukh of the new state.[150] Now his position as the constitutional head of the state was confirmed. The Nizam was paid a privy purse of Rs 12.5 million per year for life.

Earlier, it had been proposed that a Constituent Assembly would be constituted for the state and in fact the Military Governor had issued a notification to that effect. But later it was decided that, in the changed circumstances, it was not necessary and that Hyderabad could go to the polls with the rest of the country. Accordingly, under the new Constitution of India, elections were held in February 1952 in Hyderabad too. The Communist Party was still banned. So it fought under the banner of the Progressive Democratic Front, while it formed, in alliance with the Democratic People's Party, a small outfit confined to the city. Due to their work in the armed struggle, the Communists won a large number of seats in Telangana, while the Congress bagged most of the seats in the Marathwada and Karnataka regions and secured an overall majority in the State Legislature. The Congress was therefore, called upon to form the government.

For the first time, the Nizam had no say in the appointment of the government. Burgula Ramakrishna Rao, elected by the majority party of the legislature, went to the Raj Pramukh and told him who would be his ministers.

On 6 March 1952, at a brief and simple ceremony at the King Kothi, the Nizam administered the oath of office and secrecy to his new Cabinet. On that morning, for the first time, a representative government was finally installed in the state.

Born on 13 March 1899 at Burgula village of Shadnagar taluk of Mehboobnagar district, Ramakrishna Rao seemed to have all the important characteristics of Pisceans. They are gentle dreamers, sensitive, creative, understanding, friendly, and reliable. Versatile, small and dainty in physique, they also have a great sense of pity. His father was a liberal *maqtedar* that is, a small jagirdar. The family had a tradition of learning. Thus his elder brother, Venkateswara Rao, went in for the physical sciences, while the younger, Ramakrishna Rao, went to Poona for his graduation in the humanities and then to Bombay for a degree in law.

Ramakrishna Rao was a polyglot. Proficient in Telugu, Urdu, Hindi, Marathi, Kannada, Persian, Tamil, and English he felt at home, not only in the tri-lingual state of Hyderabad, but virtually anywhere in the subcontinent of India. He wrote a good deal of poetry in Telugu, both devotional and lyrical, and some in English.

He also translated the quatrains of Omar Khayyam direct from Persian into Telugu and wrote a history of Persian literature in Telugu. His articles used to be published in *Bharati*, a prestigious Telugu monthly published from the then Madras Presidency. His translation of Sufi Sarmad's works from Persian into Telugu is highly rated.

He became involved in active politics from the day he became one of the founder members of the Andhra Jana Sangh in 1921. He presided over the second session of the Andhra Mahasabha Conference in 1931. He was a member of the Provisional Committee when it tried unsuccessfully to set up the Hyderabad State Congress in 1938. He was often arrested for his politics, and when after the Police Action, a civil administration was set up under the Chief Ministership of Vellodi in 1950, he was appointed Minister for Revenue and Education. He served as the Chief Minister of Hyderabad from 6 March 1952 till the formation of Andhra Pradesh on 1 November 1956.

Burgula had never met the Nizam before he became Chief Minister. In their discussion, he and his friend, M. Narsing Rao used to refer to the Nizam as *afeemchi*—'opium-eater'. Even afterwards, when he had to deal with him officially quite often, he kept his distance.

On assuming office most radicals turn conservative. The reverse was the case with Burgula. As Chief Minister, he was responsible for the most radical reforms in the state, among which were the Hyderabad Tenancy Act, which provided protection to tenants. He also set up a Land Commission which proposed a ceiling on land holding. Both were pioneering measures in India.

He shone best in the legislature. In the mid-term elections in Andhra in 1955, he was sent as a star-performer and spoke in favour of a greater Andhra. On its formation, he bowed down to make way for Neelam Sanjeeva Reddy as the Chief Minister of the new state.

By that time he was quite disgusted with the factional politics of the Congress and did not take much interest in the state politics. The leadership, both at the Centre and the state, was also cool towards him. From June 1957 till 1962, he served successively as Governor of Kerala and of Uttar Pradesh. He was very keen to go to the Lok Sabha in 1962 and again in 1967 but the new set-up did not fancy that idea. As compensation, he was made a member of the Rajya Sabha, which he served from 1962 to 1966. He believed that politics was the art of the possible and so was not averse to making compromises.

Whether in office or out, he maintained his interest in literature and social service and served on a large number of related organizations till his death on 15 September 1967.

Gopalrao Ekbote was one of the new ministers. He had been a leading advocate and a prominent leader of the Congress. The new Chief Minister introduced him to the Nizam and said that Ekbote had a very good practice but, at the insistence of Pandit Nehru, had agreed to forego it and become a minister. Financially, it would entail considerable sacrifice on his part due to the loss of practice, he added casually.

'Why?' asked the Nizam. 'You can continue your practice while being a minister.'

'Ala Hazrat,' replied the new minister, 'it won't be proper.'

'Why? I shall issue a firman granting you an exemption. Why should you suffer a loss?'

Ekbote smiled at the naiveté of the man. He did not have the heart to tell him he could no longer issue any firman. They would all be issued by the new rulers risen from the hoi polloi henceforth.

❖ ❖ ❖

On 1 October 1953, Andhra state was formed comprising the 11 Telugu-speaking districts of the Madras state. That intensified the demand for linguistic states in India. This had been one of the planks of the policy of the Congress Party since 1920 and, though lately there had been some second thoughts on the subject in some high quarters, people were pressing for the fulfillment of the promise. On 29 December 1953, the Government of India constituted the States Reorganization Commission under the Chairmanship of Justice Fazal Ali, with H.N. Kunzru, and K.M. Pannikar as members. Its terms of reference were to suggest the reorganization of the states of India on a 'more rational basis after taking into account not only the growing importance of regional languages, but also financial, economic, and administrative considerations'.

The view of a large section of Congressmen in Hyderabad like Swami Ramananda Tirtha, V.B. Raju, Madapati Hanumantha Rao, Ramkrishna Rao, and the entire Communist Party was in favour of a larger Andhra state embracing all the Telugu-speaking people—'Vishalandhra', as they called it. K.V. Ranga Reddy and M. Channa Reddy were prominent amongst those who were opposed to it, but were subsequently won over.

Some, like Ekbote, Mehdi Nawaz Jung, and Vinayak Rao Koratkar were in favour of the retention of the identity of the Hyderabad state separately for a period of 15–20 years. They submitted a memorandum to the Commission accordingly. The Commission recommended that the Marathi-speaking districts be detached from Hyderabad and the remaining districts, which were largely Telugu speaking, be retained as Hyderabad state for the time being. A final decision might be taken after five years by a two-thirds vote of the new Legislative Assembly.

The decision of the government on this recommendation was to merge the Telugu-speaking districts of the Hyderabad state with the state of Andhra. The new state was to be called Andhra–Telangana. This hyphenated name was later abandoned in favour of compact-sounding 'Andhra Pradesh'. On 1 November 1956, the new state of Andhra Pradesh came into being along with a number of others.

Hyderabad became the capital of the fifth largest state of India. Andhra state, which had functioned from a makeshift capital at Kurnool, was the continuing state; Hyderabad was trifurcated and the Telugu speaking districts were merged in the new state. There was great onrush of persons from the Andhra area to Hyderabad. There was no city like it in Andhra. The wide concrete roads, large but low-rise mansions, parks and gardens, an equable climate, the easy graceful manners of the people and their hospitality—all were something new to the people of Andhra. The coastal people had a lot of money but for generations they had lived in the hinterland of Madras. Now they had their own capital city, older than Madras, more beautiful, and with a better climate.

The rich amongst them used to keep their city-houses at Madras. Now they turned to Hyderabad. They were used to one season—or variations in it—hot, hotter, and hottest. Here they had proper seasons. Summer was short and mild; winter was also mild. The rainy season—the best of all—was when everything turned green and the sky became overcast. Then it poured and poured from June to September. But it left no humidity in the air afterwards. For the people used to the coastline and to Madras, it seemed an air-conditioned city—or almost. There was land aplenty, vacant and cheap, waiting to be colonized. There were the Banjara Hills—oldest rocks in the world— jutting out in strange and fascinating formations. Beyond that were the Jubilee Hills. One could have land there for a song. It went by hectares—not metres. In the plain areas, in the older and not-so-old parts, there were ready-made houses, some declared 'evacuee property', because they belonged to Muslims who had gone to Pakistan.

Old nobles, jagirdars, maqtedars, and other absentee landlords, whose estates had been taken away and who had known no other way to subsist except as parasites, had started selling their remaining lands and spacious houses, their gems and jewels, and even pieces of their furniture because they could not make both ends meet. They were suddenly cast into a new unfamiliar world in which one needed to work to earn a living; petty officials from the coastal area and even the arid Rayalseema, asked in a language which sounded only vaguely familiar to them, not the names of their families, but their qualifications. What qualifications?

They asked for their level of education, and certificates, diplomas, degrees to support their claim for a job. The family connection, the upbringing, the 'culture' that comes from generations of having nothing to do for a living—all the accomplishments of gentlemen—had lost meaning. 'These tahsildars, deputy collectors, accountants, patels and officers like these used to be appointed by us to work in our jagirs. And now the same people ask us questions. How times have changed!' they moaned.

IAS probationers newly allotted to Andhra state had to come to the new capital for their departmental examinations twice a year. They came and stayed in 'Bella Vista', the former mansion of the Prince of Berar, the first son of the Nizam. It had recently been converted into a state guest house. The manager of the guest house showed off the mansion proudly to the young officers. This author, accompanied by his wife, was one among them. The manager was a little rueful at the lowly use to which the building was put now, as if it was a personal indignity inflicted on him. It had seen glorious days. The lounge used to be a ballroom with wooden flooring. I noticed that a part of the private quarters did not have adequate sunlight, 'Well, Sir,' the manager explained with a mischievous smile, 'it was deliberate. The ladies here were required not to be dressed,'

I smiled somewhat cynically. 'These stories sound rather tall, my friend,' I told the manager. The manager showed hurt at the remark and protested with a smile, 'I am no spinner of yarns, Sir. I have evidence to support whatever 1 say.' Then after a while he turned to me. 'Do you know Urdu, Sir?'.

'Yes, I do. Why?'

'I shall show you some thing which you might find interesting.'

Sure enough, in the evening, when I returned to my room, the bearer gave me an envelope. It was from the manager. I opened it. There was a newspaper clipping in Urdu. A slip attached to it read: Cutting from the *Shiraz Weekly* of 9th Jamadi-ul-Sani. 1375 H (23 January 1956). It read:

> 'Appendix to the Text of the Refreshing Tidings'
> (published last Friday in the *Shiraz*)

HEH was pleased to state that now the committee to investigate the indebtedness of Bella Vista would start its work soon under my directions.

However, the question of the ladies of Bella Vista is separate. So, everything in that connection, that is, their status, their family and on what conditions they were brought there and whether they have any written proof in favour of their claims—all these will have to be submitted before the Committee by the relatives of these ladies so that every case is scrutinized and decided on its merit. In the absence of these they will be told that since they did all this on their own volition, Nazri Bagh (Nizam's mansion in the King Kothi) has no responsibility for them. It will therefore be appropriate that they should be grateful for whatever treatment they have so far received from the Senior Prince (which is more than what their status called for), and go back to their houses. Their welfare lies in that. Clothes and jewellery worth thousands which have been given to them will not be taken back from them. Treating this as a favour, it will be for their good that they depart from Bella Vista. Otherwise they will harm themselves. If, however, there are any special cases, as has been mentioned above, they will be separately considered because all five fingers are not equal. So whatever decision is taken, it will be in the light of that and will be in accordance with some principles and rules so that it is considered just and the present complications are removed and the rest of the life of the Resident of Bella Vista can be spent in peace and comfort. To do such a thing, the head of the family considers a part of his responsibility.

I read the prolix document with incredulity. I could not wait to narrate it to my wife. The bearer was waiting. He said respectfully that his instructions were to get the paper back after I had read it. I took his pen and scribbled across the covering slip, 'Thanks. You win.' Then I handed the cover to the bearer. That night I wished I had been a guest here some years earlier—during the 'good old days'.

In the sprawling lawns on the northern side of Bella Vista, there were two swimming pools—one of normal size and one smaller—the sort in which children generally paddle. The manager explained to us that the big one was for the Princess of Berar. She was fond of outdoor life and swam regularly. The smaller one was for the Prince who used it just to cool himself. He could not bother to undertake the exertion of swimming. He exercised himself in more interesting ways. His life began in the evening and lasted through the night. Most of the day he slept to recharge himself. The Princess could not put up for long with this topsy-turvy world. So she left and went away to England. The Prince was now free to live his life the way he liked. The Nizam first cautioned him to reduce the number of women, cut down the expenditure, live within his means, and not to incur debts. The Prince would not listen. While a proposal was formally sent to the Government of India, for the conferment of GCIE (Grand Cross of the Indian Empire), the Nizam wrote a letter to the Viceroy on 6 November 1942 complaining in detail about the improvidence and indebtedness of the two Princes. He showed a copy of the letter to his Premier, the Nawab of Chhattari.[151] On 1 January 1943, he was given the title of GBE (Grand Cross of the Order of the British Empire). The Nizam threatened him. Still the Prince did not care. The Prince was impatient to succeed the Nizam. He used to send the members of the staff and even others to various Muslim shrines all over the country to pray for his early succession.

In September 1964, the Nizam was taken ill with pneumonia. The Prince believed that he would not survive the illness. He therefore wrote to the Government of India to declare him as the next Nizam. He was told that the question of succession was a matter for the Nizam to decide. The Nizam, coming to know of the move on the part of his son, decided to overlook him and nominated his grandson, Barkat Ali Khan, formally known as Prince Mukarram Jah, the eldest son of the Prince of the Berar as his successor. The Prince was crushed.

One evening, while visiting the city, we ran into a cousin of my wife at the city's main shopping centre—Abid Road. Her husband was a Major in the Army. On her insistence we moved into their house by the side of Mansab Tank. They occupied the first floor of the bungalow. On the ground floor stayed the landlord. He was a Muslim gentleman in his late 50s and had a comely wife. Their tenants addressed them as Nawab Saheb and Begum Saheba. In the compound an old Chevrolet stood jacked up on bricks, without tyres.

In the evening, from our bedroom window, we saw somebody pouring a can of petrol into the tank of the car. Someone who looked like a mechanic was fixing the tyres. A young boy opened the bonnet and an old battery was tucked in under it.

I was intrigued. My host smiled and explained that the Nawab Saheb was going to a party. Once in a while, whenever he had to go out, he would hire four tyres and a battery for the evening, wash the car himself and then drive out in style. He could not afford to buy new tyres and a battery; nor could he dare to go to a social gathering except in his own car. He had to keep up the appearances. The sherwani was still his own, so was his tuxedo. That was what the Nawab himself had told him. 'These are from the old days. Now we can't think of buying anything new.'

'Could we ever have imagined sharing a floor of our house with anyone. Or having a dilapidated car like that?' the Nawab told his host the next day when the Major invited them for a drink. 'I had two cars and four servants and once a year I drove down to my estate to spend a few days, just to collect the revenue, and to receive the homage of my subjects.'

'What a pity?' I commiserated with him.

'That's the will of Allah,' said the Nawab resignedly. 'We brought it upon ourselves. But we did not know any other world!'

'Here's to the good old days', Major Kanwal said raising his glass of brandy.

'To the new world,' replied the Nawab raising his glass of Scotch.

'Cheers!' I said. I was drinking the toast to two worlds—one that I wished I had seen, and the other which now belonged to me.

Four kilometres from Mansab Tank stood the King Kothi surrounded by walls, which had not been painted for some years. The Nizam still stayed in a portion of its compound—the 'Nazri Bagh'. He was no longer the ruler but his legend survived and even flourished. The richest man, the most miserly man, the proudest tyrant who had been humbled, the man whose word was law for close to four decades, the man who issued orders on every matter except on the rising and setting of sun. He stayed there surrounded by his family, his mistresses, their dependents, and their servants, and their dependents. A whole army of retainers catered to the whims and fancies and illusions of the one man who was still the absolute ruler within the four walls of King Kothi.

He still issued firmans in the old style, in Urdu but they pertained to his palace affairs or his private dealings. Some firmans were merely his unsolicited opinions on trivia. It was pathetic to see the descendent of Asaf Jah I, who granted concessions to the French and the British trading companies and laid down stiff conditions for their enjoyment, now issuing pointless orders just to keep up an illusion of his power and glory. The *Nizam Gazette*, used to publish them daily. So did some others like the *Shiraz*. The following are two typical firmans:

Dated 10 Rabi-ul-awal. 1376 н (15 October, 1956)

Regarding: Inayat Ali, boy aged 17 or 18, son of Khurshid Ali, servant in the palaces of the Private Estate.

Pleased to state that this child is also motherless because his mother died in his early childhood. The mother of Wasaf Ali who is a Resident of Nazri Bagh is his father's sister. Because of changed times, his father can't bear the expenses of his education. ... He had, therefore, entrusted him to my care. The child was also willing to come to Nazri Bagh. So he has joined Wasaf Ali.

Who can be there, who due to the fickleness of these times would refuse to entrust his children, whether male of female, to my care? My circumstances are known to the whole world, yet the welfare of the boys and girls staying here is apparent. It won't be out of place or considered self-praise to say that these people were lucky that they got such a master or commander who considers them his children and treats them likewise. No doubt about that.

15 Rabi-ul-Sani, 1376 H (19 November, 1956)

Regarding: Circumstances of Iqbal Jung son of the Late Maharaja Peshkar [Peshkar was Maharaja Kishen Pershad's hereditary designation] (Born of the late Guousia Begum)

Pleased to state that the upbringing and education of this boy during the lifetime of his father was not proper. But after the father's death his condition has worsened. Due to bad company and excessive drinking he developed an enlarged liver (a few years ago). Treating him as an orphan and also because of the fact that my daughter was engaged to him, he was kept in the Nazri Bagh and treated with great care at a time when there was no hope for his cure. It is a matter of satisfaction that he recovered. He was also under a large debt. That could not be discharged from the amount received by way of compensation of the Peshkar's estate. Nor could it be settled with the sale proceeds if the house (situated within the compound of the Peshkar's mansion in the city) which his father had given him during his lifetime for his stay. Out of this amount also part of his debt was discharged through a committee of the *sarf-e-khas*. Further, in spite of instructions to the contrary, he kept on taking loans without my knowledge though for a long time since his coming under my care, his personal needs did not cast any financial burden on his small income (from the compensation for the jagirs of the Peshkar). Even then he did not mend his ways (that is, he continued to incur debts).

Because of the foregoing, I had to write these few lines to bring the circumstances of his case to the knowledge of the public. After this declaration, if anyone gives him a loan, it will be at his own risk. It will not be repaid from his income, because his income which was credited by way of trust in the private estate of the *sarf-e-khas* has been fully spent (and now nothing is left of his private income). Apart from that, if this boy does not become sensible he will get embroiled in litigation. He will become notorious and will get into all sorts of troubles. Then he will be deprived of my patronage and his continued stay in the Shadi Khana will become impossible. That's all.

The Nizam also occupied himself by arranging matches for the offspring of his retainers, dependents, and servants. After the nuptials, he would send for the bedsheet to check whether the girl he had married off had in fact been a virgin. He prepared the menus for different Residents of King Kothi according to their rank and status and if someone fell ill, he would himself prescribe a medicine as well as the special diet. He was a staunch believer in the Unani—Greco-Arabic—system of medicine and his prescriptions always proved very effective because nobody dared to report otherwise. Many of his patients took his prescriptions and medicines respectfully, but supplemented them with an allopathic medicine. The credit, of course, went to the 'great healer'. Occasionally, he would still send a gift of some fruit or a part of his *khasa* and in return get nazar but that part of his business had tapered off.

The first Nizam had said in his will that he was leaving enough wealth to last seven generations—if properly spent.[152] His successors had squandered it in varying measures. The sixth Nizam created a scandal by buying the Jacob diamond for Rs 2.5 million. Osman Ali Khan set himself the task of augmenting the inheritance. He wanted so to enrich his coffers that at least two generations after him should be able to survive.

Then, while he was still on a collecting spree, he found that his world had crashed around him and that the sources of funds had all dried up. He was also painfully aware of the marked propensity of his progeny for improvidence. They spent beyond the purses fixed for them; they incurred debts from all and sundry and the ageing Nizam felt angry and embarrassed. But still he worried about what would happen to them after he was no more.

So he sat down with his Financial Adviser, Taraporewala, and called in a battery of legal experts. They suggested the creation of trusts for specific purposes which were close to his heart. So he established forty-seven trusts. They included trusts for his two sons, his two daughters, his grand sons, and his stepbrother,

Basalat Jah. They went on to provide for his stepsisters and the larger family. A trust was created for 'HEH the Nizam's Family Pocket Money'; others were set up for religious endowment, for the sacred relics, for pilgrimages, and for keeping the jewellery in good condition. There was a memorial trust for his mother, another for gifts for the wedding of his grandchildren and so on. Finally, there was a Charity Trust of Rs 50 million. No close relation of the Nizam was left unprovided for. According to the arrangement, the girls on marriage would get a house and a stipend of Rs 4,000 per month for life. There was also a trust of Rs 125,000 for the publication and sale of the Nizam's poems in Urdu and Persian. The cash trusts entailed an amount of over Rs 293 million. The jewels and sacred relics involved in the trusts were in addition to that amount.

Having created those trusts and provided for all who mattered to him as the head of a large family, and for matters which were dear to him, he issued a smug firman congratulating himself on his foresight and providence. There would be no scramble or litigation after him. 'Beneficiaries,' declared the firman published in the *Shiraz* weekly of 15th Rabi-ul-Sani 1376 н (19 November 1956), without any trace of modesty, 'will realize this with gratitude (though not today) when I shall be in the other world and shall have left behind an achievement which will be unforgettable.'

The Nizam had reconciled to a retired life. So had the rest of the world. Off and on some journalist wrote an article on him describing him as the richest man of the world—or one of the richest. That was all guesswork. There was no way of reckoning his rank amongst the wealthiest. He himself did not precisely know how much wealth he had.

His writ ran within the confines of the King Kothi as if no change had taken place in the world. The inhabitants of that small world also did not seem to be affected by changes outside. For them he was still the ruler, the Provider of Sustenance, the Dispenser of Justice, the final arbiter in every matter.

Sarfraz Ali, a District Education Officer, was one of those who still enjoyed the patronage of the Nizam. One day he begged the Nizam's permission to bring his son, Azam Ali Mirza, to kiss the feet of His Exalted Highness. On a Sunday in 1965, an appointment was fixed at 9 a.m. Azam was driven in through the dilapidated Purdah Gate of King Kothi.

The old potentate sat in the verandah in his old chair. He was wearing a lungi, a kurta, and a waistcoat. This sight overawed the young man but he was still able to note some of the details of the scene. On the three steps, which led up to the verandah, he saw numerous strewn half-burnt cigarette butts. By his side there were some newspapers and some loose papers lying in disorder. On the other side on a teapoy lay a copy of the *Band Kiwar*—the first book written in Urdu by this author in 1964. One of the stories therein related to the Nizam and his dogs—a piece of satirical fiction because the Nizam never kept any dog, and as yet the author had not seen him.

On the Nizam's left stood his son-in-law, Ali Pasha. Close to him were Qudrat Nawaz Jung and the tutor of Mukarram Jah. Some guards stood behind the Nizam at some distance.

The Nizam made polite enquires about the young man and his father. He was told what he already knew—that Azam studied at the University named after His Exalted Highness.

'Yes,' the Nizam went down his memory lane, 'I laid the foundation stone of the building in July 1934.' Then he turned to Qudrat Nawaz Jung and said: 'Qudrat Ali, do you remember?'

'Yes, Exalted Highness, very vividly,' replied the courtier. Azam Ali added that the commemorative plaque and his life-size portrait still adorned the central court of the building. 'Long since I went there,' the Nizam ruminated. He kept on chatting with the young man for some more time. Azam Ali was also impressed by the Nizam's facility in English. He heard the Nizam speak to Ali Pasha in English and responded to his salutation by saying in English: 'God bless you! Saheb.' Someone praised his command over English and said that if one heard his voice without seeing him, one would think that an Englishman was talking. The Nizam took this compliment quietly. Another sycophant tried to flatter him further on his accent.[153]

The Nizam lost his cool and snubbed him: 'You don't know any English and you have the temerity to judge my accent!' That spoiled the mood. The gathering was dismissed.

Chief Ministers Galore

The elevation of Hyderabad to the capital of the enlarged state of Andhra Pradesh in 1956 was a historic development. It made a tremendous impact on the social and economic structure of the city. Professor Manzoor Alam, who made a study of the stages of growth of the city from its founding to 1963, divides it into six stages. The formation of Andhra Pradesh was the high point of the sixth—and by then—the last stage. He observed that large vacant and green areas were 'metamorphosed beyond recognition as an endless pile of lime and stone, brick and mortar. There has been such an explosion of growth that the settlements of Hyderabad and Secunderabad have fused into each other and these two, along with their suburbs, have developed into a unified though complex urban settlement'.[154]

Some of the leaders, who were opposed to the merger of Hyderabad with Andhra, were persuaded through a 'Gentlemen's Agreement' signed by the leaders of Andhra and Telangana in Delhi on 26 February 1956. This agreement had 14 provisions. It provided, amongst others, that if the Chief Minister of the new state was from Andhra, the Deputy Chief Minister would be from Telangana and vice versa. Another important provision was the establishment of a Regional Council for the all-round development of Telangana. These provisions were given a statutory status by being incorporated into the States Reorganization Act.

Neelam Sanjeeva Reddy became the first Chief Minister of the new state. He was born in 1913 in a village in Anantapur district of the Rayalseema region. He gave up his college studies to join the freedom struggle in 1931. He played an important part in the creation of Andhra Pradesh. Three years after he became Chief Minister, he was appointed President of the Indian National Congress. Later, he became Speaker of the Lok Sabha and after a defeat in the elections for the President of India, finally, became President in 1977. It was during his Chief Ministership that the Krishna Barrage at Vijayawada was completed and the foundation stone of the Nagarjuna Sagar dam was laid. Panchayati Raj was inaugurated in the country at a function in Shad Nagar in Andhra Pradesh by Prime Minister Nehru in 1959.

He started his tenure by violating the important provision of the 'Gentlemen's Agreement'. He did not appoint a Deputy Chief Minister. He was perceived not to be favourably disposed towards Telangana. However, when the Dar-us–Salam, the headquarters of the Majlis-e-Ittehad-ul-Musalmeen located on four-and-a-half acres of prime land, was restored to it by a court order, he did not appeal against it.[155] That helped the Majlis rise from its ashes.

He was succeeded in 1960 by the first scheduled caste Chief Minister, Damodaram Sanjivayya. He was born in a poor Harijan family of a village in Kurnool and was a law graduate. After holding a government job for sometime, he entered politics. He became minister in Madras in 1952. He was Labour Minister in the Union Cabinet when he was appointed Chief Minister. He was a pleasant, mild-mannered person who could not control his ministers. One minister, Alluri Satyanarayana Raju virtually acted as the Chief Minister and often sat in the Chief Minister's chamber in the Legislative Assembly.

The Ittehad contested the elections to the Municipal Corporation of Hyderabad in 1960. It won 19 out of the 30 seats it contested, while the Congress won 30 out of all the 64 seats, thus showing a better performance proportionately. That allegedly led the government to merge the Secunderabad Municipal Corporation with its 30 seats, with the Municipal Corporation of Hyderabad. That reduced the strength of the Ittehad in the enlarged Council.[156] That was the beginning of the revival of the Majlis.Thereafter, the government started resorting to the supercession of the elected corporation, and the appointment of a 'Special Officer' enjoying all the powers of the various organs of the Municipal Corporation. From 2 August 1970 when it was first superceded, to 8 October 2004, the Corporation had an elected body only for eight years and two months, while it administered by Special Officers for 24 years and ten months. All Special Officers belonged to IAS and reported direct to the government.[157]

Sanjivayya tried to do 'justice' to the Scheduled Caste and Scheduled Tribes in respect to jobs in the government. He ordered that instead of filling up jobs reserved for candidates from the categories for which qualified candidates were not forthcoming they should be kept vacant till suitable candidates from these sections became available.

Sanjivayya lasted barely two years in office and on 12 March 1962 was sent to Delhi to be made President of the Indian National Congress, swapping places with Sanjeeva Reddy. Less than two years later, on 2 Feburary 1964, Reddy resigned on account of strictures by the Supreme Court in the case of the nationalization of road transport in the state. The Finance Minister, and a close confidant of his, Kasu Brahmananda Reddy, succeeded him.

The first major event in his tenure was the death of Nizam VII. Osman Ali Khan was taken ill in February 1967, and as usual, was treated by his physician of the Unani system. The illness was attributed to various causes like flu or broncho-pneumonia but there was no proper diagnosis. He would have none of the allopathic treatment. On 18 February, he had a relapse. Still his daughter, Shahzadi Pasha, would not allow any doctors of modern medicine to examine her father. The same afternoon, three of his wives left for the Haj pilgrimage. It was the first time they were traveling by air. So an official was sent to accompany them. The Nizam bade them goodbye and told them they wouldn't see him alive on their return. They upbraided him for uttering such inauspicious words and said they would pray for his early recovery. The next day he became very weak.

On 20 February, when he could no longer protest, Dr Waghray, his medical adviser, summoned three allopathic doctors—Bankat Chander, G.P. Ramayya, and Syed Ali—to his bedside. The bedroom was dark and filthy. Dr Ramayya felt he was entering a 'dungeon'. He took the Nizam's pulse and found he had fever. The physicians found his condition deteriorating. But Shahzadi Pasha would not allow them to give any injection, much less take a sample of his blood for tests. A cable was sent to London to his grandson and the designated successor, Mukarram Jah, informing him about the Nizam's serious condition. An anxious crowd had gathered outside the King Kothi. Police reinforcements were brought in to keep them in check.

In the midst of the results of the fourth general elections of India, health bulletins about the Nizam were issued daily. The Chief Ministers of Punjab and Bihar had been defeated in the elections. Krishna Menon and S.K. Patil had also lost the elections. Madras had thrown out the Congress and voted for the Dravida Munnetra Kazhagham. The results were pouring in from all sides. The Congress was leading at the Centre and in most states. But in Hyderabad everyone wanted to know about the Nizam. On 22 February, Mukarram Jah and his younger brother, Muffakam Jah, arrived from London and met their ailing grandfather. The Nizam was heartened to see Mukarram Jah. He held him close, but could not speak to him. He had already become unconscious. That day the doctors put him on oxygen. Princess Durreshehwar discounted the speculation that she had anything to do with the strengthening of the security in and around the King Kothi. The police authorities were acting on their own, her statement added.

On the night of 23 February, a nurse was seen coming out of the Nizam's bedroom with an oxygen cylinder. To the intelligence man on duty it seemed that she had wiped her tears. A rumour was set afoot. A news agency flashed the message that the last Nizam had breathed his last.

Syed Hashim Ali, a Deputy Secretary in the General Administration Department and Director of Protocol of the state government, received the message at midnight. He checked with Prahlad Singh, the Commissioner of Police, and learnt the news was not correct but the condition of the Nizam was indeed critical. Hashim Ali had already drafted an obituary note for the gazette extraordinary which would be issued on the death of the Nizam. Earlier, he, along with the Commissioner of Police and the sub-area Commander of the Army, Brigadier Ferris, had visited King Kothi to finalize the arrangements for the imminent funeral.

Some papers published the news of the death the next morning. It caused general confusion and considerable embarrassment.

The next morning, Hashim Ali and Prahlad Singh visited the King Kothi again. The Nizam was sinking. It was only a matter of hours. The officials of the government and those of the King Kothi met at the office of Taraporewala, the Nizam's adviser. Prince Mukarram Jah also walked in. Hashim Ali told him that they had come to discuss the arrangements in the event of the Nizam's passing away. Mukarram Jah said that it was their custom not to announce the death for three days. Hashim Ali replied that it was probably necessary in earlier times because the issue of succession had to be settled, but now that he had already been notified as the successor, it did not seem necessary to delay the announcement. In any case, the people would know from the media. Then there was the question of keeping the body in state. Mukarram Jah was opposed to that idea. It had never been done before for any Nizam. Again Hashim Ali said that there would be crowds of peoples who would want to see his face and pay their last respects. Mukarram Jah demurred, but finally agreed on both the points.

The end came at 22 minutes past one in the afternoon on 24 February 1967. Dr Ramayya put his stethoscope on the chest of the Nizam and pronounced him dead. He certified the death due to cardiac failure. Nothing more could be known because that was the first time an instrument of modern medicine had touched the Nizam's body. The richest man of the world passed away without any modern treatment. Prince Mukarram Jah, his younger brother, their mother, the Nizam's stepbrother, Basalat Jah, the three doctors, and some other members of the household were all by his bedside. An hour later the body was brought out and kept below the *shamiana* specially erected in the courtyard. As the crowds started breaking into the compound, the police formed a cordon and asked the crowd to form a queue to file past in an orderly manner.

A comic touch was provided when Azam Jah, the Prince of Berar, came to the King Kothi at 3 p.m. He ambled up to the body of his father and touched his feet as a gesture of respect. When a pressman asked him to comment on the sad event, he was at a loss for words. He looked blankly at Abdul Mannan, a retired Deputy Secretary of the Finance Department, who had become his secretary and who was standing by his side. As if on a cue, Abdul Mannan began prompting the Prince who kept on repeating whatever Abdul Mannan said: 'He was a great man. He was the architect of modern Hyderabad. He established the Osmania University. He separated the executive from the judiciary. He implemented a number of reforms in the administration. The people of Hyderabad will never forget him ... etc.' And then after a while when the secretary thought he had said enough, he whispered to ask the Prince: 'Anything more?' The Prince, thinking that it was a part of the prompting, repeated loudly: 'Anything more?'

The Nizam's second son, Prince Muazzam Jah, did not come. He was sleeping off his nocturnal vigil. When an aide tried to wake him up and told him about the Nizam's demise, he mumbled with closed eyes: 'Don't bring such unpleasant news so early in the morning'. Then he turned on his side and resumed his sleep.

Early next morning, the body was given a bath. A prayer was said and a brand new, unnumbered ambulance van cut through thousands of mourners wending its way to the Mecca Masjid. There a prayer was held. The Imam of the mosque objected to the installation of a loud speaker on the premises. That would desecrate the sacred precincts because it carried the voice of Satan he said. This created difficulties in controlling the crowds and confusion outside. The prayers over, the body was brought out and placed in a gun carriage. An estimated crowd of 200,000 people formed the procession. People hung from their balconies and occupied every possible vantage point to be witness to a historic moment.

At 11 a.m. in the morning the gun carriage reached the Judi Mosque which had been built by the Nizam in memory of his son Jawad who had died in his infancy. The Arab guards and the Sikh paltan, dressed in the uniform of the private estate of the Nizam, barefoot and holding naked swords, took charge of the body of their Supreme Commander. The members of the family gave shoulder to the coffin. A detachment of the police sounded the last post and a unit of the army reversed their arms in their last mournful salute to the Nizam.

The body was taken out from the coffin and two old servants of the Nizam—Manzoor Ali and Mohammad Bin Habel—lowered it into the four foot deep grave dug by the side of the grave of his beloved mother and his son, as the crowd droned Allah-ho-Akbar. The Nizam's sons, daughter, grandsons, stepbrother, and others threw a fistful of earth each into the grave. Osman Ali Khan, the seventh and the last Asaf Jah, was returned to dust.[158]

He was 38 days short of 81 at his death. With his passing away an era came to a close.

One Mohammad Ali Beg issued an advertisement in the papers with his own tribute. He quoted the first line of the Nizam's famous couplet:

> Sultans of old, Osman, have all died.
> By your rule are Muslims now identified.<BQ Ends>

'And now,' said the advertisement, 'the writer of this line himself had joined them.' Beg did not omit to mention that he was a Resident of Charminar and his phone number was 41019.

❖ ❖ ❖

Brahmananda Reddy had long innings as a Chief Minister—seven-and-a-half years. His first few years in office were smooth.

In the restrictive economy of that time the first spell of industrial development was started during his term. Industrialization meant the establishment of public sector units, such as Bharat Heavy Electrical, Bharat Electronics, Electronic Corporation of India. The National Institute of Nutrition, the National Geophysical Research Institute, the Railway Training Institute, the Central Institute of English and Foreign Language and some other institutes also came into being in that period.

But trouble erupted soon. He had to face three agitations during his term.

In 1966, the examiners in the medical faculty of the Osmania University upgraded a nephew of Brahmananda Reddy. The Vice-Chancellor, Dr D.S. Reddy, on coming to know of it, cancelled the orders. Incensed by that, Brahmananda Reddy had an Act passed reducing the term of the Vice-Chancellor from five to three years, and scrapped the system of panels out of which the government had to select a Vice-Chancellor. There would now be a direct appointment by the government for this post. The students, insti- gated by Dr Reddy, started an agitation against the Act alleging that it reduced the autonomy of the Universities. On a petition by D.S. Reddy, the Supreme Court ruled that his term of five years could not be curtailed. The Chief Minister thereafter had to live with a defiant Vice-Chancellor.

One effect of this agitation was that the staff and the unions came to play a part in the choice of vice chancellors. This had disastrous consequences for the future.

Next, an agitation took place for the establishment of a steel plant in Visakhapatnam. It became violent and a bronze statue of Sanjeeva Reddy in Vijayawada was pulled down. It died out with the Government of India's announcement for the establishment of the plant.

The third and the worst, the Telangana Agitation, took place in 1969.

Though the state of Andhra Pradesh was created on the basis of the bond of a common language between Andhra and Telangana, we have seen how some leaders of Telangana had reservations on the issue. The hearts of the people of Andhra and Telangana never met. The people of Telangana alleged that the 'Gentleman's Agreement' had been violated in letter and spirit. There had been gross discrimination against them in favour of the employees from the Andhra area who had been appointed to jobs in Telangana on the plea that qualified persons were not available. In early 1969, the NGOs (Non-Gazetted Officers) of Telangana threatened to launch an agitation if 6,000 Andhras occupying Telangana posts were not repatriated to Andhra. A student, named Ravinder, undertook a fast unto death in Khammam on the issue. Thus the agitation was spearheaded by students and NGOs.

Eight Congress members of the State Assembly resigned and joined the agitation. Dr M. Channa Reddy, a Telangana leader, had been a minister in Brahmananda Reddy's Cabinet. The lat- ter had him sent to the Centre in 1967 as a minister. In 1969, he resigned from the Union Cabinet upon being convicted of election offences and was disqualified from taking part in elections for six years. He then took up the leadership of the Telangana agitation and formed a party called the 'Telangana Praja Samithi' to agitate for the establishment of a separate state of Telangana. In the elections of 1971, TPS won ten out of 14 seats for the Lok Sabha from the region.

The agitation did not succeed because of the strong stand taken by the Prime Minister, Indira Gandhi. However on 30 September 1971, Brahmananda was driven to resignation.

P.V. Narasimha Rao, who succeeded him, became the first Chief Minister from Telangana. In his ministry he gave more representation to Telangana and persons from the backward classes. He had an ordinance promulgated on urban land ceilings and land reforms and later introduced a bill in the legislature. He extended the use of Telugu as the medium of instruction upto the junior college level.

His main weakness was his inability to take decisions. Files kept on piling up while he pondered the pros and cons of a particular course of action. This was later to be one of the major complaints against him. He was harassed by favour-seekers so much that he often used to go to hideouts just to dispose of files without being disturbed.

Soon after his induction, the Andhra agitation erupted in the state to protest against 'Mulki Rules'. To understand the genesis of the concept of 'Mulki Rules', we have to make a digression and go back to nineteenth century Hyderabad.

In order to modernize the administration of the feudal state of Hyderabad, the Diwan, Sir Salar Jung (1853–83), brought in a number of English-educated officials from British India to occupy most of the important jobs in the state administration. This led to much bitterness amongst the local populace. The sixth Nizam asked to be shown the list of officials with reference to their origin. The list categorized those who were from within the state as 'Mulki' and those who were from outside as 'non-Mulki'.

The seventh Nizam issued an order in 1919 that only Mulkis were eligible for jobs in the state government. 'Mulki' was defined as one who was born in the Hyderabad state or had resided there continuously for 15 years and gave an affidavit that he had no intention of going back to his native place.[159]

These Mulki rules continued to operate in the Telangana region. As a result of that, persons from the Andhra region could not be appointed in the Telangana region of the state. In 1972, some Andhra employees challenged the validity of these rules. The High Court on 14 February 1972 held that the rules ceased to be valid after the formation of Andhra Pradesh. This naturally upset the people of Telangana. Narasimha Rao's government appealed against the judgment to the Supreme Court. On 3 October 1972, the apex court reversed the ruling of the High Court and upheld the validity of the 'Mulki' rules. It was now the turn of Andhras to agitate against their being reduced to aliens in their own state. This gave rise to the 'Jai Andhra' agitation by the Andhraites demanding separation from Telangana. The agitation continued for more than two months. The Telangana Agitation had swept out an Andhra Chief Minister, Brahmananda Reddy in 1971. Two years later the Andhra agitation claimed the first Telangana Chief Minister, Narasimha Rao, as its casualty. President's Rule was imposed in the state on 18 January 1973.

A compromise in the form of '6–point Formula' was devised by Prime Minister Indira Gandhi to mollify the people from the two regions. The Mulki rules were repealed and the Constitution of India was amended in 1973.

The President's Rule was lifted on 10 December 1973 and Jalagam Vengala Rao was installed as Chief Minister.

Vengala Rao belonged to Andhra area but his family had moved to Khammam when he was a child. He left his studies to join politics and rose to the position of Chairman of the Khammam Zilla Parishad and later, President of the Chamber of Panchayati Raj. He was a simple man of few words. He presented a contrast to Narasimha Rao in the quickness of his decisions. His meetings were brief and to the point. His speeches too were short. He was the first to appoint a bright senior IAS officer as his secretary. Thus he sowed the seeds for his appointment to the Chief Minister's Secretariat. He also chose his civil servants carefully and reposed full faith in them. He had earlier served as Home Minister (1969–71) under Brahmananda Reddy and in that capacity he had dealt with the Naxal Movement in Andhra Pradesh with a firm hand.

The Naxal uprising in Andhra Pradesh was a revival of the Communist Armed Struggle, which had been withdrawn in 1951 in Hyderabad. In Andhra Pradesh, it arose in Srikakulam against the exploitation of tribals by traders and money-lenders from the plains. It was sponsored by the Communist Party of India, which initiated the formation of an association called the Girijan Sangham in 1959.

Charu Majumdar, who had started the Naxal movement in Naxalbari in West Bengal, also lent inspiration to the Maoists in Srikakulam. In 1968–9 there was an armed revolt of the CP(M) cadres in Srikakulam. The state governments of Orissa and Andhra Pradesh took concerted action to crush the movement with the help of the Government of India. The police killed the two leaders of the movement—Satyam and Kailasam—in an encounter on 10 July 1970. Including a non-militant leader, 140 persons were arrested and charged for taking part in the Srikakulam uprising. Majumdar died on 28 July 1972 in police custody. Though the armed movement was quelled in Srikakulam it did not die. On the other hand, it gradually spread to other areas, particularly the Telangana districts of the state.

Vengala Rao also had the benefit of the Emergency imposed by Mrs Gandhi from June 1975 till March 1977. Rao used it to send some of opposition leaders to jail. He also took advantage of it to weed out some corrupt and inefficient officers from service. He did not hold elections to the local bodies and controlled the cooperative bodies through appointed officials. Apart from this, the Emergency was not abused in the state.

An unprecedented cyclone hit Divi Seema in Krishna district on 19 November 1977:

The cyclone was first reported on November 14, 1977 occurring south of the Nicobar Islands. The storm took the usual route for cyclones affecting the coast traveling to west and northwest. Ultimately the cyclone crossed south Andhra coast near Chirala at 2.30 p.m. and the sea waves swept Divi and Bandar coast for over a length of 125 km of the storm track. The maximum penetration inland was 14 km. ...

Study of the tide ranges and wind strengths has shown that cyclone was closely comparable in its severity the Calcutta cyclone of 1737, the strongest ever recorded cyclone when 13 m heigh tidal waves engulfed the coast killing three lakh people. Tides of 8 to 12 m were recorded in the area during the recent cyclone. Telephone poles of 6 m height trapped hay and slush carried by the waves near Nagayalanka. The wind velocities reached the speeds of above 160 km per hour.

Wave action coupled with the high water mark of the storm were the main agencies for the destruction of property and loss of life estimated at about 10,000. Wind destruction was widespread along the storm tract in Ponnur, Chirala, Bapatla, Tenali, Repalle, Guntur, and Sattanapalli taluks of Guntur district and Vijayawada and Gannavaram, Gudivada, and Machilipatnam, and Divi taluks of Krishna district all of which are located within the storm tract. Old trees were uprooted and seen aligned in a southwesterly direction. Telephone and electrical poles were twisted and bent down at many places. Asbestos roofed industrial units and thatched huts were blown and ravaged to the ground. The winds of great magnitude blowing from 6.00 a.m. (19th) to late midnight and caused severe damage to property and life. The sea wave destruction in Divi and Masula taluks was heavy, wiping out 55 villages in the process except for some concrete structures like school buildings and temples. The worst affected villages were within the 2 to 4 km from coast from Sorlagondi in southwest to Hamsala Divi in north east. Thousands of people were swept 12 km inland by the giant sea currents entering inland through inlets and sluiceways. Tidal waves carried heavy cargo boats of 1,000 tonnes capacity berthed in Masula port to 5 km inland near Masula Railway Station.[160]

In the elections held after the Emergency was lifted in 1977, the Congress was routed and the Janata Party was voted to power at the Centre. The Congress was split and Vengala Rao deserted Mrs Gandhi's faction called Congress (I) and joined the faction led by Brahmananda Reddy called Congress (R). He showed calculated discourtesy to Indira Gandhi when she came to visit the cyclone affected areas of the state. None of his ministers received her. She was even refused accommodation in the state guest house at Vijayawada. One Congress MLA, Bapiraju, provided his car to her and a couple, Bhavnam Venkat Rama Reddy and his wife Jayaprada, offered her accommodation and looked after the comforts of the discredited leader. Indira Gandhi did not forget that gesture and Vengala Rao's discourtesy to her.

Vengala Rao continued the traditional emphasis on irrigation and power in the government's investment policies. The result was that generation of electricity took great strides, and right through the period of the Congress rule, the state had surplus power.

By the time the elections to the State Assembly were held in 1978, Channa Reddy's six-year electoral disqualification was over and after weighing his options, he joined Mrs Gandhi's faction. Vengala Rao cast his lot with the Congress (R). The Congress (I) won the election and Dr Marri Channa Reddy, having merged Telangana Praja Samithi in the Congress, became the Chief Minister of the state on 6 March 1978.

Channa Reddy was born in 1919 in Vikarabad. He graduated in medicine from Osmania University in the Urdu medium. However, he practised medicine for a short time and soon jumped into politics. As a political worker, he was imprisoned during the freedom struggle. He also edited a Telugu weekly for some time. At the age of 31, he became the youngest Member of Parliament. He served as a minister under B. Ramakrishna Rao in 1952. As Agriculture Minister he introduced a scheme in which farmers could get fertilizers on credit by certification of the village officers. He also took the initative in the establishment of the Agricultural University. He introduced the reservation of seats in the Municipal Councils and Panchayat Raj institutions for schedule castes, schedule tribes, and women. Besides, he allocated 15 per cent of the funds of local bodies for the welfare of 'Weaker Sections'. He also announced a reservation of 25 per cent for backward classes in government jobs and educational institutions. Another new scheme was that of a bus for every village.

Channa Reddy was a very intelligent and shrewd leader with vision. He liked to interact with people for new ideas. He was a good organizer and systematically followed up the promises he made to the people. However, his besetting vice was his arrogance and vengefulness. He was generous to his followers but demanded unquestioning obedience and loyalty. He took perverse pleasure in humiliating important persons. Mrs Gandhi had seen him shift his loyalties and was suspicious of him.

In 1979, his 60th birthday, *shashtipoorthi* as it is called, was celebrated lavishly as a public function. Government corporations erected felicitation arches and businessmen gave him and his wife many costly gifts. That drew considerable public criticism and contributed to the ground swell against him that led to his dismissal.

A small incident shows how crucial decisions are sometimes taken in high politics. One day, some one presented a packet of sweets to Channa Reddy by way of gratitude for some favor. One packet was also customarily left in his private secretariat and the staff there started eating the sweets. R. M. Manohar, an MLA, happened to drop by and saw that. Later that morning, Indira Gandhi's younger son, Sanjay Gandhi, was killed in an aircraft which he was flying himself. Manohar, who was not happy with Channa Reddy, reported to Indira Gandhi that Channa Reddy and his staff had celebrated Sanjay Gandhi's death by distributing sweets. She then decided to hasten his dismissal and asked G. Raja Ram to mobilize dissidents against Channa Reddy. That was done and T. Anjaiah was told in confidence in August that he would be made the Chief Minister. Anjaiah announced it in public and that caused embarrassment to Mrs Gandhi. That indiscretion on Anjaiah's part delayed the action by two months.

Channa Reddy was half-way through his term, when T. Anjaiah replaced him on 11 October 1980.

Anjaiah was uneducated and used to boast that he had started his life as a worker in the Allwyn Steel Factory in Hyderabad earning six annas—less than half of Rs 1—a day. He became a trade union leader and joined INTUC—a wing of the Indian National Congress. He became Minister for Labour under Vengala Rao. To accommodate as many MLAs as possible, Anjaiah formed a jumbo ministry of 61 ministers. When, at the behest of the Congress High Command, he had to prune it, all the ministers who were removed became dissidents.

Anjaiah introduced crop insurance and hut insurance schemes for the poor. He exempted small farmers with five acres of wet holdings from payment of land revenue. He also introduced old age pension for agricultural labourers.

When Rajiv Gandhi visited Hyderabad in 1982 as General Secretary of the Congress, Anjaiah organized a grand welcome for him. As a part of that he had welcome arches erected all over the city. Many people went to the tarmac to receive him. Rajiv Gandhi, a pilot pushed into politics, did not like all that fuss and waste of funds. He pulled up Anjaiah publicly for that. In panic Anjaiah had some of the arches removed but went into a sulk. He became a butt of jokes and ridicule in the state. One such joke narrates that on a visit to the Niloufer Hospital, when he was shown a Labour Room he expressed his appreciation for this concern for labour! While scrutinizing the comparative allocation of budgets for Andhra and Telangana regions, when he noticed an item 'Harbour' under the allocation for Andhra, he asked why no amount was allotted for any harbour in Telangana (a land locked region).

In the elections to the local bodies conducted under Anjaiah's Chief Ministership, the Congress candidates contesting without a party label lost. The Bharatiya Janata Party (BJP) won a majority in the Visakhapatnam Municipal Corporation. CPI and CPI(M) captured the majority and the deputy mayoralty, respectively of the Vijayawada Municipal Corporation. That sealed Anjaiah's fate and after less than 16 months in office, he was shown the door.

Then the time came for Indira Gandhi to reward the couple who had come to her rescue when she had come to visit the cyclone-affected areas in Vijayawada in 1977. Bhavnam Venkatram was the Education Minister whose name no one had ever heard before. He was suddenly appointed Chief Minister on 24 February 1982. He was not even a member of the Legislative Assembly. If ever there was a dark horse, Venkatram was one. According to some sources, he was the choice of P.V. Narasimha Rao whom Indira Gandhi had come to trust for his unflinching loyalty. Venkatram can be remembered only for starting the first Open University in the state—and the country. That inaugurated the era of distance learning in the country.

The office of Chief Minister became an object of mockery and held no sanctity. Chief Ministers were being 'manufactured' in Delhi and like defective pieces were being cast away one after another. Nominated by the high command of the Party in rapid succession these appointments brazenly disregarded the local sentiment. They were not leaders of their legislature party. They were the followers of the all powerful leader at Delhi. The situation was pathetically reminiscent of the last days of the Mughals in eighteenth century Delhi. The score in Andhra Pradesh was proceeding on similar lines. There was also a parallel in the Hyderabad state in the first half of the nineteenth century when the Diwans were nominated by the British Resident and served during his pleasure.

Public amusement gave way to pity, to disgust, and then to revulsion.

But the Congress (I) was the largest party. It had absolute majority in the Lok Sabha. There was hardly any opposition. But there was plenty of dissidence, which is more sinister for not being open. The situation was perfect for a revolution and somewhere it was brewing.

Politics of the Theatre

The election to the Assembly was due in January 1983 and the Congress Party suddenly realized that Venkatram would not be able to lead it in the battle of the ballot. So, three months before the election, Kotla Vijayabhaskara Reddy, a Rayalaseema leader and a Member of the Lok Sabha, was brought in as Chief Minister. He had been away from the state for about 12 years. His mandate was to win the election. But time was running out for him.

Meanwhile a film actor, Nandamuri Taraka Rama Rao, popularly known by his initials, NTR had decided to enter politics.

NTR was born in 1923 in a village Krishna district. After graduation he took up the petty job of a sub-registrar. Being a handsome man, while working there, he was offered a role in a film which he accepted. That launched him on a very successful career in films. He played mostly the roles of the heroes of Hindu mythology. By 1982, he had acted in about 300 films for 30 years, which made him a household name. People had his pictures in their houses and women worshipped them.

In 1977, M.G. Ramachandran, a Tamil actor, had become Chief Minister of Tamilnadu and Ronald Regan, an American small-time actor, had became President of the USA. Those examples inspired NTR. When he attended his friend Bhavnam Venkataram's swearing-in ceremony in the Raj Bhavan at Hyderabad, he was awed by the glamour of political power. So, he did not need much persuasion to enter politics. On 21 March 1982, he launched his political outfit—Telugu Desam Party (TDP).

The man and the moment met. The main plank of his manifesto was the self-respect of the people of the state, which had been bruised by the behaviour of the leaders of the Congress Party at Delhi. Taking a cue from Tamilnadu, he also declared that he would provide people rice at Rs 2 per kg and free mid-day meals to school children. His rival, Kotla Vijayabhaskara Reddy, in full election mode disbursed funds to local bodies liberally to help his party cadres. He also tried to pre-empt NTR by introducing the scheme of disbursing rice at Rs 1.90 per kg in Hyderabad and Vijayawada. But that was too late. Meanwhile, in 1982,

NTR started methodically building his party and contacts. He published a full page advertisement in Eenadu, a new Telegu daily, inviting all those wanting to join Telugu Desam to do so by filling up a proforma printed there, and posting it to the Party office.

NTR convened the first party *mahanadu* (general body) at Tirupati on 28 May 1982, and thereafter, began an intense familiarization tour of the state. What he did was quite novel. He travelled by a van, fitted with a public address system, two powerful lights to focus on him when he stood on the top to address a gathering at night. He had a tractor-trailer in tow housing a generator, and from morning to night, he travelled from village to village, addressing wayside public meetings from his van. This was the cheapest form of a campaign, because there was no need to erect a dias, arrange a public address system, or a lighting system or mobilise crowds. His van contained all the facilities to enable him to address a crowd of upto 5,000. Since NTR was coming from the world of films to politics, people came out of curiosity to see him, and he had the maximum exposure among politicians to the Andhra Pradesh public.

He chose two Telugu songs as his signature tunes. One was the song *Ma Telugu talliki malle poo danda* (a garland of jasmine for our Telugu mother) written by Sankarambadi Sundarachari, which is the normal prayer song in school functions, and another, *Cheyetthi jaikottu Telugoda* (Oh Telugu man, raise your hand to herald victory) written by the Communist Party leader, Vemulapalli Sri Krishna. These were old songs, but the song 'Maal Telugu talliki' was set to music to an attractive tune and sung with gusto by the eminent playback singer P. Suseela and became very popular among the crowds. About 10 minutes before NTR would enter a village, a jeep would go round the village playing the tapes of the two songs and leave, when crowds would gather on the roadside because they knew NTR was on the way, and NTR would enter the village to receive an enthusiastic reception. Nothing like this happened in Andhra Pradesh political campaigns before and people were taken in by the sheer novelty of the whole exercise.

NTR had another jeep trailer in his entourage, which travelled ahead, in which a cook travelled with cooking vessels to prepare breakfast, lunch and dinner, while there was a motor mechanic to check the transmission and electrical systems in the van with his kit of tools, and another to wash clothes. The staff would camp separately on the waysides, make breakfast, and hand it over to the driver of the van in which NTR travelled, and leave for the next station to prepare lunch. NTR was therefore self-contained, and he never went to any leader's house for lunch or dinner throughout his political career in the next 13 years. He would drink sodas, not water, frequently to quench his thirst. He would sit on top of the van in the hot sun, wiping his face with towel now and then, without regard for his glamour as a film star.

NTR would sleep in his van at nights, parked near a field or near a mango grove. He would bathe under a roadside tree in the morning, an event widely covered in the 'Eenadu'. Congress leaders did not like the campaign a bit, and called NTR a 'Drama Rao', a man who indulged in gimmicks to hog publicity, and dismissed him as of no consequence.[161]

People, tired of the long rule of Reddys, came forward to see if power could be transferred to a Kamma, the caste to which NTR belonged.

Ramoji Rao, another very innovative and successful Kamma entrepreneur, had created history in journalism by starting a Telugu daily, *Eenadu*, with separate editions for each district. It had a circulation of over a million copies. Later, he also set up a self-contained Ramoji Film City. Subsequently, he made a successful foray into private channels for TV in a number of languages. He came forward to help NTR in the choice of candidates. He prepared a panel of about 900 educated persons with a clean image for NTR to choose his candidates from for the forthcoming elections. His newspaper provided an effective publicity medium for NTR's campaigning.

In his talks with the opposition parties NTR ruled out seat sharing unless he was given 250 out of a total 294 seats of the Assembly. NTR's campaign juggernaut was rolling fast and gaining countrywide admiration.

Alarmed, the government advanced the election from March to January 1983. The TDP swept the polls and won 202 seats out of

294. The Congress Party got a bare 60 seats and other parties fared miserably.

NTR started his tenure on 9 January 1983 with an unprecedented fund of goodwill. But he squandered it liberally. He had no experience of public life.

His 'reel' life was not duplicated in real life. He was ignorant about the nuances of administration, but was unwilling to learn. As Chief Minister, law defined his powers and, unlike his screen role as mythological god, he had to listen to the people inside the legislature and heed the advice of his bureaucrats. He was not comfortable with these constraints.

He started his tenure with a number of unpopular measures. First, he reduced the age of retirement of government employees from 58 to 55. Then he banned private practice by government doctors. Next, he abolished the hereditary post of village officers. He also initiated steps to abolish the legislative council in which the Congress had a majority. He even cancelled the pension to legislators.

He abolished the three academies dealing with art, literature, and the performing arts and instead created the Telugu University which he named after Potti Sriramulu, the leader who had fasted unto death demanding the creation of a separate Andhra state. He also abolished the system of conferment of honorary titles on eminent artists and writers saying that if they were good the public would acknowledge them any way.

He was a Telugu revivalist. He erected 35 statutes of historic Andhra personages on the Tank Bund in Hyderabad. He also had a Kakatiya gate erected at the entrance of the Tank Bund Road. He wanted Hyderabad to reflect the glory befitting the capital of the Telugu state. He was so obsessed with Telugu that he prefixed it to every scheme. When latrines were provided for women, he called the project 'Telugu Women's Latrines'.

He was orthodox and eccentric. He started wearing one earring and donned saffron clothes and a turban to look like Vivekananda. In closed-door meetings with officials, if any advice did not conform to his preconceived notions, he would suddenly stand up and announce imperially that he represented 65 million Andhras. He did not read any paper or any file. Every

'case' was explained to him and he would then append his signatures to the orders with a flourish in Telugu. His understanding of public issues and policy implications was poor. Once he
ordered the merger of the Warehousing Corporation and the
Police Housing Corporation just because the word 'housing' was
common to both.

NTR enjoyed the adulation of the people and so revelled in
populist measures. The budget had no sanctity for him and the
so-called welfare measures resulted in the neglect of development. While the supply of power remained more or less static, the
demand for it kept on increasing. The state, which not long ago
was comfortable with regard to power, began to suffer increasing
deficits.

He also had a Judas in the Cabinet. When, in July 1984, NTR
went to the USA for a heart bypass surgery, Nandendla Bhaskara
Rao, his Finance Minister who had coached him in the art of
politics, engineered a coup against him. Through defections, he
claimed the support of a majority in the Assembly and staked his
claim for Chief Ministership. A pliant Governor, who belonged to
the Congress Party, accepted his claim and installed him as Chief
Minister.

NTR rushed back from the USA and, after a series of dramatic
steps which revealed the murky side of politics, won back his post
on 16 September 1984 in the midst of great public jubilation. He
then dissolved the Assembly on 22 November 1984. In the elections held in March 1985, he was returned with 202 seats in the
Assembly and won 35 out of 41 seats in the Lok Sabha in the elections held in December 1984. That was despite the nation-wide
sympathy wave in favour of Rajiv Gandhi who won more than 400
seats in the Lok Sabha due to the assassination of Indira Gandhi.

Thereafter, he became Chairman of the National Front—a
hodgepodge formation opposed to the Congress. Ironically, in
the election of 1989, while the National Front won at the national
level, NTR lost the elections in Andhra Pradesh.

Out of office, NTR was harassed by the Congress and pros-
ecuted through its local leaders. A reading of these incidents
underlines the venality prevailing not only in politics but also in
administration and the judiciary.

Channa Reddy again came back as Chief Minister on 3 December 1989. Satya Sai Baba of Puttaparthi, whom he had met before the elections, had predicted his victory. During his second term he took up the Remote Area Development Plan in January 1990. His health was not good and he spent two months in the USA for a kidney transplant and cataract surgery. During his visit, he secured a World Bank Loan for the Cyclone Emergency Reconstruction Project (CERP). A year later massive riots took place in Hyderabad and, the first time in its history, the city had to be handed over to the army. It was widely rumoured that the dissidents within the Congress Party had engineered the riots and troublemakers were specially brought for that purpose from Vijayawada and Rayalseema.

Channa Reddy was compelled to resign. He did so on 16 December 1990. However, a day before leaving he filled up 22 posts of chairmen of various corporations.

In the game of musical chairs, N. Janardhan Reddy became the next Chief Minister. When Rajiv Gandhi was assassinated on 21 May 1991 in Tamil Nadu, the Congress Party blamed NTR for that. That gave a good excuse to persecute NTR and his TDP. Violence was unleashed against him. His studio at Kachiguda and the theatre at Abid Road were set on fire. He went on a fast but was removed to a hospital by the government.

Janardhan Reddy's term too was plagued by internal squabbles and dissidence. His plan to celebrate the fourth centenary of Hyderabad on a massive scale was scuttled by his detractors. His sanction for the establishment of a dozen private medical and dental colleges in the state earned him strictures from the High Court. So Janardhan Reddy went as he came after a term just short of two years.

He was succeeded by the old horse of the Congress Party, Kotla Vijayabhaskara Reddy. He started his second term as Chief Minister on 9 October 1992. He resigned his seat in the Parliament and contested for the State Assembly from Panyam in Kurnool in an election marked by high handedness of his party and harass-ment of the TDP and its President, NTR.

As 11 years earlier, Vijayabhaskara Reddy again lost the elec-tion of 1994 to NTR, who became Chief Minister for the third time on 12 December 1994.

Despite the glory, NTR's cup of misfortune was filling up fast. His wife had died in 1984 of cancer. A married woman and a folk art performer, Lakshmi Parvathi, who was about half his age, began visiting him while he was in the Opposition. She wanted to write his biography. NTR fell to her charms and after a long live-in relationship, married her on 11 September 1993. He was then 70 and had 11 grown up children and many grandchildren. This marriage caused resentment not only amongst his children but also amongst his followers. This, coupled with his arrogant, eccentric behavior in general, disenchanted even his admirers and party members. But his charisma was so great that he still won the election in 1994. The Opposition was pulverized.

With the emergence of Lakshmi Parvathi as the mate and the conscience-keeper of the god of the TDP, the influence and patronage, which was earlier exercised largely by the two sons-in-law of NTR, passed to his wife. The favour-seekers now sought not Chandrababu Naidu, the General Secretary of the Party, nor the other members of the family, but the new Queen. They therefore revolted against NTR. Chandrababu Naidu, the great organizer of the party and the successful manager of the earlier crisis of 1984 when Bhaskara Rao had tried to dislodge NTR, revolted and started mobilizing the party legislators against his father-in-law. On 24 August 1995, out of a total of 220 MLAs of TDP, 144 elected him as the leader of the Legislature Party. A series of dramatic developments followed in which the Speaker of the Assembly, the Governor, and the High Court played their respective roles—some not entirely creditably. With his shrewdness Naidu managed to ride through all and was sworn in as Chief Minister of the state on 1 September 1995.

Some astrologer had told Lakshmi Parvathi and NTR that if a son were born out of their union, either he or NTR would rule the country. To make that happen, the lady tried to have her sterilization undone and fed him steroids. The operation on her did not succeed; his drug took its toll.

Buffeted around by Fate, disowned by the family, denounced by the Party, sucked dry by an ambitious second wife, turned away by the Governor, rejected by the High Court, NTR died on the night of 18 January 1996. Thus passed into history a man who played hero on the screen till his 60th year and who created real-life drama for 13 years following that. NTR was a man born to rule—but to die in exile. A man used to cheering crowds and fawning politicians, breathed his last in the bed of a woman who was the only one left with him in his last hours.

Handsome, arrogant, eccentric, unschooled in politics, living in a world of make-believe, NTR gave the people of Andhra a feeling of identity and a role which they had lost after the fall of Kakatiyas eight centuries ago. He also broke the hegemony of a monolithic political party and conferred a legitimacy of role on regional powers in the politics of the country. He shifted the centre of gravity of political power of the state from the far away Delhi to Hyderabad. The nature of politics in Andhra Pradesh was forever changed by NTR.

The e-Governor

Nara Chandrababu Naidu was born on 20 April 1950 of middle-class, illiterate, agricultural parents in a village in Chittoor district of Andhra Pradesh. His father, owner of 24 acres of land, sold part of it to educate his two sons—Chandrababu and Ramamurthy.

Chandrababu did his MA in Economics and enrolled for M.Phil at the Sri Venkateswara University. His thesis was on the famed Andhra leader, N.G Ranga's concept of rural development. But politics claimed him midway. He won the Legislative Assembly elections in 1978 on a Congress Party ticket. After spending two years as MLA, he became a junior minister under Anjaiah in 1980 with a portfolio which included cinematography. That fortuitous circumstance brought him in touch with NTR who was being wooed by the government of Andhra Pradesh to help shift the film industry from Chennai to Hyderabad.

NTR came to like the keen young minister. He was from a modest background and was good in his habits. NTR was rich and glamorous but was also very disciplined in his habits—and a teetotaler. His third daughter, Bhuvneshwari, was married to Naidu in 1981. When NTR launched TDP in 1982, Naidu was in the Congress Party. In the election later that year Naidu contested against his father-in-law's party and lost. Thereupon, he joined TDP and became a confidant of NTR.

In the introduction to the book *Plain Speaking* that Naidu wrote with Sevanti Ninan, he comes off as a master strategist. She says, 'As they tell you about this party in Andhra Pradesh, NTR founded it and Chandrababu Naidu built it'.[162] He showed his political acumen and organizing abilities during the crisis of 1984 when Nandendla Bhaskara Rao betrayed NTR. Ironically, in 1989, Naidu won the election, but NTR lost. Again Naidu worked out the strategy for NTR during his year in the opposition. In 1993, when NTR, on being suspended from the Assembly along with his Party MLAs, vowed not to sit in the Assembly, Naidu virtually became the leader of the Opposition in the Assembly. In 1994, when NTR recaptured power Naidu was appointed Minister for Revenue, Finance, and Power. Naidu used his organizing ability and his gift for intrigue and manoeuver to dislodge NTR from power in 1995 and became the Chief Minister of the state. He had four years out of NTR's remaining term to rule.

Naidu continued the three major schemes of NTR—namely, supply of rice at Rs 2 per kg, introduction of total prohibition and a flat rate of Rs 50 per hp of power for tube well irrigation. He had an advantage over NTR in the new political equation emerging at the national level. The successive Prime Ministers of the Congress governments had humiliated NTR no end. With the defeat of P.V. Narasimha Rao in the national election in 1996, the United Front was formed comprising a conglomerate of non-BJP parties. Naidu was elected its Convener and after Jyoti Basu was not allowed by his Party—CPI(M)—to accept the Prime-Ministership, it was offered to Naidu. Seeing the fragility of the Front, he shrewdly declined the offer. He wanted first to consolidate his position at home.

In the 1998 mid-term elections, the BJP emerged as the largest single party in the Lok Sabha. It led a National Democratic Alliance (NDA) with 23 other parties. Naidu's support to it was crucial since his party had 12 MPs in the Lok Sabha. He agreed to support it without joining the government on the basis of a Common Minimum Programme. His sudden somersault into NDA annoyed the leftists in Delhi. They dubbed him an opportunist to the core.

The arrangement with NDA gave Naidu strong leverage which he used to get special treatment and crucial concessions for the state. He was conscious of the abuse and corruption involved in the supply of rice at Rs 2 per kg and the flat rate for supply of power for tube wells. Prohibition too led to bootlegging and corruption. Besides, all three schemes cost the exchequer a huge amount. They had to be reviewed.

In 1996, Naidu led his Party to a reasonable success in the Lok Sabha despite a cut into his vote share of 10.66 per cent by NTR's widow, Lakshmi Parvathi, who had floated her own party. That established his legitimacy and he turned his attention to various aspects of administration needing reforms. He started looking at various modes of economic development outside, studied the impact of subsidies involved in various schemes, and gave serious thought to area needing reforms.

Naidu approached the World Bank for aid. He agreed to its condition for reducing subsidies and raising tariffs. In accordance with advice given by the experts of the World Bank, he raised power tariff, increased the price of subsidized supply of rice from Rs 2 to 3.50, and reduced the quantum per family from 5 to 4 kgs. In 1997, he scrapped prohibition. The receipts from taxes also increased. While all these measures improved the finances of the state and earned a pat from the World Bank, they were not popular. The Opposition criticized them and ridiculed him as a puppet of the World Bank.

There was widespread speculation that, because of his bold steps to bolster the economy of the state, he had alienated the voters and he might lose the elections of 1999. But to everyone's surprise, Naidu won a handsome victory and this time rode back to power in his own right. He returned to his unfinished agenda with redoubled vigour and self-confidence.

His pragmatism, the boldness of his approach, and his publicity blitz won him many admirers both in India and abroad. Articles were written on him and his 'vision' in prestigious papers and magazines of the western world and in India. His vision is elaborated in his book *Plain Speaking* written with Sevanti Ninan in 2000. Naidu felt that NTR had spent too much on welfare. The attention now needed to be diverted to development. Also till 1999 he believed that money was important to win elections. His success in the elections of 1999 made him realize that money alone was not enough. At the same time, for economic development of the state, the assistance of institutions like the World Bank was a good thing. It also exposed the economy and the people to new thinking, which went in to the making of developed countries. He came to believe in the virtues of competitive economy which promoted efficiency and better services to the consumers. That meant a curtailment of freebies and levy of user charges for services.

He subjected his ministers and senior bureaucrats to spells of training both in India and abroad.

After 1999 he became less accessible to his colleagues and party cadres. He stopped consulting them and even ignored them in the formation of the Cabinet and distribution of patronage. That resulted in extreme centralization of authority which defeated many of his objectives. His lavish expenditure on publicity, which was again largely focused on himself, proved counterproductive.

He persuaded local and foreign leaders in business to establish some institutions of excellence. Starting with HITEC City (Hyderabad Information Technology and Engineering Consultancy City) in 1998, he went on to set up the Indian School of Business in collaboration with Kellogg School of Management and The Wharton School in the United States of America, and London Business School, UK; the Indian Institute of Information Technology; and ICICI Knowledge Park. He addressed various fora of business, both national and international, and made power point presentations to them highlighting the potential for investment in Andhra Pradesh.

In the field of governance Naidu computerized the Land Revenue and Commercial Taxes departments which increased their efficiency, reduced corruption, and enhanced revenue. The most citizen-friendly innovation was the E-seva centers. There the citizens could pay bills for any department of government. That reduced queues in collection counters spread over various parts of the city.

He gave a special boost to IT, Biotechnology, and Tourism. To improve the state, he started with the capital. The newer part of the city of Hyderabad was beautified. Malls sprang up on the main road from Secunderabad to Hyderabad. The area in which latest facilities were set up was made into a separate zone and named 'Cyberabad' to rhyme with Hyderabad. These initiatives won him accolades. But the Opposition criticized them as elitist. They benefited the urban rich, they alleged, not the common man. He took up special programmes for the poor.

In 1999, he distributed one million new LPG connections to women with a subsidy of Rs 500 for the deposit for the gas cylinder. There were however no takers for these in the second round in 2003. The Rythu Bazar (Farmers Market) scheme eliminated the middleman between the producers and the consumers of vegetables and fruits. He initiated the scheme of 'Janamabhoomi' under which officers of various departments descended on one area and took up its total development. To establish a direct connection with people for feedback, he had weekly phone-in programmes on radio and TV. He used to have a regular video conference with Collectors and other officials.

Rural areas, however, suffered for lack of adequate attention. Hyderabad had no power cuts. But there were prolonged spells of blackout in rural areas. The farmers did not get adequate water from their tube wells for want of power. Recurrent drought for three years—from 2001–3 compounded their misery. Many farmers could not repay their debts because they could not raise crops. Hundreds of them committed suicide. So while Naidu's image abroad soared, it suffered at home. While he was included in the 'dream Cabinet' of the world, in his own state he was dubbed as some one who was out of touch with the realities of the life of the poor.

He also antagonized the People's War Group by banning it and mounting a relentless campaign against them. He was determined to eliminate them. He was accused of encouraging fake encounters by the police authorities. The People's War Group resolved to remove him from the scene. They struck with claymore mines under his bulletproof car at Alipiri when he was going to Tirumala for worship on 1 October 2003. It was a miraculous escape for him. He was shaken and called his survival in the attack as his rebirth. He declared that he would devote his life to the service of the poor.

People condemned the attack on him and offered him their sympathy. Expecting the sympathy for him to translate into votes, the politician in him decided to advance the elections. On his recommendation the State Assembly was dissolved on 15 November 2003—ten months ahead of the scheduled elections. Much to Naidu's discomfiture, the Election Commission did not agree to hold elections in January 2004 on the plea that the electoral rolls were under revision.

Meanwhile, the NDA government at the Centre won elections in three out of the four states which went to the polls in December 2003. Elated, it announced the dissolution of the Lok Sabha on 6 February 2004. The Election Commission decided to club the Lok Sabha election with the Assembly election in Andhra Pradesh by April 2004. By that time the assassination attempt on Naidu had been forgotten and the sympathy factor that he hoped to capitalize on had dissipated.

From the date of the dissolution of the Assembly, Naidu became a 'care-taker' Chief Minister. That prevented him from taking policy decisions. After the announcement of the election schedule by the Election Commission, he was prevented by the model code of conduct even to announce new schemes or to attend functions to celebrate the completion or the inauguration of any new project. He thus couldn't claim credit for increasing the drinking water supply to Hyderabad from the river Krishna by 20 mgd or over 12 per cent. That was a major achievement and normally there would have been a media splash about it. But it largely went unnoticed because of the ban of the Election Commission.

Thus he entered the election fray of April–May 2004 virtually as a lame duck Chief Minister with both hands tied at the back. His support in 1999 to the BJP-led government at the Centre from outside had earlier drawn flak from Muslims. That tarnished his image of a secular leader. In 2004, Naidu openly aligned his party with the NDA led by BJP. That added to the alienation of Muslim voters.

The suicides of the farmers in the state were blamed on his anti-farmer, anti-poor policy.

❖ ❖ ❖

The Congress Party was led by Dr Y.S. Rajasekhara Reddy. Popularly known as 'YSR', he was born in 1949 in Pulivendula, a small town in Kadapa district of the Rayalseema region of Andhra Pradesh. His father, Y.S. Rajareddy, was the sarpanch of the village Panchayat and was known for his daredevilry as a mass leader. He was murdered in 1998 by a rival political faction.

Rajasekhara Reddy graduated in medicine from Gulbarga in Karnataka. He began his political career as secretary of the District Youth Congress in 1975. He was first elected to the State Assembly in 1978. Never losing an election, YSR was elected four times to the Lok Sabha and for an equal number to the State Assembly. For some time, he and his arch political rival Chandrababu Naidu's political careers ran parallel when both served as ministers under T. Anjaiah during 1980–2. He was appointed twice as President of the State Congress Committee.[163]

Though a Christian, he enjoyed wide support across religious lines, particularly of the powerful Reddy community. For his audacious behaviour, he was popularly called the 'Kadapa Tiger'.

His family set up a polytechnic and a degree college besides a number of educational and training centres in and around Pulivendula. In 1973, YSR established a 70-bed hospital at Pulivendula in the name of his father.

In the height of summer in 2003, YSR undertook a grueling 68-day *pada yatra* (foot march, generally for a good purpose), covering 1,400 kilometers across the state.[164] During that dramatic marathon, he offered people a change and asked for a chance to provide it.

Suddenly the old demand for Telangana rose its head in 2001. The man behind it was 57-year-old Kalvakuntla Chandrasekhar Rao (KCR).

Born in Chintamadaka village in Medak district of Andhra Pradesh in 1954, KCR did an MA in Telugu literature.

He started his political career with the Congress in 1970. He joined TDP in 1983 and was elected to the State Assembly continuously from 1985 to 2004. He served as a minister of state in the TDP ministry during 1987–8 and as a Cabinet Minister during 1997–9. He served as deputy speaker of Andhra Pradesh Assembly during 1999–2001.

On 27 April 2001, KCR resigned from his post and quit. TDP alleged that the people of Telangana region were being suppressed by Seemandhra (a compact term employed for the combined coastal Andhra and Rayalseema regions) leaders. He declared that bifurcation of the state of Andhra Pradesh was the only solution for the Telangana people. He launched the Telangana Rashtra Samithi (TRS) with the one-point agenda of securing statehood for Telangana.

The TRS made a good show of its strength in the Panchayat and Zilla Parishad elections of 2001.

The Congress Working Committee acknowledged the merit in the demand for Telangana in its meeting on 30 October 2001. It favoured the creation of a state reorganization commission to examine the issue. That gave hope to KCR and he entered into an alliance with the Congress for the elections in 2004.

The Congress–TRS alliance proved very beneficial to both partners in the elections of 2004. Out of 42 seats in the Lok Sabha, Congress won 29 seats, and its ally, TRS, 5. Out of a total of 294 seats in the State Assembly, Congress won 185 seats and TRS 26. TDP won 47 seats, the Majlis 4, CPM 9, CPI 6, and BJP 2. Independent candidates won 11 seats.

Chandrababu Naidu' party, TDP, lost in all the three regions and across all social categories.

The Seething Cauldron

Out of consideration for the pre-poll alliance with TRS, the Congress offered TRS one Cabinet and one Minister of state berth at the Centre and six Cabinet seats in the state. KCR joined the Union Cabinet as labour minister.

YSR became Chief Minister of the state on 13 May 2004. Immediately after his swearing in at a massive public function in the Lal Bahadur Stadium, he signed the first file in public view providing free power to farmers and waiving arrears of loans taken by them.

Apart from that, he reintroduced the scheme of the supply of rice at Rs 2 per kg for the poor, he also initiated a number of other important welfare schemes. For example, the Rajiv Arogyasri was a health insurance scheme providing up to Rs 200,000 for all persons below the poverty line. The Pavala Vaddi scheme enabled the poor to take loans from financial institutions at rates as low as 3 per cent. Under the Indiramma Illu scheme, the government subsidized the construction of houses in rural areas. The Jala Yagnam scheme provided water to ten million acres of land, resulting in the conversion of wasteland into cultivable land.

✠ ✠ ✠

However, there was no progress on the Telangana issue. In protest, all the TRS ministers in the state resigned in 2005. That was followed by KCR's resignation in 2006. In the ensuing by-elections, KCR was re-elected to the Lok Sabha by a huge margin.

That too did not elicit any response from the Congress to KCR's demand for Telangana. Frustrated, all four MPs and 16 MLAs of TRS resigned their seats in March 2008. Meanwhile, reports of internal squabbling in TRS and allegations of whimsical and dictatorial behaviour against KCR also began to emerge. KCR expected that the resultant by-elections would be clubbed with the general elections due in April 2009, which would give him enough time to mobilize the required resources. However, the Election Commission ordered an immediate by-election. In a comparatively poor showing, TRS could win only two Lok Sabha and seven Assembly seats. The Telangana sentiment thus seemingly suffered a setback.

All the parties started preparing for the upcoming elections in 2009. K. Chiranjeevi (b. 1955), a megastar of Telugu films, founded the Praja Rajyam Party in August 2008. It was generally expected that he would replicate the NTR miracle of 1982. A flurry of political realignments ensued. Most political parties including TDP declared their support for the cause of Telangana. The state government itself declared in February 2009 that it had no objection in principle to the formation of a separate Telangana and constituted a joint committee of the two houses of the legislature to look into that issue.

For the elections of 2009, TDP formed the Mahakutami (Grand Alliance) against the Congress. It comprised the third front and the left-wing parties. Since it had declared its support for Telangana, KCR also joined the alliance. However, TRS could win only two seats in the Lok Sabha and ten seats in the State Assembly. Congress won 156 out of 294 seats in the Assembly and thus was able to form the government easily.

The Congress victory was a personal triumph for YSR.

❖ ❖ ❖

Four months later, YSR was killed in a helicopter crash on 2 September 2009.

The next day, Finance Minister K. Rosaiah was sworn in as Chief Minister.

Within hours of that, a clamour rose for the succession of his son Y.S. Jaganmohan Reddy as Chief Minister.

Born in 1972, Jagan was elected a Member of Parliament from Kadapa in 2009. He started a Telugu daily newspaper and a TV channel under the banner of *Sakshi*. He was also the chief promoter of Bharathi Cements.

The sympathy wave for Jagan was so strong that the State Cabinet passed a unanimous resolution for his appointment as Chief Minister. A representation to that effect was made to the President of the Congress Party and many loyalists of the aspirant held demonstrations in different parts of the state in favour of the demand.

❖ ❖ ❖

KCR made a dramatic move on 29 November 2009. He demanded that the UPA government at the Centre introduce a bill in the Parliament for the formation of Telangana. To press his demand, he proceeded on a fast unto death.

Student organizations, employee unions, and various other organizations joined the movement. A general strike shut down Telangana on 6 and 7 December 2009. In an all-party meeting called by the state government on the night of 7 December to discuss the situation arising out of KCR's fast, all the parties except CPI(M) extended their support to the demand for Telangana.

Alarmed by the medical bulletin on KCR's health, Union Home Minister P. Chidambaram announced late on the evening of 9 December 2009 that the government of India would initiate the process of forming a separate Telangana state. While people in Telangana hailed the statement, it led to violent reactions including resignations of legislators from the Seemandhra region.

Responding to the negative reaction from Seemandhra, the Union Government backtracked a fortnight later. Thereupon, the Seemandhra legislators withdrew their resignations while those from Telangana put in theirs.

Thereupon, the Central Government appointed a five-member committee headed by Justice B.N. Srikrishna on 3 February 2010 to examine the demand for Telangana comprehensively.

After touring the state and meeting a large number of people from the cross section of society, the committee submitted its report to the government on 30 December 2010. The report discussed six possible solutions to the problem. Its preferred option was to keep the state united by simultaneously providing specific statutory measures for the socio-economic development and political empowerment of the Telangana region, including the creation of a statutory Telangana Regional Council. Its second-best option was the bifurcation of the state into Telangana and Seemandhra as per existing boundaries, with Hyderabad as the capital of Telangana and a new capital for the latter. An interesting aspect of the report was a chapter numbered eight submitted by the committee separately in a sealed cover to the Union Government.

TRS launched a non-cooperation movement on 17 February 2011, which lasted 16 days. About 300,000 government employees participated in it. The session of the State Assembly was boycotted during February and March and the Parliament session was disrupted for several days by MPs from Telangana.

The Telangana Joint Action Committee organized a 'Million March' in Hyderabad on 10 March 2010. Despite the police move to foil the march, around 50,000 people managed to reach Tank Bund, the venue of the march. The activists damaged 16 out of 33 statues of famous personalities representing Telugu culture and language and threw some of the damaged pieces into the Husain Sagar Lake.

On 4 July 2011, as many as 81 of 119 Telangana MLAs, 12 out of 15 Telangana ministers in state, 13 out of 17 Telangana members of the Lok Sabha, 1 Congress member of the Rajya Sabha, and 20 members of the State Legislative Council resigned their seats protesting delay in the formation of Telangana.

TRS launched a general strike in the Telangana region on 13 September 2011. Sixty thousand coal miners of the Singareni Collieries Ltd joined the strike. Lawyers started boycotting courts. On 14–15 September, nearly 450 movie theaters in Telangana were closed on the call given by the Telangana Film Chamber. Government teachers joined the strike on 16 September. Private school managements declared a holiday in support of the strike. On 19 September, the employees of the State Road Transport Corporation and the State Power Generation Corporation in Telangana joined the indefinite strike.

A 'Rail Roko' agitation was carried out at various places in the city. Road blockades on national highways were set up throughout Telangana. The Auto Rickshaw Union also joined the strike on 24 September, adding to the disruption of transport services. Virtually all sections of people joined this strike. It resulted in an unprecedented power crisis in the state.

On 11 October 2011, the police registered criminal cases against KCR for delivering inflammatory speeches and disturbing the peace and harmony in different places.

After 42 days, the government employees' unions called off the strike on 24 October 2011.

❖ ❖ ❖

While the state was engulfed in the Telangana agitation, Jagan's sideshow was stepped up. Not getting any response even six months after YSR's death, Jagan embarked upon what he called a 'condolence yatra'. He went around the state offering condolences to the families of those who had allegedly either committed suicide or died of shock after hearing the news of YSR's death. Defying the direction of the Congress Party to call off his yatra, he resigned from the party on 29 November 2010. He and his mother also resigned from the Parliament and the Assembly respectively. On Mach 2011, he founded the YSR Congress Party (YSRC) under his presidency.

In the resultant by-elections, both won back their seats by huge margins.

Meanwhile, two leaders filed petitions in the High Court of Andhra Pradesh alleging that Jagan had illegally amassed wealth by tactics such as pressurizing companies to invest in his business ventures in return for various favours from his father's government. Some investors filed affidavits supporting the allegations. On the court's orders to conduct a thorough investigation into the allegations, the Central Bureau of Investigation (CBI) conducted countrywide raids and searches on Jagan's offices and residences.

On 27 May 2012, while he was busy campaigning for by-elections due in June 2012, Jagan was taken into custody by the CBI. However, such was the strength of the sentiment in his favour that his party, YSRC, won 15 out of 18 State Assembly seats and the sole Lok Sabha seat.

That led to many Congress and TDP leaders joining the YSRC.

Jagan remained in jail for 16 months and was released on bail on 28 September 2013 after the completion of the CBI's investigation.

✤ ✤ ✤

On 10 November 2010, the speaker of the Andhra Pradesh Assembly, Nallari Kiran Kumar Reddy, was elected the 16th Chief Minister of Andhra Pradesh, succeeding K. Rosaiah.

Kiran Kumar hails from a political family of Nagaripalle in Chittoor district. His father, N. Amaranth Reddy, served as a minister in Andhra Pradesh during 1978–82.

He was born in Hyderabad in 1960. A law graduate, he represented the South Zone in national and international cricket tournaments.

Kiran Kumar was elected to the State Assembly on his father's death in 1989. Except for 1994, he was re-elected thrice, till 2009. In that year, he was elected speaker of the State Assembly and thereafter he was appointed as Chief Minister.

Kiran Kumar's job was to ensure that the demand for Telangana was kept at bay.

✤ ✤ ✤

Meanwhile, the Telangana cauldron continued to seethe. The normal course of life was frequently disturbed, often violently. Hundreds of people, including a large number of students, committed suicide.

A long and exhausting agitation was followed by a lull after 24 October 2011.

All eyes were set on the next elections to be held in 2014.

Birth of Telangana

The official intelligence reports and other surveys indicated to the Congress Party that it had little support left in Seemandhra. It, therefore, tried to shore up its prospects in Telangana. Accordingly, it announced its acceptance of the demand for Telangana on 30 July 2013. It hoped to thereby earn KCR's gratitude and anticipated that he might merge his party with the Congress in the coming elections.

As the battle lines were drawn for the 2014 polls, TDP and YSRC withdrew their earlier decision in favour of the formation of the state of Telangana.

However, an open revolt erupted within the Congress Party by its members and legislators from Seemandhra who bitterly opposed the decision.

The bill for the creation of Telangana was introduced in the Lok Sabha on 13 February 2014.

The proceedings in both houses of the Parliament were marred by unprecedented hooliganism by members of the ruling party from Seemandhra. Somehow, with the support of the BJP, the bill was passed by Lok Sabha on 18 February 2014. Thereupon, Kiran Kumar Reddy resigned from Chief Ministership. The Rajya Sabha passed the bill two days later. Andhra Pradesh was placed under the President's Rule on 1 March 2014.

Far from merging with the Congress, TRS did not even enter into an alliance with it. It decided to contest the elections on its own.

The results of the elections were declared on 16 May 2014. TRS won 63 of 119 seats in the State Assembly and 11 out of 17 seats in the Lok Sabha

In the Seemandhra region, TDP won 102 seats out of 177. The Congress Party was wiped out in Seemandhra and won only 23 seats in Telangana.

Andhra Pradesh was formed on 1 November 1956 by merging the state of Hyderabad into Andhra. After 57 years, on 2 June 2014, it reversed the merger and divided Andhra Pradesh into two states—creating the new state of Telangana.

❖ ❖ ❖

K. Chandrasekhar Rao took over as the first Chief Minister of Telangana on 2 June 2014. He declared that his aim was to transform the new state into `Bangaru (golden) Telangana'.

The occasion was celebrated by illumination and fireworks all over the state in the evening. As if by magic, the daily power cuts disappeared after that.

Alongside, he also declared that 20,000 MW of power generation would be added within the next five years through conventional and renewable sources.

On the other issue of water supply, he assured an increase of 172 MGD shortly with the completion of the Godavari Project.

A snap one-day socio-economic survey was conducted all over the state on 19 August 2014. Its aim was to have reliable data on the basis of which welfare programmes could be properly targeted.

This was followed by the publication of two books. The first *Reinventing Telangana—The First Steps*, 2015, dealt with the socio-economic outlook for 2015. The second, *Human Development in Telangana State—District Profiles*, 2016, was the first of its kind and was intended to help in the specific development of each district of the state.

Some of the other important measures taken up in different fields are mentioned below.

In addition to an increase in their salaries, government employees were also provided cashless medical treatment at designated hospitals.

An ambitious scheme for providing cheap two-bedroom houses at a unit cost of Rs 350,000 was launched.

Three universities, namely Kaloji Narayana Rao University of Health Sciences in Warangal, Sri Konda Laxman Telangana State Horticultural University in Hyderabad, and P.V. Narsimha Rao Telangana Veterinary University, Karimnagar, were established. Loans taken by farmers and power-loom weavers of upto Rs 100,000 were waived. In addition, a market intervention fund of Rs 4 billion was set up to ensure remunerative prices to farmers for their produce.

The quantum of subsidized rice supply at Re 1 per kg was enhanced from 4 kgs to 6 kgs per head per month without any limit on the size of the family. The eligibility limit for the beneficiary families was enhanced from an annual income of Rs 60,000 to Rs 150,000 in rural areas and from Rs 75,000 to Rs 200,000 in urban areas.

A monthly pension of Rs 1,000 was announced for the poor such as weavers, toddy tappers, *beedi* workers, AIDS patients, widows, and old-aged persons. Similarly, a monthly pension of Rs 1,500 was sanctioned for aged artists and persons with disabilities.

Financial assistance of Rs 51,000 for girls belonging to Scheduled Castes, Scheduled Tribes, and minorities families at the time of their marriage was announced.

The Arogya Lakshmi programme provided one full nutritious meal daily to lactating mothers through Anganwadi centres.

To rid Hyderabad city of traffic congestion, construction of skyways, major corridors, roads, and flyovers, with an estimated cost of Rs 216.84 billion, was planned.

An integrated Inter-City Bus Terminal is being set up at Miyapur. In addition, two logistics parks are being set up outside the city on the Vijayawada and Nagarjunasagar roads for freight operators, cargo handling, trucks, and warehouses.

To improve the infrastructure facilities in Hyderabad, a 158 km-long, eight-lane Outer Ring Road has been taken up at a cost of Rs 66.96 billion.

In addition, 33 radial roads have been identified for improved connectivity between Inner Ring Road and Outer Ring Road. Out of these, more than half have been completed.

To provide better policing, 4,433 new vehicles equipped with modern technology were provided to the Hyderabad and Cyberabad Police. In addition, 1,500 motor cycles were provided to the Cyberabad Police.

Further, 550 vehicles have been provided to all districts of the state. These will ensure police response to calls for help within 10 minutes. A hundred thousand CCTV cameras are under installation in various points in the city to monitor traffic and other offences.

Modernization of police stations was undertaken in the city, district headquarters, and villages through a monthly grant of Rs 75,000, Rs 50,000 and Rs 25,000 respectively.

It was proposed that Hyderabad would be made a slum-free city by providing better housing to slum dwellers.

❖ ❖ ❖

Since its coming into power in June 2014, the TRS party won all the by-elections to the Lok Sabha State Assembly. A number of leaders from other parties have joined the ruling party.

In the elections for the Greater Hyderabad Municipal Corporation held in February 2016, TRS won 99 out of 150 seats. That was the best performance by any party in the history of the Corporation.

On the day of the Dasara festival on 10 October 2016, the number of districts in the state was increased from 10 to 31.

KCR claimed that the move would help in the effective implementation and monitoring of public welfare schemes.

❖ ❖ ❖

The first election of the Telangana State Assembly was due in May 2019. That meant it would become part of the general elections to the Lok Sabha. Presumably, in order to avoid having to fight on two fronts simultaneously, KCR decided to advance the state election by six months. On his advice, the Governor dissolved the

Assembly on 6 September 2018. The state elections were held on 7 December 2018.

KCR's gamble paid off and he won 88 out of 117 Assembly seats, improving his tally from 63 in 2014.

It turned out later that this was part of his bigger strategy. After assuming charge as Chief Minister of Telangana for the second time on 13 December 2018, KCR announced the appointment of his son, K.T. Rama Rao, as the working President of TRS. That, he said, would enable him to devote more time at the national level in order 'to bring about a qualitative change in national politics'.[164] It made two things clear: his ambition for a national role and his son's succession as Chief Minister of Telangana.

The Parliamentary elections were held in April/May of 2019. Most of the opposition parties made a joint front against the ruling BJP. However, KCR launched what he called the 'Federal Front' and invited other opposition parties to join it. He declared that he would rid the country of both, the BJP and the Congress. He advocated more powers for states. However, his party won only nine out of 17 seats in the Lok Sabha. This upset his grand plans.

His mood was lifted soon when the results of the election to local bodies were announced on 27 May 2019. The TRS had made a clean sweep by winning 449 out of 538 seats in the Zila Parishad Territorial Constituencies, and 3,548 out of 5,817 seats in the Mandal Parishad Territorial Constituencies.

All this shows that while KCR remains the undisputed master in the state, his national ambition will have to wait.

In the neighbouring state of Andhra Pradesh, the ruling TDP of N. Chandrababu Naidu was routed. It secured only 23 seats in the Assembly, losing 151 to the YSRC of Jaganmohan Reddy. In the Lok Sabha it won only 3 seats against 23 won by the YSRC.

After ten years of unremitting toil, of which 16 months were spent in jail, Jaganmohan Reddy became the Chief Minister of Andhra Pradesh on 30 May 2019.

Epilogue

For some decades after 1956, Hyderabad grew faster than most other cities of India. The large-scale immigration from parts of the old Andhra state changed its old character drastically. The former inhabitants of Hyderabad, who prided themselves on their gracious manners and courteous behaviour, who enjoyed their leisurely, laid-back style of life were exposed to sudden competition. A confused generation, nursing a sense of hurt, could not cope with the new situation in which they had lost their primacy.

For a decade after the Police Action, there was fear amongst the old ruling group. Then the Majlis-Ittehad-ul-Musalmeen was revived. It started protesting against what it perceived as discrimination against the Muslim minority, and the consequent lack of opportunities open to them. Then it contested elections for the Municipal Corporation of Hyderabad and on making a good showing, it went to the State Legislature and then to the Parliament. Given the concentration of the community there, the old city virtually became its pocket borough.

Some Muslims migrated to Pakistan fearing reprisals or discrimination in Hyderabad or hoping for better openings there.

The oil boom in West Asia opened new opportunities. Beyond West Asia there were other lands—England; America, the great melting pot, and Canada with its vast virgin lands. Australia relaxed its old, all-white immigration policy. The exodus, which had earlier headed for Pakistan, spread further and became a diaspora. Low-tech people, skilled and even semi- and un-skilled persons made it to the Gulf, where all sorts of jobs like lift-operators, carpenters and cleaners for men, and maids for women were available with the rich sheikhs. There was a sprinkling of doctors, engineers, and architects too but most of such people preferred to go further west where opportunities, compensation, and scope for the education of their children was better. In West Asia, there is only money, in Western Europe and America there is 'freedom' too, and there are opportunities for growth which freedom affords. Those Hyderabadis who went for higher education stayed on; they secured work-permits in England, green cards in United States of America, and their equivalent in other countries. Once they settled down comfortably they called their brothers and sisters and multiplied their clan. To cope with the out-bound traffic, the Government of India had to open a passport office in Hyderabad.

The Arab sheikhs come to Hyderabad to shop for young brides. There is no dearth of poor girls with no prospects of marriage because their parents have no money to give for *ghora* and *jora*—dowry. The Arab men started coming and picking up girls young enough to be their granddaughters. That brought temporary prosperity to some impoverished families. But in many cases, it brought grief and misery when some of the new brides, having spent a few nights with their husbands, stayed on waiting for a call from their new grooms—calls which never came. Some who went with them returned soon as poor as they had been earlier—even poorer—because they had been robbed of their 'virtue' and loaded with children.

Expatriates from Hyderabad constitute the largest number after Kerala. The new lands claimed them. They don't want to come back and even if they do, their children—a whole new generation born and brought up there—don't. The old parents are left alone back home. Some have died waiting, hoping. Others are approaching their end.

That is what happened to Syed Hashim Ali, former Vice Chancellor successively of Osmania and Aligarh Muslim Universities. His three children are settled in the United States of

America. Whenever he visited them, he became, in his own words, an old fogey in one house, a telephone operator in the second, and a piece of furniture in the third. He always came back as soon as he could. One evening his wife suddenly died of cardiac arrest while they were watching television after dinner at their home in Hyderabad. The children flew down to him and within a fortnight disposed of all his belongings and took him away from his roots. For ten years he longed to return to Hyderabad, and then passed away in Chicago.

The case of Professor Akbar, whose sons are also in the USA, is typical of thousands of parents in Hyderabad. He is over 80. His diminutive stature is accentuated by his lean figure. On a couple of occasions he had to take help from Narottam, a senior IAS officer. Once, when some local toughs had encroached upon Prof. Akbar's land, Narottam spoke to the Commissioner of Police and got the problem sorted out.

Narottam said it was no bother when Akbar thanked him, but then asked him: 'Why did you send them abroad? Surely it was your decision?' There was the hint of an accusation about the professor's decision to send his sons to the USA.

'Yes. It was,' the old man admitted. 'Actually I had wanted to send only two boys. I thought the third would stay here with us. But he went on a visit and saw his two brothers making so much money. So he too went away.' Akbar's neat planning had not worked.

As Narottam went out to see him off, Akbar asked him sheepishly if he could reverse his car for him. 'At this age, you know, it is a little difficult.'

'No problem,' Narottam said, as he put the car in position for the small, dainty man to drive out.

Then Akbar started dropping in off and on and repeating his same old stories. Narottam reversed the car for him as a matter of course. If ever Akbar rang up to ask if he could come, Narottam made some excuse to avoid him. So he started coming without calling. Narottam did not have the heart to tell him that he was a bore because he knew that he was really senile and that because Akbar's children had practically deserted him and his wife with a retarded girl.

That is the paradox of the prosperity and poverty of Hyderabad, like of many cities of India.

People going to the Gulf are almost all Muslims. Saudi Arabia alone has close to a million persons from Hyderabad. People have worked there for decades but have not been able to get citizenship. A large number keep their wives and children in Hyderabad and visit them once or twice in a year. Some cannot even afford that. They send remittances for the upkeep of the family. The Government of India opened a large number of schools in the Gulf which are integrated with the Indian school system. But the host countries do not allow extending similar facilities for the university education. So the expatriates have to either send their children to the western countries, which is expensive, or back to India. That entails setting up a separate establishment. Often the wife has to come back to stay with the children. Separation from their spouses and children creates problems of loneliness at both ends—and family tensions.

The Hyderabadi diaspora transmits home a mixed set of new influences and old values simultaneously. While the immigrants in the USA and Europe bring liberal influences, those in the Gulf generally tend to reinforce religious orthodoxy. Today in Hyderabad there are more women in burqas and hijabs and more men in skullcaps than ever before.

The parents of Gulf NRI's indulge in conspicuous consumption. They spend extravagantly on ceremonies and weddings. That is their way of showing to the world that their progeny is doing well abroad. The NRIs themselves are a worried lot. Those who are merely subsisting abroad face the bleak prospect of returning home without even a house of their own.

Business Process Outsourcing has changed the life-styles of many persons in Hyderabad. They make money but have to work at night. Women particularly are not at ease with that situation, but for many there is no option.

Many NRIs have made investments in real estate and business. Shops and malls are springing up all over. Various loan schemes for cars, houses, white goods, and other miscellaneous items have landed many young persons into debt traps. The number of vehicles on the roads is increasing just as is the number of road accidents. Crime is on the increase. The civic infrastructure has not kept pace with the growth in population and housing complexes. A city once known for its greenery and garden houses has now turned into a concrete jungle. Names of localities like Bagh Lingampalli, Bashir Bagh, and Kundan Bagh seem misnomers. Beautification of the city is a misnomer for erratic and haphazard schemes.

Of course, the situation in Hyderabad is no different from that in other cities of India. But the demographic composition of the city adds a new dimension to the plethora of problems. Today ironically, the Muslim minority talks in an idiom once used by the Hindu majority before the merger of Hyderabad with India. They talk of the lack of opportunities, of discrimination, and of open prejudice against them.

Despite all that, Hyderabad continues to attract people from all over India for a variety of reasons. Its climate, its cosmopolitanism, its growth—particularly in the IT, Biotechnology, and Pharma sectors—serve as a magnetic pull for new immigrants. While it enhances its cosmopolitan character, it also adds to the pressure on its precarious civic amenities.

More than 2,000 years ago, Heraclitus the Greek philosopher said, 'You can not bathe in the same river twice—no, not even once'. Because a river is water and water keeps flowing. It is not the same water when you entered as when you come out of the river.

One feels the same about Hyderabad. People who have lived here for 50, 40, 30, 20, or even 10 years feel they are not living in the same city. It is changing, changing fast, too fast and that is taking away some of its old charm. According to the Aristotelian dictum quoted earlier, a city's raison d'être is to make life better. It seems to many that this justification holds no more.

The city was conceived by its founder as a 'replica of heaven on earth'.

Today one wonders whether it is the same city. It was Bhagnagar of Mohammad Quli and Bhagmati—and yet where is Bhagnagar, 'O Bird of time!'

Chief Minister of Hyderabad

		Period in Office
1.	B. Ramakrishna Rao	6–3–1952—1–11–1956

Chief Ministers of Andhra Pradesh

1.	Neelam Sanjeeva Reddy	1–11–1956—11–11–1960
2.	Damodaram Sanjivayya	11–1–1960—12–3–1962
3.	Neelam Sanjeeva Reddy	12–3–1962—29–2–1964
4.	Kasu Brahmananda Reddy	29–2–1964—30–9–1971
5.	P.V. Narasimah Rao	30–9–1971—18–1–1973
	President's Rule	18–1–1973—10–12–1973
6.	Jalagam Vengala Rao	10–12–1973—6–3–1978
7.	Dr Marri Channa Reddy	6–3–1978—11–10–1980
8.	Tanguturi Anjaiah	11–10–1980—24–2–1982
9.	Bhavanam Venkatram	24–2–1982—20–9–1982
10	K. Vijayabhaskara Reddy	20–9–1982—9–1–1983
11.	N.T. Rama Rao	9–1–1983—16–8–1984
12.	Nadendla Bhaskara Rao	16–8–1984—16–9–1984
13.	N.T. Rama Rao	16–9–1984—9–3–1985
14.	Dr Marri Channa Reddy	3–12–1989—17–12–1990
15.	N. Janardhana Reddy	17–12–1990—9–10–1992
16.	K. Vijayabhaskara Reddy	9–10–1992—12–12–1994
17.	N.T. Rama Rao	12–12–1994—1–9–1995
18.	N. Chandrababu Naidu	1–9–1995—13–5–2004
19.	Dr Y.S. Rajasekhara Reddy	13–5–2004—2–9–2009
20.	K. Rosaiah	3–9–2009—24–11–2010
21.	N. Kiran Kumar Reddy	25–11–2010—24–2–2014

President's Rule	24–2–2014—2–6–2014
22. N. Chandrababu Naidu	8–6–2014—23–5–2019
23. Y.S. Jaganmohan Reddy	30–5–2019—present

Chief Minister of Telangana

| 1. K. Chandrasekhar Rao | 2–6–2014—present |

Notes

1. Mullah Vajahi, *Qutb-o-Mushtari* (ed.), Maulvi Abdul Haq, New Delhi: Anjuman-e-Taaraqqi-e-Urdu. 1939, p. 22.
2. A fruit with white seeds.
3. All the similes and metaphors have been taken from Mohammad Quli's poems. His *kulliyat*—complete works—were first edited with an introduction by Syed Mohiyuddin Qadri Zore and published by Maktaba-e-Ibrahimia Machine Press in Hyderabad in 1940. See also Syeda Jaffar, 'Introduction', in *Kulliyat–e–Mohammad Quli Qutb Shah*, New Delhi: Taraqqi–Urdu Board, 1985.
4. Mohammed Qasim, Ferishta, *History of the Rise of Mohammedan Power in India*, vol. II, trans. John Briggs, London: Longman, Rees, Orme, Brown & Green, 1829, p. 173.
5. 'Mir Jumla', 'Peshwa', and later 'Diwan' all mean 'Prime Minister' and are used interchangeably in this book according to the demands of the occasion.
6. According to some, the Sultan's decree that the city should be 'a replica of heaven' was taken literally by Mir Momin and he tried to recreate an architectural metaphor for the Islamic heaven. See in this connection Jan Pieper, 'A Quranic Paradise in Architectural Metaphor in the Environmental Design', *The Journal of the Islamic Design Research Centre*, Special Issue, January 1983, pp. 46–51.
7. These were the experts from Iran who assisted Mir Momin in the project. See Fiazuddin, 'Daur-e-Qutb Shahi ki Tashkeel-e-Shehar', in S.M.Q. Zore (ed.), *Nazar-e-Mohammad Quli Qutb Shah*, Hyderabad: Idara-e-Adabiyat-e-Urdu, 1958, pp. 27–32.

8. In a monogram, *Mohammad Quli Qutb Shah —Founder of Hyderabad,* (Bombay: Asia Publishing House, 1967), the late Professor Haroon Khan Sherwani dismissed the story of Bhagmati as mere fiction. Many scholars contested that. See, for example, Masud Husain, *Mohammad Quli Qutab Shah,* Delhi: Sahitya Akademi, 1989, pp. 19–26. For a full demolition of Sherwani's thesis, see my article: 'On the Historicity of Bhagmati', in the bi-annual *Research Journal of the Salar Jung Museum* (vol. xxix–xxx, 1992–3).

9. Hakim Nizam-ud-Din Geelani, *Hadiqa-tus-Salateen,* trans. Khwaja Mohd. into Urdu, Sarvar, Hyderabad: Idara-e-Adabiyat-e-Urdu, 1968, p. 27.

10. Geelani, *Hadiqa-tus-Salateen,* p. 30.

11. Geelani, *Hadiqa-tus-Salateen,* pp. 33–5.

12. Abdul Majeed Siddiqu, *History of Golconda,* Hyderabad: n.p., 1956, p. 135.

13. Server-ul-Mulk, *My Life,* trans. Nawab Jeevan Yar Jung, London: Arthur H. Stockwell, n.d., p. 95. Also, Haroon Khan Sherwani in n. 267 in *The History of Medieval Deccan 1295–1724,* vol. 1, Hyderabad: Government of Andhra Pradesh, 1973, p. 483.

14. Geelani, *Hadiqa-tus-Salateen,* pp. 80–2.

15. Mohd. Qasim Ferishta, *History of the Rise of the Mohammedan Power in India: Till the Year AD 1612,* vol. iii, 1829, p. 335.

16. W.M. Moreland, *Relations of Golconda in the Early Seventeenth Century AD 1608–1622,* London: Hakluyt Society, 1931, p. 23.

17. Jean-Baptiste Tavernier, *Travels in India,* trans. V. Ball, 2nd edn. London: Macmillan & Co., 1889 [1676]; Delhi: Atlantic Publishers and Distributors, 1989.

18. Mons. de Thevenot, *The Travels into the Levant,* vol. iii, trans. A. Lovell, London: H. Paul, 1687, pp. 94–8.

19. Abbe Carre, *The Travels of Abbe Carre in India in the New East 1672–74,* vol. i & ii, Delhi: Asian Educational Services, p. 329.

20. Niccolao Manucci, *Storia Do Mogor,* trans. William Irvine, London: John Murray, 1913 [1705], p. 192.

21. Manucci, *Storia Do Mogor,* p. 195.

22. William Foster, *Early Travels in India, 1583–1619,* Delhi: S. Chand & Co., 1968, p. 131.

23. For a detailed account of the mourning during Muharram and celebrations on the Prophet's birthday by a contemporary chronicler, see Geelani, *Hadiqa-tus-Salateen,* pp. 51–4.

24. *Adab-I Alamgiri,* Salar Jung Museum Persian Manuscripts, ff. 2b to 68b.

25. H.D. Love, *Vestige of Old Madras*, London: John Murray, 1913, quoted in Sherwani, *History of Medieval Deccan 1295–1724*, vol. I, Hyderabad: Government of Andhra Pradesh, 1973.

26. Mohd. Sleman Siddiqui, 'Two Neglected Chishti Saints of Golconda', in M.L. Nigam (ed.), *Glimpses of Qutab Shahi Culture*, Hyderabad: Golconda Society, 1986, pp. 8–20.

27. K.V. Bhupala Rao, *The Illustrious Prime Minister Madanna*, Hyderabad: Savitri Sadanmu, 1984, pp. 53–4.

28. Rao, *The Illustrious Prime Minister Madanna*, pp. 70–4.

29. Rao, *The Illustrious Prime Minister Madanna*, p. 124.

30. Rao, *The Illustrious Prime Minister Madanna*, p. 84.

31. Jagannadha Rao (ed.), *Ramdasu Kirtanulu*, Hyderabad: Andhra Pradesh. Sangeet Natak Academy, 1975. Also see B. Rajnikanta Rao, *Andhra Vagyakara Charitrumu*, Vijayawada: Visalandhra Pracharuna, 1958.

32. Chinna Nookala Satyanarayan, 'Bhadrachalam Ramdas', M.Litt. thesis, Madras University, 1960.

33. Rao, *The Illustrious Prime Minister Madanna*, pp. 43–4, Sherwani note on p. 485.

34. Rao, *The Illustrious Prime Minister Madanna*, p. 306.

35. Rao, *The Illustrious Prime Minister Madanna*, 1984, p. 207.

36. Rao, *The Illustrious Prime Minister Madanna*, p. 213.

37. Hashim Khan and Khafi Khan Nizam-ul-Mulki, *Muntakhib-ul-Lubab*, vol. II, Calcutta: Asiatic Society of Bengal, 1874, pp. 322–72. An abridged verion of that in English is available in Elliot and Dowson, *The History of India as Told by its Own Historians*, London: Trubner & Co., 1867. A very brief account is given in Mohd. Saqi Mustaid Khan, *Ma'asir-e-Alamgiri*, trans. Moulvi Mohd. and Fida Ali Talib, Karachi: Nafis Academy, 1962, pp. 297–300.

38. Khafi Khan Nizam-ul-Mulki, *Muntakhib-ul-Lubab*, 1874, p. 322.

39. Nizam-ul-Mulki, *Muntakhib-ul-Lubab*, p. 353.

40. Nizam-ul-Mulki, *Muntakhib-ul-Lubab*, p. 354. For an eye-witness satirical account of the siege, see N.H. Ansari, *Chronicles of the Siege of Golconda Fort*, Delhi: Idarah-i-Adabiyat-i-Delhi, 1975.

41. Ansari, *Chronicles of the Siege of Golconda Fort*, p. 359.

42. Yusuf Husain, *The First Nizam—The Life and Times of Nizam-ul- Mulk Asaf Jah I*, Bombay: Asia Publishing House, 1963, p.132.

43. Mohd. Abdul Hai, *Mamlakat-e-Asafiya*, vol. I, Karachi: Idara-e-Mohibban-e-Deccan, 1978, pp. 103–4.

44. Hai, *Mamlakat-e-Asafiya*, vol. I, pp. 105–6.

45. *Maasir-i-Nizami;* Nizam-ul- Mulk's testament quoted by Husain, *The First Nizam,* p. 199.

46. Mansa Ram, *Maasir-e-Nizami,* Persian manuscript, quoted in P. Setu Madhaa Rao, *Eighteenth Century Deccan,* Bombay: Popular Prakashan, 1963, p. 106.

47. Gordon Mackenzie, *A Manual of the Kistna District,* Government of Madras, 1883, Government of Andhra Pradesh, 1992, pp. 93–4.

48. John William Kaye, *Life and Correspondence of Major-General John Malcolm,* London: Smith Elder & Co., 1856, pp. 100–1.

49. H.C. Briggs, *The Nizam—History and Relations with the British Government,* London: Bernard Quatrich, 1861, p. 100.

50. For an account of his marriage, see, Edward Stachey, 'The Romantic Marriage of Major James Achilles Kirkpatrick', *Blackwoods Magazine,* July 1893. Also see William Dalrymple, *White Mughals,* London: Viking, 2002.

51. Philip Meadows Taylor, *The Story of My Life,* London: Oxford University Press, 1920, p. 274.

52. J.D. Gribble, *History of the Deccan,* vol. ii, London: Lizac & Co., 1924, New Delhi: Rupa & Co., 2002, pp. 209–10.

53. Gribble, *History of the Deccan,* vol. ii, p. 220.

54. P.M. Taylor, *Confessions of a Thug,* London: Richard Bentley, 1839, Delhi: Asian Educational Services, 1988.

55. Taylor, *Confessions of a Thug,* p. 149.

56. Karen Isaksen Leonard, *Social History of an Indian Caste—The Kayasths of Hyderabad,* Hyderabad: Orient Longman, 1994, p. 23. The year of the construction of the temple—1802—differs from that given by Rao in *Bostan-e-Asafiya*—1812. The archives of the Andhra Pradesh Government contain two documents relating to this temple. One is from Daftar-e-Istifa dated 6th Rabi-ul-Awwal, 1231 Hijri corresponding to AD 1816. This sanctions a daily grant of Rs 2 to the persons who looked after the temple. The other, issued on 28th Safar, 1239 Hijri corresponding to AD 1822 is in favour of Raja Bhavani Pershad and is for the amount of eight anas, and four pies (a little more than Rs 2,093.50 in today's currency) to meet the expenditure for maintenance of the temple.

57. Mir Karamat Ali Khan, 'Asaf Jahi Daur ki Shahi Mamaen', unpublished paper, 1990. Also Tamkeen Kazmi, 'Hyderabad ki Mamaen', in Abid Ali Khan (ed.), *Dakkan Des,* Hyderabad: Siasat Publications, 1980, pp. 46–50

58. Henry George Briggs, *The Nizams—His History of Relations with the British Government,* London: Bernark Quartich, 1861.

59. Hyderabad State Committee, *The Freedom Stuggle in Hyderabad*, vol. II (1857–1885), Hyderabad, 1956, pp. 8–9.
60. Ibid. p.15 quoting Hyderabad Residency Records, vol. 93
61. *The Englishman*, 27 June 1857.
62. Harriet Ronken Lynton, *My Dear Nawab Saheb*, Hyderabad: Orient Longman, 1991, pp. 92–6 and passim.
63. Lytton's letter to Salsibury of 24 September 1877 quoted in V.K. Bawa, *The Nizam Between Mughals and British—Hyderabad under Salar Jung I*, New Delhi: S. Chand & Company Ltd. 1986, p. 199.
64. Nawab Server-ul-Mulk Bahadur, *My Life*, trans. Nawab Jiwan Yar Jung Bahadur, London: Arthur H. Stockwell, n.d., pp. 89–104 and passim.
65. Server-ul-Mulk, *My Life*, pp. 187–8.
66. Server-ul-Mulk, *My Life*, p. 141.
67. Server-ul-Mulk, *My Life*, pp. 121, 146, 155.
68. Moulvie Syed Mehdi Ali (ed.), *Hyderabad Affairs 1879*, vol. III, pp. 469–78.
69. Server-ul-Mulk, *My Life*, p. 228.
70. Habeeb Zia, 'Maharaja Sir Kishen Pershad Shad—Hayat aur Adabi Karname', Ph.D thesis, Osmania University, 1978.
71. M. Visvesvarayya, The Flood of 1908 at Hyderabad—An Account of the Flood, Its Causes and Proposed Preventive Measures, Hyderabad, 1 October 1909.
72. Sayyad Ahmed Husain Amjad, *Jamal-e-Amjad*, Hyderabad: National Fine Printing Press, 1384H/1964, pp. 92–103. A less personal account of the devastation caused by the flood can be seen in Mirza Farhatullah Beg Dehlvi, *Meri Dastan*, Hyderabad: privately printed, n.d., pp. 49–61.
73. Hyderabad State Congress Committee, *The Freedom Stuggle in Hyderabad*, vol. III (1885–1920), Hyderabad, 1957, p.18.
74. Hyderabad State Congress Committee, *The Freedom Stuggle in Hyderabad*, vol. III, pp. 27–9.
75. Hyderabad State Congress Committee, *The Freedom Stuggle in Hyderabad*, vol. III, pp. 170–6.
76. Late Abid Ali Khan, Editor of the *Siasat* Urdu Daily in an interview to the author.
77. Late Abid Ali Khan interview, pp. 62–73.
78. Late Abid Ali Khan interview, p. 176.
79. Late Abid Ali Khan interview, pp. 151–6.
80. R.J. Rajendra Pasad, 'Chloroform Controversy—a Century Ago', *The Hindu*, 1 May 1988. Also a note by D.A. Ramachari on 12 October 1993.

81. R.L. Megroz, *Ronald Ross, Discoverer and Creator,* London: George Allen & Unwin, 1931, p. 74.

82. E.F. Dodd, *Sir Ronald Ross and His Fight Against Malaria,* London: Macmillan, 1956, pp. 7–71.

83. See the table of the geneology of the dynasty in Meherunisa Husain, *The Unhappy Prince-Nashad Asafi,* New Delhi: Vikas, 1997.

84. Sidq Jaisi, *Darbaar-e-Dürbaar,* Hyderabad: Hussami Book Depot, 1961. Translated from Urdu by Narendra Luther under the title *The Nocturnal Court: The Life of a Prince of Hyderabad,* New Delhi: Oxford University Press, 2004, pp. 69–75, 94.

85. Visveswarayya, The Flood of 1908 at Hyderabad.

86. M. Visveswarayya, *City Improvements Schemes,* Hyderabad: Deccan, Bombay, 3 February 1930.

87. Sibte Hasan, *Shehar-e-Nigaran,* Karachi: Maktab-e-Danyal, 1984, pp. 57–8.

88. Sidq Jaisi, *Shehar-e-Nigaran,* 1961, pp. 124–9.

89. Ali Jaleeli (the poet's son) in an interview to the author in Hyderabad in 1990.

90. The ghazals of the Nizam were translated by the scholar–administrator, Sir Nizamat Jung. Some of them were reproduced by D.F. Karaka in his book, *Fabulous Mogul, Nizam VII of Hyderabad,* London: Derek Verschoyle, 1955.

91. Sibte Hasan, *Shehar-e-Nigaran,* Karachi, 1984, pp. 93–5.

92. The author has translated this book and provided the introduction and notes to the text. See Narendra Luther, *The Nocturnal Court.*

93. Excerpt quoted in Hyderabad State Congress Committee, *The Freedom Struggle in Hyderabad,* vol. IV (1921–47), Hyderabad, 1966, pp. 3–4.

94. Miza Zafarul Hasan, *Zik-e-Yar Chale,* Hyderabad: Hussami Book Depot, 1979, pp. 266–2.

95. Hyderabad State Congress Committee, *The Freedom Struggle in Hyderabad,* vol. III, p. 240.

96. Hasan, *Shehar-e-Nigaran,* pp. 91–2.

97. Sheikh Mohd. Abdullah, *Atish-e-Chinar—An Autobiography,* Srinagar: Ali Mohd. & Sons, 1988, p. 256.

98. Nazeer-ud-Din Ahmed, *Swaneh Bahadur Yar Jung,* Hyderabad: Bahadur Yar Jung Academy, 1968, p. 221.

99. For details of these developments, see Hyderabad State Congress Committee *The Freedom Struggle in Hyderabad,* vol. IV.

100. Hyderabad State Congress Committee *The Freedom Struggle in Hyderabad,* vol. IV, p. 143.

101. Hyderabad State Congress Committee *The Freedom Struggle in Hyderabad,* vol. IV, p 151.

102. Hyderabad State Congress Committee *The Freedom Struggle in Hyderabad*, vol. IV, p. 107.

103. Hyderabad State Congress Committee *The Freedom Struggle in Hyderabad*, vol. IV, p. 112, quoting the *Daily News* of 18 Januay 1939.

104. Hyderabad State Congress Committee *The Freedom Struggle in Hyderabad*, vol. IV, p. 186.

105. Hyderabad State Congress Committee *The Freedom Struggle in Hyderabad*, vol. IV, p. 189.

106. Ahmed Sayeed Khan of Chhattari, *Yad-e-Ayyam*, vol. III, Aligarh: privately printed, n.d., p. 69.

107. Khan, *Yad-e-Ayyam*, vol. III, p. 69.

108. Khan, *Yad-e-Ayyam*, vol. III, pp. 71–2.

109. Khan, *Yad-e-Ayyam*, vol. III, p. 79.

110. Hasan, *Shehar-e-Nigaran*, 1984, p. 97.

111. Based on an interview with the late Abid Ali Khan. A signed copy of the note is available with the author.

112. V.K. Bawa, *The Last Nizam—The Life and Times of Mir Osman Ali Khan*, New Delhi: Viking, 1991, pp. 105–7.

113. Mirza Ismail, *My Public Life—Recollections and Reflections*, London: George Allen & Unwin, 1954, pp. 105–8.

114. Ismail, *My Public Life*, p. 107.

115. Philip Mason, *A Shaft of Sunlight: Memories of a Varied Life*, Delhi: Vikas, 1978, pp. 200–1.

116. See Syed Abdul Latif, *Bases of Islamic Culture*, Hyderabad: Institute of Indo-Middle East Cultural Studies, 1959.

117. A copy of the speech was made available to the author by the late Rasheedudin, son of Nawab Akbar Yar Jung with his letter dated 20 July 1992.

118. A copy of this letter kindly made available by his daughter, Fatima Alam Ali, is with the author.

119. Author's interview with Mehdi Ali on 02 July 1992.

120. Fareed Mirza, *Pre- and Post-Police Action Days in the erstwhile Hyderabad State—What I saw, felt and did*, Hyderabad: privately printed, 1976. Also interview with him on 01 July 1992.

121. Razvi's speech on 17 April 1948, in K.M. Munshi, *The End of An Era*, 3rd edn., Bombay: Bharatiya Vidya Bhavan, [1957] 1998, p. 141.

122. Wilfred Cantwell Smith, 'Hyderabad: Muslim Tragedy', in Omar Khalidi (ed.), *Hyderabad After the Fall*, Wichita: Hyderabad Historical Society, 1998, p. 13.

123. This and the following information about the Police Action is based on *Operation Polo: The Police Action Against Hyderabad*, Ministry of Defence, Government of India, New Delhi, 1972.

124. Munshi, *The End of An Era*, p. 63.

125. Mir Laik Ali, *The Tragedy of Hyderabad*, Karachi: Pakistan Cooperative Book Society, 1962, p. 283.

126. Based on author's interviews with Khusro Yar Khan and Naidu. The latter joined the Indian Police Service later.

127. Zafarul Hassan, *Deccan Udas hai Yaro*, vol. III, Hyderabad: Hussami Book Depot, 1978, pp. 97–8.

128. Hassan, *Deccan Udas hai Yaro*, vol. III, pp. 194–5.

129. Mir Laik Ali, *The Tragedy of Hyderabad*, pp. 202–03.

130. Mir Laik Ali, *The Tragedy of Hyderabad*, p. 305.

131. Munshi, *The End of An Era*, 1998, p. 229–30.

132. Ministry of Defence, Government of India, *Operation Polo*, 1972.

133. Author's interview with Syed Hashim Ali on 12 September 1992. He had served under Pimputkar.

134. Mirza, *Pre- and Post-Police Action Days in the Erstwhile Hyderabad State*, pp. 38–49.

135. Khalidi, *Hyderabad after the Fall*, p. 99.

136. Mohd. Murtuza Ali Khan (ed.), *Suragh Rasani aur Taftish*, Hyderabad: n.d., pp. 285–91.

137. Narrated by Zahid Ali Kamil to the author in a series of interviews in 1990.

138. AIR (S.C.) 1953, p. 156.

139. B. Narsing Rao (ed.), *Telangana: The Era of Mass Politics—A Felicitation Volume dedicated to Ravi Narayana Reddy*, Hyderabad: Ravi Narayan Reddy Felicitation Committee, 1983, p. 53.

140. Rao, *Telangana: The Era of Mass Politics*, pp. 55–6.

141. Arutla Ramachandra Reddy, *Telangana Stuggle: Memoirs*, trans. B. Narsing Rao, New Delh: People's Publishing House, 1984, pp. 68–9.

142. Rao, *Telangana: The Era of Mass Politics*, pp. 29–32.

143. Rao, *Telangana: The Era of Mass Politics*, pp. 70–2.

144. Based on Rao, *Telangana: The Era of Mass Politics*.

145. Shaz Tamkanat, *Makhdoom—Hayat aur Karname*, Hyderabad: Maktab-e- Shair-o- Hikmat, 1986. See also Alexis Sukhachev, *Makhdoom Mohiuddin*, trans. Ussama Farooqi, Hyderabad: Maktaba-e-Sheir-o-Hikmat, 1993. The account was supplemented by interviews with Raj Bahadur Gaur on 11 August 1992, and others.

146. Razvi, Jawad, Interview with Raj Bahadur Gaur unpublished manuscript, 15 July 1999.

147. Interview with Chandra Rajeshwar Rao on 12 August 1992.

148. A detailed discussion on this is given in P. Sundarayya, *Telangana Peoples Struggle and its Lessons*, Calcutta: Desraj Chadda, 1972, pp. 391–436. A background reference is also found in the interview of

K.L. Mahendra in Mallikarjuna Sharma (ed.), *In Retrospect*, vol. 5, part I, Hyderabad: Ravi Sai Enterprises, 2002, pp. 291–2. This is called the Kishen Document. Also see Mohit Sen, *A Traveller And The Road: The Journey of an Indian Communist*, New Delhi: Rupa & Co., 2003, pp. 125–6.

149. Manuscript note by his grandson Mohd. Mohiuddin, given to the author on 19 August 1992. Numerous references to him are found in various books by Zaffarul Hassan, Sidq Jaisi, and others.

150 In the original Constitution of India, there were two categories of states. While the British Indian provinces were classified as Part A States, the erstwhile India states were categorized as Part B States. The head of Part A State was called Governor, while that of Part B State was called Raj Pramukh. This distinction was abolished with the reorganization of states in 1956.

151. Chhattari, *Yad-e-Ayyam*, pp. 121–2.

152. Husain, *The First Nizam*, 1963, p. 245.

153. Azam Ali Mirza, 'Asaf-e-Sabeh—My Meeting and Impressions', *Siasat Urdu Daily*, 12 March 1967.

154. Manzoor Alam, 'The Growth of Hyderabad City: A Historical Perspective', in Haroon Khan Sherwani (ed.), *Dr Ghulham Yazani Commemorative Volume*, Maulana Abul Kalam Azad Oriental Research Institute, 1966, pp. 212–20.

155. Theodore P. Wright Jr., 'National Integration and Modern Judicial Procedure in India: The Dar-us-Salam Case', in Omar Khalidi (ed.), *Hyderabad: After the Fall*, Wichita: Hyderabad Historical Society, 1988, p. 145.

156. Theodore P. Wright Jr., 'Revival of the Majlis Ittehad-ul–Mulimin of Hyderabad', in Khalidi, *Hyderabad: After the Fall*, pp. 136–7.

157. Records supplied by the Municipal Corporation of Hyderabad.

158. Based on interviews with Sayed Hashim Ali in May 1992.

159. Appendix N, Rule 39 of the Hyderabad Civil Service Regulations.

160. 'Studies on November, 1977 and May, 1979 Cyclones of the Southern Andhra Costal Areas', Paper by K.N. Prasad, M.D. Karimmuddin, et al., Geological Survey of India, Rec., vol. 115, Pt. 5.

161. R.J. Rajendra Prasad, *Emergence of Telugu Desam: An Overview of Political Movements in Andhra*, Hyderabad: Master Minds, 2004, pp. 39–41.

162. N. Chandrabau Naidu and Sevanti Ninan, *Plain Speaking*, New Delhi: Viking, 2000, p. xvi.

163. Wikipedia entry for Y.S. Rajasekhara Reddy, available at: http://en.wikipedia.org/wiki/Y.S. Rajasekhara Reddy (accessed 7 April 2020).

164. Hams India, 15 December 2018.

Bibliography

Abdullah, Sheikh Mohd., *Atish-e-Chinar,* Srinagar: Ali Mohd. & Sons, 1988.

Ahmed, Hasan-ud-Din, *Anjuman,* Hyderabad: Vila Academy, 1974.

Ahmed, Mohammad Ziauddin, 'The Relations of Golconda with Iran 1518–1687', Ph.D thesis, University of Poona, 1979.

Ahmed, Nazeer-ud-Din, *Swaneh Bahadur Yar Jung,* Hyderabad: Bahadur Yar Jung Academy, 1968.

Ahmed, Zahir, *Life's Yesterdays: Glimpses of Sir Nizamat Jung and His Times,* Bombay: Thacker & Co., 1945.

Akbar, S. Ali (ed.), *Mehdi Nawaz Jung Memorial Volume,* Hyderabad: Maulana Abul Kalam Azad Oriental Research Institute, 1970

Ali, Abdullah Yousuf, *The Holy Quran: Text, Translation and Commentary,* 2 vols., Hyderabad: Hussaini Book Depot, n.d.

Ali, Fatima Alam, *Yadash Bakhair,* Hyderabad: privately printed, 1989.

Ali, Mir Laik, *Tragedy of Hyderabad,* Karachi: Pakistan Co-operative Book Society Ltd., 1962.

Ali, Moulvi Syed Mehdi, (comp.) Hyderabad Affairs, vol. III (n.d.) vol. IV (1983), Hyderabad: State Archives.

Ali Yavar Jung, *Commemoration Volume,* Bombay: A.K. Azad Oriental Research Institute, 1983.

Alladin, Bilkiz, *For the Love of a Begum,* Hyderabad: Hydeca, 1989.

'Araiz-wa Ittihad Namajat wa Faramin-i-Abdullah Qutb Shah', Persian manuscript, Salar Jung Museum Library, Hyderabad.

'Armughan-e-yom-e-Mohammad Quli Qutb Shah', Diamond Jubilee Souvenir of the Osmania University by Idara-e-Adabiyat-e-Urdu, Hyderabad, 1958.

Asaf Jah I, *Dewan-e-Asaf Jah*, 1354 H/AD 1935.

Asaf Jah I, *Dewan-e-Shakir*, 1357 H/AD 1938.

Ashahari, Moulvi Syed Amjad Ali, *Swaneh Umri Ala Hazrat Mehboob Ali Khan*, Lahore: Khadim-ul-Taleem Steam Press, 1911.

Ashraf, Syed Dawood, *Auraq-e-Muwarrikh*, Hyderabad: Shagoofa Publications, 1998.

————, 'Beroni Mashaheer-e-Adab aur Hyderabad', *Siasat Urdu Daily*, 1990.

————, *Guzishta Hyderabad—Archives Ke Aine Mein*, Hyderabad: Shagoofa Publications, 2003.

————, *Hasil–e-Tehqiq*, Hyderabad: Shagoofa Publications, 1992.

————, *The Seventh Nizam of Hyderabad—An Archival Appraisal*, Hyderabad: Moazam Hussain Foundation, 2002.

Bahadur, Mohd. Wazir Ali Khan, *Samar-e-Hyat Sultan-ul-Hukma Bahadur*, Hyderabad: Maktba-e-Saheb-e-Deccan, n.d.

Bailey, T. Grahame, *History of Urdu Literature*, London: Oxford University Press, 1932.

'Baras Baras Roshan—Chronology of 400 Years of Hyderabad', unpublished manuscript.

Barrett, Douglas and Basil Gray, *Indian Painting*, London: Macmillan, 1978.

Basham, A.L., *A Cultural History of India*, Delhi: Oxford University Press, 1975.

Bawa, V.K., *The Last Nizam—The Life and the Times of Mir Osman Ali Khan*, Delhi: Penguin, 1992.

————, *The Nizam Between Mughals and British: Hyderabad under Salar Jung I*, New Delhi: S. Chand & Co., 1986.

Benichou, Lucien D, *From Autocracy to Integration— Political Developments in Hyderabad State 1938–1948*, Hyderabad: Orient Longman, 2000.

Bernier, Francis, *Travels in the Mughal Empire*, 2 vols., trans. Irving Brock, London: Willing Pickering, 1826.

Bilgrami, Hosh, *Mushahdat*, Hyderabad: Inquilab Press, 1950.

Bilgrami, H. and S.A. Asghar, *Landmarks of the Deccan Hyderabad*, Hyderabad: Government Central Press, 1927; rpt., Delhi: Manas Publications, 1984.

Briggs, Henry George, *The Nizam*, London: Bernard Quaritch, 1861.

Campbell, Claude A., *Glimpses of the Nizam's Dominions*, London: C.B. Burrows, 1898.

Danish, Dilwar Ali, *Rayaz-e-Mukhataria Saltanat-e-Asafiya*, Hyderabad: Azam Steam Press, 1942.

Dehalvi, Mirza Fahutullah Beg, *Meri Dastan*, Hyderabad: Mirza Sharafat Ullah Beg, n.d.

Dehalvi, Sayyed Yousuf Bukhari, *Yaran-e-Rafta*, Karachi: Makhatab Usloob, 1987.

Desai, V.H., *Vande Matram To Jana Gana Mana—Saga of Hyderabad Freedom Struggle*, Bombay: Bharatiya Bhavan, 1990.

Dodd, E.F., *The Story of Sir Ronald Ross and His Fight Against Malaria*, Madras: Macmillan India, 1960.

Ferishta, Mahammed Kasim, *History of the Rise of Mohammedan Power in India till* AD *1612*, vol. III, trans. John Briggs, London: Longman, Rees, Onme, Brown & Green, 1829.

Frazer, J.S., *Memoirs of General Frazer*, London: Whiting & Co., 1884.

Gauhai, Moulvi Ghulam Samdani Khan, *Hayat-e-Mah Laqa*, Hyderabad: Nizama-ul-Maktaba, 1906.

Gilani, Hakim Nizamuddin Ahmed, *Hadiqutus Salateen*, trans. Khawaja Mohammad Sarvar, Hyderabad: National Fine Printing Press, 1986.

Gour, Raj Bahadur, *Glorious Telangana Armed Struggle*, New Delhi: Communist Party Publications, 1973.

———, *Random Writings*, Hyderabad: Makhdoom Society, Pranchee Publications, 2002.

———, *Tricolour Shall Fly Over Hyderabad*, Bombay: People's Publishing House, n.d.

Government of Hyderabad, *The Classified List of the Civil Department of HEH the Nizam's Government*, Hyderabad: Government Press, 1948.

———, *The Report of the Hyderabad Chloroform Commission*, Bombay: The Times of India Steam Press, 1981.

Government of India, *Report of the States Reorganization Commission*, New Delhi: Government of India Press, 1955.

Gribble, J.D.B., *A History of the Deccan*, 2 vols, London: Luzar and Co., 1896.

Haig, Sir William, *Cambridge History of India*, vol. III, Delhi: S. Chand & Co., 1979.

Handa, R.L., *History of Freedom Struggle in Princely States*, New Delhi: Central News Agency, 1968.

Hasan, Mirza Zafarul, *Deccan Udas Hai Yaro*, Karachi: Idara-e-Yadgare-e-Ghalib, 1978.

———, *Zik-e-Yar Chale*, Hyderabad: Hussami Book Depot, 1979.

———, *Woh Qurbaten Si Woh Fasle Se—Safar Nama-e-Deccan*, Hyderabad: Hussami Book Depot, 1987.

Hasan, Sibte, *Shahar-e-Nigaran*, Karachi: Maktaba-e-Danyal, 1984.

Hashmi, Mohammed Nasiruddin, *Al-musammi beh Al-Mahboob*, Hyderabad: privately printed, 1996.

Hashmi, Nasiruddin, *Deccan Mein Urdu*, 4th edn., Lahore: Nizam-e-Deccan Press, 1952.

Hijr, Ghulam Inam Khan, *Tarikh-e-Rashiduddin Khani*, Hyderabad: Shamsul Umra Press, 1286 H/AD 1865).

Huizinga, Johan, *Men and Ideas*, London: Eyre and Spottiswoode, 1960.

Husain, Masood Mohd., *Quli Qutb Shah*, Delhi: Sahitya Akademi, 1981.

Husain, Yusuf, *The First Nizam: The Life and Times of Nizam-ul-Mulk Asaf Jah I*, Delhi: Asia Publishing House, 1963.

Hyderabad Affairs, vols. III and IV, State Archives, Hyderabad.

'Hyderabad in 1890 and 1891'. Comprising All the Letters on Hyderabad Affairs, Written to *The Hindu*, Madras, by its Hyderabad Correspondent During 1890 & 1891, Bangalore: Laxton Press, 1892.

Imperial Gazetteer of India: Provincial series, Hyderabad State: Superintendent of Government Printing, 1909.

Irwin, William, *The Later Mughals*, vol. II, Jadunath Sarkar (ed.), Calcutta: M.C. Sarkar and Sons, 1922; rpt, New Delhi: D.K.Publishers and Distributors, 1995.

Ismail, Sir Mirza, *My Public Life: Recollections and Reflections*, London: George Allen & Unwin, 1954.

Jaffar, Syeda (ed.), *Kulliyat-e-Mohammad Quli Qutub Shah*, New Delhi: Taraqqi-e-Urdu Bureau, 1985.

Jaisi, Sidiq, *Darbaar-e-Dürbaar*, Hyderabad: Hussami Book Depot, 1960.

Jaleeli, Ali Ahmed, *Fasahat Jung Jaleel Manakpuri: Hayat, Shaksiyat aur Fun*, Ph.D. thesis, Osmania University, 1989.

Jalibi, Jamil, *Tareekh-e-Adabe-Urdu*, vols 1 and 2, Delhi: Educational Publishing House, 1977 and 1984.

Johnson, Alan Campbell, *Mission with Mountbatten*, London: Robert Hale, 1952.

Joseph, T. Uma, *Accession of Hyderabad: The Inside Story*, Delhi: DK Publishers, Distributors, 2007.

Joshi, P.M., and M.A. Nayeem, *Studies in the Foreign Relations of India: From the Earliest Time to 1947*, State Archives, Hyderabad: Government of Andhra Pradesh, 1975.

Jung, Mehdi Nawaz, *Maharaja Kishen Pershad*, Hyderabad: n.p., 1950.

Jung, Nasir, *Dewan-e-Nasir Jung*, n.p., n.d.

Jung, Sir Nizamat, *Ghazals of Nizam VII of Hyderabad*, Hyderabad: Government Printing Press, 1919.

Kamtar, Shah, *Mathnavi Dastan-e-Nizam Ali Khan*, Hyderabad: Asaf Jahi Society of Oriental Studies, n.d.

Karaka, D.F., *Fabulous Mogul: Nizam VII of Hyderabad*, London: Derek Verschoyle, 1955.

Khalidi, Omar (ed.), *Hyderabad: After the Fall*, Wichita: Hyderabad Historical Society, 1988.

Khan, Hashim Ali (Khafi Khan Nizamul Mulki), *Muntakhab-ul-Lubab*, Part III trans. Mohd. Ahmed Farooqui, Karachi: Nafees Academy, 1963.

Khan, Masud Hussain, *Muqaddama-e-Tarikh-e-Zaban-e-Urdu*, Aligarh: Educational Book House (7th rpt.), 1987.

Khan, Mir Osman Ali, *Intekhab-e-Kalam-e-Asaf-e-Sabeh*, Hyderabad: HEH the Nizam's Trust, 1975.

Khan, Mohammed Nooruddin, *Yaddasht*, Hyderabad: Adabistan-a-Deccan, 2003.

Khan, Mushatq Ahmed, *Zawal-e-Hyderabad Ki Ankahi Dastan*, Lahore: S.A. Alam & Sons, 1986.

Khan, Raza Ali, *Hyderabad 400 Years*, Hyderabad: privately printed, 1990.

————, *Hyderabad: A City in History*, Hyderabad: privately printed, 1986.

Khan, Sadath Ali, *Brief Thanksgiving*, Delhi: Asia Publishing House, 1959.

Khan, Sayyed Hafiz Mohd. Ahmed, *Yad-e-Ayyam*, 3 vols, Aligarh: Muslim Educational Press, n.d.

Khan, Nimat Ali, *Chronicles of the Seige of Golconda*, trans. N.H. Ansari, Delhi: Idara-e-Adabiyat-e-Dilli, 1975.

Khanam, Khaleda Adeeb, 'Androon-e-Hyderabad', *Inside India* tr. into Urdu by Maulvi Sayed Hashmi, Hyderabad: Anjuman-e-Ishaet, Urdu, 1936.

Khandalevala, K. and Rehmat Ali Khan, *Gulshan-e-Mussavari*, Hyderabad: Salar Jung Museum Publications, 1986.

Khobrekar, V.G. (ed.), *Tarikh-e-Dilkusha*, trans. Jadunath Sarkar, Bombay: Department of Archives, 1972.

Krishnan, Usha R. Bala, *Jewels of the Nizam*, Delhi: Department of Culture, 2001.

Kulkarni, A.R. and M.A. Nayeem (eds.), *History of Modern Deccan 1724 –1948*, vol. I, Unpublished typescript, Hyderabad: Maulana Abul Kalam Azad Oriental Research Institute, 1990.

Latif, Syed Abdul, *Bases of Islamic Culture*, Hyderabad: Institute of Indo-Middle East Cultural Studies, 1959.

Leonard, Karen Isaksen, *Social History of an Indian Caste: The Kayasths of Hyderabad*, 2nd edn., Hyderabad: Orient Longman.

————, 'Hyderabad: The Mulki-Non-Muliki Conflict' in Jeffrey Robin (ed.), *People, Princes and Paramount Power: Society and Politics in the Indian Princely States*, New Delhi: Oxford University Press, 1978.

————, 'Construction of Identity in Diaspora: Emigrants from Hyderabad, India', in Carla Petiench (ed.), *Expanding Landscapes: South Asians in Diaspora*, New Delh: Manohar, 1994.

Luther, Narendra, *Prince, Poet, Lover, Builder: Muhammad Quli Qutb Shah*: *The Founder of Hyderabad*, Delhi: Publications Division, 1991.

―――, *Raja Deen Dayal: Prince of Photography*, Hyderabad, Creative Point, 2004.

―――, *The Nocturnal Court: The Life of a Prince of Hyderabad*, New Delhi: Oxford University Press, 2004.

―――, 'Hyderabad Through Foreign Eyes' in Sachidananda Mohanty (ed.), *Travel Writing and the Empire*, New Delhi: Katha, 2003.

Lynton, Harriet Ronken and Mohini Rajan, *The Days of the Beloved*, Los Angeles: University of California Press, 1974.

Lynton, Harriet Ronken, *My Dear Nawab Saheb*, Hyderabad: Orient Longman, 1991.

'Makateeb-i-Sultan Abdullah Qutb Shah', Persian manuscript at the Salar Jung Museum Library, Hyderabad.

Malleson, G.B., *History of the French in India*, Delhi: Gian Publishing House, 1909.

Mamlakate-Asafia, 2 vols., Karachi: Idara-e-Muhibban-e-Deccan, 1989.

Mannucci, Niccolao, *Storia Do Mogor*, vol. 2, trans. William Irvine, London: John Murray, 1913; rpt, Delhi: D.K. Publishers, 1996.

Mason, Philip, *A Shaft of Sunlight: Memoirs of a Varied Life*, Delhi: Vikas, 1978.

Mazhar, Mohammad, *Tazkara -e-Bab-e-Hakumat* (1338H to 1363H), Hyderabad: Azam Steam Press, 1932.

Megroz, R.L., *Ronald Ross: Discoverer and Creator*, London: George Allen & Unwin, 1931.

Menon, K.P.S., *Many Worlds Revisited: An Autobiography*, Bombay: Bharatiya Vidya Bhavan, 1981.

Menon, V.P., *The Story of the Integration of Indian States*, New Delhi: Orient Longman, 1956.

Mirza, Fareed, *Pre- and Post-Police Action Days in the Erstwhile Hyderabad*, Hyderabad: privately printed, 1976.

Ministry of Defence, *Operation Polo: The Police Action Against Hyderabad*, Delhi: Government of India, 1972.

Mohammed, Abul Mukarram, *Sir Salar Jung-e-Azam*, Hyderabad: Sabras Kitab Ghar, 1950.

Mohammed, Faiz, *Nawab Imad-ul-Mulk Syed Hussain Bilgrami*, Hyderabad: Idara-e-Adabiyat-e-Urdu, 1940.

Mohiuddin, Makhdoom, *Baggi ke Peechee Chhokra* (ed.), Zahid Ali Khan, Hyderabad: Siasat Publications, 1980.

―――, *Bisat-e-Raqs*, Hyderabad: Urdu Academy, 1986.

Moreland, W.M., *Relations of Golconda in the Early Seventeenth Century* AD *1608–1622*, London: Hakluyt Society, 1931.

Mudiraj, K. Krishnaswamy, *Pictorial Hyderabad*, Hyderabad: privately printed, 1934.

Mujalla-e-Osmania—Maharaj Number, Hyderabad: Osmania University, 1940.

Munshi, K.M., *The End of an Era*, 3rd edn., Bombay: Bharatiya Vidya Bhavan, [1957] 1998.

Nag, Kingshuk, *Battleground Telangana—Chronicle of an Agitation*. New Delhi: Harper Collin Publishers India, 2011, pp. 126–7.

Nagar, Murtaza Ali Khan, *Detection and Investigation*: *Memoirs of Lati Khan Fazal Rasool Khan Nagar*, Hyderabad, n.d.

Naidu, Sarojini, *The Sceptered Flute*: *Songs of India*, Allahabad: Kitabistan, 1943.

Narayan, S. Venkat, *N.T.R.*: *A Biography*, New Delhi: Vikas, 1983.

Narisetti, Innaiah, *A Century of Politics in Andhra Pradesh*, Hyderabad: Rationalist Voice Publications, 2002.

Nayeem, M.A. and Dharamender Prasad, *The Salar Jungs*, Hyderabad: The Salar Jung Museum, 1986.

Nehru, Jawaharlal, *A Bunch of Old Letters*, Bombay: Asia Publishing House, 1958.

Ninan, Sevanti and Chandrababu Naidu, *Plain Speaking*, Delhi: Penguin, 2000

Orme, Robert, *Historical Fragments of the Mogul Empire of the Morattoes and of the English Concerns in Indostan from the year* MDCLIX, London: Wingrane in the Strand, 1705.

Pataudi, Sher Ali, *The Elite Minority Princes of India*, Lahore: Syed Mohin Mahmud & Co., 1989.

Prasad, Babu Ishari, *Complete Proceedings of the Case of Nawab Mehdi Hasan vs. S.M. Mitra* (Part 1), Aminabad: Munshi Gang Prasad Verma & Brothers Press, n.d.

Prasad, Dharmender, '*Place-names of Hyderabad City*', unpublished manuscript, Hyderabad, 1987.

Prasad, R.J. Rajendra, *Emergence of Telugu Desam*, Chennai: Master Minds Academic Press, 2004

Prasad, Rajendra H., *The Asaf Jahis of Hyderabad: Their Rise and Decline*, New Delhi: Vikas, 1984.

Raj, Sheela, *Hyderabad in the Days of the Nizams 1828–1896*, Hyderabad: Narhari Pershad Charitable Trust, 1996.

Rao C.P. (ed.), *Census of India 1981*, Andhra Pradesh: Special Report on Hyderabad City, Directorate of Census Operations, Hyderabad, 1989.

Rao, B. Nageshwar, *Torch Bearers of Freedom Movement*, Hyderabad: Institute of Historical Research of Freedom Struggle, 1991.

Rao, B. Narsing (ed.), *Telangana: The Era of Mass Politics. A Felicitation volume dedicated to Ravi Narayan Reddy*, Hyderabad: Ravi Narayan Reddy Felicitation Committee, 1983

Rao, B. Rajnikanta, *Andhra Vagyakara Charitrumu*, Vijayawada: Visalandhra Pracharuna, 1958.

Rao, D. Sudershan, *Dr Burgula Ramakrishna Rao*, Secunderabad: Jyotirmayi, 1999.

Rao, V. Krishna, *Swami Ramananda Tirtha and the Hyderabad Struggle*, Warangal: Shri Sai Publishers, 1988.

Rao, I. Venkata, *Okade—Okadu*, Hyderabad: Monica Books, 2000.

Rao, I. Venkata, *Okadu*, Hyderabad: Monica Books, 2003.

Rao, Jagannadha Manechala, *Ramadasu Kirtanalu*, Hyderabad: Andhra Pradesh. Sangeet Natak Academy, 1975.

Rao, K. Aravinda, *Naxalite Terrorism—Social and Legal Issues*, Madras: East West Books, 1996.

Rao, K.V Bhupala, *The Illustrious Prime Minister Madanna*, Hyderabad: privately printed,1984.

Rao, Kondal Velachala et al. (eds), *The Telangana Struggle for Identity.* Hyderabad: Telangana Cultural Forum Publication, 2010, pp. 44–7.

Rao, M.B. (ed.), *Documents of the History of the Communist Party of India*, vol. VII (1948–50), New Delhi: People's Publishing House, 1976.

Rao, P. Setu Madhava, *Eighteenth Century Deccan*, Bombay: Popular Prakashan, 1963.

Rao, P.R., *History of Modern Andhra Pradesh*, New Delhi: Sterling Publishers, 1988.

Rao, Vithal Manik, *Tarikh-e-Bostan-e-Asafiya*, 8 vols., Hyderabad: Chistia Press, 1372H / AD 1925.

Ray, Bharati, *Hyderabad and British Paramountcy*, Bombay: Oxford University Press, 1988.

Razvi, S.M. Jawad, *Political Awakening in Hyderabad: Role of Youth and Students*, Hyderabad: Visalandhra Publishing House, 1985.

———, *Riyasat Hyderabad Mein Jaddojahd-e-Azadi*, New Delhi: Taraaqui-e-Urdu Bureau, 2000

Reddy, Arutla Ramachandra, *Telangana Struggle Memoirs*, trans. B. Narsing Rao, New Delhi: People's Publishing House, 1984.

Reddy, K.V. Ranga, *The Struggle and the Betrayal—the Telangana Story (An Autobiography)*. Hyderabad: Vignana Sarovara Prachurnanalu, 2010, pp. 139–47.

Regani, Sarojini (ed.), *Who's Who in Freedom Struggle in Andhra Pradesh*, 3 vols., Hyderabad: Government of Andhra Pradesh, 1978.

———, *Nizam-British Relations*, Hyderabad: Book Lovers, 1963.

Rehman, Habib-ur, *Chand Yaddashten*, Karachi: Bahadur Yar Jung Academy, 1986.

Rocco, Shah, *Golconda*, Hyderabad: Salar Jung Museum Library, n.d.

Reddy, Suvarnam Pratap, *Life of Raja Bahadur Venkatarama Reddy*, trans. Anand Rao Thota, Hyderabad: Raja Bahadur Venkatarama Reddy Centenary Celebration Committee, 1996.

Sadiq, Mohd., *History of Urdu Literature*, 2nd edn., Delhi; Oxford University Press, 1984.

Sarma, Modali Nagabhushana, et al., *History and Culture of the Andhras*, Hyderabad: Telugu University, 1995.

Server-ul-Mulk, Nawab Bahadur, *My Life*, trans. Nawab Jiwan Yar Jung Bahadur, London: Arthur H. Stockwll, n.d.

Satyanarayana, Nukala Chinna, *Bhadrachala Ramadas*, M.Litt. Dissertation, Madras University, 1961.

Saxena, Bhaskar Raj, *Hyderabad ke Bansi Raja*, Hyderabad : Maktaba-e-Sheir-o-Hikmat, 1995.

Saxena, Bhaskar Raj (ed.), *Hyderabad Nizam Kal ke Bhakt Kavi AD 1762–1957: Hindi ke Paanch Ratn*, Hyderabad: Maan Publications, 2002.

Saxena, Manohar Raj, *Historic Telangana Peasant's Struggle and the Legal Battle*, Hyderabad: Telangana Martyr's Memorial Trust, 2000.

Saxena, Raman Raj, *Asman Jah Ka Hyderabad*, Hyderabad: Hussaini Book Depot, 1991.

———, *Tazkara-e-Darbar-e-Hyderabad*, New Delhi: Taraqqi-e-Urdu Bureau, 1988.

Sen, Mohit (ed.), *Documents of the History of the Communist Party of India*, vol. VIII (1951–6), New Delhi: People's Publishing House, 1977.

———, *A Traveller and the Road*, New Delhi: Rupa & Co., 2003.

Sengupta, Padmini, *Sarojini Naidu: A Biography*, Bombay: Asia Publishing House, 1966.

Shakeb, Badar, *Hyderabad ka Urooj-o-Zawal*, Karachi: Osmania Academy, 1964.

Shamshad, Syed Ghulam Panjatan, *Hyderabad Ke Bade Log*, Hyderabad: Idara -e-Adabiyat-Urdu, 1957.

Sherwani, H.K. (ed.), *Ghulam Yazdani Commemoration Volume*, Hyderabad: Moulana Abul Kalam Azad Oriental Research Institute, 1966.

———, *History of Golconda*, Hyderabad: The Literary Publications, 1956.

————, *History of Qutb Shahi Dynasty*, Delhi: Munshiram Manoharlal, 1974.

————, *Mohammad Quli Qutb Shah: The Founder of Hyderabad*, Bombay: Asia Publishing House, 1967.

Sherwani, H.K. and P.M. Joshi (eds.), *History of Medieval Deccan*, vols. ɪ and ɪɪ, Hyderabad: Government of Andhra Pradesh, 1973 and 1974

————, *Cultural Trends in Medieval India*, Bombay: Asia Publishing House, 1968.

————, *Tarikh-e-Golconda*, Hyderabad: Aijaz Printing Press, 1964.

Sherwani, Moulana Mohd. and Habibur Rehman Khan, *Viqar-e-Hayat*, Aligarh: Muslim University Press, 1344 ʜ/ᴀᴅ 1925.

Showkat, Samnia, *Mah Laqa*, Hyderabad: Aijaz Printing Press, 1959.

Siddiqui, Abdul Majeed, *Muqqadama-Tareekh-e -Deccan*, Hyderabad: Idara-e-Adabiyat-e-Urdu, 1940.

Siddiqui, Mohd. Akbar-ud-Din, *Intekhab-e-Mohammad Quli Qutab Shah*, New Delhi: Maktaba-e-Jamia, 1972.

Singh, Sant Nihal, *The Nizam and the British Empire*, New Delhi: privately printed, n.d.

Soorat Garan-e-Deccan, Hyderabad: Siasat Publications, 1979.

Sukhachev, Alexis, *Makhdoom Mohiuddin*, trans. Mohd. Ussama Farooqi, Hyderabad: Idara-e-Shair-o-Hikamat, 1993.

Sundarayya, P., *Telangana People's Struggle and its Lessons*, Calcutta: Desraj Chadda, 1972.

Sykes, W., Stanley, *Essays on the First Hundred Years of Anaesthesia*, vol. ɪɪɪ, London: Churchill Livingstone, 1982.

Taley, Sayyad Murad Ali, *Mal Wale*, Hyderabad: Azam Steam Press, 1944.

Talib, Mohammad Sirajuddin, *Meer Alam ki Swaneh Zindagi*, Hyderabad: n.p., 1930.

Tamkanat, Shaz, *Makhdoom Mohiuddin: Hayat aur Karname*, Hyderabad: Maktaba-e-Shaire-o-Hikmat, 1986.

Tareekh-e-Majlis-e-Ittehad-ul-Musalmeen, Hyderabad: Drul Inshait Siasiat, 1941.

Tavernier, Jean Baptiste, *The Six Voyages*, vol. 1 (1676), trans. V. Ball, London: Macmillan, 1889.

Taylor, Philip Meadows, *Confessions of a Thug*, London: Richard Bentlay, 1839, rpt, New Delhi: Asian Educational Services, 1988.

————, *The Story of My Life*, London: Oxford University Press, 1920.

The Classified List of Officers of the Civil Department of HEH the Nizam's Government', Hyderabad: Government Press, 1948.

The Hyderabad State Committee, *The Freedom Struggle in Hyderabad*, vol. I (1800–1857), vol. ɪɪ (1857–85), vol. ɪɪɪ (1885–1920) Hyderabad, 1956,

1956, 1957 respectively. vol. IV, The Andhra Pradesh State Committee, 1966.

Thevenot, *The Travels into the Levant*, vol. III, trans. A. Lovell, London: H. Clark, 1687.

Tirtha, Swami Ramananda, *Memoirs of Hyderabad Freedom Struggle*, Bombay: Popular Prakashan, 1967.

Urfani, Sheikh Yakub Ali, *Hayat-e-Usmani*, vol. I, Hyderabad: Azam Steam Press, n.d.

Vajahi, Mulla, *Qutb-o-Mushtari*, (ed.) Maulvi Abdul Haq, New Delhi: Anjuman-e-Taraqqi–e-Urdu, 1939.

Vasumati, *Telugu Literature in the Qutb Shahi Period*, Thesis submitted to Maulana Abul Kalam Azad Oriental Research Institute, Hyderabad, n.d.

Wahid, Mohammad Abdul, *Tazkara-e-Wahid*, Hyderabad: Taj Press, n.d.

Wilmot, C. and Syed Hossain Bilgrami, *Historical and Descriptive Sketch of His Highness the Nizam's Dominions*, vols. I and II, Bombay: Times of India Steam Press, 1833.

Zia, Habib, Maharaja Sir Kishen Pershad Shad: *Hayat and Adabi Khidmat*, Ph.D. Thesis, Osmania University 1978.

Zore, S.M.Q., *Deccani Adab Ki Tareekh*, 3rd edn., Hyderabad: Idara-e-Ibrahimia Machine Press, 1982.

———, *Hayat-e-Mohammad Quli Qutb Shah*, Hyderabad: Azam Steam Press, Hyderabad, 1940.

———, *Kulliyat-e-Mohammad Quli Qutb Shah*, Hyderabad: Maktab-e-Ibrahimia Machine Press, Hyderabad, 1940.

———, *Nazar-e-Mohammad Quli Qutb Shah*, Hyderabad: Idara-e-Adabiyat-Urdu, 1958.

———, *Farkhunda-Buniyad*, Hyderabad: Idara-e-Adabiyat-Urdu, 1952.

———, *Mir Mohammad Momin* , Hyderabad: Idara-e-Adabiyat-Urdu, 1941.

ARTICLES AND PAPERS

Abbasi, Shahid Ali (ed.), *Islamic Culture*, Special 75th Anniversary Issue, 2002, vol. LXXVI, no. 2.

Ali, Hashmi Amir, 'The Last of the Salar Jungs: Personal Reminiscences of a Bygone Era', *Salar Jung Museum Bi-Annual Research Journal*, 1976–7, vol. IX–X, pp. 1–10.

Azeem, Azeem-ur-Rehman, 'Sukhan Banam-e-Hyderabad', *Sabras*, December 1991, pp. 27–9.

Cowsjee, Hurmuz, 'Musi Nadi—1908 ki Tughyni ke Baad se Aab Tak', *Siasat Urdu Daily*, 19 October 1970

Deccan Chronicle, Daily files, Secunderabad.

Ghaffar, Qazi Mohd. Abdul, *Letter to Nizam VII*, 1948 (from the private papers of Fatima Alam Ali).

Gour, Raj Bahadur, 'Influence of Socialist Thought on the People's Movement in Hyderabad State', Essay given to the author by Dr Gaur, 1990.

————, *The Glorious Telangana Struggle. What It Meant? What It Achieved?*, New Delhi: People's Publishing House, 1975.

Hasan, Akther, 'Razakars, A Blot on the History of Hyderabad', *Deccan Chronicle*, 15 August 1997.

Jung, Nawab Akbar Yar, 'Shri Krishna, the Prophet of Hind', Address delivered on the occassion of Janmashtami organized by the Young Men's Kayasth Association at Hyderabad, Hyderabad, 11 August 1936.

Kaushik, Vandana, 'Hyderabad in the Early 19th Century'. Paper presented at the seminar on 400 years of Hyderabad at the Salar Jung Museum, Hyderabad, Hyderabad 1–3 April 1991.

————, 'Religious and Cultural Synthesis in the 19th Century Hyderabad', Proceedings of the Indian History and Cultural Society, November 1990.

Khan, Maqsood Ali, 'Bhadur Yar Jung', *Siasat Urdu Daily*, 2 October 2000.

Khan, Mir Karamat Ali, 'Asaf Jahi Mamas' *Siasat Urdu Daily*, 11 August 1990.

Leonard, Karen Isaksen, 'Banking Firms in Nineteenth Century Hyderabad Politics', *Modern Asian Studies*, 1981, vol. 15, no. 2, pp. 1177–201.

————, 'The "Great Firm" Theory of the Decline of the Mughal Empire', *Comparative Studies in Society and History*, April 1979, pp. 151–67.

————, 'The Hyderabad Political System and its Participants', *Journal of Asian Studies*, May 1971, vol. 30, no. 3, pp. 569–82.

————, 'The Deccani Synthesis in old Hyderabad: An Historiographic Essay', *Journal of Pakistan Historical Society*, October 1973, vol. xxi, no. iv, pp. 205–18.

Luther, Narendra, 'Four Hundred Years of Hyderabad', *Readers Digest*, December 1991.

————, 'Hyderabad Through the Ages', *Yojana*, October 1990.

————, 'Mohammad Quli and His City', Lecture organized by the Sarojini Devi Memorial Trust, Hyderabad, 1990.

————, 'On the Historicity of Bhagmati', Special Issue of *Vignan Saraswati*, Oriental Manuscript Library, Hyderabad, October 1992.

————, 'A Paradise to be Reclaimed', *Frontline*, 13 February 1992.

————, 'The Changing City—The way we were in the 60s', *Deccan Chronicle*, 15 May 1997.

————, 'Poet and Pulisher', *The Hindu*, 17 September1997.

————, 'Politics given a new dimension', *The Hindu*, 9 March 1999.

Mirza, Azam Ali, 'Asaf-e-Sabeh: My Meeting and Impressions', *Siasat Urdu Daily*, 12 March 1967.

Mohiuddin, Mohammad, 'A Note on Syed Jamaluddin', unpublished manuscript.

Murthy, K.S.R., 'References to Bhagyanagar in the Contemporary Telugu Literature of the Qutb Shahi Period'. Paper presented at the seminar on 400 years of Hyderabad at Salar Jung Museum, Hyderabad, 1991.

Pawar, Narayan Rao, 1987, 'Daredevil of Hyderabad', *Deccan Chronicle*, 15 August 1997.

Pershad, Mohan, 1987, 'Musi Nadi Ki Tughyani', *Siasat Urdu Daily*, 28 September 1987.

Quadri, Mahir-ul, 'Yad-e-Raftgan: Nawab Mir Osman Ali Khan, Asaf Jah Sabeh, Nizam -e-Deccan Marhoom', *Faran*, April 1967.

Rahbar-e- Deccan', Urdu Daily files in the State Central Library, Hyderabad.

Ramachari, A. and Abhay Patwari, 'Edward Lawrie and the Hyderabad Chloroform Commissions', in Richard S. Atkinson and Thomas B. Boulton (eds.), *The History of Anaesthesia*, London: Parthenon Publishing Group, 1988.

————, 'Milestones of Medical History of Hyderabad', *Journal of the Indian Medical Association*, n.d., vol. III, no. 4, pp. 208–12.

Razvi, S.M. Jawad, 'Dr. Raj Bahadur Gour: Some Impressions', *Siasat Urdu Daily*, 24 July 1991.

Razvi, Shafqat, 'Dagh Dehlvi Hyderabad Mein', *Siasat Urdu Daily*, 22 August 1995.

————, 'Khanwada-e-Asafiya mein Shairi ki Rivayat', *Siasat Urdu Daily*, 20 December 1997.

Roosa, Jhon B, 'Lal Salaam : Nationalism Painted Red', *Deccan Chronicle*, 15 August 1997.

Sarkar, Jadunath, 'General Raymond of the Nizam's Army', *Islamic Culture*, January 1933, vol. VIII, pp. 93–113.

————, 'Hyderabad and Golconda in 1750—As seen Through French Eyes', *Islamic Culture*, 1936, vol. x.

Sequeira, Isaac, 'The Mystique of the Mushaira', *The Journal of Popular Culture*, 1981, vol. 15, no. 1.

Shiraz, Urdu Daily files in the State Central Library, Hyderabad.

Sriharsha, V., 'A Traveller's Tale', *Indian Express*, 22 December 1990.

Strachey, Edward, 'The Romantic Marriage of Major James Achilles Kirkpatrick', *Blackwoods Magazine*, July 1893, pp. 18–29.

Sabras, Mohammad Quli Number, Magazine of Idara-e-Adabiyat-e-Urdu, Hyderabad, 1959, and 1961.

Oral History References

ABBASSI, NOOH*
Freedom fighter. Member of the Socialist Party of India. Participated in the Quit India Movement and suffered imprisonment.

AFZAL, SYED GHULAM (BIYABANI)
A senior police officer of the Hyderabad state who was a witness to some of the incidents during the Police Action.

AHMED, HASAN-UD-DIN
Son of Nawab Deen Yar Jung who was the Director General of Police during the Police Action. He joined the Hyderabad Civil Service and was promoted to IAS later. Author of some books.

AHMED, SIRAJUDDIN
A social and political worker who has seen both pre- and post-Police Action days.

ALI, FATIMA ALAM
Daughter of Qazi Abdul Ghaffoor, writer and editor of *Payam*. Later Director of Information. Author of a collection of reminiscent articles in Urdu—*Yadash Bakhair*. He wrote a strong letter to the Nizam advising him to join the Indian Union and then left Hyderabad to escape the latter's wrath.

ALIKHAN, ASAF
Son of Professor Hosain Alikhan and Masooma Begum. He became a minister under the Sanjeeva Reddy government in Andhra Pradesh.

ALI, SYED H.
A well-known oncologist of Hyderabad who was close to Dr M. Channa Reddy and also had some reminiscences of the last Nizam.

ALI, SYED HASHIM
An IAS officer who became successively Vice Chancellor of the Osmania and Aligarh Universities. An eye-witness to the death of the last Nizam, and in charge of the arrangements for his funeral.

ALI, SYED MEHDI
A Hyderabad Civil Services officer who defied the Razakar and suffered both during and after the Police Action.

BAWA, OUDESH RANI
A scholar of Urdu who studied in Moscow. Close to the CPI and is very knowledgeable on Hyderabad.

BILGRAMI, SYED NAQI
Secretary of the Department of Communications and Transport under the last Nizam. Later an IAS officer.

COWSJEE, HURMUZ
An officer in charge of the maintenance of the palaces of the Nizam. Was very knowledgeable on the details of the life of the Nizam and the history of Hyderabad. An avid collector of coins, stamps, and other memorabilia pertaining to the Nizams.

DEVI, RANI KUMUDINI
Daughter of the last Deputy Prime Minister of Hyderabad under the Razakar regime. A companion to the Princess of Berar. Now a keen social worker and philanthropist.

DITTIA, B.F.
A Parsee IAS officer well versed in the old customs and traditions of the Hyderabad state.

EKBOTE, GOPALRAO
Lawyer, freedom fighter, became minister in the first popular Congress Government of Hyderabad in 1952. Retired as Chief Justice of the Andhra Pradesh High Court.

GOUR, RAJ BAHADUR
A medical graduate who joined the Communist Party and became a prominent trade union leader. Suffered imprisonment. Became member of the Rajya Sabha for two terms. Scholar of Urdu.

GOUR, TAMARA
Daughter of Dr Gour. Medical graduate from Moscow. A favourite of Makhdoom Mohiuddin.

HABEEBUDDIN, COMRADE *
Member of the Communist Party of Hyderabad. Was underground for a long time.

HASAN, AKHTAR **
Communist leader and member of the Progressive Writers' Association. Became member of the Andhra Pradesh Legislative Assembly.

HUSSAIN, ABID
IAS officer, Became member of the Planning Commission and India's ambassador to the United States of America.

HYDER, GHULAM
Journalist, member of the CPI who infiltrated the Majlis-e-Ittehad-ul-Mussalmeen and rose to be a member of its top deliberative body.

JALEELI, ALI AHMED
Son of Jaleel Manikpuri, the poetic preceptor of the last two Nizams. Himself a respected poet, he did a Ph. D. thesis on his father.

JIGAR, MEHBOOB HUSAIN
Progressive writer. Co-founder of the Urdu daily *Siasat* and its joint editor.

JUNG NAWAB KAZIM
Popularly known as Ali Pasha. He was the favourite son-in-law of Nizam VII.

KAMIL, ZAHID ALI **
A senior advocate. Most loyal follower of the Razakar leader, Kasim Razvi. Very well informed about the politics of pre-integration Hyderabad.

KHAN, ABID ALI **
An officer of the Information Department who resigned to found the leading Urdu daily of Hyderabad, the *Siasat*, in 1948. Had mature understanding of the problems of Hyderabad. Awarded the Padma Shree.

KHAN, (COL) KHUSRO YAR
Officer of the Hyderabad army. Saw action in the Police Action. Married the wife of the half-brother of the last Nizam.

KHAN, MIR AHMED ALI *
Member of the Congress Party. Became a minister in Andhra Pradesh.

KHAN, MIR AKBAR ALI **
Bar-at-Law. Prominent politician during the Nizam's rule. Worked for the integration of Hyderabad with India. Became Member of Parliament and later Governor, successively of Uttar Pradesh and Orissa.

KHAN, MOHD. ABDUL SAMAD
An avid collector of books and documents in Urdu and about Hyderabad.

LATIFF, BILKEES
Adoptive granddaughter of Sir Akbar Hydari, Prime Minister of Hyderabad, daughter of Nawab Ali Yawar Jung, Governor of Maharashtra, wife of Air Chief Marshal Latiff, who was successively Governor of Maharashtra and Ambassador to France.

LEONARD, KAREN ISAKSEN
Professor of Anthropology and Social Sciences, University of California at Irvine. An expert author on Hyderabad. Author of a number of books on the subject.

MIRZA, FAREED
A Revenue Officer of Hyderabad who resigned in protest against the atrocities of the Razakars on the Hindus. Rehabilitated, but

did not get his due after Police Action. Resigned again and did private business. Has documented his work for communal harmony in a booklet.

MOHIUDDIN, SYED MOHD
Social worker, journalist

NATH, KASHI
Journalist, social worker. Recipient of the first Yudhvir Foundation Award.

NIZAMUDDIN, MOHAMMAD
Member of the Communist Party, freedom fighter, and journalist.

PERSHAD, MOHAN
Officer in the Labour Department. Very knowledgeable on historical sources and anecdotes about Hyderabad.

PRASAD, DHARMENDER
Professor of Geography, Nizam College. An authority on the history and customs of Hyderabad.

PRASAD, R.J. RAJENDRA
Deputy Editor of *The Hindu* for a long time. Author of the book *The Emergence of Telugu Desam.*

RAJ, LAKSHMI DEVI
Social worker. Expert on handicrafts. Authority on the dress, manners, and customs of old Hyderabad

RAMACHARI, A.
Physician. Historian of medicine, especially of Hyderabad

RAMAN, B.N.
IAS officer. Authority on general history and anecdotes of Hyderabad.

RAMAYYA, G.P.
Physician in the Hyderabad Medical Service. Eyewitness to the last day of the Nizam's life. Certified his death.

RAO, B. NARSING
Political worker and social activist. A nephew of the first popular Chief Minister of Hyderabad.

RAO, RAJA J. RAMESHWAR
Last ruler of the principality of Wanaparthy, a tributary of the Nizam. First to join the Indian Union. Later, Chairman of Orient Longman, a reputed publishing house.

RAO, C. RAJESHWARA
Joined the Andhra Mahasabha, predecessor of the Communist Party of India. He and his wife donated all their property to the Party. Retired voluntarily as the General Secretary of the Party in 1992.

RAO, CH. RAJESHWAR
Joined the Communist Party of India at a young age. Lived in mosques during his underground years and so became well versed in the traditions and rituals of Islam.

RAO, I. VENKATA
Chief reporter and later editor of the Telugu daily, *Andhra Jyothi*. Became Chairman of the Press Academy of Andhra Pradesh. Author of a biography each of NTR and Chandrababu Naidu in Telugu.

RAZVI, S.M. JAWAD
MA from Osmania University. Joined the Hyderabad Students' Federation. After 1956, left the Communist Party and became a librarian in the Salar Jung Museum, Hyderabad.

REDDY, RAVI BHARATI
Daughter of the legendary leader, Ravi Narayana Reddy. Worked as lecturer in Telugu at the Raja Bahadur Venkata Rama Reddy College for Women, Hyderabad.

REDDY, M. CHANNA **
Fiery leader of Telangana. Became Union Minister, twice Chief Minister of Andhra Pradesh, and Governor of many states.

REDDY, RAVI NARAYANA *
A landlord, a social worker and a vastly popular political leader. President of Andhra Mahasabha. Donated 500 acres of his land for distribution to the landless. Won the Parliamentary election of 1952 with the largest majority.

RAHMAN, FAZLUR
First director of Radio Deccan. An intellectual and a translator.

RAHMAN, HABBEBUR
Social worker. Donated all his landed property for the founding of the Urdu Arts College.

SAJIDA, ZEENAT
An erudite and very popular teacher of Urdu at the Osmania University. An authority on the Dakhni language. A rebel against traditional mores.

SANGHI, PARMANAND
A member of an old banking family of Hyderabad. Storehouse of old tales

SAXENA, GURUCHARAN DAS
A social worker interested in the history of Hyderabad

SAXENA, MANOHAR RAJ
An eminent senior advocate. Very close to the Communist Party of India. Fought many cases to defend the accused in the Telangana Armed Struggle. Author of a book based on these cases.

SAXENA, RAMAN RAJ
Son of Satguru Prasad Saxena, author of *Hyderabad Farkhunda Bunyad*. Very close to the Congress Party.

SHERWANI, H.K. *
Professor of History at the Osmania University. An authority on medieval Deccan on which he wrote extensively

SHROFF, GOVINDA RAO *
A Congress leader of the Marathwada region of Hyderabad. Took part in the freedom struggle in Hyderabad and agitated for the integration of the state with India.

TABASSUM, MUGHANI
Formerly professor of Urdu, Osmania University. Secretary General of Idara–e-Adabiyat–e–Urdu, and editor of Urdu monthly literary journal *Sabras*.

VITHAL, B.P.R.
An IAS officer, became member of the Tenth Finance Commission.

Yusuf, Hafiz Abu **
Social worker and a politician. Author of a book on the personalities of old Hyderabad.

* Through recorded tapes of interviews available with the Indian Council of Social Sciences Research, Southern Regional Centre, Osmania University, Hyderabad.
** Tapes, as above, and personal interviews.

Index

About the Author

Narendra Luther, a writer, author, columnist, and former civil servant, is the best living authority on Hyderabad. His focus lies in the history and culture of the erstwhile Hyderabad state and its rulers, topics on which he has written several books. He has been the president of the Society to Save Rocks, Hyderabad. During his tenure in the civil service he has served in various departments including tourism, industries, and municipal corporation.

His important books include *Legendotes of Hyderabad* (2014), *Lashkar: The Story of Secunderabad* (2010), *Raja Deen Dayal: Prince of Photographers* (2003), and *The Rockitecture of Andhra Pradesh* (2003). He has also translated from Urdu into English Sidq Jaisi's *Darbaar-e-Durbaar* under the title *The Nocturnal Court: The Life of a Prince of Hyderabad* (2004). Luther has also authored an autobiography, *A Bonsai Tree*, and a novel, *The Family Saga*. Some of his own books have also been translated into Urdu, Telugu, Hindi, and Oriya.